Melanie Phillips is a *Daily Mail* and former *Sunday Times* columnist and a regular panellist on Radio 4's *The Moral Maze*.

'[A book] shot through with Phillips' customary clarity . . . [she] shows beautifully that the vote was really symbolic of a far wider range of issues on which women were struggling to find a public voice. There is not a page of this book that does not reverberate in the present . . . this fine book simply reminds us that in many ways we keep having the same old arguments' Suzanne Moore, *Evening Standard*

'Melanie Phillips reanimates the complexities of the period . . . this highly enjoyable history gives an excellent sense of the vivid feuds, ideological divides and disputes which fractured and enlivened the progressive Victorian feminist movement . . . and sheds an amusing sidelight on the preoccupations of our own' Caroline Moore, *Sunday Telegraph*

'By wearing her scholarship lightly and employing a clear, incisive style, Phillips has produced a very readable and important book' Declan McCormack, *Irish Sunday Independent*

'Her reading of the suffragette movement is both thorough and interesting' Rebecca Abrams, *Sunday Times*

'A gripping and rather magnificent new book' Maureen Freely, *The Times*

'A richly detailed history' Claudia Fitzherbert, *Daily Telegraph*

D0109029

THE ASCENT
OF WOMAN

A HISTORY OF THE
SUFFRAGETTE MOVEMENT
AND THE IDEAS BEHIND IT

Melanie Phillips

ABACUS

First published in Great Britain in 2003 by Little, Brown
This edition published in Great Britain in 2004 by Abacus

13 15 17 19 20 18 16 14

Pictures reproduced by kind permission of: Camera Press (p. 10, top; p. 13, top;
p. 14, bottom); Mary Evans (p. 1, top left; p. 2, bottom; p. 3, bottom left; p. 4,
top and bottom left; p. 5; p. 6, top left, top right; p. 7, top right; p. 8, top left;
p. 9, bottom; p. 10, bottom; p. 12, middle; p. 14, top right); Hulton Getty (p. 1,
top right, bottom; p. 2, top left, top right; p. 3, top and bottom right; p. 4,
bottom right; p. 7, top left; p. 8, top right, bottom; p. 10, middle; p. 11, bottom;
p. 12, top right, bottom; p. 13, bottom; p. 14, top left; p. 15; p. 16, top);
Popperfoto (p. 6, bottom right; p. 7, bottom; p. 9, top; p. 11, top; p. 16,
bottom); Museum of London (p. 6, bottom left; p. 12, top left)

A CIP catalogue record for this book
is available from the British Library.

ISBN 978-0-349-11660-0

Typeset in Sabon by M Rules
Printed and bound in Great Britain by
Clays Ltd, St Ives plc

Papers used by Abacus are from well-managed forests
and other responsible sources.

MIX
Paper from
responsible sources
FSC
www.fsc.org
FSC® C104740

Abacus
An imprint of
Little, Brown Book Group
100 Victoria Embankment
London EC4Y 0DY

An Hachette UK Company
www.hachette.co.uk

www.littlebrown.co.uk

CONTENTS

'We do not know how it sprang to life, no one explanation is entirely satisfactory, certainly not the theory that it was the work of "leaders". It began all over the country, in silent, lonely places. It was a spiritual movement and had fire, not form . . . It released vast stores of unconscious energy . . . it was not premeditated or controllable – it *happened*.'

Quoted in Betty Balfour (ed.),
Letters of Lady Constance Lytton, 1925

PREFACE

In August 1916, with the war in Europe raging, an apparently impenetrable blockage in the British constitutional system suddenly started to shift. The British government, after more than fifty years of obduracy, indicated that at long last it was prepared to give women the parliamentary vote. Herbert Asquith, the Liberal Prime Minister, who had been the most implacable foe of women's suffrage, appeared to have changed his mind. As a result of the war, new legislation was needed to enfranchise soldiers and sailors whose residency qualification for the vote would have expired by the next general election. Asquith had indicated votes for women would be introduced on the back of this legislation. But it was still far from certain that his government would honour this commitment. Indeed, one proposal that was in the air left the women's movement aghast. This would have 'rewarded' servicemen by making the vote conditional on their war effort, a move which, apart from being undemocratic, would of course block votes for women once again.

At this critical juncture a voice was raised against giving the vote to women. This defender of the male preserve insisted that votes were required not for women but for fighting men. 'The men had proved their claim to the vote by making it possible to keep a country in which to vote. Could any woman face the possibility of the affairs of the country being settled by conscientious objectors, passive resisters and shirkers?'[1]

The author of these reactionary sentiments was not one of the legion of diehard opponents of women's suffrage. It was Emmeline Pankhurst, leader of the militant suffragette movement, martyr of repeated jail terms and hunger strikes for the cause and the supreme heroine of feminism.

Mrs Pankhurst's volte-face was not the only development to cause heads to turn in astonishment. Her daughter Christabel, the strategist and inspiration behind the militant suffragettes, also seemed to have lost all interest in votes for women and instead was devoting her energies to rousing men to war. The woman who had mounted a ferocious onslaught on British men, accusing them of spreading 'the great scourge' of venereal disease to infect the nation's women and children, had returned from France, where she had fled at the height of the militancy she had organised, to pronounce: 'We suffragists do not feel that Great Britain is in any sense decadent. On the contrary we are tremendously conscious of strength and freshness.' As for women's lack of political rights, the cause she had helped symbolise, she now declared: 'In the English-speaking nations under the British flag woman's influence is higher, her political rights more extended than in any other part of the world . . .'[2]

How could Emmeline and Christabel Pankhurst, the most visible and potent symbols of the great struggle for women's suffrage, have performed such an astonishing about-turn – and at such a crucial moment? From the start, the Pankhursts' own part in the story was a psychodrama of its own. It is customary to separate the militancy they represented from the constitutional battle for women's suffrage fought by Millicent Fawcett and others. However, the themes that animated the Pankhursts around the turn of the twentieth century and which seemed so extreme in these last years of the suffrage campaign, imperialist notions of the English race and the noxious character of male sexuality, were in fact not only intimately related to each other but were integral to the wider movement for female emancipation.

For the suffragist movement was about far more than the parliamentary vote. It was about more, even, than improving the general condition of women. At base it was a spiritual movement whose goal was to elevate the character of the human race by altering male behaviour and redefining the relationship between women and men. It was not trying to make women equal with men. It was rather an attempt to revolutionise the entire social system by getting it to adopt the moral values of women, and in so doing raise the whole public sphere and human nature itself to a higher moral plane of existence. It therefore encapsulated the double standard at the heart of feminism which persists to this day: the simultaneous argument that women are the equals of men *and* that women are men's moral superiors.

When I first started looking at the history of the women's suffrage campaign, this is not what I expected to find. Like many others, I knew the bare bones of the story – the constitutional campaign led by Mrs Fawcett, the militant movement spearheaded by Mrs Pankhurst, the marches and petitions, the hunger strikes and forced feeding, the final, staggered victory when the vote was eventually granted to women on equal terms with men. But when I started delving below this familiar narrative I discovered a far wider array of women beyond the campaign itself, whose stories also played an integral role in the great movement of thought that propelled the suffrage cause. For the vote was not the fundamental issue. It was rather a means to an end: a society – and, above all, a male sex – transfigured by women's apparently distinctive values of spirituality, self-restraint and sensibility.

Moreover, this feminist movement was deeply split over virtually every issue. Suffragists passionately disagreed not just about tactics, but about the issues themselves. There were those who were fighting a sex war against men, and those who were working alongside men, shoulder to shoulder; there were those who wanted to enfranchise married women, and those who wanted to restrict the vote to single women and widows; there were those who saw the suffrage as part of a sexual purity crusade, and those who wanted women to be sexually liberated; there were those who supported marriage, and those who thought it was a form of slavery. The parliamentary vote was like a tree, on whose branches were hung the issues that arose from a society in constant flux and ferment and about which women, fighting for their public voice, were so often radically divided.

This book is an attempt to chart the ideas behind the movement for female suffrage. It does not pretend to ground-breaking scholarship;

there are many authoritative books dealing with the events of the campaign itself, and many eminent writers have chronicled the political debates and intellectual controversies that engulfed Victorian and Edwardian England. This is an attempt to marry the two, to seek to explain the women's suffrage campaign in the context of the ideas that animated the age from which it sprang. In attempting such a task, I have drawn widely upon the work of many scholars, to whom I am deeply indebted and to whom I hope I have given due acknowledgement.

I am also very grateful to Alan Samson, my editor at Little, Brown, whose idea this was, and to Stacey McNutt for her incisive editorial guidance; to Christopher Sinclair-Stevenson and Luigi Bonomi, who provided me with valuable advice; to David Doughan at the Fawcett Library for his unsurpassed knowledge; to the staff at the British Library for their courteous efficiency; and to my long-suffering family, Joshua, Gabriel and Abigail, who endured the effects of a more than usually protracted outbreak of deadline fever with their usual aplomb.

MELANIE PHILLIPS
LONDON, DECEMBER 2002

I

HOW IT BEGAN

The radicalisation of women developed against a background of social and political ferment. It is a popular myth that the Victorian era, that great age of empire and economic achievement, was one of invincible superiority and self-confident poise. In fact, the nineteenth century was marked by repeated periods of near pathological insecurity about a likely breakdown in social order and corresponding fear of the mob. In particular, anxieties were heightened by the pressure to widen the franchise, and by the strengthening movement by Irish radicals to repeal the union between Ireland and Britain.

The cult of the individual and promotion of human rights that had started with the Enlightenment in the seventeenth century led inevitably to a reassessment of the role of women and to calls for recognition of their equal rights. It accelerated the move towards women's education which was already gathering pace with the rise of literacy. This provoked deeply hostile and fearful reactions. Female intellectualism was regarded as profoundly suspect. Rousseau defined the terms of sexual engagement in 1762 when he wrote: 'the woman is made specially to please the man', and that learning in a woman was 'unpleasing and unnecessary'.[1]

Nevertheless, in the second half of the eighteenth century a group of spirited women who wanted to break out of the stultifying round of social visits and trivial pursuits began to hold literary evenings to which they invited well-known men of letters to encourage discussion. This group was called the Bluestockings, reputedly because one of their male guests, Benjamin Stillingfleet, turned up to their evening salon in blue worsted stockings because he was too poor to afford the black silk stockings gentlemen wore for evening occasions. The group, which consisted of the finest female intellects of the age, such as the future best-selling author Fanny Burney, the noted linguist Elizabeth Carter and the religious writer and philanthropist Hannah More, cultivated moral and intellectual rigour and philanthropic activities.

As a result, they had to run the gauntlet of mockery and ridicule. Mrs Carter, who single-handedly tutored her brother Henry to gain him admission to a Cambridge college in 1756, was said to talk Greek 'faster than any woman in England'.[2] Lady Mary Wortley Montagu advised her daughter to conceal her learning as if she were hiding crookedness or lameness.[3] She complained to her daughter about woman's lot and said women like her were sold as slaves.[4]

Yet in the main even the Bluestockings subscribed to the prevalent notions of the limited rational capacity of women, female chastity and submission and their proper domestic sphere.[5] Mrs Carter, Fanny Burney, Hannah More, the author and powerful social hostess Mrs Elizabeth Montagu, and the writer Mrs Anna Barbauld refused to be associated with feminism. Mrs Barbauld declined to join Lady Mary Wortley Montagu's scheme to found a women's college, saying: 'The best way for a woman to acquire knowledge is from conversation with a father or brother and such a course of reading as they may recommend.'[6] Hannah More thought that women should be educated to become better mothers. But she didn't believe women were men's equals. 'Far be it for [sic] me to make scholastic ladies or female dialecticians,' she said. Only 'the vulgar and ill informed' struggled for power. And she was contemptuous of the woman who, 'vain of her wit', tried to 'vindicate the rights of women'. The more a woman's understanding improved, 'the more accurate views will she take of the station she was born to fill'.[7]

Despite their conventional views, however, the Bluestockings were helping lay the foundations for a revolutionary way of thinking which would have shocked them profoundly. For what they did was to open up women's horizons beyond the bounds of social calls and domestic pre-occupations. Hannah More and other such women took themselves off to Somerset to teach the wild children of the Cheddar Hills. Even though such education was intended to teach the children to be contented with their lot, the activity itself hardly upheld the status quo since it meant that women were going out to teach. Once women began to look outside their own drawing rooms, they were bound to revolt against their own decorative futility.[8] Limited though this may seem today, in the context of the times it had radical potential.

The new individualism invested education for women with a respectable purpose and added impetus. The old system of dynastic marriage had waned. In its place arose companionate marriages entered into for love, which gave women the ability to choose their husbands. This new, more equal type of marriage fundamentally altered not just relationships between men and women but the way women saw themselves. Even women who were devout Christians and believed that wives were naturally subordinate to men wanted to be better educated in order to become better companions to their husbands. By the end of the eighteenth century a consensus had been reached about the ideal education for women who came from the gentry and the upper bourgeoisie. The purpose of women's education was to produce neither a frivolous mother and possibly adulterous upper-class wife, nor a middle-class Bluestocking. It was rather to produce a well-informed and well-motivated woman with a desire to please her husband and provide him with friendship and intelligent companionship. Yet of course this particular genie, having been let out of the bottle, could not be constrained. By 1810 women were proclaiming their educational superiority to men, a notable reversal in the space of just one century.[9]

This astonishing leap from subservience to superiority was rooted in the paradox at the very heart of feminism – a paradox which was evident even in the eighteenth century, long before the organised movement for women's rights was to start. For, surprising as it may seem, the notion of female superiority over men arose from precisely that separate domestic sphere in which women were trapped and from which feminism offered the means of escape. It all stemmed from the growth of sensibility and refinement, characteristics intimately related to women and their place in the home. Although these are commonly associated with the Victorian era, their roots stretch back to the previous century, which laid the foundations for what was to become the predominant view of nineteenth-century womanhood and its distinctive and superior characteristics.

In the latter part of the eighteenth century a vast change in manners occurred as the cult of feelings took hold. Originating in the discovery of the nervous system, the cultivation of sensibility became invested with spiritual and moral significance. Feelings, after all, differentiated human beings from animals. With church authority in retreat, morality started to become a matter of inward impulse and therefore needed to be outwardly demonstrated. Hearts now had to be worn on sleeves. Emotion was taken as proof of fine feelings and of virtue.[10] Sexually coarse behaviour was taken as evidence of callous attitudes. Sexuality now had to be refined and conducted with decorum, and was increasingly expressed through the elevated language of sensibility and ardour.

Crucially, the cult of sensibility became associated with women. It was women who were to write and buy in great number the new romantic novels, which provided a huge impetus for the desire to marry for love. It was women who were believed to harbour these prized feelings of sympathy, delicacy and refinement. The nervous system of women which invested them with these virtues was held to be different from the nervous system of men. Delicacy, or desexualisation, was urged upon women in order to protect them. John Bennett wrote in 1789: 'Delicacy is a very general and *comprehensive* quality. It extends to everything where woman is concerned. Conversation, books, pictures, attitude, gesture, pronunciation should all come under its salutary constraints.'[11] At the same time, those with the most refined nerves were most susceptible to nervous disorders. So women were both morally superior and weaker than men; indeed, their very weakness was the source of their superiority, an ambiguity that was to lie at the heart of both the campaign for women's rights and its opposition.

The rise of sensibility resulted in two important movements which were to exercise a crucial influence over the women's movement in the next century. The first was romanticism, which viewed sexuality as gross and materialistic, idealised love and women and elevated passion to a spiritual plane. The second was evangelicalism, which wanted to banish hedonism in general and sexuality in particular from respectable consciousness and public life.[12] Both of these movements had one thing in common. They both associated female virtue with a higher plane of being. Women's moral virtue thus became a weapon of social reform.

By the end of the eighteenth century this championing of private and domestic virtues had put women at the head of a moral-rearmament movement. Women had become the guardians of morality.[13] Novels propagated this new ideology of femininity, associating sensibility with sympathy, compassion, benevolence, humanity and pity. The figure of the mother in her domestic setting became a symbol of virtue. As G. J. Barker-Benfield has noted, all the suffering addressed by humanitarian reformers in the late eighteenth century could be laid at the door of the masculine world against which the culture of sensibility defined itself and which its advocates wished to enter and change: cruelty to animals; mistreatment of the sick, children and insane; public floggings and executions; duelling, war and imperialism; abuse of the poor, political corruption and the slave trade.[14] Female virtue was therefore presented as the antidote to male vice. The domestic sphere inhabited by women was invested with a mission to civilise the public sphere of men.

Evangelical Christians took up the virtues of the home as a defence against sexuality. Their vanguard was the élite Clapham Sect in London, headed by merchants and bankers such as William Wilberforce, Zachary Macaulay and John Thornton. Starting with the home, they aimed to re-Christianise society by promoting hard work and the deferral of gratification.[15] They campaigned for a wide range of deserving causes: better public health and hospitals, the moralisation of the poor and the abolition of the slave trade. And it was women, whose voices could not be heard in the public sphere, whose virtues were nevertheless being trumpeted as the means of its salvation.

Across the Channel, however, an event was to occur which was to have seismic repercussions on British society and to define the political and social debates in the coming Victorian era. It was to give rise to the founding text of the women's movement, the banner under which women would spend much of the following century fighting to enter the public sphere and break out of the gilded cage of the home. Yet both this event, and the landmark text it produced, were to provoke such a hostile reaction that the cause of women was to be all but buried for some fifty years before it re-emerged into political debate. The text was Mary Wollstonecraft's *A Vindication of the Rights of Woman*, and the event was the French Revolution.

2

MARY WOLLSTONECRAFT AND
THE FRENCH REVOLUTION

To English radicals, the French Revolution seemed to augur a new moral
order within human relations. Its promise to end medieval obscurantism
and free individuals from despotic authority made it the supremely fashionable cause in literary and artistic circles. In particular, it provided an
ideological justification for abandoning sexual constraint. Licentiousness
had been commonplace in the eighteenth century; now it became
invested with political significance. The revolt against convention was
very profound and led to a self-conscious intellectual bohemianism
which set out to defy accepted moral codes.[1] Radical circles which
included the political theorist William Godwin, the novelist Mary Hays
and the publisher Joseph Johnson practised sexual freedom as a political
statement.

Into this intellectual, political and sexual ferment drifted a young
woman in long, black worsted stockings and dishevelled hair, and with a
deep-rooted sense of personal misery and grievance which left her prone
to violent mood swings. Mary Wollstonecraft was not a prepossessing
figure, which was hardly surprising given her family background. Born in
1759, Mary felt unappreciated and unloved. Her mother doted on
Mary's elder brother and her father Edward was often violent. Although

Mary would throw herself between her parents, the mother she was trying to protect seemed to be an all too willing victim.[2]

Supporting her father after her mother's death, Mary set up a school in Newington Green, north London, which was also host to a community of liberal intellectuals and dissidents, including Dr Richard Price, an enthusiastic supporter of the American and French Revolutions. She subsequently became a writer and fell in with a group of radical dissenters including the Swiss painter Henry Fuseli, William Godwin, the poet William Blake and the political philosopher Thomas Paine. Here she fell in love with Fuseli, who was married, and who described her at first sight as 'a philosophical sloven, with lank hair, black stockings and a beaver hat'.[3]

In 1789 Dr Price delivered a lecture rejoicing in the prospect of civil and religious liberty for France as a result of the Revolution, which he thought would bring about universal benevolence and realise the perfectibility of man. Horrified by this euphoria, the political thinker Edmund Burke published a reply the following year with his *Reflections on the French Revolution*, prophesying instead chaos and terror for France. This in turn prompted enormous controversy, centred around Tom Paine's riposte in 1791 in *The Rights of Man*. The most prominent name linked with Paine in the rebuttal of Burke was Mary Wollstonecraft. In 1790 she published an angry polemic, *A Vindication of the Rights of Men*, in which she championed the new doctrines of civil and religious liberty and attacked the aristocracy.[4] But she also attacked Burke for the treatise he had published in 1757, *A Philosophical Inquiry into the Origin of Our Ideas of the Sublime and Beautiful*, which had upheld traditional distinctions between men and women, masculinity and femininity. The applause she received for this work spurred her on to cast herself as the champion of half the human race.[5] In 1792 she published *A Vindication of the Rights of Woman*, an argument for female emancipation which she had written in six weeks, distilling 'thirty years' rage' about her life.[6] The book provoked instant flak. Hannah More wrote that there was something so ridiculous in the very title she had no intention of reading it.[7] But the controversy did the book no harm; it quickly proved a best-seller, and Mary became a celebrity.

Mary dedicated her book to the French revolutionary bishop Charles Talleyrand because he had just proposed a system of state education only for boys; she wanted this 'flaw in the constitution' addressed and her own proposals for female education to be adopted by the French legislative assembly.[8] So much did she identify with the new French moral and political order that after her book was published she went to live in Paris, ostensibly to improve her French but actually to witness at close quarters the new dawn of human virtue.

But as the dedication she had herself written to Talleyrand implied, the gap between what she imagined the Revolution was about and what was actually happening was enormous. For the initial wish to give women equality before the law went as sour as the Revolution's other ideals. The original talk had been of the patriarchal family being recast, and of women being given the same property rights as men and an equal voice in family matters. Women's clubs were formed to deliver services to the community. In 1791, after Olympe de Gouges published her *Déclaration des Droits de la Femme et de la Citoyenne*, there were the first stirrings of anti-feminist protest. In 1792 the Jacobin Club gave an attractive young woman self-publicist called Théroigne de Méricourt an admiring reception. But the Société des Républicaines Révolutionnaires, a women's club of the extreme left, began patrolling the streets in red-and-white-striped trousers and bits of military uniform, physically attacking anyone to whose appearance they took exception. A reaction set in. Women began to be accused of talking too much and of immoral behaviour, and in 1793 an article appeared claiming that the women's clubs had become the bane of domestic happiness. The Jacobins turned savagely against women. Théroigne, who founded a mixed club, was attacked by a band of *citoyennes* in the Tuileries gardens and sustained such bad head injuries that she later ended up in a lunatic asylum. Olympe was already in prison. A proposed civil code giving women equality and independence was rejected. By the end of 1793, the French feminist movement was crushed.[9]

On all these events, of such central importance to her own feminist agenda which she was constructing on the very principles that were being dismantled before her eyes, Mary Wollstonecraft remained silent. She was deeply shocked by the carnage at the guillotine, and in February 1793 wrote to her publisher, Joseph Johnson, doubting her theory of a more perfect state, fearing that vice or evil is 'the grand mobile of action' and lamenting the blood being shed and the frivolity of the French. Nevertheless, within a year she had managed to exorcise such Burkean thoughts by arguing that the Revolution was an outcome of the Enlightenment, which would proceed gradually through people's minds, freeing them so they could eventually become politically liberated.[10]

The quest for the perfectibility of mankind was at the core of her argument in *A Vindication of the Rights of Woman*. The perfection of human virtue could not be attained without reason and knowledge. So to be virtuous, women had to have equal rights to develop their reason, which was equal in capacity to the reason of men. Women should be able to rise as high as their work and intelligence could take them.

She accompanied this with a vitriolic onslaught on the way girls and women were conditioned to lead useless lives by the emphasis on delicacy and sensibility, the means by which they were trapped in their domestic prison. They thereby degenerated into 'mere parasites' who, confined in cages like birds, had nothing to do but preen themselves and had exchanged health, liberty and virtue in exchange for food and raiment. Women, said Mary, had become idle, decorative accessories; 'the toys of man' who 'must jingle in his ears whenever, dismissing reason, he chooses to be amused'.[11]

She wanted women to be educated in reason, not in manners. Their ostensible virtues of 'gentleness, docility and a spaniel-like affection' could only inspire a 'vapid tenderness' which easily descended into contempt. Instead of being socialised to depend on men, she said, women should have an independent capacity to earn a living. Unsparing in her withering criticisms of frivolous or immoral women, she nevertheless blamed men for any female misconduct. Thus, women adapted their behaviour to the voluptuousness required by men so that they were unable to discharge the proper duties of a mother.

Morality depended on equality. 'It is vain to expect virtue from women till they are in some degree independent of men ... While they are absolutely dependent on their husbands they will be cunning, mean and selfish; and the men who can be gratified by the fawning fondness of spaniel-like affection have not much delicacy, for love is not to be bought ...' Virtue at home would grow with a civic identity. So women should be physicians as well as nurses, study politics and pursue business. 'Would men but generously snap our chains, and be content with rational fellowship instead of slavish obedience, they would find us more observant daughters, more affectionate sisters, more faithful wives, more reasonable mothers – in a word, better citizens. We should then love them with true affection, because we should learn to respect ourselves; and the peace of mind of a worthy man would not be interrupted by the idle vanity of his wife, nor the babes sent to nestle in a strange bosom, having never found a home in their mother's.'[12]

Notably, Mary emphasised the importance of women's role in the home. In this and many other instances her writing reflected the conflicts and dilemmas that were to characterise the women's campaign she inspired. She believed, for example, that mothering was crucial to perfecting civilisation; yet she also wanted women to be educated and have a role in the public sphere. She reconciled the two by claiming that only through rational motherhood could women look after their children properly. To be a good mother, a woman must have 'sense and independence of mind', and 'meek wives' were in general foolish mothers.[13]

Like most of the leaders of the women's suffrage movement in the next century, Mary directed her argument only towards middle-class women. Aristocratic women, she thought, were incapable of redemption through education; the poor she ignored altogether, with the implication that they were simply too brutalised. It was the middle class that would redeem mankind, a key assumption of the women's movement and of Victorian society.

It was on the subjects of sex and marriage that Mary set out views which were later to be associated with the most extreme suffragettes, but which in fact were woven into the complex tapestry of the women's movement from its earliest times. Sexuality, Mary thought, was wrong in itself; it was imposed by men upon women, since men were more under the influence of their sexual appetites. Marriage was nothing other than legal prostitution; prostitutes undermined the chastity of good women by encouraging them to think they must hold their husbands' affection by sexual means.[14]

Human perfection, indeed, lay in chastity, by which she meant sexual continence. 'To render the human body and mind more perfect, chastity must more universally prevail, and that chastity will never be respected in the male world till the person of a woman is not, as it were, idolised, when little virtue or sense embellish it with the grand traces of mental beauty or the interesting simplicity of affection.' Chastity was not only the key to human perfection but the lack of it was all men's fault. 'The little respect paid to chastity in the male world is, I am persuaded, the grand source of many of the physical and moral evils that torment mankind, as well as of the vices and follies that degrade and destroy women . . .'[15]

Such a view went far beyond a call for equality between the sexes, far-reaching in itself though that was. It went way beyond a protest at the way women were treated as inferiors by men. This was an infinitely more inflammatory accusation: that the very essence of men, their sexuality, was responsible for the evils of the human race. And it followed from this that women were the key to perfecting human nature through the female insight that male sexual incontinence needed to be restrained. Even though Mary acknowledged that women were not created 'to save [man] from sinking into absolute brutality by rubbing off the rough angles of his character', it was nevertheless 'time to effect a revolution in female manners . . . and make [women], as a part of the human species, labour by reforming themselves to reform the world'.[16]

Yet at the same time that Mary was making grandiose claims to utopia in human relations, her own were proving disastrous. Indeed, there was as much discrepancy between what she was writing and her private life as there was between her enthusiasm for French revolutionary liberty and the bloody carnage on the guillotine. While she was reaffirming in print the innate goodness of man, she fell in with an unscrupulous fortune-hunter, Gilbert Imlay, whom she met in Paris and lived with there and in Le Havre and by whom she had a daughter, Fanny, in 1794. She put Imlay on a pedestal of honour and worth;[17] but he soon tired of her and abandoned her for a woman from a strolling theatre company. So deep was Mary's desire to believe the best of human nature, she deluded herself for months that he would return to her. In 1795, when she could no longer ignore the truth, Mary tried to kill herself by jumping into the Thames from Putney Bridge, but was pulled out by a passer-by.[18]

In 1796 Mary resumed her acquaintance with the political philosopher William Godwin. The relationship had not got off to a good start when they first met in 1791 at a party thrown by Joseph Johnson for Tom Paine after publication of *The Rights of Man*. As Godwin later described it, although Paine was the principal attraction Mary hogged the limelight to such an extent that Godwin was quite unable to hear what Paine was saying.

Nevertheless, in 1796 Mary and Godwin became lovers. Since both held strong views about independence and disapproved of marriage, they maintained separate homes. When Mary discovered she was pregnant, however, they married to avoid social stigma. It was a symbolic union. Godwin, who was at the peak of his career, was a thinker who showed scant regard for the reality of human existence.

In 1793 he published *An Enquiry Concerning Political Justice and its Influence on General Virtue and Happiness*, which proclaimed the perfectibility of mankind. Godwin not only believed that marriage would prevent the development of perfectly rational and moral human beings who were free and equal, but he thought that sex itself would become redundant. As men grew more rational, superior intellectual joys would drive out inferior bodily pleasures. This would not threaten the regeneration of the species, since life would be infinitely prolonged through being in a state of permanent perfection. The vision of immortality aside, the replacement of carnal sexuality by a mystical spirituality was an aspiration that would resurface at the heart of the feminist movement a century later.

This marriage of true minds was tragically cut short. Mary died of complications after the birth of their daughter, the future Mary Shelley, in 1797. She left behind her the first sustained critique of the social and economic system which had created double standards of achievement for men and women and which relegated women to inferior status. Early assessments of her contribution were generous and favourable, recognising her talents. An article in the conservative *Gentlemen's Magazine* paid handsome tribute to 'the soundness of her understanding and sensibility of heart', despite not supporting her politics.[19]

But this posthumous acclaim was unintentionally shot to pieces by Godwin himself. In 1798 he published his *Memoirs of the Author of the Vindication of the Rights of Woman*. This revealed that Mary had been thwarted in her attempt to have an affair with Henry Fuseli, a married man; that she had had a child by Gilbert Imlay; that she had attempted suicide, become pregnant by Godwin before marrying him and ignored religion on her deathbed.

Godwin's candour appalled his readers. Why he had written such a memoir 'stripping his dead wife naked', as Robert Southey accused him, is unclear. Some have speculated that his frankness arose from his anarchistic principles of sincerity and plain speaking.[20] In any event, he was so widely and bitterly attacked that he never again wrote so freely.

The furore he created played into the hands of his political enemies to such an extent that not only his own reputation but the legacy of Mary Wollstonecraft too was dealt an enduring blow. For the terror in France had inflamed paranoia about a French invasion of Britain. Since Jacobinism was linked to sexual licentiousness, Godwin's enemies claimed that his philosophy, 'by leaving women to the exercise of . . . their natural and social rights . . . would take away powerful restraints on the promiscuous intercourse of the sexes . . . dissolve the rites of marriage, one of the chief foundations of political society, and then promote Jacobinical politics'.[21] So Godwin's own words had turned both himself and Mary Wollstonecraft into emblems of an English Jacobinism that threatened the destruction of domestic, civil and political society. He had wanted to defend her. Instead Mary was portrayed as the embodiment of sexual and personal licence and the equivalent of the viragos of revolutionary France. To the writer Horace Walpole, she was 'the hyena in petticoats'.

The ferocious reaction against the French Revolution swept away the embryonic women's movement with such force that it would not emerge again for many decades. Even a periodical like *The Lady's Monthly Museum*, which campaigned for women's rights and education, was driven to denounce the anonymous *Appeal to the Men of Great Britain on Behalf of Women* in 1797 for demanding 'unqualified equality' with men. 'An opinion thus preposterous and inimical to the monarchical constitution of matrimony is one of the last qualities, almost, any man would wish to find in his wife', it thundered. It also attacked 'a Wollstonecraft, who squared her principles to her conduct', and said 'the champions of female equality . . . are no longer regarded as sincere and politic friends, but as base and insidious enemies'.²²

Fear of the growing power of the mob made the respectable classes deeply insecure. Suddenly Enlightenment optimism had given way to a nightmare vision of the upright individual beset by a host of uncontrollable forces – class antagonism, population explosion, starvation wages and a crisis of overproduction. In such a climate the licentious morality of the Georgian period seemed scandalous and inflammatory. Instead stricter family discipline, paternal authority and sexual propriety were called for.²³ A new type of middle-class reformer emerged. The growing body of evangelical Christians called for a revolution in 'manners and morals' to elevate the behaviour of the dissolute upper classes and control the lower. The moral malaise of Jacobinism could only be cured by godliness, clean living and patriotism.

In such a struggle over evil, women were pivotal. A friend wrote to Hannah More: 'If our women lose their domestic virtues, all the charities will be dissolved, for which our country is a name so dear. The men will be profligate, the public will be betrayed, and whatever has blessed or distinguished the English nation on the continent will disappear.'²⁴

3

THE ANGEL IN THE HOUSE

During the nineteenth century the fundamental tenets of women's role were to be challenged in several ways: by attacking inequalities in marriage and family; by questioning the role motherhood played in women's lives; by opening up work and politics to women; and by challenging the very notion of masculinity to which the domestic conception of femininity had been set in opposition.

In 1823 the journalist and father of John Stuart Mill, James Mill, published an article in the *Encyclopaedia Britannica* which said that since the interests of women and children were bound up with those of their husbands or fathers, women could be denied political rights 'without inconvenience'.[1]

James Mill's argument provoked an explosive reaction. William Thompson, a wealthy Anglo-Irishman who was acquainted with Mill and other leading political thinkers, had formed a close friendship with Mrs Anna Wheeler, daughter of a radical Irish Protestant archbishop, wife of a drunkard and great-grandmother of the noted suffragette Lady Constance Lytton. Anna, who bore six children and educated herself in French and German philosophy, became infatuated with the French Revolution. Disraeli, who met Mrs Wheeler at dinner, described her as 'something between Jeremy Bentham and Meg Merrilees, very clever but awfully revolutionary'.

Mrs Wheeler was so enraged by Mill's article that in 1825 she got Thompson to write a book called *An Appeal of One Half of the Human Race, Women, Against the Pretensions of the Other Half, Men, to Retain Them in Political and Thence in Civil and Domestic Slavery*. This comprehensive title was followed by a thumbnail epigram: 'Tis all stern duty on the female side; on man's, mere sensual lust and surly pride'; a sentiment whose severe impact was only marginally dented by the printing of 'lust' as 'gust'.[2]

Mrs Wheeler's anger was reflected in the book's ferocious attack on men and marriage. Men, wrote Thompson with contempt, only know the pleasures of animal appetite and of 'the boundless misuse of uncontrolled power till its victims are reduced at least to the condition of Negroes in the West Indies'. His recurring theme was that women were slaves and that marriage was their bondage. From adolescence until marriage, women were considered as capable as men of self-government.

'But as soon as adult daughters become wives, their civil rights disappear; they fall back again, and remain all their lives – should their owners and directors live so long – into the state of children or idiots, the passive property of their owners; protected by the law in some few respects only, like other slaves, from the excessive abuse of despotic power.'[3]

Unlike Mary Wollstonecraft, Thompson did not value the domestic virtues but saw the home as a place where men incarcerated their women slaves. 'Home, except on a few occasions, chiefly for the drilling of a superstition to render her obedience more submissive, is the eternal prison-house of the wife: the husband paints it as the abode of calm bliss, but takes care to find, outside of doors, for his own use, a species of bliss not quite so calm, but of a more varied and stimulating description . . . The house is *his* house with everything in it; and of all fixtures the most abjectly his is his breeding machine, the wife.'

Women were compelled in marriage 'to be the literal unequivocal slave of the man who may be styled her husband'. It was a monstrous pretence that wives' happiness was involved with that of their husbands.

Marriage was a superstition called in aid by men when they wanted to admit women to the honour of becoming their 'breeding machines and household slaves'.[4]

Thompson also turned his coruscating ire against the sexual double standard, particularly after marriage, by which men were afforded sexual licence while women were given none. 'To man married, for breach of the vain and insulting promise of fidelity to his wife, no penalty is awarded by law; while public opinion extenuates the venial offence, or smiles upon it; while to woman married, the breach of the compulsory vow of slavish obedience is punished at command of the husband, even by aid of the civil power; and the vow of fidelity – no empty vow to her – ie, enforced by the united ruin and degradation of law and public opinion, both created by man for his exclusive benefit and unrelentingly enforced.'

Wives were protected only against absolute desertion, starvation or life-threatening violence. Men must be obeyed while women were not permitted to feel or to desire. 'Not satisfied with superiority of strength, man makes it but the basis on which to erect his system of sexual exclusions to gratify his unhallowed lust of domination.'[5]

The only way women could win civil and domestic rights, Thompson concluded, was through legal and political equality with men. Accordingly, he incited them to revolt. 'Women of England! Women, in whatever country ye breathe – wherever ye breathe, degraded – awake!' They should demand, he urged, the removal of disadvantages, the same education as men, equal protection from assault, the same punishments, and the same political and civil rights. And, crucially, he presented women's liberation as the way to elevate the moral position of men.

'Shall none be found with sufficient knowledge and elevation of mind to persuade men to do good, to make the most certain step towards the regeneration of degraded humanity, by opening a free course for justice and benevolence, for intellectual and social enjoyments, by no colour, by no sex to be restrained? As your bondage has chained down man to the ignorance and vices of despotism, so will your liberation reward him with knowledge, with freedom and with happiness.'[6]

Here were set out all the key arguments that were to surface in the campaign for the suffrage – the list of grievous wrongs and disadvantages suffered by women in sexual bondage, the presentation of men as their brutish slave-owners, the sexual double standard, the moral superiority of women and the belief that only through full civil and political equality could men be reformed and humanity saved. In Thompson's seminal text, therefore, lay the real message of the not-yet-born suffrage campaign – that the women's vote was the means not to equality between the sexes but to the liberation of women and the transformation of men and humanity in general.

This ambition was rooted in the prevailing view among nineteenth-century progressives. At the beginning of the century the French socialist Charles Fourier constructed an elaborate theory of mankind's evolution through a series of historical stages to which, he argued, the progressive liberation of women within marriage was fundamental. 'Social progress and changes of period are brought about by virtue of the progress of women towards liberty, and social retrogression occurs as a result of a diminution in the liberty of women,' he wrote. This argument was repeated over and over again in feminist writings. 'Women, however high or low in the scale of cultivation, hold the destinies of mankind,' wrote Frances Wright in 1829.[7]

Followers of the radical socialist Robert Owen believed that improving the social position of women was the index of humanity's progress from savagery to civilisation, and that women would be the standard-bearers of a new moral culture. Fettered women were mental and moral cripples who contaminated all around them and who were so degraded they couldn't even recognise their own servitude. Once freed, women's 'more refined sentiments and moral capabilities', in Wheeler's words, would become a spiritual lever elevating society as a whole. Femininity itself would become a regenerating force. 'So true is it that though men make the law, it is women who mould the manners and morals of society; and according as they are either enlightened or ignorant, do they spin the web of human destiny.' The only way to emancipate women, argued the Owenites, was to end female dependency; housework would be collectivised, and new forms of communal living would remove the economic basis of male dominance.[8]

Such revolutionary sentiments were given additional impetus by the pressures of demography. For a major problem of much of the Victorian period was a surplus of unmarried women. From the late 1840s concern grew. Periodicals were full of articles discussing what to do with England's old maids. The 1851 census showed there was a surplus of 365,000 women over men. This was due partly to a higher male mortality rate and partly to emigration. The census also showed that twenty-nine per cent of women over twenty were unmarried. In 1851 there were 2,765,000 unmarried adult women, in 1861 2,959,000 and in 1871 3,228,000.[9] This was largely because men put off marriage because they couldn't afford it.[10] As the standard of living rose, so did the cost of supporting a wife. Children cost more as they were living longer. So men who aspired to social status postponed marriage until they had enough money for the middle-class lifestyle: the suburban villa, the large dinners, the servants, the balls and parties.[11]

The main problem with these spinsters was lack of money. 'A single woman with a narrow income must be a ridiculous old maid, the proper sport of boys and girls; but a single woman of good fortune is always respectable, and may be as sensible and pleasant as anybody else,' noted Jane Austen in Emma in 1816. Upper- and middle-class women couldn't work as this was socially unacceptable. Women who remained unmarried were social failures. They often had to live on a small pension in obscure and lonely lodgings, seeking consolation in religious devotion and charitable good works. The lesser gentry could become companions, a practice denounced by Mary Wollstonecraft as 'odious' since it obliged women to live with strangers who were 'so intolerably tyrannical. It is impossible to enumerate the many hours of anguish such a person must spend. She is alone, shut out from equality and confidence.'[12]

There was considerable prejudice against women working. The writer William Greg thought that women could never master any profession because their minds and health would break down; as a solution to the problem of surplus women, he suggested they should emigrate.[13]

It was no surprise that spinsters were to form the backbone of the organised feminist movement. So much of the impetus for reform had its roots in the dearth of opportunities for unmarried middle-class women.

Such chronic female unemployment was exacerbated by the development of the separate spheres of home and work as a result of the Industrial Revolution. Opportunities for productive work at home lessened, and women ceased to be economic partners to their husbands as work migrated to the factories. Now that the home was no longer a workshop, women devoted themselves to home-making and childcare. The idea grew that a man should be paid a family wage, and that a married woman made an adequate economic contribution through running the home and family.[14] Domestic activities became the woman's preserve. Even that great feminist John Stuart Mill performed only one domestic chore: he made the tea when he returned home in the evening.[15]

Working-class women frequently worked in overcrowded and insanitary conditions; London dressmakers and milliners worked eighteen to twenty hours a day for months at a time. The national conscience was aroused by descriptions of women engaged in unsuitably heavy labour in the mines or in sweatshops. There was also a widespread belief that work lowered the moral tone of girls through giving them feelings of independence. Many Victorians would have withdrawn women from all forms of factory labour, so shocked were they by the new class of women workers, and they reiterated that a woman's place was in the home. 'Girls quickly become depraved . . . It seems almost an impossibility that a girl who has worked for a single season in a gang can become a modest and respectable woman . . . the effect of gangs on the married women employed in them is destructive of all the domestic virtues,' wrote one commentator.[16]

Nevertheless, working women did make some gains in economic and social independence. Those who worked in the factories, usually before marriage, learned punctuality, obedience, and hardiness. Such work brought out their capacities for comradeship and taught them self-respect, self-reliance and courage. Every woman received her own earnings as a matter of course, which gave women a new sense of freedom and prompted many to leave home at an early age.[17]

Middle-class women, however, were prescribed a life of idleness and were limited to the genteel occupations of dressmaker, milliner or governess. In 1853 Margaretta Greg wrote in her diary: 'A lady, to be such, must be a mere lady, and nothing else. She must not work for profit, or engage in any occupation that money can command, lest she invade the rights of the working classes, who live by their labour.'[18]

The home was viewed by Victorian men as a refuge and an antidote to the savage, competitive, grimy world of industry and work. Home was the temple of virtue. The family became the shrine of Victorian life. So women, the guardians of home and family, were set on a corresponding pedestal of sanctity and idealisation, summed up in Coventry Patmore's poem 'The Angel in the House' and in the extravagant hyperbole of John Ruskin. For Ruskin, home was a sacred place which repelled a hostile outside world, and his view of women was exaggeratedly romantic, based on an elevated chivalric view of both men and women.

So precious were women, Ruskin believed, they had to be protected by men from the public sphere. In *Sesame and Lilies* he wrote:

> The man's power is active, progressive, defensive. He is eminently the doer, the creator, the discoverer, the defender. His intellect is for speculation and invention; his energy for adventure, for war and for conquest, wherever war is just, wherever conquest necessary. But the woman's power is for rule, not for battle – and her intellect is not for invention or creation, but for sweet ordering, arrangement and decision. She sees the qualities of things, their claims and their places. Her great function is praise; she enters into no contest but infallibly adjudges the crown of contest. By her office and place she is protected from all danger and temptation.[19]

Woman, he wrote, must be incapable of error, incorruptibly good, infallibly wise – but 'not that she may set herself above her husband, but that she may never fail from his side . . .' Indeed, her whole divine purpose was merely to be the helpmate of man. So she should be educated like men 'only so far as may enable her to sympathise in her husband's pleasures, and in those of his best friends'.[20]

Ruskin's divine pedestal was a pretty bleak promontory for a woman of flesh and blood. Ruskin's own marriage was never consummated. He was impotent. In a letter to his lawyer he explained that he did not consummate his marriage on his wedding night because he was repelled by the sight of his wife's body. It was 'not formed to excite passion'.[21]

This paradoxical view, which identified the highest virtue with women's weakness, was widespread in the Victorian age and central to the resistance to women's suffrage. It was feminine weakness which was said to make men behave well towards women. One commentator wrote: 'In all modern civilised communities, and especially in the most refined and cultivated portion of those communities, women are treated by men with peculiar deference, tenderness and courtesy. Do they owe this treatment to their strength or to their weakness? Undoubtedly to the latter.'[22] And their role was essentially to make other people happy. In his best-selling manual *Manners Makyth Man*, the Reverend Edward Hardy wrote: 'Sweetness is to woman what sugar is to fruit. It is her first business to be happy – a sunbeam in the house, making others happy . . . Girls and women are willing enough to be agreeable to men if they do not happen to stand to them in relation of husband, brother or father; but it is not every woman who remembers that her raison d'être is to give out pleasure to all as fire gives out heat.'[23]

In 1839 the writer Alexander Walker managed to idealise women's alleged intellectual inferiority. Woman was the sacred epitome of sensibility, instinct and feelings; man was a slave to mere reason, which gave men a hallucination of mental supremacy. Yet he also maintained there was a vast difference between the brains of men and women, a natural inferiority of female intellect compensated by a vast superiority in instinct. 'Woman's perception of what is fitting, her politeness, her vanity, her affections, her sentiments, her dependence on and knowledge of man, her love, her artifice, her caprice, being chiefly instinctive, reach the highest degree of perfection; whereas her friendship, her philanthropy, her patriotism and her politics, requiring the exercise of reason, are so feeble as to be worthless.'[24]

Here were the arguments which would be used time and again by the opponents of women's suffrage: women lacked reason, they were guided instead by instinct, they weren't patriotic, their relationship to their country was adequately discharged through their husbands. Women as well as men viewed such disqualifications as virtues. The popular writer Sarah Stickney Ellis stated in 1839 that married women must accept 'the superiority of your husband, simply as a man'. Even though men were selfish, allowances should be made because they were trained to be superior. 'The love of woman appears to have been created solely to minister; that of man, to be ministered to.' A man should never have his dignity infringed. 'It is unquestionably the inalienable right of all men, whether ill or well, rich or poor, wise or foolish, to be treated with deference, and made much of in their own houses.'[25]

Women, she wrote, had to work for the happiness of others by guarding the comfort of the home. The house must be not only neat and clean but ordered through the minutest calculation to suit the tastes of all.[26] The woman's role was to inspire virtue and train children's souls for immortality.[27] In this lay not inferiority but influence.

'The women of England, possessing the grand privilege of being better instructed than those of any other country in the minutiae of domestic comfort, have obtained a degree of importance in society far beyond what their unobtrusive virtues would appear to claim. The long-established customs of their country have placed in their hands the high and holy duty of cherishing and protecting the minor morals of life, from whence springs all that is elevated in purpose, and glorious in action.'[28]

Mrs Stickney Ellis intended to rouse women against the developing threat of feminist subversion. Yet the arguments she advanced were the mirror image of the arguments advanced by feminists themselves. Like them, she expressed the widespread view that women counteracted the morals of masculine lives preoccupied with worldly goods and ambitions. Since the life of a businessman lowered and degraded the mind and promoted materialism and selfishness, she wrote, a wife should be 'a companion who will raise the tone of his mind from ... low anxieties and vulgar cares' and who will 'lead his thoughts to expatiate or repose on those subjects which convey a feeling of identity with a higher state of existence beyond this present life'.[29]

The moral elevation of man was so closely identified with feminine duty that, in his sermons, the moralist James Baldwin Brown blamed women for the moral deterioration of men under the hard influence of business. Women had succumbed to mean desires for money or the ridiculous phantom of women's rights when their true power was 'to love, to serve, to save'. But many women, he added, were still faithful to their role as a fountain of courage and inspiration to hard-pressed men and sent them forth each morning with new strength for their conflict.[30]

By the mid-nineteenth century the evangelicals were presenting women as more moral and virtuous than men. But men's intellectual powers were considered different and superior. Men had courage, boldness, discretion, honesty and sobriety. They had no choice but to act responsibly in looking out for the 'weaker vessel'. Women's vanity, affectation, ambition, artifice, confidence and stubbornness were vices, although virtues in men. Men were selfish and haughty, and male lust was recognised as a fact of life. Women were expected to stay at home, since children and domestic responsibilities were considered better suited to the more compassionate and tender sex. But men, while earning a living, were also expected to govern their families, protect and comfort their wives and lead the whole family in prayer. Women, busy at home, were expected to have a positive moral influence on the wider society. According to *The English Matron*, women had the potential to effect 'a great moral revolution ... in society'.[31] Conduct books encouraged wives to 'endeavour to correct any deviation from the path of Christian rectitude';[32] to 'mildly correct' husbands who were behaving uncharitably;[33] and 'gently to combat all that is faulty and weak in her husband's character'.[34]

Through such arguments the evangelicals were, ironically, providing a huge impetus for the argument of their arch-enemies. It was an argument that would be crucial to the battle for the suffrage. Women would lead men and all humanity on to a higher moral plane. According to Eliza

Farnham, women had spiritual courage, they were braver, steadier and calmer than men and they honoured their obligations more deeply. Nature meant woman to be the chief agent for improving human behaviour by moving man from savagery to civilisation. She wrote: 'Woman will grow into fitness for the sublime work which Nature has given her to do; and man, through her help and persuasion, will spontaneously assume the relation of a co-operator in it . . . And this will be the era of woman . . . with this theory of life, of its ends and means, it follows that the grandest era of humanity must be that which is dominated by the feminine qualities; especially that essential love of truth in motive, action and speech, which will make all these godlike in each individual, and give to their concrete expression the character which alone will justly entitle any system to the grand name of civilisation.'[35]

The view was beginning to be commonly expressed that humanity was gradually evolving towards perfection. In 1844 Robert Chambers had written that there would emerge 'a nobler type of humanity, which shall complete the zoological circle on this planet, and realise some of the dreams of the purest spirits of the present race'.[36] Herbert Spencer wrote in 1851: 'The ultimate development of the ideal man is logically certain, certain as any conclusion in which we place the most implicit faith: for instance, that all men will die.'[37] It may have been an age of radical insecurity but it was also an age of optimism. It was generally believed that Charles Darwin affirmed this idea of 'evolution' in *The Origin of Species*:

And as natural selection works solely by and for the good of each being, all corporeal and mental endowments will tend to progress towards perfection . . . Thus, from the war of nature, from famine and death, the most exalted object which we are capable of conceiving, namely, the production of the higher animals, directly follows. There is grandeur in this view of life, with its several powers, having been originally breathed into a few forms or into one; and that, while this planet has gone cycling on according to the fixed laws of gravity, from so simple a beginning endless forms most beautiful and most wonderful have been, and are being, evolved.[38]

Upon this general belief that humanity was evolving from a state of savagery towards scientific perfection middle- and upper-class women staked their claim that female emancipation would make them the catalysts for utopia. Prosperity had relegated women from these classes to the position of a status object. With servants taking care of the drudgery of domestic life, these women were ladies of leisure.

In her unpublished autobiographical novel *Cassandra*, Florence Nightingale wrote in 1852 about the intolerable nature of such a life. Mornings, she wrote, were spent sitting round a table in the drawing room, looking at prints, doing worsted work and reading little books. Afternoons were spent on drives. At night, she said, women 'suffer – even physically . . . the accumulation of nervous energy, which has had nothing to do during the day, makes them feel every night when they go to bed as if they were going mad. The vacuity and boredom of this existence are sugared over by false sentiment', by which she meant romanticism and fantasy.[39]

The energies of these women were to be channelled into revolt against their gilded subjugation and against the men who kept them there. They were going to discover their voice, their self-respect and their power.

The first notable challenge was made to women's position in law, and it came about through a society scandal. In law, married women had no separate personality at all. Property, earnings, liberty and conscience all belonged to their husbands. Crimes women committed in the presence of their husbands, apart from murder and high treason, were presumed to have taken place under coercion, so women were guiltless. Women could be locked up by their husbands, and had no rights at all over their children – unless they were illegitimate, in which case the mother alone had to shoulder their upkeep. By contrast, the father of a child born in wedlock was entitled to the entire control and custody of the child, regardless of the man's behaviour, and could bar the mother from all access. William Blackstone had written about coverture, the legal doctrine under which married women had no separate legal identity from that of their husbands and, as a result, could not own property: 'The disabilities a woman lies under are for the most part intended for her protection and benefit, so great a favourite is the female sex in the laws of England.'[40] To which one might say: thanks for nothing. Alexander Walker had it rather better. 'Thus wives in England are in all respects as to property, person and progeny in the condition of slaves. Thus has man made woman a slave, and himself at once a tyrant, and his slave's companion, not less degraded than she is.'[41]

When women married, they were placed in the same category as under-age children, wards, lunatics, idiots and outlaws. This legal limbo was bad enough. But it also gave rise to a number of baroque myths about the extent to which men could and did ill-treat them. For example, there was a widespread belief that a man could rid himself of his wife by selling her and exhibiting her with a halter round her neck; but this repellent display was actually a misdemeanour punishable by fine or imprisonment.[42]

As the head of the household, said Blackstone, husbands possessed the right of 'moderate correction' and could restrain their wives by 'domestic chastisement'. But this, he said, was 'confined within reasonable bounds and the husband was prohibited from using any violence towards his wife'.[43] The problem was, however, that many jurists upheld that it was *not* outrageous for a husband to beat his wife. But this was not in fact allowed by law. There was more legal protection for wives than was generally acknowledged; for example, wives could safeguard their property through trustees. The legal position of women was undoubtedly parlous and unjust. But their situation was made worse because so few were familiar with what the law actually provided.

One woman, however, found herself on a very steep learning curve indeed. Caroline Norton was a society beauty who took London society by storm in the season of 1826. The granddaughter of the playwright Richard Sheridan, she was witty, brilliant and fascinating. A fashionable political hostess whose house was frequented by Whig politicians, she developed a friendship with their leader, Lord Melbourne. Her husband George, however, was not only a Tory but was abusive and cruel and jealous of his wife's liaison. While Caroline was visiting her sister, George spirited away their three children, aged six, four and two, to live with a cousin, who barred their mother from seeing them at all.

Caroline then discovered that a woman had no rights over her own children and that a husband could do what he liked with them. Her letters asking for news of her children were returned to her. She once managed to meet them by stealth in St James's Park, but then they were sent to live in Scotland. Worse still, in 1836 George sued Lord Melbourne for 'criminal conversation' with his wife. A jury dismissed the charge, but not before Caroline discovered that she had no legal standing in the trial. Penniless, she found that George refused to give her any of the money or property that were historically hers, but over which by law he had ownership.

So Caroline determined to change the laws from which she had suffered so much. As she wrote in 1854: 'I have learned the law respecting married women piecemeal, by suffering every one of its defects of protection.'[44] She took to writing passionate pamphlets calling for mothers to keep their children if adultery was not proved against them. Championed by the MP for Reading, Thomas Talfourd, a lawyer who had represented husbands in such cases and whose legal victories had violated his sense of justice, she inspired the Infants' Custody Act which Parliament passed in 1839 and which allowed an innocent mother to have the care of her children until they were seven, even though the father remained the guardian at law. She subsequently agitated for legal protection of the property and earnings of separated women against seizure by their husbands.[45] In 1839 Norton agreed to let Caroline see the children from time to time, although one child died through his neglect.[46]

Yet for all that she had suffered, Caroline Norton remained staunchly anti-feminist. 'I for one (with millions more) believe in the natural superiority of man, as I do in the existence of God . . . I never pretended to the wild and ridiculous doctrine of equality,' she wrote.[47] 'The natural position of woman is inferiority to man. Amen! That is a thing of God's appointing, not of man's devising. I believe it sincerely, as a part of my religion; and I accept it as a matter proved to my reason. I never pretended to the world any ridiculous notion of equality. I will even hold

that (as one coming under the general rule that the wife must be inferior
to the husband) I occupy that position . . .'[48]

Others were to draw a far more radical lesson from the Norton scandal. The outrage over her treatment and the absence of equality for
women before the law prompted upper-middle-class women and others
to press for divorce law reform. The reformers were led by Caroline
Norton's close friend Lord Lyndhurst, the octogenarian ex-Lord
Chancellor. Ranged against them were pious Christians led by William
Gladstone, then in a period of political opposition in the House of
Commons and for whom all divorce was anti-Christian. There were
three crunch issues here for women: the ability of women to defend
themselves in court, the protection of married women's property and
access to divorce on equal terms with men.[49]

The latter two issues, as Lawrence Stone has noted, hit the Victorian
nerve over home and family. The demand for equal access to divorce
struck at the foundation of the sexual double standard under which men
were held to be blameless for sexual misbehaviour for which women
were penalised. Giving married women control over property, moreover,
threatened the strategic manipulation of marriage to advance property
interests. In the financial top ten per cent of society, married women
already kept control over their own property through trustees. The proposal to extend this to the rest of the population struck terror into the
hearts of the legislators.[50]

The subsequent Divorce Reform Act of 1857 introduced some very
limited reform on these fronts. Some protection was given to the property
of separated wives, and the grounds on which wives could sue for divorce
were extended. But more far-reaching proposals for giving married
women rights over their property were defeated and the double standard
of sexual conduct remained. Men could obtain a divorce if their wives
merely committed adultery. Women, by contrast, could obtain a divorce
only if their husbands had committed incest or adultery with desertion,
cruelty or unnatural offences.

Gladstone, who was opposed to divorce root and branch, nevertheless
argued against this double standard. He thought it was 'not so much

designed in the spirit of preventing a sin as by way of the assertion – I must add, the ungenerous assertion – of the superiority of our position in creation . . . [which] results from the exclusive possession of power and from the habits of mind connected therewith.' But supporters said in the debate on the bill that the distinction was 'consistent with the intuitive feeling of mankind. In all ages it had been felt that the adultery of the wife brought ruin on the married state, but not so much the simple unfaithfulness of the husband'.[51] It was of course an irony that Gladstone, who opposed divorce reform, supported female equality on this issue while Caroline Norton, who crusaded for divorce reform, fervently supported the absolute superiority of men over women.

This issue of the sexual double standard was absolutely crucial to the development of the women's movement and the fight for the suffrage. It was the 1857 Divorce Act which propelled it on to centre stage. For this reforming measure not only gave it the imprimatur of Parliament at a time when women were beginning to demand fair treatment as equal citizens. By making divorce more common, it turned the double standard into a repeated and visible irritant in the public sphere and transformed it into a female *casus belli*. For central to the feminist cause was the plain unfairness of treating women differently under the law and ignoring or even condoning sexual misbehaviour in men which for a woman spelled social and economic ruin.

In particular, the divorce courts brought to light the fact that violence could be committed by husbands. The issue was not so much male violence, which was a given, but the fact that it could be perpetrated by members of those social classes which had been assumed to be a breed apart from the atavistic savagery of the lower orders. The suffragist Frances Power Cobbe wrote:

Who imagined that the wives of English *gentlemen* might be called on to endure from their husbands the violence and cruelty we are accustomed to picture exercised only in the lowest lanes and courts of our cities, where drunken ruffians, stumbling home from the gin-palace, assault the miserable partners of their vices with curses, kicks and blows? Who could have imagined it possible that well-born and well-educated men, in honourable professions, should be guilty of the same brutality? Imagine a handsomely furnished drawing-room, with its books, and flowers, and lights, and all the refinements of civilised life, for the scene of similar outrages. Imagine the offender a well-dressed gentleman, tall and powerful as English gentlemen are wont to be; the victim shrinking from his blows – a gentle, high-bred, English *lady*! Good God! Does not the picture make every true man set his teeth and clench his hand?[52]

Miss Cobbe concluded that marriage would become more and more rare, and that the Englishman of the twentieth century would abandon claims of marital authority and bring to marriage a nobler and more tender conjugal love. The Englishwoman, meanwhile, would learn to 'rise above her present pitiful ambitions of social advancement and petty personal vanity' and become true and brave and prepared to cope with poverty.[53]

Yet the paradox behind the double standard, which had surfaced as far back as Mary Wollstonecraft's work, was once again all too visible. The critical point which emerged from the battles over divorce reform was that, for legislators, the dangerous sex was not female but male. If divorce was made easy and respectable, it was feared, this would lead to serial polygamy because of the promiscuous sexual appetite of the human male. This was a view with which women were very much in agreement.[54] It was a view that was to contradict the claim that the women's movement was about 'equality'. For while feminists went to war against the ill-effects on women of the double standard, at the very same time they were to maintain that male sexual behaviour was dangerous and predatory while female sexual behaviour was benign and moral. It was a paradox which was to allow their opponents to open up a deadly front against them – by agreeing that women were special, and had to be kept so.

4

THE EMBERS SMOULDER

In the wake of the industrial revolution, the pace of change was so bewildering that many found it difficult to get their bearings. Economic, social, intellectual and religious life all seemed in a state of flux. Developing urbanisation led to the rise of pressure groups: the Chartists, the Anti-Corn Law League, the trade unions. The sanctity of private property was challenged by thinkers such as Robert Owen and John Stuart Mill, Thomas Carlyle and John Ruskin. But it was only radicals like these who were enthusiasts for democracy. For others, the notion carried connotations of communism or dictatorship, as in France.[1] Yet agitation was building to give women the vote. The embers of the revolt were beginning to smoulder.

In 1831 the *Westminster Review* published an article by a young woman, later Mrs Mylne, advocating women's suffrage. In a preface to a later edition published in 1872, she described how she had got the idea from reading the work of the utilitarian philosopher Jeremy Bentham, who had proposed universal suffrage in the 1820s. When she was invited to air her ideas, however, the paralysing conventions which prevented women from expressing themselves in public almost destroyed her health. She went into a decline and only completed the article under doctor's orders as the best cure for her complaint.[2] In 1832 William Johnston Fox, MP for Oldham, published a pamphlet saying the same thing.

By 1830 Thomas Arnold was predicting that the pressures for male franchise reform were threatening revolution. Panic carried the 1832 Reform Bill into law.[3] But this was very limited in scope. Although the ruling Whigs were reformers, both they and the Tories agreed that democracy was so dangerous that landed property was important in guaranteeing the stability of the social order.[4] So the bill proposed only a limited franchise to men owning or tenanting property above a certain value. It was passed not to subvert the old order but to consolidate it and to relieve the danger of revolution. News that the Reform Bill had passed into law was met throughout the country by banquets, illuminations and the ringing of church bells.[5]

The irony was that the 1832 Reform Act, that first step on the road to democracy, actually debarred women from the franchise for the very first time. Under Tudor and Stuart law, a woman freeholder or burgess had been entitled to vote at parliamentary elections. During the eighteenth century, when women's dependence on men increasingly became seen as natural and inevitable, this had fallen into disuse.[6]

During the debate on the Reform Bill, Henry 'Orator' Hunt, the most advanced radical in the House of Commons, presented a petition from Miss Mary Smith, a lady of enormous wealth from The Ridings, Yorkshire.[7] This proposed that every unmarried female meeting the bill's property requirements should be given the vote. The response from MPs was swift and condign. The parliamentary draftsmen altered the bill's wording from 'persons' to 'male persons', thus explicitly restricting the suffrage to men.[8] For the rest of the century women would be battling not for new rights but for the restoration of old ones.

After the Reform Bill was passed, working people began to campaign for universal male suffrage and the removal of all property qualifications. In 1838 the Chartists, who were to be a potent radical force for a decade, published their petition which suggested an end to all monopoly and oppression, including 'the existing monopolies ... of paper money, of

machinery, of land, of the public press, of religion, of the means of trav-
elling and transit'.[9] The cabinet-maker William Lovett, secretary of the
London Working Men's Association, included female suffrage in the first
draft of the petition, but it was rapidly struck out as it was thought this
might hold back the suffrage of men.

The Chartist cause changed the nature of politics. It covered the
country with a network of political associations, and gave rise to petitions, mass meetings, conventions and riots. By the winter of 1840 at
least five hundred Chartist leaders were in jail.[10] And, crucially, women
were becoming involved in the campaign, forming political associations
to further the charter.[11] Women were also being swept along with the
great middle-class cause of the times, the Anti-Corn Law League. As
depression, protest and revolt spread throughout the land, Manchester
radicals and businessmen such as Richard Cobden and John Bright
turned the campaign against the Corn Laws into a moral and religious
crusade. The League had a massive influence on the political landscape,
monopolising pressure-group politics for much of the 1840s. Its style
owed much to the movement for the abolition of slavery, giving rise to
violent denunciations of Parliament by inflammatory speakers. And,
importantly, it encouraged women to help organise its teas, fêtes and
bazaars.[12] It was a most significant apprenticeship. Women were not
merely starting to dip their toes into the political maelstrom; they were
listening and learning how most effectively to mobilise and manipulate
public opinion.

In mid-century this was febrile. In 1848 unrest on the continent was
reflected in riots in London, Liverpool, Glasgow and other cities. Troops
under the Duke of Wellington barricaded Downing Street and bridges
over the Thames in London and garrisoned the Bank of England. The
Chartists' humiliating collapse provoked radical despair at achieving
anything through national politics, and channelled forces for reform into
other outlets such as municipal politics or temperance agitation.[13]

In 1844, in his novel *Coningsby*, Disraeli depicted a governing class
falling into helplessness in the face of the unfranchised clamouring for the
vote. There was an intensifying passion for a science of society to explain

and solve everything. The emergence of cults such as Christian Science and theosophy illustrated the frantic need for guides through modernity.[14] Émile Zola wrote in a letter that the time was characterised by 'impetuosity, devouring activity; activity in the sciences, activity in commerce, in the arts, everywhere: railroads, electricity applied to telegraphy, steam making vessels move, balloons launching themselves in the air . . . Thus the world is hurling itself into the path of the future, running and eager to see what awaits it at the end of its race.'[15]

Science was delivering a hefty blow to organised religion. Sir William Paley's theory of natural theology had emphasised the order and design of a creative intelligence, and the romantic sensibility had found the divine spirit rolling through all things. But then Sir Charles Lyell's *Principles of Geology*, 1830–3, Robert Chambers's *Vestiges of Creation* in 1844 and Charles Darwin's *The Origin of Species* in 1859 turned nature into a visceral battleground. All intellectual theories were deeply insecure, and morality itself seemed to be threatened. Was there a God? Was He a person or a force? Were there heaven and hell? Was there a true religion, theism or Christianity? What sort of Christianity? Did man have free will or not? Was he merely a higher form of ape?[16] Looking back from the vantage point of the 1880s, James Froude summed it up: 'All round us, the intellectual lightships had broken from their moorings, and it was then a new and trying experience. The present generation which has grown up in an open spiritual ocean, which has got used to it and has learned to swim for itself, will never know what it was to find the lights all drifting, the compasses all awry and nothing left to steer by except the stars.'[17]

The decline in Christianity and the rise of atheism were assumed to mean the destruction of morality and the resulting disintegration of society. Evangelicals dwelt morbidly upon moral imperfections in themselves and others, not to mention their terror of hell and damnation. Reviews of *The Descent of Man* in 1871 severely censured Darwin for 'revealing his zoological conclusions to the general public at a moment when the sky of Paris was red with the incendiary flames of the commune'.[18] Beleaguered Victorians clung ever more compulsively to Christianity's outward form. The churches gained many converts. Piety became fashionable.[19] Moral reform became a spiritual end in itself, and gained all the intensity of religious zeal.

The importance of religion to the Victorian political and social reform movements, including female suffrage, cannot be overestimated. Evangelicalism in the nineteenth century was a movement of enormous psychological power and physical energy in spreading its message throughout society. It called upon those who were already saved to join others in the common work of alerting individuals to spiritual danger and opening for them the gates of salvation. The movement took a number of forms, and got its philanthropic and crusading institutions going by dint of assembling backers and guarantors of funds, publicising its causes, sermonising, collecting subscriptions, using the networks of evangelical lecture tours, societies and public occasions, bringing together capital and administrative expertise and recruiting a huge amount of voluntary help.[20]

In this way middle-class liberals were given the apparatus of political activism. The use of magazines and tracts, the staging of public meetings, the appeal to public opinion and the creation of voluntary societies all paved the way for the highly organised middle-class political movements later in the century.[21] There was one other factor which was particularly relevant to the great cause of female suffrage. The Society of Friends, known as Quakers, were prominent philanthropists and radicals. And right from their origins in the seventeenth century, Quaker men had treated their women as equals.

Evangelicalism stressed in particular the importance of charitable conduct. The rise of Victorian philanthropy was a key factor in propelling women into the public sphere. In the early nineteenth century it was virtually unheard of for a woman to make a public speech. Some men discouraged women from even attending public meetings. At a meeting of the Society for the Propagation of the Gospels in the 1820s, several ladies had attended hidden behind the organ. 'A bishop was publicly rebuked by a baron of the exchequer for bringing in his own wife upon his arm,' noted one Christian paper.[22]

But middle-class, moneyed women needed something of interest to do. Their houses were run by servants. With little suitable employment other than writing and governessing, they had time on their hands. They were also increasingly regarded as agents of social improvement. Social reformers from Hannah More onwards argued that women's domestic virtues of morality, self-denial and compassion were what was needed in English public life. The suffragist and anti-vivisectionist Frances Power Cobbe wrote of woman's contribution: 'We want her sense of the law of love to complete man's sense of the law of justice; we want her influence inspiring virtue by gentle promptings from within, to complete man's external legislation of morality. And, then, we want woman's practical service. We want her genius for detail, her tenderness for age and suffering, her comprehension of the wants of childhood to complete man's gigantic charities.'[23]

All this of course greatly reinforced female stereotypes. The claim by women to moral authority and greater social recognition depended on public belief in their special qualities.[24] Female publicists argued that it was woman's duty to rescue men from the sensual morass which imperilled their souls. In 1839 Sarah Lewis argued that 'the moral world is ours . . . ours by the very indication of God himself'.[25] Numerous novels were published which examined women's emotional lives and conduct within the home and emphasised the moral influence they could exert.[26]

So the woman of leisure turned to philanthropy. As that indefatigable chronicler of female manners Sarah Stickney Ellis maintained: 'Men, engaged in the active affairs of life, have neither time nor opportunity for those innumerable little acts of consideration which come within the sphere of female duty, nor are they by nature so fitted as woman for entering into the peculiarities of personal feeling, so as to enable them to sympathise with the suffering or the distressed.'[27]

It was above all the domestic virtues of home and family with which women were to civilise the public sphere. Florence Nightingale told her nurses: 'While you have a ward, it must be your home and its inmates must be your children.'[28] As the family was built up more and more into the paramount social unit, women's sense of mission became more pronounced. Christian philanthropists were to impose middle-class norms of domesticity on the working class; and only women could do it. Benevolent women believed that they could turn the poor into better wives and mothers and into imitations of themselves. So they set out to indoctrinate the inmates of institutions through tracts, prayer meetings and Bible readings to replace deceit and pride with guilt. They believed they would act as 'physicians of the soul' to return the nation's pariahs back to society. Eliza Lynn Linton observed: 'There is scarcely a woman who does not think herself a minor St Peter with the keys of heaven and hell at her girdle; and the more conscientious she is, the narrower the door she unlocks'.[29]

The process turned some women into public figures. Ellen Ranyard, who helped set up the London Bible and Domestic Mission in 1857, recruited poor Bible-women for work in districts considered impenetrable by male reformers. Women, she said, had to take the lead in missionary work because only women could penetrate deep into the hearts of the poor. 'Why are they so wretched in their circumstances and in their habits in our great metropolis of civilisation? Because the middle-class which ought to civilise them has known so little of them. This knowledge is now being daily attained in a womanly way. The women make their homes – and it is these who must be influenced.'[30]

Louisa Twining, born in 1820 to a wealthy family, was so shocked by the slums and by workhouse conditions that she started the Workhouse Visiting Society, which paved the way for the 1875 act which enabled women to be Poor Law guardians. Mary Carpenter, born in 1807 and educated in her father's boys' school, opened the first of her ragged schools in Bristol in 1846, and by the 1850s was running reformatories. Angela Burdett Coutts became a great philanthropist, and in 1871 was raised to the peerage in recognition of her benevolent work. In 1857 Florence Nightingale returned from her pioneering nursing work in the Crimea to a storm of popularity unknown by any woman previously. That same year the National Association for the Promotion of Social Science was established and admitted women to

membership. In 1869 Octavia Hill founded the Charity Organisation
Society which believed mass misery arose from indiscriminate doles. All
of this delivered a huge impetus to the activities of public-spirited
women.[31]

The formation of professions like medicine and public administration
produced even more sharply differentiated roles for the sexes. Wives
were expected to oil the wheels of their husbands' careers. Some such
men viewed their wives as secondary and inferior. But there were also
couples bound together by companionship and mutual affection and
respect, which gave wives considerable informal influence. Jane Simon,
for example, the wife of a reforming doctor, was intellectually formidable, competing as an equal with Ruskin, Darwin and the social analyst
Owen Chadwick at regular salons and dinner parties organised by her
husband John.[32]

From the 1850s there was a growing dialogue between male experts
and female social reformers. Edward Sieveking, a fellow of the Royal
College of Physicians, used Florence Nightingale to prove that women's
involvement in sanitary reform – public cleanliness and personal
hygiene – was a natural extension of their domestic role for 'what we
claim for the woman in the house we would also claim for her beyond its
walls'.[33] Women could help show the correlation between 'temperance,
equable temper, and other moral virtues' and 'intemperance, vice and
misery'. The Rev Frederick Maurice, the socialist founder of the London
Working Men's College, found that a middle-class lady's presence in
the Poor Law hospitals provided a 'softening, humanising, health-giving
influence', teaching a man that 'in whatever abyss he may be sunk he is
still capable of health and resurrection'. Women hospital visitors were
able to supervise the medical regime, administer medicines, scrutinise the
nurses and enquire into the moral habits of poor patients.[34]

Middle-class women were being used to provide links between the
classes and promote social and political stability. Maurice believed that
if men recognised the importance of philanthropy, this would stem the
growing demand for female emancipation. Such anxiety reflected the
fact that philanthropy had given women an enlarged social role,

employment opportunities and the experience to reflect on their position which fed into feminist campaigns.[35]

But as more and more women became involved in social problems, they became more dissatisfied with their own powerlessness. The embers of revolt began to glow more fiercely.

5

THE LADIES OF LANGHAM PLACE

In 1855 women started to get organised. Florence Nightingale's cousin, Barbara Leigh Smith Bodichon, gathered around her a group of feminist women who during the next decade met in Langham Place in central London, the meeting place which was to become the cradle of the women's movement. Mrs Bodichon was the daughter of Benjamin Smith, the radical MP for Norwich, and came from an enlightened and well-connected family. She was tall, handsome, intelligent and vigorous. She was also a woman of independent means, since her father gave her an income of £300 per year.

In 1856 she got together a small group of women to sign a petition in favour of the Married Women's Property Bill, which, at her instigation, Sir Erskine Perry MP was about to introduce. The very existence of a committee of women was a startling novelty. Mrs Bodichon managed to collect some twenty-four thousand names, even though she knew nothing of committee procedure and kept no minute book. The reaction was very strong on both sides. It was claimed that such a measure would disrupt society, destroy the home and turn women into loathsome, self-assertive creatures, but in 1857 it passed its Second Reading. At the same time, however, the Marriage and Divorce Bill was going through

Parliament and the two bills clashed. Caroline Norton, who wanted women who were obliged to leave their husbands to retain their own property, repudiated the 'ill advised public attempts on the part of a few women to assert their "equality" with men'. The divorce bill cut the ground from under the property bill; if injured wives were protected, what did uninjured wives want with their property?[1] So Mrs Bodichon's property bill was blocked. But battle had been joined.

Mrs Bodichon then turned her attention to women and work. She wrote a paper which said women should be clerks, doctors and nurses. She was howled down. A woman's profession, said her critics, was marriage. If single life was remunerated, marriage would decline and the home would collapse. In 1857 Mrs Bodichon started the *Englishwoman's Journal* expressly to repudiate this viewpoint.[2] This publication, which printed articles advocating women's suffrage, became a mouthpiece of feminism.

Almost no jobs were open to educated women except teaching and needlework, both of which offered deplorable pay and conditions. Nursing was just beginning, secretarial work didn't exist, shop assistants were all men, female journalists, apart from the political economist and philosopher Harriet Martineau, could find no openings and there were no women civil servants. Women couldn't be doctors, lawyers or architects; if they wrote they often did so under men's names and if they painted they couldn't get exhibited unless they belonged to a family of artists.

So Mrs Bodichon and her friends set up in Berners Street, in central London, an employment bureau, training centre and reading room. They started classes in arithmetic, law copying and printing; they interviewed employers, placed apprentices and dealt with streams of unemployed gentlewomen. They tried to make office and clerical work, as well as printing, telegraphy and hairdressing, respectable for middle-class women. There was a tremendous outpouring of energy to promote female type compositors, hotel managers, wood engravers, house decorators, watchmakers, telegraphists. Augusta Webster, admitted to art school in South Kensington, nearly dashed women's art prospects when she was expelled for whistling. Louie Garrett reported that she had asked the man who was washing her hair whether this was a suitable trade for women. 'Impossible, madam!' the man cried in horror. 'Why, it took *me* a fortnight to learn it.'[3]

Soon, however, Mrs Bodichon and her friends realised that the lack of education for girls and the political disabilities of women were crucial factors behind the barriers to employment.[4] Education, indeed, was the key that would unlock the political sphere.

Education was a particularly middle-class grievance, since middle-class girls received a worse education than their working-class counterparts. Working-class girls went to co-educational elementary schools where they were taught by trained teachers. Middle-class girls either went to small boarding schools or had governesses teaching French, music, drawing and deportment. Boys went to school as a preparation for active life but this was considered unnecessary for women. On 1 May 1848 the first public action to give middle- and upper-class girls an equal education was taken by the Rev Frederick Maurice, a professor at King's College, London. He opened Queen's College in Harley Street, which offered to governesses free evening classes in maths, geography, Latin, history, theology and mental and moral philosophy. Among the students were Frances Buss and Dorothea Beale.[5]

These two women were to become pioneers in girls' education and were thus to unlock the doors of female ambition. In 1850 Miss Buss founded North London Collegiate School; in 1858 Miss Beale founded Cheltenham Ladies' College. Miss Buss wrote: 'The terrible sufferings of the women of my own class for want of a good elementary training have more than ever intensified my earnest desire to lighten, ever so little, the misery of women brought up "to be married and taken care of" and left alone in the world destitute. It is impossible for words to express my fixed determination of alleviating this evil – even to the small extent of one neighbourhood only.'[6]

Blackheath School, in south London, run by Miss Browning, gave its girls an unusually broad education, including literature, art and music. One of its pupils was Elizabeth Garrett, one of ten children of a merchant and ship owner from Snape, Suffolk, and another was Elizabeth's younger sister, Millicent. Elizabeth, a bright and politically engaged character, was a great influence on young Milly. Elizabeth talked to her younger siblings about Garibaldi's freeing of Italy from the Austrians, Carlyle's *Cromwell* and Macaulay's *History of England*. She also talked about modern politics, and particularly about women's rights.[7]

She had a great friend called Emily Davies, the only daughter of the Rector of Gateshead, who, if anything, had even stronger views. Emily said the whole position of women was fundamentally wrong, and so Elizabeth and Emily decided to change it. The younger Garrett children disliked Emily and dreaded her visits because 'she was too positive and rational, too severe and dry'. But her ideas transmuted through Elizabeth's voice were absorbed nevertheless by the Garrett children. 'Slavery was wrong, liberty was desirable and the position of women must be changed.'[8]

In 1859 Elizabeth Garrett and Emily Davies, who had met Barbara Bodichon in Algiers, turned up at Langham Place.[9] Elizabeth noted the work of the women's employment bureau, read the *Englishwoman's Journal*, heard about the campaign for the Married Women's Property bill and contacted the National Association for the Promotion of Social Science; the world opened out for her. She attended a lecture delivered by Dr Elizabeth Blackwell, who had gained a medical degree in America and was to become Britain's first woman doctor. The most important listener there, said Dr Blackwell, was 'the bright, intelligent young lady whose interest in the study of medicine was then aroused – Miss Elizabeth Garrett'. Elizabeth became determined to be a doctor herself. Her mother was totally unsympathetic. She feared her daughter would become a social outcast and a figure of fun. But her father loved a stand-up fight and backed her with money and moral support, although sometimes he would burst out to the other children: 'I don't think I can go on with it; it will kill your mother.'[10]

There is a story, possibly apocryphal, about a conversation Emily Davies once had with the Garretts. 'Well,' said Emily, 'it is clear enough what is to be done: you, Elizabeth, must open the medical profession to women, I must see about higher education and as the vote will follow after the other two, Milly here, who is younger than we are, must attend to that.'[11] In due course, that is precisely what the three of them were to do.

While women were becoming radicalised and educated, pressure was growing for female suffrage. In 1843 Mrs Henry Reid published *A Plea for Women*, calling for the vote. She wrote that women required representation because of the many laws passed to protect them from their nearest male relatives. 'The weaker they are, the greater is their need of equal rights, that they may not fall under the tyranny of the stronger portion of their race.'[12] In 1846 the first of a deluge of leaflets supporting women's suffrage poured from the pen of Ann Knight, a Quaker from Chelmsford active in anti-slavery and other radical causes.

And already there was fierce opposition from both men and women. The female author of *Women's Rights and Duties*, published in 1840, anonymously spelt out the argument. Women were unfit for the vote, they didn't need it and it would unfit them as women. Women's interests, which were no different from those of men, would not be served by the franchise but would bring women into collision with men. 'Nothing could possibly be devised more disastrous to the condition of women. They would be utterly crushed; the old prejudices would be revived against their education, or their meddling with anything but household duties . . .'[13]

In 1848 Joseph Hume moved a resolution in the Commons extending the vote to householder women. Benjamin Disraeli spoke in favour. By 1850 it was these rumbles of revolt which provoked Mrs Stickney Ellis and others to publish a flurry of books anxiously restating women's domestic role.

But the rumbles had materialised into an earthquake across the Atlantic. Elizabeth Cady Stanton, Lucretia Mott and others prominent in the fight against slavery and against liquor met in 1848 in Seneca Falls, New York State, and, with a thousand people present, drew up the first public protest against women's political, social and economic inferiority. They resolved that every human being whose property or labour was taxed was entitled to a direct share in government; that women were entitled to the suffrage and to be considered eligible for office; that civil and professional employment should be thrown open to them; and that wives should have equal rights to property.[14]

Elizabeth Cady Stanton believed in the anthropological theories of Lewis Henry Morgan, who held that savage cultures in the 'mother age' had been matriarchies, and that women had once been free and independent, after which there was a long period of male dominance. Her conclusions, though, were illogical. If centuries of such oppression had left women just as capable of self-rule as men, the oppression couldn't have been as severe as claimed; but if women had been left as a result inferior to men, they could hardly claim the franchise as equals.[15] Despite such niceties of reasoning, however, the start of the feminist revolt in America was to have a decisive effect upon two radicals eagerly watching events from Britain: Mrs Harriet Taylor and her very close friend, the eminent philosopher John Stuart Mill.

In 1851 Mill published his *Enfranchisement of Women*, in which he based his argument for female suffrage on the need for equality. Society was only now getting rid of Negro slavery, monarchical despotism, the hereditary feudal nobility and religious disabilities, he wrote, and it was treating men as citizens. So women could not be excluded. Women did not have a 'proper sphere' of their own, he maintained. Where motherhood was incompatible with a public role, this would sort itself out. Many women were wives and mothers only because no other career was open to them. Women should contribute at least some income to the family so that they were not dependent on men for subsistence. Unbridled power over women, according to Mill, had corrupted the psyche of the man.

'He [Man] was a patriarch and a despot within four walls, and irresponsible power had its effect, greater or less according to his disposition, in rendering him domineering, exacting, self-worshipping, when not capriciously or brutally tyrannical.'[16]

Despite this unprepossessing profile, men, it seemed, were closer to women than ever before. 'They have now scarcely any tastes but those which they have in common with women, and for the first time in the world, men and women are really companions.' However – and this was a remarkable twist in Mill's argument – the fact that women were weaker than men meant that unless the gap between the sexes was eradicated, the closeness between them presented a threat to the male sex. 'Those who are so careful that women should not become men do not see that men are becoming, what they have decided that women should be – are falling into the feebleness which they have so long cultivated in their companions. Those who are associated in their lives tend to become assimilated in character. In the present closeness of association between the sexes, men cannot retain manliness unless women acquire it.'[17]

In other words, female emancipation was necessary to prevent men from becoming unmanned through corruption by exposure to a weaker sex. Similarly, education for women was necessary because if men had intellectual communion only with those to whom they could lay down the law, they would fail to get any wiser. A woman, after all, was on a higher intellectual plane than a man: 'There is one person, often greatly his superior in understanding, who is obliged to consult him and whom he is not obliged to consult.' The influence of the unemancipated wife, however, was usually illiberal and anti-popular and so when a man married he usually 'declines into conservatism and sympathises with the holders of power and authority'. The emancipation of women was therefore necessary for the interests of men as well as women.[18]

In the space of a few paragraphs, therefore, this essay managed to convey that women were superior to men, that marriage was a thoroughly reactionary state and that female emancipation would be doing men a great favour. It was hardly surprising, then, that the novelist Charlotte Brontë believed the *Enfranchisement* had been written by a harsh representative of her own sex.

'When I first read the paper,' she wrote, 'I thought it was the work of a powerful-minded, clear-headed woman who had a hard, jealous heart, muscles of iron and nerves of bend leather; of a woman who longed for power and had never felt affection.' Discovering it had been written by Mill, Charlotte Brontë conceded its 'admirable sense', although she thought Mill would make a 'hard, dry, dismal world of it'. His head 'is, I dare say, very good, but I feel disposed to scorn his heart'.[19]

But Charlotte Brontë had effectively been right the first time. For Mill was later to attribute the *Enfranchisement* to Harriet Taylor, who had become his wife. On 20 March 1854 he wrote to Harriet that the essay would appear in a collection of articles accompanied by a preface 'which will show that much of all my later articles, and all the best of that one, were, as they were, my Darling's'.[20] Mill's concern over the status of women, to be expressed again in 1869 in his book *The Subjection of Women*, was greatly deepened by Harriet Taylor. In his autobiography of 1873 he claimed that Harriet's interest in him was due to his sharing these beliefs. He wrote: 'But that perception of the vast practical bearings of women's disabilities which found expression in the book on the "Subjection of Women" was acquired mainly through her teaching. But for her rare knowledge of human nature and comprehension of moral and social influences, though I should doubtless have held my present opinions, I should have had a very insufficient perception of the mode in which the consequences of the inferior position of women intertwine themselves with all the evils of existing society and with all the difficulties of human improvement.'[21]

Indeed; for, as the historian Gertrude Himmelfarb has noted, Harriet Taylor manipulated both her husbands, with her domestic bullying matched only by her intellectual arrogance.[22]

Mill was twenty-four and Harriet thirty-three when they first met. She was the wife of a prosperous merchant and mother of two, with a third child born the following year. Harriet lived apart from her first husband, but she stayed with him in town from time to time and even received Mill there. Mill took trips abroad with her, and paid extended visits to her in the country, where her husband rarely joined her. Mill insisted that it was years before the relationship became intimate, but it was clear that this occurred almost immediately. For almost twenty years

Harriet was his 'incomparable friend' despite her being married. In 1831 a 'reconciliation' took place between Mill and Mr Taylor; the following summer Mill wrote Harriet a love letter. He docilely acquiesced to her telling him what subjects to write about, the order in which he should write them and the points he should stress.[23]

Naturally enough, anti-feminists who feared the loss of the separate female role were deeply opposed to such arguments for women's emancipation. In the 1860s they claimed that such reforms would make women unwilling to marry. W. R. Greg wrote:

> To endeavour to make women independent of men; to multiply and facilitate their enjoyment; to enable them to earn a separate and ample subsistence ... to induct them generally into avocations, not only as interesting and beneficent and therefore appropriate but specially and definitely as lucrative; to surround single life for them with so smooth an entrance ... that marriage shall almost come to be regarded not as their most honourable function and especial calling, but merely as one of many ways open to them ... would appear to be the aim and theory of many female reformers ... Few more radical or fatal errors, we are satisfied, philanthropy has ever made.[24]

But support among female pioneers was also far from unanimous. Even some feminists were worried that women might lose their femininity. George Eliot wrote to Emily Davies: 'There lies just that kernel of truth in the vulgar alarm of men that women should be unsexed. We can no more afford to part with that exquisite type of gentleness, tenderness, possible maternity suffusing a woman's being with affectionateness, which makes what we mean by the feminine character, than we can afford to part with the human lobe, the mutual subjection of soul between a man and a woman.'

One of the most virulent opponents of female suffrage was that rebel against the domestic incarceration of women, Florence Nightingale. At first she opposed a movement which seemed merely to want to replicate what men did rather than to fulfil women's particular vocation. In

Notes on Nursing, in 1859, she attacked the 'jargon about the rights of women' which 'urges women to do all that men do including the medical and other professions merely because men do it, and without regard to whether this *is* the best that women can do; and of the jargon which urges women to do nothing men do, merely because they are women'.[25]

By 1861 she was feeling lonely and discouraged; she was bitter that women were not flocking to help in her crusade to establish nursing standards. As her health approached collapse she poured out a diatribe against women, who, she said, possessed no sympathy. Her doctrines had taken no hold among women. Her sister, aunt and female cousins had never 'altered one hour of her existence for me'. 'It makes me mad,' she raged, 'the "Woman's Rights" talk about the "want of a field" for them – when I know I would gladly give £500 a year for a woman secretary ...' Her own family, she claimed, didn't even know the names of Cabinet ministers, which churches had Bishops and which men of the day were alive and which dead. Women, she alleged, craved not to love but to be loved. 'They scream at you for sympathy all day long, they are incapable of giving *any* in return, for they cannot remember your affairs long enough to do so ... They cannot state a fact accurately to another, nor can that other attend to it accurately enough for it to become information ... I am sick with indignation at what wives and mothers will do of the most egregious selfishness. And people call it maternal or conjugal affection, and think it pretty to say so.'[26]

When she thought that her reform of workhouse nursing would collapse for want of anyone to work as nurses, she wrote in 1865: 'The more chattering and noise there is about Woman's mission, the less of efficient women we can find. It makes me mad to hear people talk about unemployed women. If they are unemployed it is because they won't work.' In September 1860 Mill asked her to support the movement to enable women to qualify as doctors on the same basis as men. She was unsympathetic and said she believed women had more opportunities than they were using. She was intensely feminine and preferred men to women. Equality meant little to her. Stupidity, not sexual stereotypes, frustrated her. Exaggerated praise lavished on female achievement exasperated her. When Dr Elizabeth Blackwell qualified and became a celebrity as Britain's first woman doctor, Nightingale wrote that she would be 'inferior as a third rate apothecary of 30 years ago'. She thought women in men's fields could only achieve as much as very inferior men. Women, she thought, made third-rate doctors and first-rate nurses; there were plenty of doctors and not enough nurses.[27]

In July 1867 Mill asked Nightingale to join the committee of the London National Society for Women's Suffrage. She refused. It was not that she opposed female suffrage on principle. She wrote on 11 August 1867: 'That women should have the suffrage, I think no-one can be more deeply convinced than I. It is so important for a woman to be a "person", as you say.' However, it would be years before this happened and meanwhile there were other evils which pressed more on women. 'Till a married woman can be in possession of her own property there can be no love nor justice.' She didn't believe that giving women the vote would be a panacea for anything. 'If women were to get the vote immediately, Mr Mill would be disappointed with the result,' she wrote. Eventually, though, her attitude softened. In 1868 she joined the London National Society, and in 1871 her name was added to the general committee. In 1877 she retracted her harsh opinion of women doctors and signed a memorial urging the admission of women to medical degrees at London University. However, she was never emotionally stirred by the emancipation of women or considered it as important as public health reform in India and England.[28]

The issue of domestic public health, however, was to become inextricably associated with feminist radicalism and the push for the female suffrage. In 1864 the all-male Parliament passed the Contagious Diseases Act, which it extended further in 1866 and 1869. This measure required prostitutes to be examined for venereal disease. The passionate campaign engendered against this measure challenged not just the law but the whole basis of Victorian sexual morality, the double standard of behaviour by men and women and the relationship between the sexes. It turned women into steely, well-organised radicals and propelled them into public controversy, vilification and the likelihood of violence. Without it, the story of the struggle for the suffrage would have been entirely different. But to make sense of the Contagious Diseases Act and the fury it provoked, we must first examine Victorian attitudes to sex and marriage.

THE SEXUAL DOUBLE STANDARD

6

THE SEXUAL DOUBLE STANDARD
OF VICTORIAN ENGLAND

At the heart of the movement for women's suffrage was an argument about women's place in the world. And at the heart of that was an intense, prolonged and indeed never-resolved debate about relations between the sexes and the sexuality of women. Caricature would have us believe that the ultra-respectable nineteenth century never discussed sex openly and that the Victorian woman was a repressed prude, flinching from sexual relations with men and even clothing the piano legs in modesty drapes. The reality was very different and much more complex.

One might conclude instead that the Victorians were utterly obsessed with sex. Major advances in biology and medicine created considerable public discussion of sexual matters. These were endlessly explored in public through a proliferation of texts of all kinds – tracts and pamphlets, medical treatises, sex manuals, sybaritic poetry and novels and a great deal of pornography. Young, middle-class women devoured the novels of Georges Sand, denounced by others as the height of sensuality and impropriety. In 1859, five years before John Stuart Mill published his great protest against the alleged stifling conformity of the age in *On Liberty*, a sex manual entitled *The Elements of Social Science: Physical, Sexual and Natural Religion* preached sexual licence: 'If a man and a woman conceive a passion for each other, they should be morally entitled to indulge it, without binding themselves together for life'.[1]

Among the upper classes such sentiments were certainly acted upon. The memoirs of the Countess of Cardigan and Lancaster, published in 1909, described an extramarital ménage during the 1850s known as the Parrot Club, consisting of two ladies and a commoner with their three lovers. In such circles a philosophy of free love was commonplace. Extensive physical intimacy was also common in courtship. Texts written in the 1860s repeatedly emphasised the 'fastness' or flirtatiousness of young girls, who wanted to be mistaken for a 'femme du demi-monde'. By 1859 some working-class young Londoners were developing a libertine ideology about love being supreme and marriage a humbug.[2]

The received wisdom that Victorian women found sex vile and marriage oppressive is simply not borne out by the evidence. The prominent suffragette Emmeline Pethick-Lawrence wrote of her mother that when she married she was completely ignorant of what was expected of her as a wife, 'but that after her marriage her lover initiated her in such a way that, during her honeymoon, she was so blissfully happy that she felt that she was "walking on air"'.[3] Victorian women may have been ignorant and even nervous of sex before marriage, but many subsequently found it a source of deep satisfaction.

There were many successful middle-class marriages in which sensuality was very important. The constant refrain was the elevation of sexual intercourse on to a spiritual plane. Sex was thought uplifting; it served a higher purpose by producing a sense of oneness with another person. Love was central. One woman said she had once thought children to be the sole legitimate object of intercourse. But experience had taught her that 'the habitual bodily expression of love has a deep psychological effect in making possible complete mental sympathy, and perfecting the spiritual union that must be the lasting "marriage" after the passion of love has passed away with the years'.[4]

Far from the modern stereotype of miserable unions between cruel and oppressive husbands and violated wives, Victorian marriages were commonly close and loving. The ideal seemed to be domestic unions which combined mutual interest and strong affection. Marriage was a total relationship of mind, spirit and body. People were widely contented in their marriages even when conditions were harsh; the labouring poor still managed to find room for affection and mutual respect.[5]

The enormously popular and influential manual *The New Whole Duty of Man* laid out the nature of Christian marriage based on love and the primacy of the husband-wife relationship. Men were obliged to love their wives and keep love alive by exercising 'great delicacy'. William Cobbett noted in 1837 that 'in general, English wives are more warm in their conjugal attachment than those in France'.[6] Many accounts of the intense grief felt by widows indicated the extent to which women felt bound up with their husbands and how deeply they valued conjugal love.[7]

The close bonds of love and companionship in English marriages were remarked upon by visitors from abroad. In 1784 La Rochefoucauld wrote that, in England, 'husband and wife are always together, they belong to the same society. It is extremely rare to see one of them without the other . . . They do all their visiting together. It would be more ridiculous in England to do otherwise than it would be in Paris to go around always with one's wife. They give the impression of the most perfect harmony.' Another French writer, Hippolyte Taine, observed: 'every Englishman has, in the matter of marriage, a romantic spot in his heart. He imagines a "home" with the woman of his choice, the pair of them alone with their children. That is his own little universe, closed to the world.'[8]

True, husbands generally had authority over their wives, and there was a division of labour between the sexes. But, during the eighteenth century, the status of husbands was often qualified by the conduct-book writers as their authors tried to reconcile authority with the growing importance of marital companionship. So they encouraged equality, and the need for spouses to please each other. The anonymous author of *The English Matron* wrote in 1846 that: 'marriage was never intended to be a state of subserviency for women . . . the very word "union" implies a degree of equality'.

So if things were so good, how come they were so bad? For sexuality was to be the battleground on which nineteenth-century feminists were to rally behind the crusade to end the subjection of women. From Mary Wollstonecraft onwards, many Victorian and Edwardian feminists viewed marriage as 'legalised prostitution' and argued that male sexuality was responsible for female oppression. But if women by and large enjoyed contented, sexually fulfilling marriages to considerate husbands, why was the feminist movement to become so hostile to marriage and to male sexuality?

Some have sought an explanation in the often appalling experience women had of multiple pregnancies, excruciating confinements and infant bereavements. As a result, it is said, they developed fantasies of fleeing the home altogether or forcing their husbands into a regimen of sexual continence or birth control.[9] Despite such undoubted privations, however, this explanation is not convincing. After all, childbirth was just as dangerous and child mortality even more common in previous centuries. Yet there was no equivalent groundswell of hostility then towards marriage or male sexuality.

The real reason was surely to be found in how the nineteenth century came to think about what it meant to be a human being. The recoil from sexuality had nothing to do with female prudery or frigidity, nor indeed the boorish or brutal behaviour of men. It developed instead from the belief that carnal sexuality, identified with the male instinct, was behaviour associated with savages and animals while spirituality, identified with delicate female sensibilities, was the most elevated expression of the human spirit.

This belief, that sexuality was essentially animal and spirituality was essentially human, ran as a common thread throughout the century. It linked the utopian socialism of the Owenites, the developmental thinking of the zoologist Jean-Baptiste Lamarck, the political science of Thomas Malthus, and the evolutionary theories and eugenic doctrines propagated by Francis Galton towards the end of the nineteenth century. What all this thinking shared was a profound anxiety, as science took a sledgehammer to the biblical narrative of creation, that there might be really no

difference between human and animal, between civilisation and savagery. So it was very important to find such a difference; and the
distinction between sexuality and sensibility served the purpose. Spiritual
values, it was believed, would lift the human race on to a higher level of
existence. Since characteristics (according to Lamarck) could adapt and
be passed on to subsequent generations, it was vital to develop the spiritual side of human nature and suppress the carnal. Men, with their
incontinent sexual urges, were therefore universally perceived as the
problem; and the virtues of continence and self-restraint embodied by
women would supply the solution.

Fuelling such concerns was the apocalyptic prognosis of Thomas
Malthus which was to cast its baleful shadow across the whole of the
nineteenth century. The population was rapidly expanding because of
improvements in food and sanitation, the foundation of hospitals and the
development of medicine. In 1801 John Rickman, a friend of Jeremy
Bentham, published the first population census, which showed an
increase of one and a quarter million to 10,488,000 within ten years.[10]
Malthus was a Christian clergyman who opposed both the utopian idea
of perfectibility espoused by William Godwin and the suggested extension of the Poor Laws. In 1798, in his *Essay on the Principle of
Population*, he set out his bleak doctrine that the population would
always outstrip the food supply. This would mean increased poverty,
and only natural disasters like war, pestilence or famine could maintain
the balance of nature.[11] Implacably opposed to birth control, by the
time of the second edition of his book in 1803 Malthus advocated
instead postponed marriages and 'moral restraint', or chastity – an ironic
concession to his arch-adversary Godwin, who bizarrely believed that the
human sex drive would in time disappear altogether.[12]

The combination of the rise in population, the revolutionary agitation
for democracy and the dire warnings of Malthus combined to create
among the educated classes a profound dread of the mob and the view
that sexuality was downright dangerous. It was not only that sex led to
procreation and population increase. There were also deep fears that
sexual licence would slide into general disorder and anarchy. These fears

expressed themselves in a deep and widespread anxiety about the sexual habits of the poor.

Declining church attendance among urban dwellers coupled with the filth and degradation of slum life seemed to threaten sexual profligacy and social breakdown. Owen Chadwick recorded that gross overcrowding, with adults and children sharing the same bed, gave rise to promiscuity, incest and depravity. Once degraded, girls took to the streets as prostitutes.[13] In 1834 the Poor Law Commissioners were told: 'It is scarcely possible in a civilised country, and nowhere Christianity is professed, for there to be less delicacy on the point of chastity than among the class of females in farm service and the labouring community generally ... The moral sanction is wholly ineffective among the labouring classes.'[14]

Such moral and political anxieties were given dramatic shape and focus by medical science. As religious certainty crumbled, professional authority stepped into the vacuum to explain human behaviour. Morals and medicine combined to explain the links between debauchery and disease. The urban poor were viewed as agents for spreading contagion. There was medical evidence that both their environment and their physical and moral habits stimulated disease. The cholera epidemics in the 1830s were seen as punishment for those who had sinned through drunkenness or dirt.[15] James Phillips Kay, senior physician at the Ardwick and Ancoats dispensary in Manchester and a strong evangelical, linked sexual immorality to disease, filth, depravity, political sedition and the threat of an oppositional culture. In a pamphlet published in 1832 he wrote: 'There is, however, a licentiousness capable of corrupting the whole body of society, like an insidious disease, which eludes observation, yet is equally fatal in its effects. Criminal acts may be statistically classed ... but the number of those affected with the moral leprosy of vice cannot be exhibited with mathematical precision. Sensuality has no record.'[16]

With sexual immorality linked so explicitly to disease, the hospital was attributed with powers going beyond physical remedy. The 'lock hospital' in particular, which treated venereal disease, was said to promote 'benevolent principles consonant to sound policy and favourable to reformation or to virtue'.[17] Since the practice of medicine was linked to the promotion of sexual morality, doctors became an influential pressure group campaigning for moral reform, a development that was all the more welcome to a new profession trying to enhance its status and authority.[18]

The physical and moral squalor associated with the poor became a dominant preoccupation of social reformers, whipping up a terror of contagion. Dirt and filth also served as a metaphor for social disorder. For example, the 'miasma' theory promoted by Florence Nightingale, James Phillips Kay and Owen Chadwick, held that under certain circumstances the atmosphere could become charged with an epidemic influence which turned malignant when combined with the effluvia of organic decomposition from the earth, producing bodily disease. This theory encompassed both insanitary conditions and immoral practices. Immorality, blamed upon a lack of self-reliance and immoral habits, was both the cause and the effect of squalor.[19]

Specific warnings against sexual excess figured prominently in numerous tracts and pamphlets. Almost invariably these injunctions were addressed to men. Doctors viewed male sexuality as dangerous, not just because of the effect on the nation's morals but because of their 'scientific' belief that sexual excess was harmful to men. It would cut men off in their prime, and lead to mental and bodily infirmity or madness and even consumption. Sexual excess destroyed nerve tissue, sapped the body fibres and thinned the blood. The most influential medical authority of the age, Sir William Acton, was particularly worried by the waste of vital spermatic fluid, which was believed to use up a finite store of male energy. Even in marriage, men could waste away through spermatorrhoea. A man's intellectual qualities, he thought, were usually in an inverse ratio to his sexual appetites. 'It would almost seem as if the two were incompatible; the exercise of the one annihilating the other.' That was why, apparently, so many unmarried men were intellectuals.[20]

So what were men to do to protect themselves against this terrifying list of sexually generated infirmities? The answer was sexual abstinence. Not permanent abstinence, since retention of sperm or ovarian fluid was thought to send people mad in old age, but moderate sexual activity punctuated by periods of abstinence was thought to be the healthiest pattern of behaviour. Marriage was held to be the surest way of providing a moderate sex allowance and discouraging licentiousness. As a result, all young men above twenty-five were advised to marry as soon as circumstances allowed.[21]

Self-restraint was the key. The regular and temperate habits among the middle classes, it was claimed, were 'one of the great causes why the middle classes of society have more of real soundness of mind, as well as body, than either the highest or the lowest'.[22] Middle-class restraint was the key to moral and social order; working-class men were described as semi-barbarous and close to nature. When it came to working-class women, however, the analysis became more confused. On the one hand, they were condemned as moral pollutants, on the grounds of their class; on the other, they were hailed as agents of moral reform, on account of their sex. Factory commissioners believed that women were made depraved by their employment in mines and factories and by their close and indecent proximity to men. 'I have no doubt the debauchery is carried on,' an employment commissioner wrote in 1842, 'for there is every opportunity; for the girls go constantly, when hurrying, to the men . . . I think it scarcely possible for girls to remain modest who are in pits, regularly mixing with such company, and hearing such language as they do. I dare venture to say that many of the wives who come from pits know nothing of sewing or any household duty, such as women ought to know . . . all classes of witnesses bear testimony to the demoralising effect of females underground . . . the girls and boys and the young men and even married women and women with child, commonly work almost naked.'[23]

By contrast, the home – woman's natural and proper sphere – was presented as a temple of cleanliness, sobriety and moral virtue. Home was the antidote to the moral and physical contagion of public life. And because woman was the high priestess of this temple, her own sexuality could not be admitted for fear she might be tempted to abandon her calling. 'I should say that the majority of women (happily for society) are not much troubled by sexual feeling of any kind,' declared Acton. 'Many of the best mothers, wives and managers of households, know little or are careless about sexual relations. Love of the home, children and of domestic duties are the only passions they feel. As a general rule, a modest woman seldom desires any sexual gratification for herself. She submits to her husband's embraces, but principally to gratify him; and were it not for the desire of maternity, would far rather be relieved from his attention.'[24]

Woman's sexual pleasure was therefore denied. Instead her sexuality was identified with childbearing, which in turn was used to define female identity. The uterus, for example, was held to be the seat of female hysteria brought on by enforced abstinence.[25] Woman's purpose was to bear children and reproduce the race. Like men, women were damned both by sexual licence and by abstinence. What was required of women was to play their role of mother and home-maker.

It would be a mistake, however, to view such an attitude as evidence of male triumphalist oppression. On the contrary, male insecurity was the motif of the age. Victorian men felt themselves to be under siege. Their world was already being turned upside down by the industrial revolution, the march of science and the buckling of religion, and the demands from working men to widen the franchise. Now the home, the very temple of reassurance and security, was being threatened too by women who were apparently intent on turning their backs on it. Women were petitioning for divorce under the 1857 divorce law; they were demanding rights to property and custody of children in matrimonial disputes; they were beginning to press for the vote; maybe they were even demanding greater sexual satisfaction.[26] It was in the light of such profound male insecurities that Acton's infamous remark about female sexuality needs to be viewed. For in claiming that women had no sexual feelings, he was trying to reassure men anxious about the sexual demands of marriage that 'no nervous or feeble young man need, therefore, be deterred from marriage by any exaggerated notion of the duties required of him'.[27]

Nevertheless, the fact remains that female sexuality was defined in the Victorian era by male doctors who were themselves heavily caught up in the rampant insecurities of their sex and of the age. Indeed, Acton insisted that sexuality could only be understood by doctors. A vast literature insisted that male sexuality was instinctual and proved the biological link between man and the lower mammals, while women were without sexual desire. In 1886 Dr Richard Freiherr von Krafft-Ebing claimed in *Psychopathia Sexualis* that women's sensual desire was small. Women craved love more than men, but this was a spiritual rather than an erotic need. This became the prevalent view. In 1881 H. Newell Martin, in his authoritative textbook *The Human Body*, said not only that sex was 'a nuisance to most women belonging to the most luxurious classes of society', but that many suffered pain from it. The American educational reformer William Alcott condemned lewd publications for spreading the erroneous impression that woman was 'naturally sensual, like the other sex'.[28]

W. R. Greg wrote in 1850 that, except in the case of fallen women, sexual desire in women was dormant 'always till excited by undue familiarities; almost always till excited by actual intercourse ... Women whose position and education have protected them from exciting causes, constantly pass through life without ever being cognisant of the promptings of the senses ... Were it not for this kind decision of nature, which in England has been assisted by that correctness of feeling which pervades our education, the consequences would, we believe, be frightful.'[29]

Smith H. Platt enjoined wives to sacrifice their health to their husbands' sexual needs, 'even though the sacrifices may *seem* to be a species of immolation, abhorrent to the sensibilities of her nature'. But 'no true husband will behold such sacrifice for *him* without feeling the noblest instincts of his manhood stirred to their profoundest depths', and he will restrain himself to 'nullify to the last possible degree the necessary infliction, and in that which seems inevitable to deepen his love and tenderness for the noble woman who not only has given herself to him, but given herself for him'.[30]

Although doctors defined women by their sexual functions, which they deemed to be morally superior to those of men, they did not similarly define men by their sexual functions but by their brains. Men had a higher intellectual faculty than women, they averred, because they had an allegedly larger brain; women were more physical, instinctual and emotional because they were dominated by their sexual functions. Some saw in this evidence of female superiority. In 1883 Alfred Wiltshire, in his *Lecture on the Comparative Physiology of Menstruation*, said that menstruation indicated a higher evolutionary stage of reproductive function in the human female compared with other mammals, thanks to civilisation. Elsewhere the love of a wife and mother was said to be 'of that higher and more fervent emotion which fills the whole soul of woman when devoted to religion' and was linked to the 'fundamental doctrine of Christianity, the love of God to man'.[31] But Charles Darwin thought that woman's intuitiveness was typical of children and the lower races.[32]

This 'scientific' proof of female intellectual inferiority lay at the core of the argument against women's education and employment in the professions. The American physician and Harvard professor Edward Clarke provoked a fierce dispute with the pioneering woman doctor Elizabeth Garrett Anderson (as Elizabeth Garrett became, on marriage in 1871) when he argued against female education. Clarke said the struggle to improve women's educational opportunities implicitly conceded that woman was inferior to man, and that her condition could only be bettered by making her into a man. The current relationship was equal but different. 'Man is not inferior to woman, nor woman to man. The relation of the sexes is one of equality, not of better and worse, or of higher and lower. By this it is not intended that the sexes are the same. They are different, widely different from each other, and so different that each can do, in certain directions, what the other cannot.'[33] Gender roles had to be kept distinct otherwise women would be masculinised and social stability threatened.[34]

The desire to show that women were indeed quite different from men led doctors from the 1840s onwards to investigate the function of the ovaries. These were thought to be the autonomous control centres of sex and reproduction from which all differences between the sexes flowed. However, if womanhood was admirable and moral, and the ovaries were the source of these virtues, then it followed that when the ovaries stopped functioning those virtues vanished. So after the menopause, women stopped being attractive and moral and instead became hideous. 'With the shrinking of the ovaria,' wrote one doctor, '. . . there is a corresponding change in the outer form . . . With this change in the person there is an analogous change in the mind, temper and feelings. The woman approximates in fact to a man, or in one word she is a virago . . . This unwomanly condition undoubtedly renders her repulsive to man, while her envious, overbearing temper renders her offensive to her own sex.'[35]

Without a functioning reproductive system, in other words, women were regarded as repulsive and worthless. Not only did the medical profession seek to define femininity by sexuality, but it came close to defining female identity in terms of disease. The female nervous system was deemed very susceptible to a wide range of physical, moral and environmental stimuli. Professor Edward Clarke opposed women's entry into medicine because he thought such intellectual work would reduce the supply of nerve energy to the female reproductive system, producing 'monstrous brains and puny bodies; abnormally active cerebration and abnormally weak digestion; flowing thought and constipated bowels'. The English psychiatrist Henry Maudsley thought the over-expenditure of vital energy in mental activity by women would cause menstrual derangements leading to hysteria, epilepsy and chorea.[36]

Gynaecological disorders were thought to be a direct cause of insanity. A number of gynaecological treatments were aimed to manage women's minds. The obstetrician Isaac Baker Brown believed that masturbation led to madness and that the surgical removal of the clitoris could cure it. He actually put this theory into grisly practice between 1859 and 1866, but eventually he was expelled from the Obstetrical Society. In the 1880s gynaecologists in Britain and America started advocating the removal of healthy ovaries to cure a range of conditions from dysmenorrhoea and uterine fibroids to incipient insanity and epilepsy. By the end of the century doctors were proposing the appointment of gynaecologists to the staff of insane asylums. Such an attempt to create a science of womanhood led to an 'obstetric jurisprudence'.

The obstetrician Henry MacNaughton-Jones asked: 'Is it not true that the gravest issues, even those of life and death, liberty, loss of character and reputation . . . frequently hang upon the evidence of the gynaecologist?'[37]

There was, however, one doctor who challenged this bizarre and misleading view of female sexuality. This was hardly surprising since this doctor was a woman. She was the living refutation of her profession's assumptions about female intellectual inferiority, and on a personal level had taken on the entrenched prejudice of the medical profession – and won. Elizabeth Blackwell emigrated from Britain to America as a child and trained there as a doctor. In January 1859 the newspapers announced that she was to visit England. One columnist wrote: 'It is impossible that a woman whose hands reek with gore can be possessed of the same nature or feelings as the generality of women.'[38]

Dr Blackwell, who belonged to several philanthropic and moral purity organisations, had an ambivalent relationship with the feminist movement. On the one hand, she thought women should become doctors because their very distinct moral position would counter the male materialist science of men.[39] She herself became a doctor in part at least to avoid marriage; she remained a spinster because she was 'repelled' by the implications of a lifetime's intimate association with any individual. She hated domesticity, as well as the requirement to be ladylike and display 'feminine' accomplishments. 'I felt more determined than ever to become a physician, and thus place a strong barrier between me and all ordinary marriage,' she wrote. Yet at first she was critical of the women's movement, blaming women themselves for their inferior position, and she said marriage and motherhood were women's natural and most important role. She told women medical students they must not be like men but must bring to medicine feminine maternal values.[40]

She shared the mainstream view about the dangers of male sexual excess. Sexual activity, she agreed, expended a huge amount of nervous energy in men at the expense of other achievements. Masturbation caused nervous exhaustion. Continence and self-restraint were therefore essential.

This healthy limitation of physical secretion in men sets free a vast amount of nervous force for employment in intellectual and active practical pursuits. The amount of nervous energy expended by the male in the temporary act of sexual congress is very great; out of all apparent proportion to its physical results, and is an act not to be too often repeated . . . Even in strong adult life there is great loss of social power through the squandering of adult energy, which results from any unnatural stimulus given to the passion of sex in the male. The barbarous custom of polygamy; the degrading habit of promiscuous intercourse; and all artificial excitements which give undue stimulus to the passion of sex, divert an immeasurable amount of mental and moral force from the great work of human advancement.[41]

In holding these views Dr Blackwell was very much a woman of her time. But when it came to female sexuality, she parted company with her colleagues. For her, women had very similar sexual desires to those of men, but female sexuality was more elevated and spiritual. Physical passion was not evil but a 'rich endowment of humanity' that had been divinely created. She saw marital love as an amalgam of tenderness and desire. 'The severe and compound suffering experienced by many widows who were strongly attached to their lost partners' was, she wrote:

well known to the physician; and this is not simply a mental loss that they feel but an immense physical deprivation. It is a loss which all these senses suffer, by the physical as well as moral void which death has created. Although physical sexual pleasure is not attached exclusively, or in woman chiefly, to the act of coition, it is also a well-established fact that in healthy loving women, uninjured by the too-frequent lesions which result from childbirth, increasing physical satisfaction attaches to the ultimate physical expression of love. A repose and general well-being results from the natural occasional intercourse, whilst the total deprivation of it produces irritability. I have known this physical loss severely felt for years after the death of a beloved husband.[42]

How could anyone claim, after reading such testimony, that the Victorian woman recoiled from sex with her husband?

Female sexuality, wrote Dr Blackwell, was, however, superior to male because of the spirituality of motherhood and the maternal instinct, which led women to put the interests of husbands and children above their own. 'This profound depth of maternity in women gives a sacredness to their appreciation of sex, which has not yet been utilised for the improvement of the family,' she observed.[43] And it was spirituality, that distinctly female virtue, which elevated human sexuality above brute behaviour:

> Those who deny sexual feeling to women, or consider it so light a thing as hardly to be taken into account in social arrangements, quite lose sight of this immense spiritual force of attraction, which is distinctly human sexual power, and which exists in so very large proportion in their nature . . . The different form which physical sensation necessarily takes in the two sexes, and its intimate connection with and development through the mind (love) in women's nature, serve often to blind even thoughtful and painstaking persons as to the immense power of sexual attraction felt by women. Such one-sided views show a misconception of the meaning of human sex in its entirety.[44]

Women, she observed, located sexual pleasure in rather more than the actual act of coition:

> The affectionate husbands of refined women often remark that their wives do not regard the distinctively sexual act with the same intoxicating physical enjoyment that they themselves feel, and they draw the conclusion that the wife possesses no sexual passion. A delicate wife will often confide to her medical adviser (who may be treating her for some special suffering) that at the very time when marriage love seems to unite them most closely, when her husband's welcome kisses and caresses seem to bring them into profound union, comes an act which mentally separates them, and which is often either indifferent or

repugnant to her. But it must be understood that it is not the special act necessary for parentage which is the measure of the compound moral and physical power of sexual passion. It is the profound attraction of one nature to the other, which marks passion; and delight in kiss and caress – the love-touch – is physical sexual expression, as much as the special act of the male.[45]

The erroneous general belief that men had sexual appetites and women did not created a deeply rooted double standard of behaviour which women like Dr Blackwell regarded as a deep injustice and wrong against their sex. The double standard meant that sexual licence was regarded as an understandable and even pardonable lapse by men, who were after all at the mercy of their instincts, but an unpardonable and very serious offence by women, who were betraying theirs.

Wives were expected to be virgins on their wedding night; men, by contrast, were expected to gain sexual experience before marriage and any later infidelities by them were treated as venial sins best overlooked. Sexual misbehaviour by both sexes was condemned by the church, but the double standard was built into law. Husbands were entitled to use restraint to force their wives to have sex, whereas wives could only get a court order. Conduct books treated adultery involving married women as a crime far worse than theft; if husbands committed adultery, however, women were told not to complain but reform their husbands by setting a virtuous example.[46] The 1857 Matrimonial Causes Act, which held that a man could divorce his wife for adultery alone but a wife needed additional grounds such as cruelty or desertion, was an open sore, implicitly holding that adultery was a natural act when committed by men, but unnatural when committed by women. Dr Blackwell was later to comment: 'In our own country the unjust condonation of adultery by law in 1857, against the strenuous opposition of far-seeing statesmen, has educated more than one generation in a false and degrading idea of physiology.'[47]

The double standard was rooted in more than a belief in male sexual instincts. Female sexual fidelity and trustworthiness were crucial in establishing beyond doubt the paternity of a child when it came to inheritance.

In addition, a wife was seen as a husband's property; a girl's loss of virginity reduced her saleable value, and the corruption of a wife was viewed as a kind of theft.

This of course posed a problem. If men had sexual instincts which needed to be satisfied but respectable women needed to be virginal or chaste, what were men to do? The answer was female prostitution. The situation was summed up in W. E. H. Lecky's backhanded tribute to the prostitute in his 1913 *History of European Morals*. 'Herself the supreme type of vice, she is ultimately the most efficient guardian of virtue. But for her, the unchallenged purity of countless happy homes would be polluted and not a few who, in the pride of their untempted chastity, think of her with an indignant shudder, would have known the agony of remorse and despair. On that one degraded and ignoble form are concentrated the passions that might have filled the world with shame. She remains, while civilisations rise and fall, the eternal priestess of humanity, blasted for the sins of the people.'

And it was prostitution, and the response to it by the male worlds of medicine and government, that detonated the explosive issue of the sexual double standard and created an unstoppable momentum for women's rights.

By the middle of the nineteenth century prostitution had become a 'great social evil' that threatened respectable families and the social order. Estimates varied, but it is clear that the trade was huge and highly visible. In the late 1830s there were said to be some seven thousand prostitutes in London, more than nine hundred brothels and 850 houses of ill fame (brothels with no resident staff).[48] In 1841 the Chief Commissioner of Police estimated there were 3,325 brothels in the Metropolitan District of London alone.[49] In 1872 Taine wrote of Shadwell, in London's East End: 'All the houses, except one or two, are evidently inhabited by harlots . . . Every hundred steps one jostles twenty harlots; some of them ask for a glass of gin; others say "Sir, it is to pay my lodgings". This is not debauchery which flaunts itself but destitution – and such destitution . . .'[50] Howard Vincent, Director of the CID at Scotland Yard, told a committee of peers in 1881: 'I should think that prostitution in England is considerably in excess of the prostitution in other countries.' From mid-afternoon, he said, it was impossible for a respectable woman to walk from the top of Haymarket to Wellington Street off the Strand, as the West End was thronged with prostitutes openly soliciting.

Many reasons have been offered for the phenomenon. Men tended to marry late, and there was a belief that prostitution was a necessary evil to satisfy men's sexual needs. There was a lack of legal protection for girls; the age of consent was fixed at twelve in 1861, and although brothels were illegal it was necessary for two ratepayers to complain before any action was taken. Poverty and low wages undoubtedly played a major part, along with the expansion of domestic service and the migration from the countryside to the cities, which shattered the traditional moral restraints of family, neighbours and church, exposing girls to easy seduction.[51]

According to Dr Elizabeth Blackwell, there was a great army of domestic servants surrounded by constant temptations to supplement their wages. They drifted into prostitution through a combination of exhausting work, the privations of their backgrounds and their undeveloped sense of social duties, as well as the special danger posed by rich, careless establishments. 'The five shillings secretly gained at night becomes an important addition to scanty wages, the stolen pleasures an intoxicating relief to drudgery,' she noted. And each 'fallen' woman corrupted others.[52]

Most prostitutes drifted into their trade through lives of promiscuity. Droves of girls were described huddled along Regent Street, Piccadilly and Haymarket, urinating and defecating in public.[53] Many shop girls took part in the trade, with some West End dress-shop managers encouraging them into high-class prostitution and hiring out dresses to them for advertising. Respectable employers assumed that *any* intercourse between men and work girls was evidence of impropriety, simply because there was so much of it about.[54]

The phenomenon gave rise to endless scandalised discussion and concern, which fuelled the inflammatory grievance at the heart of sexual politics. The women who worked as prostitutes were held to blame for corrupting the nation's morals, whereas the men who patronised them were merely satisfying their natural inclinations while keeping respectable women pure. William Tait, author of a study of prostitutes in Edinburgh, accused prostitutes of lying, stealing, swearing and being prone to drinking. They were prostitutes, he claimed, because of their licentious desires, pride, indolence and love of dress.[55] The physician Michael Ryan, on the other hand, wrote that women were not depraved by inclination but because they were seduced. 'It is therefore, in my opinion, a most glaring defect in our legislation,' he wrote, 'to exonerate the male sex from all responsibility and punishment for seduction and bastardy, because this sex is by far the most guilty and vicious; for all physiologists admit that amorous impulse is stronger in the males than in the females of all grades of the mammiferae, from the lowest to the human species.'[56]

Over the course of the next few decades the climate of opinion was to change dramatically in Dr Ryan's direction. Originally held to be responsible for vice, prostitutes came to be seen as the victims of male sexual profligacy and social injustice.[57] The double standard by which prostitution was viewed as a necessary evil for men but a source of shame and disgrace for the 'fallen' women involved, was challenged in a bitter and even violent campaign which radicalised women and provided crucial ammunition for their struggle for the vote.

The leaders of this campaign were the evangelicals. They saw male sexual licence as a direct threat to conjugal love and the family. So they made an uncompromising demand for a single standard of sexual conduct and for the purity of sexual relations. Adultery and resorting to prostitutes constituted a grievous injury to the 'holy and inviolable union' of marriage.[58] And they set out to 'rescue' prostitutes wherever they could, even though many women refused to take on such a task as they thought it indelicate and unfeminine. Reformers would seek out girls on the streets, give them tracts and plead with them to change their ways. No class or denomination had a monopoly on this work: there were middle- and upper-class evangelicals, working-class Bible-women and home missionaries, Catholic sisters and Anglican deaconesses, Jewish

women and the women of the Salvation Army.[59] The Liberal leader
William Gladstone walked the streets at night to persuade prostitutes to
accompany him to his home, where his wife gave them food and shelter.
Houses of refuge tried to reform such girls by training them in laundry,
domestic work and cooking. Large rescue and reformatory societies were
formed. But all this activity achieved only a small drop in the volume of
prostitution.[60]

The crucial point, however, was that the evangelicals wanted to save
these girls' souls by reforming them; they did not want them punished.
And they wanted to stamp out prostitution completely – which meant
challenging head-on the sexual double standard which turned a blind eye
to male licentiousness. This brought them into direct conflict with the
male medical profession, and particularly with the leading writer on sexuality, Sir William Acton.

Acton was a typical Victorian. Earnest, morally austere, liberally
inclined, sincere and open-minded, he believed it was his duty to allevi-
ate human misery. Born in 1813 in Shillingstone, Dorset, the second son
of a clergyman, he became a surgeon and devoted himself to the study of
the urinary and generative organs. He believed that prostitution could
never be eradicated as it was an inevitable aspect of society. Instead, he
suggested in his classic book on the subject, published in 1857, that its
attendant evils could be mitigated. Prostitution, he said, could be managed and regulated by the state.

He was not unsympathetic to the prostitutes themselves. On the contrary, he wanted the rest of society to regard them as fellow human
beings. Girls largely turned to such a trade, he said, through destitution
and 'cruel biting poverty'.[61] But he didn't think anything could ever stop
women selling their bodies, nor prevent men from using them in this way.
Unlike the evangelicals, he saw prostitution as a social problem rather
than a moral evil. His principal concern was with the effects it would
have on the rest of society. For he thought that prostitutes, far from
being social outcasts, would pollute and corrupt the respectable classes
and threaten the very temple of social order itself, the family.[62]

Acton spelled this out in his book:

Vice does not hide itself, it throngs our streets, intrudes into our parks and theatres and other places of resort, bringing to the foolish temptation, and knowledge of sin to the innocent; it invades the very sanctuary of home, destroying conjugal happiness and blighting the hopes of parents. Nor is it indirectly only that society is injured; we have seen that prostitutes do not, as is generally supposed, die in harness; but that, on the contrary, they for the most part become, sooner or later, with tarnished bodies and polluted minds, wives and mothers; while among some classes of the people the moral sentiment is so depraved, that the woman who lives by the hire of her person is received on almost equal terms to social intercourse. It is clear, then, that though we call these women outcasts and pariahs, they have a powerful influence for evil on all ranks of the community. The moral injury inflicted on society by prostitution is incalculable; the physical injury is at least as great.[63]

The physical injury that so frightened Acton and his fellow Victorians was venereal disease. By the mid-Victorian period, VD was considered to be a serious health hazard to the population at large. Much of the concern centred around the very high rates of the disease among the armed forces. As Acton pointed out, one of the most important causes of prostitution was the virtual ban on marriage for soldiers, from the fear that married men would lack the will to fight. Troops returning from India were a particularly grave source of infection; it was estimated that two-thirds of the military hospital patients at Baroda in 1824 had VD and thirty-one per cent of the army's strength in Bengal was infected in 1828.[64] Military returns showed a steady increase in VD in the armed forces since then. During the Crimean War of 1854–6 the British had more casualties in hospital than on the battlefield. This focused attention on the dreadful sanitation in the barracks and the very high rate of VD among the military. In 1864 one in three cases of sickness in the army was due to VD; in the navy in 1862, one in eleven.[65]

Before Acton's book was published, however, prostitution was an unmentionable subject outside the medical journals. The dominant attitude towards the subject was expressed by Samuel Solly, a member of the council of the Royal College of Surgeons. Far from seeing syphilis as evil, he regarded it as a blessing, and believed that it was inflicted by the Almighty to act as a restraint upon the indulgence of evil passions. 'Could the disease be exterminated, which he hoped it could not, fornication would ride rampant through the land . . .'[66]

But it was disease, not fornication, that people were frightened was running rampant. Acton's book opened up the subject to public debate and changed attitudes almost overnight. There was, in any event, a new enthusiasm for intervening in the lives of the poor on medical and sanitary grounds. Sir John Simon, Medical Officer to the Privy Council, was a firm believer in 'sanitary science'. The improvement of the moral and physical health of individuals was considered important not just for an industrial nation but as the duty of a Christian country, since the standard of public health reflected the degree of civilisation attained by the state.[67]

In his speech to the Royal Medical Society in 1860, Acton said that since philanthropists and the clergy had failed to stem prostitution, they should hand the problem over to scientific regulation.[68] Far from the state sanctioning male vice, such regulation would improve sanitary health and so remoralise the nation.[69]

The public authorities were convinced that such preventive measures were urgently needed. The illness was spreading through contact with diseased prostitutes, and the techniques existed to diagnose and treat the sources of infection. However, in 1859 compulsory medical investigation of soldiers was abandoned because the men were hostile to such intimate investigation. So the same thing was proposed for the women instead.[70] The problem was that this defined women as the agents of social infection.

It was France which showed Acton, Simon and their colleagues the way forward. France had subjected vice to state regulation since 1802 through its *police des moeurs*, or morals police. Ever since then the Belgians had pressed for such regulation to be spread through Europe. Prince Albert, however, disapproved, and a similar law was only pushed through in Britain when Queen Victoria was distracted in early widow-hood.[71]

The Society for the Suppression of Vice attacked the police for inertia and looked to the continent for models of regulation. In 1862 Florence Nightingale told the committee investigating the problem of VD that the continental system was disgusting and unworkable. She opposed the examination of prostitutes. Instead she wanted lock hospitals, improvements to sanitary conditions in the barracks and penalties for concealing, but not for contracting, VD. But Gladstone disagreed.[72]

In 1864 the first Contagious Diseases Act was passed by a sparsely attended House of Commons and without debate. It applied to certain ports and garrison towns, where the police were given the power to arrest common prostitutes, order them to undergo an internal examination and, if they were diseased, detain them until they were pronounced cured. If a woman refused, she could be jailed after a trial in which she had to prove she was virtuous. In 1866 the Act was extended to provide compulsory three-monthly examinations of prostitutes on the sworn evidence of one policeman, and it introduced compulsory regular examinations of suspected women within ten miles of the protected area. Again, this law was passed without debate. In 1869 it was extended to all garrison towns, and permitted also five days' incarceration before examination without committal or trial and with no release permitted under habeas corpus.

There was no doubt that the condition of these prostitutes was dire. They went 'on the game' at puberty and survived on pitiful earnings, riddled with VD, until they were wrecked by beatings, hunger and delirium tremens. One venereologist described the prostitutes who lived in the sand caves outside Aldershot military camp as half-naked and semi-insensible with liquor. 'The women were very dirty – in fact, filthy, covered with vermin, like idiots in their manner, very badly diseased; they almost burrowed in the ground like rabbits, digging holes for themselves in the sandbanks.'[73]

So the Contagious Diseases Acts were considered by some to be a moral duty and act of benevolence. But in practice they were far less attractive. The process of internal examination was hurried and brutal, and at Devonport it could be observed through the windows by jeering crowds of dockyard workers.[74] It was also difficult to decide who was a prostitute and who was not, a problem which gave rise to the intrusive activities of plainclothes spies. Inevitably, innocent women and children were arrested and examined. One such, Mrs Percy, was subsequently driven out of her job in a music hall and in 1875 committed suicide.[75]

There was a further aspect of the procedure which roused its opponents to incandescent fury and horror. A speculum was used in the internal examination of the prostitute. This touched on some very deeply rooted fears. The speculum was said to be a danger to women's health. Robert Lee, a professor of midwifery, argued in May 1850 that the speculum was used unnecessarily. He recounted a horrific example of a woman affected by paraplegic symptoms which were thought by her doctor to be the result of a uterine inflammation. He examined her by speculum, but her hymen was unbroken and the doors of the house had to be closed to prevent her screams from being heard. She later died of a brain inflammation with nothing wrong with her uterus at all. Professor Lee argued that doctors were not far from committing a form of rape for their own vicarious sexual gratification.[76]

Indeed, the use of the speculum transgressed deep taboos about female propriety and modesty. For it exposed and penetrated a woman's 'private parts', which wounded and even 'blunted' women's modesty. For women's virginity was not only physical but also a mental and moral state. Dr Elizabeth Blackwell protested about the speculum: 'Its reckless use amongst the poor is a serious national injury ... I have known the natural sentiment of personal modesty seriously injured amongst respectable people by the resort to a succession of incompetent advisers.' Doctors should acknowledge the interaction of mind and body, she said, and cherish 'the great conservative principle of society, personal modesty and self-respect'.[77] The experimental physiologist Marshall Hall argued that such an examination therefore caused the 'dulling of the edge of virgin modesty and the degradation of pure minds of the daughters of England', which had to be avoided as 'the female who has been subjected to such treatment is not the same person in delicacy and purity as she was before'.[78]

Indeed, this corruption of sexual innocence was even held to cause a woman to develop sexual fetishes. Robert Brudenell Carter wrote in an influential study of hysteria in 1853: 'I have more than once seen young unmarried women of the middle classes of society reduced, by the constant use of the speculum, to the mental and moral condition of prostitutes; seeking to give themselves the same indulgence by the practice of solitary vice; and asking every medical practitioner, under whose care they fell, to institute an examination of the sexual organs.'[79]

Acton, however, insisted that the speculum was of the greatest value in detecting VD. Because it was not used enough, women were not being treated properly and were infecting fresh men; but he and others making such an argument found themselves in the minority.[80]

The country finally woke up to all this in the autumn of 1869 when the doctors tried to extend the Contagious Diseases Acts to the civilian population across the land. This provoked huge public meetings and petitions to abolish the Acts with hundreds of thousands of signatures, one alone signed by a quarter of a million women. Now the great accusation of female slavery, reminiscent of the arguments of William Thompson and others in the previous century, came roaring back into public discourse. Dr Blackwell did not mince her words in making the comparison, nor in identifying the slave owners.

Women were being bought and sold like slaves, she argued, by a 'mighty army of vicious men' who thought there was nothing wrong in buying temporary physical gratification. It was men who were thus undermining marriage. 'The irresponsible polyandry of prostitution with its logical acceptance and regulation of brothels has replaced in the west the polygamy of the east. In both degradation, discouragement of marriage and injustice to women create a fatal barrier to permanent national progress.' It not only harmed the characters of both men and women, but struck at the integrity of humanity itself. 'This evil tends in women to produce the vices of the slave, viz., deceit, falsehood and servility; in men it tends to foster the vices of the slave-holder, arrogance, selfishness and cruelty. In both it engenders that deadly sin – hypocrisy . . . The cruel vice of fornication, protected by hypocrisy, is sowing moral scrofula broadcast, and like an insidious poison producing generations of feeble ricketty wills and maniacal monsters. It is the degeneracy of the race!'[81]

Acton fiercely defended the Contagious Diseases Acts. He too loved liberty and religion, he said, but this kind of interference was necessary for the sake of women and of the community. It was mitigating the evils of prostitution. And he suggested other reforms aimed at diminishing prostitution itself, such as addressing overcrowding in families, making better provision for female relief and employment, and making a woman's seducer legally responsible for any offspring. He also wanted to 'heal the sick prostitute and cleanse her moral nature', since she would eventually become a wife and mother. Recognition and regulation, however, were not the same as licence and did not encourage vice.[82]

Support for Acton's views came from a notable heretic in the feminist camp. Elizabeth Garrett didn't believe that voluntary treatment or individual attempts at reform could defeat VD. She saw the Acts as an attempt to diminish injury to public health and their aim as the relief of physical suffering. The evidence, she wrote, 'can only be fully appreciated by those who have had medical experience'. She believed compulsory treatment was necessary because women refused to enter hospital early enough or to stay long enough. She thought the powers of arrest were a useful check on ignorant young girls who failed to see the danger of disease, and she ridiculed the idea of police persecution. 'It is difficult to believe anyone can seriously credit women with such a degree of helplessness,' she tartly observed. She wrote with compassion of her prostitute patients as being 'without health, without character, without friends, without money. Could their position be more forlorn?' And she pointed out the injustice of leaving innocent women and children to suffer from VD. 'Degradation cannot be taken by storm, and the animal side of nature will outlive crusades.'[83]

However, there were more powerful feminist voices raised in fierce opposition. Both Florence Nightingale and Harriet Martineau raised the standard of revolt. Harriet Martineau wrote: 'There is evidence accessible to all that the regulation system creates horrors worse than those which it is supposed to restrain. Vice once stimulated by such a system imagines and dares all unutterable things ... we shall have entered upon our national decline whenever we agree to the introduction of such a system.'[84]

But vice was still unmentionable in public. This was a campaign which, if it was to have any chance of success, had at all costs to avoid offending the sensibilities of middle-class society. It needed to be fought by an ultra-respectable person whose claim to virtue was unassailable. In other words, it needed to be fought by a mother. Just such a person was now unwillingly to have her destiny thrust upon her.

7

JOSEPHINE BUTLER AND THE
REVOLT OF THE WOMEN

In October 1869 some seventy campaigners against the Contagious Diseases Acts, including the redoubtable reformer Elizabeth Wolstenholme, met at the Social Science Congress in Bristol. After the meeting Elizabeth sent a telegram to her friend Josephine Butler. Would Josephine, she asked, 'haste to the rescue' of the campaign against the Acts?

It was an inspired choice. Josephine Butler had precisely the combination of qualities required for such a difficult campaign. She was also charismatic, strong-minded and beautiful, and she always dressed in the height of fashion. She was also a wife and mother, most suitable therefore – as the crusading editor W. T. Stead later observed – to plead for the inviolable sanctity of a woman's right to her person.[1]

When she received the call from Elizabeth Wolstenholme, however, Mrs Butler was reluctant. Profoundly conservative, she believed her first duty was to her husband and children. This was still an era where women did not speak in public. The very subject of prostitution was considered obscene. For a woman to campaign on such a theme would be considered so shockingly disreputable that she would expose herself and her family to public odium and social ostracism. It was not a risk that an ordinary woman would seriously consider taking. But Mrs Butler was by no means ordinary.

She was born in Northumberland in 1828, the seventh child of John and Hannah Grey. The family was intelligent, radical and well connected. Her father was a great agricultural reformer and anti-slavery campaigner. From her mother, a Moravian, she gained her attachment to evangelical Christianity. Lord Grey, the Whig leader during the struggle for the Reform Act 1832, was her father's cousin. Her aunt, Margaretta Grey, was a strong-minded feminist who was so disgusted at not being allowed to enter the precincts of the Houses of Parliament to see her cousin in action, that she dressed as a boy to gain admission.[2] Despite her family's connections, however, Josephine was always hostile to the London élite, preferring the company of working men.

When she was seventeen, Josephine experienced a religious crisis after seeing a man hanging from a tree when she was out riding. He had been dismissed from his job. This prompted a crisis of faith, the precursor of a life to be dogged by periodic breakdowns and ill health. In 1851 she married George Butler, an educator and Anglican clergyman. It was very much a marriage of equals. They had four children, three boys and a girl. When the American Civil War broke out in 1856, the Butlers supported the Union and the abolition of slavery and found themselves ostracised as a result. It was Mrs Butler's first experience of political agitation in an unpopular cause.

One day tragedy struck. Mrs Butler had been impatient with her six-year-old daughter, Eveline. Later in the day the child rushed out to meet her parents but fell down the stairs and was killed. After a visit to Italy with her sister Harriet to get over the bereavement – in the course of which she fell ill with a mysterious, probably nervous, affliction – Mrs Butler said: 'I became possessed with an irresistible desire to go forth and find some pain keener than my own, to meet with people more unhappy than myself and to say (as now I knew I could) to afflicted people, "I understand; I too have suffered."'[3] She found people more unhappy than herself in the workhouse, where destitute prostitutes picked oakum in appalling conditions. She took religion to them, and to the prostitutes she met at the dockside. She founded a refuge for prostitutes, instructing the matron to be a mother to the girls rather than an overseer. She even took some of the more desperate cases home to care for them. It was perfectly clear that this was very much an attempt to expiate her own profound personal distress. To one prostitute called Marion, who was dying of TB, she said: 'Will you come with me to my home and live with me? I had a daughter once.' Not surprisingly, perhaps, in the light of what was driving her, she became convinced that these girls were more sinned against than sinning. As a result, she scorned other rescue work for blaming prostitutes for their own degradation and for treating them as a class rather than as individuals.[4]

The Contagious Diseases Acts were therefore anathema to her. Here were vulnerable, maybe even dying, prostitutes being treated as criminals and subjected to apparently barbaric sexual assault, while men remained free to use them to satisfy their lustful instincts. Finally, therefore, she decided to answer the call to lead the crusade – but not without asking for approval from her devoted husband, whose reputation and career would also be threatened by such a move. George did not hesitate. 'Go, and the Lord be with you,' he said.[5] Mrs Butler told a meeting in Carlisle: 'I believe we are called, in this our day, to labour for the abolition of harlotry – that great and soul-devouring evil, that huge Typical Sin.'[6] Later she was to write: 'A crisis had arrived in the moral history of England that for good or evil would affect, it might be for all time, the position of their sex . . . For woman ever represents the Ideal, and the rude realities of her abasement are the measure of the degradation even of the aspirations of man.'[7]

In the course of what was to follow, Mrs Butler was to stand accused of going to apparently perverse and bewildering lengths to allow the trade of prostitution to continue by opposing moves to shut it down altogether. This can only be understood in terms of her personal motivation. As W. T. Stead was later to observe, she was driven principally by compassion for the lost daughters of other mothers. 'Other labourers in this most difficult and more dangerous field have been impelled thither by a desire to save souls, or to rescue women,' he wrote. 'Mrs Butler always wanted to save DAUGHTERS. Motherhood is to her the sacredest thing in the world.'[8] Yes, she wanted to abolish 'harlotry'; but she was to fight like a mother to protect the well-being of the harlots.

On New Year's Day 1870, 140 women, including Florence Nightingale, Harriet Martineau, Josephine Butler, the penal reformer Mary Carpenter, the suffragist Lydia Becker, notable ladies from the Society of Friends and many from the literary and philanthropic world, signed a protest against the Contagious Diseases Acts. This manifesto, a powerful and unprecedented blow against the sexual double standard, could be considered another foundation document of feminism. It declared that the Act removed security from women and put their reputation, freedom and person in the power of police; it was unjust not to punish the sex who were the main cause of vice while punishing women by arrest, forced medical treatment and where they resisted imprisonment, hard labour; it made evil easier for men as it provided a convenience for the practice of vice; it violated and further brutalised women; and it would not diminish disease, whose condition was moral, not physical.[9]

The protest caused a sensation. There was a storm of shocked hostility and consternation that women had gone public on such an indecent and distasteful matter. The *Saturday Review* attacked the 'shrieking sisterhood'.[10] Even reformers thought the campaign exceedingly ill-advised. John Morley, the radical editor of *Fortnightly Review*, warned that the manifesto 'encouraged the presumptuous notion, current among men of the world, that resort to declamatory *a priori* methods is the incurable vice of women when they come to political subjects'.[11]

But it had struck home. The protesters formed a campaigning body, the Ladies' National Association (LNA). Within a few months every major city had its repeal societies, and many had ladies' committees devoted to the cause. In March a campaign newspaper, *The Shield*, was started by a northern doctor, Dr Hoopell.[12] The great French novelist and poet Victor Hugo wrote from Paris urging the women: 'Protest! Resist!' While the slavery of black women had been abolished in America, he said, slavery of white women continued in Europe 'and laws are still made by men in order to tyrannise over women'.[13]

Among politicians there was consternation of a different kind. One MP said to Mrs Butler: 'We know how to manage any other opposition in the house or the country, but this is very awkward for us – this revolt of the women. It is quite a new thing; what are we to do with such an opposition as this?'[14] It was a question that was to reverberate for more than half a century. This was just the beginning.

Mrs Butler had set herself against not just the Contagious Diseases Acts but the entire concept of officially institutionalised vice and the state regulation of prostitution. Economics, she claimed, lay at the root of practical morality. Lack of industrial training and good openings for women were responsible for prostitution, as were overcrowding and lack of decency in homes. She wanted seduction punishable by law, equal legislation for men and women, the bastardy laws amended and equal laws to check street solicitation by either sex, in addition to the repeal of the Contagious Diseases Acts themselves.[15]

The Acts, she wrote, would encourage prostitution and enshrined the unpardonable double standard. This had arisen because men 'are driven away at an early age from the society of women, and thrown upon the society of each other only – in schools, colleges, barracks etc; and have thus concocted and cherished a wholly different standard of moral purity from that obtaining among young women. Even those men who are personally pure and blameless become persuaded by the force of familiarity with male profligacy around them that this sin in *man* is venial and excusable.'[16] She drew an explicit analogy with the slave trade through the 'traffic in flesh' which was condoned, if not encouraged, by a large section of middle-class men.

What made Mrs Butler's attack so emotionally supercharged, however, was the internal examination by speculum. LNA literature denounced this, in a hyperbolic image, as the 'espionage of enslaved wombs'.[17] Mrs Butler wrote: 'For myself, I had much rather die than endure it . . .'[18] It wasn't just the actual use of the speculum that caused her distress, but the fact that such an intimate procedure was carried out upon women by men. This turned a medical procedure into a sexual attack.

This recoil from male physicians became clear in dealings she had with Elizabeth Garrett, before this doctor declared herself a supporter of the Contagious Diseases Acts. Mrs Butler often became emotionally involved with the girls she was rescuing and after the death of one of them, Fanny, she was on the verge of a nervous breakdown. She consulted Dr Garrett about her ailments, and later wrote:

I must say of her that I gained more from her than from any other doctor ... *because* I was able to tell her so much more than I ever could or would tell to any *man* ... O, if only men knew what women have to endure, and how every good woman has prayed for the coming of a change in this. How would any modest *man* endure to put himself in the hands of a woman medically as women have to put themselves into the hands of men? And are women less modest than men? God forbid. They are *not*, and believe me, the best and the purest feelings of women have been torn and harrowed and shamefully wounded for centuries, just to please a wicked *custom*, while those women who are not intrinsically noble and good are debased, insensibly, by such custom.[19]

It was to be sixteen years before the Acts were finally repealed. During that time, the campaign transformed the political landscape. It challenged social and sexual conventions which had never been publicly discussed, radicalised many women, toughened them against public hostility and ignominy and gave them an infrastructure of political protest.

A majority of the LNA's national leaders were already experienced feminists. Twelve out of thirty-three on the executive board were single, another six were widowed and twenty were known to have been childless. Most came from families who had been deeply involved in the political agitations of the 1830s and 1840s, and several male relatives were outstanding feminists too. Margaret Tanner and Mary Priestman were sisters-in-law to John Bright, the leading Quaker politician. He, in fact, opposed both repeal and women's suffrage, even though many feminists had learned the tactics of political agitation decades earlier while helping him in the Anti-Corn Law struggle.[20]

Most LNA leaders observed strict standards of personal conduct, a necessary protection against the implication that any association with prostitution was morally tainted. There were a few exceptions, most notably Elizabeth Wolstenholme, who modelled herself on Mary Wollstonecraft and became pregnant by Ben Elmy in 1875. She was persuaded by Mrs Jacob Bright to marry for fear of harming the suffrage cause. Most LNA leaders became feminists through the slavery and temperance crusades. Elizabeth Pease Nichol, for example, had been among the British female delegates to the 1840 world anti-slavery convention who were outraged by their exclusion. LNA leaders were also active in the National Association for the Promotion of Social Science, which, during the 1860s, sponsored a series of activities designed to advance women in education, law and other professions.[21] Though members of the board tended to be secular London radicals, most repealers were northern nonconformists from the Liberal radical wing, the same groups involved in other reform movements.[22]

The tactics used by the LNA became a template for the later suffrage campaign. Parliamentary candidates were picked out for harassment, and a notable scalp was taken at the Colchester by-election in 1870. Although the repealers were mostly Liberals, they had been infuriated when the party had given the Newark seat to Sir Henry Storks, an ex-governor of Malta. He had enforced the Contagious Diseases Acts there with great zeal, remarking: 'I am of the opinion that very little benefit will result from the best devised means of prevention until prostitution is recognised as a necessity.'[23] Newark was placarded and Storks withdrew on election day, with a new candidate pledged to repealing the Acts being successful. However, Storks was put up again in Colchester in 1870. This time the repealers ran a third candidate, split the vote and let in the Conservative by a large majority.[24]

The electioneering in Colchester was led by the then obscure Mrs Butler and James Stuart, a fellow of Trinity College, Cambridge, and later a maths professor and a Liberal MP. They were repeatedly attacked by the mob and placed in danger of their lives. On one occasion Mrs Butler had to leave the hotel where she was staying under an assumed name when the mob attacked the building in the middle of the night and threatened to burn it down. In 1872 H. C. E. Childers, First Lord of the Admiralty, had to seek re-election at Pontefract, where he was a popular local figure. The Admiralty had shocked many by its zealous prosecution of the Acts. Demonstrations by repealers were met with violence; in the worst incident Mrs Butler and another campaigner were trapped in a hayloft. Childers was returned, but with a massively cut majority. Such a result caused a sensation. The press, although hostile to the repealers, gave them credit for the result.[25]

And the worse the violence, the more publicity and the more support Mrs Butler got. Her glamorous appearance and demeanour, coupled with the taboo-breaking claims she was making about 'instrumental rape' and so forth, had an electrifying effect on the public. Mrs Butler's crusade showed the intoxicating results of threatening parliamentary candidates with ruin unless they supported the cause. It showed how male politicians could be hopelessly wrong-footed by women on a public platform. And it showed how public sympathy could be manipulated by exposing women to violence and danger. These lessons were not to be lost on the militant suffragettes.

The immediate success of these tactics went to the campaigners' heads. They set out to forge an electoral machine which would, in Mrs Butler's words, 'make these fellows afraid of us'.[26] But their growing self-importance blinded them to the fact that they were still only a small pressure group, overwhelmingly reliant on the Liberals and with no purchase on the Conservatives. The tactic of giving the Liberals a bloody nose rebounded badly when in January 1874 the Liberals were badly beaten in the general election by the Conservatives and as a result the repealers lost those MPs who had been sympathetic to their cause.[27] The repealers had shot themselves in the foot.

Mrs Butler herself played down the sexual politics of her great crusade. 'It was as a citizen of a free country first, and as a woman secondly, that I felt impelled to come forward in defence of the right,' she wrote later. 'I never myself viewed this question as fundamentally any more a woman's question than it is a man's. The legislation we opposed secured the enslavement of women and the increased immorality of men; and history and experience alike teach us that these two results are never separated.'[28] But the fact remained that her campaign radicalised women and taught them for the first time how to organise, as she herself acknowledged:

Thus the peculiar horror and audacity of this legislative movement for the creation of a slave class of women for the supposed benefit of licentious men forced women into a new position. Many, who were formerly timid or bound by conventional ideas to a prescribed sphere of action, faced right round upon the men whose materialism had been embodied in such a ghastly form, and upon the government which had set its seal upon that iniquity; and so, long before we had approached near to attaining to any political equality with men, a new light was brought by the force of our righteous wrath and aroused sense of justice into the judgement of society and the councils of nations, which encouraged us to hope that we should be able to hand down to our successors a regenerated public spirit concerning the most vital questions of human life, upon which alone, and not upon any expert or opportunistic handling of them, the hopes of the future must rest.[29]

The result of this radical awakening was that the campaign gave rise to other reform groupings to work against injustices and disabilities affecting women. So Mrs Wolstenholme Elmy formed a society to obtain for poorer married women the right to possess their own wages, a campaign which eventually led to the passing of the Married Women's Property Act in 1870. Feminists were attracted to other reforms, including anti-vivisection and anti-vaccination, water cures and dress reform.[30]

Mrs Butler herself became involved in specifically feminist agitation. Between 1867 and 1873 she was president of the North of England Council for Promoting the Higher Education of Women. In 1869 she edited a book of essays, *Women's Work and Women's Culture*. In her introduction she acknowledged that women's sphere was the home but she called for the diffusion of home influence into the general society. She celebrated the feminine form of philanthropy, 'the independent, individual ministering, the home influence' against the masculine form, 'the large comprehensive measure, the organisation, the system planned and sanctioned by Parliament'. She wanted women to have a legal, political and economic identity outside the home but she also wanted to exploit women's moral pre-eminence. Women's mission was to defend home and family and promote a single standard of chastity in the political arena.[31] So Mrs Butler embodied the paradox at the heart of the feminist movement. She wanted to end the sexual double standard and promote an equality of continent behaviour between the sexes; but she also wanted to impose women's moral superiority upon men.

The state had defined women as the source of contagion. Through regulating them, it thought it could make sexual immorality safe for men. It appeared to have no concern whatsoever for the well-being of the women involved. As W. T. Stead expostulated, it created 'a class of "Queen's women"', virtually licenced and safe to sin with and periodically violated.[32] But the despised Acts of Parliament that embodied this belief were not the only targets of the campaign. It was male sexuality that was squarely in the sights of these reformers. It was male sexuality that had reduced women to the status of slaves. Mrs Butler wrote: 'The cry of women crushed under the yoke of legalised vice is not the cry of a statistician or a medical expert; it is simply a cry of pain, a cry for justice and for a return to God's laws in place of these brutally impure laws invented and imposed by men ... The slave now speaks. The enslaved women have found a voice in one of themselves ... It is the voice of a woman who has suffered, a voice calling to holy rebellion and to war.'[33]

For the Social Purity Alliance, founded in 1873, male vice lay at the heart of the problem of immorality. It was men who had to be made to meet their moral obligations. Many believed this meant transforming the whole public climate into one founded on moral and religious principle. The family had to be made into the paradigm of ethical government. The source of moral contagion wasn't women but men, backed up by a medical profession which wanted to define and control femininity itself. Indeed, in a mirror image of those men who conceived femininity in terms of disease, Mrs Butler claimed that men were intrinsically polluted. 'Among men the disease is almost universal at one time or another,' she wrote, so 'to try to stem disease by curing women who are immediately infected by men' was a hopeless task.[34] More than forty years later Christabel Pankhurst was to earn a reputation as a pathological man-hater by expressing very similar sentiments.

The sex war was thus profoundly religious in origin, and was at root not a fight for equality. It was rather a crusade to redeem human beings from evil, which was conceived as male lustfulness, and it was women who would be the agents for national moral regeneration. Mrs Butler wrote in *The Shield* in 1871: 'But it is the buyers who have the first interest in prostitution. It is this stronghold which must first be attacked if we are ever to hope to stem the torrent of evil which threatens to overflow us. The great thing that is to be done is to create a pure moral tone among men.'[35] In order to attack society's unjust laws, the campaign had to take an axe, she said, to the roots of vice: the absence of male chastity and the 'creation of woman as a mere vessel of dishonour for the brutal instincts of man'.[36]

The Butler crusade thus audaciously wrenched the whole agenda for social reform away from the problem of women, and reconceived it instead as the need to deal with the problem of men. William T. Malleson, chairman of the Social Purity Alliance, said in 1880: 'It is the rescue and reform of men that is really the question of our society today . . . and for the rescue and reform of men we look to the power and devotion of women . . . It is to women as mothers, to women as sisters, to women in private life, and in public life, that we must look for the new force on this question, to give a new impulse, to take the matter into their own hands in order to save Society, to save England, to save India, and I almost say to save the future of the world.'[37]

Despite dismissing the idea that she was involved in the sex war, Mrs Butler was quite clear that it was men who were the wellspring of female misery and the degradation of prostitutes.

I recall the bitter complaint of one of these poor women: 'It is *men, men, only men*, from the first to the last, that we have to do with! To please a man I did wrong at first, then I was flung about from man to man. Men police lay hands on us. By men we are examined, handled, doctored and messed on with. In the hospital it is a man again who makes prayers and reads the bible for us. We are had up before magistrates who are men, and we never get out of the hands of men till we die!' And as she spoke I thought: 'And it was a Parliament of men only who made this law which treats you as an outlaw. Men alone met in committee over it. Men alone are the executives.' When men, of all ranks, thus band themselves together for an end concerning women, and place themselves like a thick impenetrable wall between women and women, and forbid the one class of women entrance into the presence of the other, the weak, the outraged class, it is time that women should arise and demand their most sacred rights in regard to their sisters.[38]

Since sexual injustice for women had been created by a political arena which excluded them, it was an obvious next step to conclude that sexual justice for women could only be achieved if they were allowed to enter that political arena to speak up for their rights. Indeed, Mrs Butler – who had said that if she wasn't working for repeal of the Acts, she would throw her whole force into getting the suffrage – wrote passionately in favour of women obtaining the vote. In her Address to the Electors at the 1885 general election, she pointed out that women were unable to have a share in making the laws by which they and their children would be governed.

We have listened to cynical arguments in favour of the protection of male vice from men in that House of Commons, whose illegitimate children and cast-off paramours we have sheltered and nursed in their disease and poverty and destitution, and the victims of whose seductions we have laboured hard to restore to hope and a new life. Sometimes, after looking down from the ladies' gallery there, or vainly arguing with some hardened sinner in the lobby, we have returned to our almost hopeless work among their victims and have been driven in a moment of darkness to ask, 'Is there indeed a God in Heaven?'

I have seen a good mother, wild with grief, kneeling by the dead body of her young daughter in my own house, where my husband and I had received the dying outcast, and heard that mother shriek the name of the man, the gentleman, the 'honourable member for—', who had ruined her child. 'If that man could but see her now!' she cried. 'O God, keep me from thoughts of revenge and blood!' How little do some good people understand the demand of women to be put just on a level with the poor agricultural labourers, and to be granted that little favour, the parliamentary vote! They prate about women coveting power, and stepping out of their sphere; while what we are craving for, with aching hearts, is but to be able to protect ourselves and our children from male destroyers, not only from their deeds of shame but from their evil influence in the legislature. There is a French saying that it is 'women who make the morals of a country'. That is not true; it cannot be true, so long as MEN ALONE MAKE THE LAWS.[39]

The sexual purity campaign was not the same as the campaign for women's suffrage. But the two were nevertheless intimately connected, and not merely because some of the same women were involved in both. For both sexual moralists and suffragists, the best way to end prostitution, reform men and deliver social and sexual justice for women was for women to have a voice in the contaminated public sphere and thus purify it by elevating public morals.

The moral reform societies of the late nineteenth century wanted to regenerate family life by transforming relations between the sexes. Josephine Butler, Catherine Booth, Mrs Bramwell Booth, Frances Power Cobbe, Ellice Hopkins, Margaret Lucas, Mary Steer and others campaigned for the suffrage in the hope it would enable women to transform England into a more civilised society. The temperance worker Mary Anne Clarke said: 'We see a well-educated woman with wealth and property at her command classed by the law with minors, idiots and felons while the man who opens her carriage door or drives her horses may have a voice in the legislation of the country, be he ignorant, drunken or depraved.'[40]

Ellice Hopkins wanted women to legislate for their own protection. She compared the state to the family and said that as women had evolved a more prominent place in the home, they should be more prominent by men's side in national affairs. 'May we not find in the larger family of the state that the work of the world is best done by the man and the woman together, each supplying what is lacking in the other, the man the head of the woman, the woman the heart of the man?'[41] Votes for women were to her simply the means to make society more compassionate and relations between men and women more holy. If women had political power, she thought, men might rise to the standard women set for them.[42]

Nevertheless, many suffragists viewed all this with horror and alarm. For the subject matter was simply too incendiary. Respectable people thought it was indecent, and anyone who put forward such arguments was by definition disreputable. Mrs Butler's crusade had provoked fierce reactions. She was condemned as 'frenzied, unsexed and utterly without shame', and accused of gross irresponsibility. Lord Dufferin, the Viceroy of India, said 'the shrieking sisterhood . . . who have constituted themselves the champions of military chastity' would 'allow death and disease to be propagated wholesale throughout the British army', and he scorned those who demanded chastity outside marriage.[43] Mrs Butler's support for prostitutes was thought perverse, especially as she was an evangelical and most of her contemporaries thought harlotry was avoidable by work and prayer.[44] John Morley who wrote in the *Pall Mall Gazette*, complained: 'To sacrifice the health and vigour of unborn creatures to the "rights" of harlotry to spread disease without interference is a doubtful contribution towards the progress of the race. This sentimental persistence in treating permanently brutalised natures as if they still retained infinite capacities for virtue is one of the worst faults of some of the best people now living.'[45]

Under attack from the repealers, supporters of the Acts hardened in their hostility to prostitutes. Those who supported extending the Acts attacked the 'immoral' literature distributed by the 'shrieking sister-hood'. Anti-suffragists seized upon the campaign as a portent of what would happen if women became involved in politics. The repealers added fuel to the fire. Mary Hume-Rothery, a prominent LNA speaker, explic-itly associated bourgeois marriages with prostitution. In an open letter to Gladstone she looked forward to the day 'when women shall dare poverty, loneliness, contempt, starvation itself rather than sell them-selves, whether to wealthy husbands or less eligible purchasers'.[46]

In 1875 Sir William Acton warned against the threat posed by advo-cates of women's rights to the sexual supremacy of men in marriage. He noted the case of a 'lady who maintains women's rights to such an extent that she denied the husband any voice in the matter, whether or not cohabitation should take place. She maintained most strenuously that as the woman bears all the consequences . . . a married woman has a perfect right to refuse to cohabit with her husband.'[47]

Anti-suffragists were using the prostitution campaign to smear cam-paigners for the vote as women of loose morals. Votes for women therefore had to be dissociated from the repeal campaign. It was an argument that was to split the infant suffrage cause, which just a few years previously had coalesced into a movement as circumspect as it was revolutionary.

8

THE CHALLENGE TO POLITICS

In 1865 the Kensington Ladies' Discussion Society was formed with fifty members, united by their common interest in opening up higher education to women. It was composed largely of gifted members of the Langham Place group, including Mrs Bodichon, Miss Emily Davies, Miss Buss and Miss Beale, Miss Jessie Boucherett, head of the Society for Promoting the Employment of Women, Miss Sophia Jex-Blake, Miss Frances Power Cobbe, Miss Elizabeth Garrett and Miss Helen Taylor, the stepdaughter of John Stuart Mill.[1]

That November they debated the subject of women's suffrage and discovered that they were all ardent supporters. Emily Davies was the most wary, since she was committed to opening up the universities to women and didn't want to harm that particular cause by attracting 'wild people' who 'would insist on jumping like kangaroos'.[2] However, Barbara Bodichon was a friend of the radical John Stuart Mill, who had just been elected as an MP. When she asked him to help, he replied that if she could get a hundred signatures for a petition he'd hand it in. With Jessie Boucherett, Rosamond Hill and Elizabeth Garrett, Mrs Bodichon promptly formed the first Women's Suffrage Committee to get up a petition.

Immediately, though, they hit a problem. Did they want votes for all women householders, or only those who were unmarried? Emily Davies, mindful of the need to avoid antagonising the public, said asking for votes for married women would cause a storm. Mill, however, would not dilute the principle of equality. So a form of words was found which was satisfyingly ambiguous.[3] On 28 April 1866 Barbara Bodichon, Emily Davies and Jessie Boucherett drafted a petition asking for 'the enfranchisement of all householders, without distinction of sex, who possess such property or rental qualification as your Honourable House may determine'. This implicitly excluded married women, who couldn't be householders. Within a fortnight it was signed by 1,499 women and taken to Mill, who, with another radical, MP Henry Fawcett, presented it to the House of Commons on 7 June.[4]

This was not a demand for democratic rights in the sense we understand the term today. The vote was to be restricted to owners of property, including unmarried women. So although it was a demand for female suffrage, it was only for some women. It was not based on an understanding of sexual equality. It did not seek to breach the conventions of the time: that citizenship was not universal but was based on property, and that women lost its entitlements upon marriage. This was a deeply middle-class campaign, which produced its own ironies. As the weekly journal *Truth* pointed out, the vote was to be showered on courtesans but not on married women.[5] The argument between universalism and the property vote was to bedevil and split the women's movement for decades.

In 1867 Mrs Bodichon's group turned into the London Society for Women's Suffrage. In Manchester the advanced feminist Elizabeth Wolstenholme Elmy brought together local suffrage groups under the umbrella of the National Society for Women's Suffrage. This was full of radical thinkers, many of whom had campaigned against slavery or had been members of the Anti-Corn Law League, such as the Manchester MP Jacob Bright, his wife Ursula and Dr Richard Pankhurst, a barrister and champion of all progressive causes.[6] Its secretary was Miss Lydia Becker. Born in 1827, she was already an 'old maid' when she joined the group.

Plain and solid in appearance, with heavy features and severely dressed hair, she seemed typical of the kind of strong-minded woman who wanted to take part in politics. She was involved in the campaigns against the Contagious Diseases Acts and for property rights for married women. In October 1866 she had attended a meeting of the National Association for the Promotion of Science in Manchester at which Mrs Bodichon read a paper on the 'reasons for the enfranchisement of women'. On the spot, Lydia Becker became committed to a campaign that was to give meaning to a restricted and lonely life.[7]

In 1867 a measure was passed by Parliament that was to become a Trojan horse for constitutional, political and social transformation. The Reform Act did more than extend the franchise: it transformed British politics. It established household suffrage, giving the vote to urban male householders who paid their rates. It thus enfranchised skilled manual workers but excluded those deemed incapable of political and economic independence: women, lunatics, agricultural labourers and the residuum of the casual poor. But in the late 1860s and 1870s the courts increasingly widened the terms of the franchise. This extension gave rise to a new type of politics based on mass organisation and the rise of interest groups.[8] The result was the stimulation of a wave of political activism among middle-class nonconformists and working-class radicals.

On to this great political reform John Stuart Mill tried to graft the rights of women. On 20 May 1867 he proposed an amendment which sought to replace the word 'man' in the bill by the word 'person'. He was defeated by 194 votes to 73. But the speech he made was to be a benchmark for the struggle to come. Women householders, he said, hardly presented a danger to the state. Women paid taxes, and taxation and representation should go together. A stake in property meant the same for men and women. As for the claim that politics was not a woman's business, this was absurd.

'The ordinary occupations of most women are domestic; but the notion that these occupations are incompatible with the keenest interest in national affairs, and in all the great interests of humanity, is as utterly futile as the apprehension, once sincerely entertained, that artisans would desert their workshops and their factories if they were taught to read . . . this claim to confiscate the whole existence of one half of the species for the supposed convenience of the other appears to me, independently of its injustice, particularly silly.' A silent, domestic revolution was taking place, Mill said, in which the two sexes were growing closer together. For a man, 'the wife is his chief associate, his most confidential friend and often his most trusted adviser . . .' An unworthy stigma had to be removed from an entire sex, that women were frivolous and not capable of undertaking serious things.[9]

In 1869 Mill expanded on his feminist theme in his essay *The Subjection of Women*. This was to be a seminal text for the women's movement and repays close attention. For, as Gertrude Himmelfarb has pointed out, Mill subtly but crucially shifted his ground as he developed his argument.[10] This shift in the governing principle, from equality to freedom, anticipated the very question that the suffrage movement itself was to beg. Did women want to be like men – or did they instead want to be free of men altogether?

At the beginning Mill based his argument for women's rights squarely on the principle of equality. The subordination of one sex by the other was wrong in itself, he said, and one of the chief hindrances to human improvement; it should be replaced by the principle of perfect equality. Inequality between the sexes was grounded in nothing other than the superior strength of men. All women were brought up to believe that their ideal of character was the very opposite to that of men; not self-will and government by self-control but submission and yielding to the control of others. Told to live entirely for others, they were also told that meekness, submissiveness and resignation were essential to sexual attractiveness. 'What is now called the nature of women is an eminently artificial thing – the result of forced repression in some directions, unnatural stimulation in others.'[11]

Men, said Mill, treated women worse than Roman slaves, and marriage was the mechanism of their bondage. Wives had no legal personality. Husbands could force them to have sex, compel them to return if they left, and had sole rights over their children. The ferocity with which Mill tore into his own sex leads one to detect the hand of Harriet Taylor hovering above the page:

> When we consider how vast is the number of men, in any great country, who are little higher than brutes, and that this never prevents them from being able, through the law of marriage, to obtain a victim, the breadth and depth of human misery caused in this shape alone by the abuse of the institution swells to something appalling. Yet these are only the extreme cases ... Absolute fiends are as rare as angels, perhaps rarer; ferocious savages, with occasional touches of humanity, are, however, very frequent: and in the wide interval which separates these from any worthy representatives of the human species, how many are the forms and gradations of animalism and selfishness, often under an outward varnish of civilisation and even cultivation, living at peace with the law, maintaining a creditable appearance to all who are not under their power, yet sufficient often to make the lives of all who are so, a torment and a burthen to them![12]

If men were brutes, the family was a temple not of sympathy and tenderness but of male 'wilfulness, overbearingness, unbounded self-indulgence and a double-dyed and idealised selfishness'. Lower-class men were the worst of all in subjecting their wives to disrespect and indignity. 'This self-worship gets more intense the lower down the scale of humanity and worst of all among men who can be raised above no-one except wife and children.' Moral cultivation was only possible between equals. Women should be free to work – but not if they were married. Wives who worked couldn't look after the children and household. Their husbands would force them to work and look after the family while spending most of their time in drinking and idleness; instead, 'on earnings, the common arrangement by which the man earns the income and the wife superintends the general expenditure seems to me in general the most suitable division of labour between the two persons'.[13]

It was marriage that was squarely in Mill's sights. 'Marriage is the only actual bondage known to our law. There remain no legal slaves, except the mistress of every house.' All evils were blamed on marriage. 'All the selfish propensities, the self-worship, the unjust self-preference, which exist among mankind, have their source and root in, and derive their principal nourishment from, the present constitution of the relation between men and women.' If marriage was a form of slavery, then it followed that women had to be liberated from it. Equality was therefore merely the means; liberty was the desired end.[14]

The Subjection of Women became a bible for the feminist movement. And yet at its core lay a profound ambivalence about women. For Mill did not subscribe to the assumption that was to run like a thread through the women's rights campaigns: that women were the moral superiors of men. On the contrary, his view of women was hardly complimentary. Women were so useless, grasping, shallow and destructive that it was imperative, it seemed, to raise their intellectual game to prevent them from doing any more harm to men. 'A man who is married to a woman his inferior in intelligence,' he wrote, 'finds her a perpetual dead weight, or worse than a dead weight, a drag upon every aspiration of his to be better than public opinion requires him to be.'[15] This echoed what he had told Parliament in 1867: 'Sir, the time is now come when, unless women are raised to the level of men, men will be pulled down to theirs. The women of a man's family are either a stimulus and a support to his highest aspirations, or a drag upon them.'[16]

This was, to put it mildly, a contradictory argument. On the one hand, Mill claimed that men held women in bondage; on the other, he portrayed women as a ball and chain around men's feet. The key to the puzzle lay, perhaps, in Mill's relationships with his mother and his wife. His autobiography notably omitted his mother, who in early drafts – before she was excised from the narrative – was portrayed as painfully submissive. It was his mother, not his father, whom Mill blamed for the lack of affection in his family life, for the distance between himself and his father, and for a childhood lived in the absence of love and the presence of fear. In an early draft he wrote: 'That rarity in England, a really warm-hearted mother, would in the first place have made my father a totally different being, and in the second would have made the children grow up loving and being loved. But my mother with the very best intentions, only knew how to pass her life in drudging for them. Whatever she could do for them she did, and they liked her, because she was kind to them, but to make herself loved, looked up to, or even obeyed, required qualities which she unfortunately did not possess.'[17]

Here, surely, lay the seeds of Mill's later political view that the passive role and inferior status of women was a deadly threat to men's progress. Nevertheless, the woman he was to marry, Harriet Taylor, who effectively co-authored *The Subjection of Women*, believed passionately that men were the cause of female oppression. One of Mill's friends observed that he was in a 'state of subjection' to his wife. So *Subjection*, the sacred text of the women's movement, managed to present women as the victims of men, whose lives they nevertheless held in their own bound female hands. Such were the contradictions of an author struggling to reconcile his wife and his mother in his mind; and they were to be among the many contradictions of the women's movement itself.

Mill's amendment in 1867 had no chance against the deep insecurities of the time. The Reform Act was passed against a background of a financial crash, unemployment and riots. The harvest was ruined by rains, meat prices were high from an outbreak of disease, cholera broke out and there were Fenian disturbances. The resulting volatility of public opinion provoked the Prime Minister, Benjamin Disraeli, to push through the Reform Act fast in order to see off the opposition. Many feared such a great increase in democratic power, believing that dangerous forces would be unleashed.[18] The last thing people were inclined to do was to revolutionise the position of women as well.

Nevertheless, the fact that the amendment was put and Mill's speech made at all galvanised the suffrage societies. In November 1867 the London and Manchester societies formed a loose federation called the National Society of Women's Suffrage.[19] Its members believed that with some eighty MPs supporting Mill's amendment, victory was only a few years away. As naïve as they were high-minded, they had absolutely no idea how politics worked, or of attitudes beyond the rarefied radical circles in which they moved.[20] They never foresaw how difficult it would be to persuade people of their cause.

Moreover, many believed that the new Reform Act actually enfranchised women. Suffragists claimed that under an earlier law the use of the word 'man' had been taken to include women unless specified to the contrary. At a by-election in Manchester in 1867 a woman's name, Lily Maxwell, was accidentally allowed to remain on the electoral register, and under the escort of Lydia Becker she voted for Jacob Bright. Before the general election of 1868 a large number of women householders claimed to be on the register of electors: in Manchester alone, 5,346 women signed the claim. In a few places their votes were indeed allowed. Lady Scarisbrick and twenty-seven women tenant farmers voted in south-west Lancashire for Gladstone. However, in November 1868 this brief suffrage idyll was brought abruptly to an end when the Court of Common Pleas in the case of *Chorlton v Lings* ruled that 'every woman is personally incapable' of recording a vote.[21] The case for the women was presented by Dr Richard Pankhurst, who argued that 'man' included women on the grounds that 'man' derived from the Latin 'homo', meaning a human being. His argument fell on deaf ears.[22]

As the century wore on, the male franchise was progressively widened and so more and more salt was rubbed into the wound. (By the third Reform Act in 1884, between sixty-three and sixty-six per cent of adult men were able to vote.[23]) Society was transforming the way it organised itself, but was nevertheless excluding half the population. By identifying rate paying with voting, the Reform Act made more glaring the inconsistency of enforcing rates upon women while refusing them the right to vote. It was this transformation that was crucial in fomenting the sense of injustice. For women were not suddenly demanding a set of settled rights that had been hitherto restricted to men. It was rather that men, or rather the vast majority of them, were progressively being turned into democratic citizens for the first time, a new status that women were denied. The intense focus on the creation of democracy made the exclusion of women from this momentous change an intolerable injustice. To add insult to injury, some of these enfranchised men were drawn from the labouring classes. In an era which viewed property ownership and good breeding as badges of social fitness, giving lower-class men the vote while excluding upper-class women was the last straw.

So the suffrage committees started to organise. Their tactics were based on the Anti-Corn Law League struggle of Cobden and Bright, and they used itinerant lecturers, indoor public meetings, handbills and propaganda. Cobden's daughters Annie and Jane became active feminists; after Mill lost his parliamentary seat in 1868, Jacob Bright became the leader of the suffragists in the Commons. The societies set up meetings first in drawing rooms and then on public platforms, with the first public meeting held on 14 April 1868 at the Free Trade Hall in Manchester. This required a degree of courage, since it was simply not done for women to speak in public. When they did so, the appearance of these suffragists mattered enormously since it was crucial to avoid shocking or outraging the public. Some of them were young and beautiful, but, observed the suffragist historian Ray Strachey, 'it cannot be denied that among these brave and devoted women there were a few who were not only plain but positively uncouth to the outward eye'. They didn't realise the bad impression given by their thick boots, untidy hair and crumpled dress. This indifference to the way they were perceived gave rise to the legend of the strong-minded, rather hirsute female with spectacles and large feet, which figured as an anti-suffrage stereotype in the satirical press for twenty-five years.[24]

So profound was the public's antipathy to the whole phenomenon of women agitating in public for the suffrage, it was dangerous for the rest of the infant women's movement to let the public recognise the close connection between the campaign for the vote and the other politically sensitive agitations for education and medical reform – so much so that Elizabeth Garrett wanted her name kept out of the suffrage campaign altogether. Nevertheless, in the last third of the nineteenth century the public sphere slowly opened up to the women clamouring at its gates. The surplus of women over men in the population meant more middle-class women were looking for alternatives to marriage in education, philanthropy and the professions. In all classes women were affected by 'that wave of desire for a personal working life' described by Clementina Black, president of the Women's Industrial Council. The enormous growth of charities, churches, pressure groups and artistic, political and self-improvement societies brought thousands of women into a quasi-public sphere.[25]

From 1870 women gained a toehold in local government which they exploited to get involved in the administration of the Poor Law, sanitation and public health, and they gained legal rights over property and children.[26] More women found employment as clerks and secretaries, many from the work done by Jessie Boucherett's Society for Promoting the Employment of Women, and with the growth of commercial firms such opportunities for women expanded.

In 1871 women gained the right to sit on school boards. The first elections to these boards returned the women most identified with the suffrage campaign: Elizabeth Garrett, Emily Davies, Lydia Becker and Miss Flora Stevenson. Elizabeth Garrett had an immense majority, polling forty-seven thousand votes. Lydia Becker retained her seat until her death in 1890 and Flora Stevenson until her death in 1905.[27]

The battles to open up education and medicine were harder, but slowly the opposition was worn down. In 1865 girls were admitted to Cambridge local examinations, followed by Oxford, after a campaign by a committee chaired by Emily Davies. By 1869, her schoolmistresses' associations were entering hundreds of girls for junior and senior exams. In 1872 Maria Grey and her sister, Emily Shirreff, started the Girls' Public Day Schools' Trust. By 1890, there were eighty endowed schools for girls. In 1869 Emily Davies founded what would become Girton College. The college, which moved from Hitchin, Hertfordshire, to Cambridge in 1873, examined its women students on the same papers as men, even though women's degrees were not yet recognised. At various universities, progressive men set up extramural lectures for women.[28] In January 1878 London University admitted women to degrees, followed two years later by Cambridge.[29]

The fight for medical education was even tougher. The very idea of women doctors was considered indecent, dangerous and brazen. The pioneer was Elizabeth Blackwell, who was born in Bristol in 1821 but brought up and trained in America, where she was awarded her degree in 1849. She was placed on the British Medical Register in 1859, and her lectures inspired Elizabeth Garrett to start training. But in 1860 the British Medical Register excluded anyone from practising who had a foreign degree. An English medical degree, though, was impossible for women to obtain as they were excluded from the universities. Undeterred, Elizabeth Garrett bought private tuition and qualified for the diploma of the Apothecaries' Society, which in 1865 gave her a licence to practise, following which she obtained her MD in Paris in 1869. During such a struggle she remained very conscious of the importance of appearance. She wrote to Emily Davies about another female student: 'She looks so awfully strong-minded in walking dress . . . she has short petticoats and a close round hat and several dreadfully ugly arrangements . . . It is abominable, and most damaging to the cause.'[30]

The real battle for medical education, however, was fought by Sophia Jex-Blake. She led a small group of women who persuaded the professors of medicine at Edinburgh University to teach them but were then turned on by their male fellow students. She failed her exams, but eventually fought her way on to the British Medical Register after taking degrees in Berne and Dublin. In 1875 a bill was passed enabling universities to admit women, and women medical students were then admitted to London University and the Royal Free Hospital.[31]

Meanwhile women's claim to an independent legal existence was slowly gaining ground. In 1868 a bill giving property rights to married women was blocked after being carried in the Commons by just one vote. In 1870, however, a successor bill made it through Parliament but was transformed when it reached the House of Lords. Instead of allowing women to keep all their own wealth, the bill let them keep only what they had earned. Their lordships didn't care about the principle of equality or the injustice of a man owning his wife's property. They did, however, think it unjust that if a woman had worked to support herself and her children, a husband who may have ill-used her could still take all her earnings. This first Married Women's Property Act was a significant milestone; but it was also a Pyrrhic victory for the campaigners led by the redoubtable Elizabeth Wolstenholme Elmy. For they had now lost the leverage provided by the really hard cases, and were left to fight on the bald principle of equality, which was far harder to sell.[32]

That same year the wife of Henry Fawcett, a Liberal MP, made a speech in her husband's Brighton constituency in support of women's suffrage. Fawcett's constituency officers were aghast as they thought such an outrageous event would injure his electoral prospects. Fawcett, however, was made of sterner stuff. A professor of political economy at Cambridge, he was blind from a shooting accident and was to display remarkable bloody-mindedness in support of the causes in which he believed. In 1873 he managed to defeat Gladstone over religious freedom. Gladstone wanted to amalgamate the Irish colleges into a single university whose curriculum would exclude theology, moral philosophy and modern history. Fawcett fought this and despite the huge Liberal majority in Parliament, defeated Gladstone by 287 votes to 284, a staggering blow to the Liberals for which Gladstone probably never forgave him.[33]

Fawcett's wife was to emerge as even more formidable. Indeed, Millicent Garrett Fawcett was to become the leader of the constitutional battle for the suffrage that was to be waged over the next half-century. A woman who hated speaking in public, which she always said 'takes it out of me', she was nevertheless a class act. She had a clear and distinct voice, was always beautifully dressed and her whole performance was disarming.[34]

Millicent Garrett was born in 1847, the seventh or eighth child (she didn't know which since a brother died before she was born) and the younger sister of Elizabeth. The year of her birth saw the terrible Irish famine and the repeal of the Corn Laws. These tremendous events, she later wrote, 'may possibly have had an electrifying effect upon the whole atmosphere in which I found myself as a little child'. Her father, Newson Garrett, a merchant who owned a fleet of trading vessels, transferred his political allegiance in the early 1860s from Conservative to Liberal. He was 'brave to rashness', vehement, quarrelsome, political and full of fun.

In September 1855 he came in to breakfast with a newspaper in his hand, looking gay and handsome, and called out to his little brood: 'Heads up and shoulders down. Sebastopol is taken!' Her mother, a strict evangelical, was opposed to Elizabeth's ambition to become a doctor but reluctantly went along with it.[35]

Brought up in Aldeburgh and Snape, Suffolk, Millicent inherited a love of strong winds and high waves, along with a Puritan reserve and an obstinate individualism. At the age of twelve she went to Blackheath School, in London, and although for money reasons she left at fifteen, she had a room to herself at home and was allowed to study in the mornings by her mother. Millicent later remarked that she had been a suffragist from her cradle. In 1865, when she was eighteen, she attended one of John Stuart Mill's election meetings. She was much impressed by his 'delicate, sensitive physique, united as it was with a very unusual degree of moral courage'; when he was heckled and asked whether he had written that the characteristic fault of the British working man was untruthfulness, he replied: 'I did.' This kindled tenfold, said Millicent, her enthusiasm for women's suffrage.[36]

She was highly political. During the American Civil War she and Elizabeth were staunch supporters of the North, and she studied carefully arguments proving that the real cause of the war was slavery.[37]

One night she was at the home of the radicals Peter and Harriet Taylor when news came through of the murder of Abraham Lincoln. Henry Fawcett, who was a fellow guest, heard Millicent remark that the murder of Lincoln was a greater loss than that of any crowned head in Europe – and at that point fell in love with her. In 1867 they married and, as the wife of a Liberal MP, Millicent was catapulted into the heart of London's radical political society, becoming a good friend of Mill.[38] Moreover, her political education accelerated as a result of having to act as Fawcett's eyes, reading and writing for him and attending Commons debates.[39]

She later claimed that she was much moved to fight for women's political and social equality by two small, overheard conversations. While dressing for a dance before she was married, she heard two women discussing the failure of the marriage of another. One said to the other: 'I

cannot see what she has to complain of. *Look how he dresses her.*'
(Millicent's italics). Millicent was appalled and kept thinking about the
shame and degradation of the remark. 'I did not know anything at that
time about "kept women",' she wrote, 'but "Look how he dresses her"
was of its essence.' The second conversation took place at Ipswich station
after her marriage. Two clergymen's wives were making small articles of
lace to be sold for the benefit of schools. Asked what sold best, one said:
'Oh, things that are really useful, such as butterflies for the hair!'
Millicent hoped for a time when intelligent and active-minded women
would cease to regard such things as useful.[40]

In 1877 an incident at Waterloo Station further sealed her determination to fight for women's rights. A young man tried to steal her purse. He
was caught and charged with 'stealing from the person of Millicent
Fawcett a purse containing £1 18s 6d, the property of Henry Fawcett'.
When she saw the charge, Mrs Fawcett commented: 'I felt as if I had
been charged with theft myself.'[41] Thus was a constitutional revolutionary created.

Like Millicent Fawcett, a number of suffragists were the wives or
daughters of prominent Liberal politicians, and many were nonconformists. Most shared friendship circles and held similar religious
and political beliefs. This brand of feminism reflected a highly optimistic
view of the world, a middle-class commitment to opportunity, and a liberal faith in liberty and progress which had motivated the anti-slavery
and free-trade crusades.[42]

The times were right for turning the world upside down. The 1860s
and 1870s were a key period for Victorian intellectual tumult. The sense
of a hierarchy of human beings was accentuated by the rise of the intellectual classes, characterised by their common attitudes of superiority,
aloofness and detachment.[43] From this elevated stratum of society
poured forth newspapers, magazines, broadsides and tracts, all promul-
gating a torrent of preventative doctrines to control the working class.
Men of science were considered the leading British intellectuals of the
period. But even scientists disagreed among themselves.

9

THE AGE OF CRUSADES

Everywhere old certainties were being torn up and replaced by new uncertainties. Insecurity was in the ether. Walter Bagehot observed in 1872: 'One peculiarity of this age is the sudden acquisition of much physical knowledge. There is scarcely a department of science which is the same, or at all the same, as it was fifty years ago. A new world of inventions – of railways and telegraphs – has grown up around us which we cannot help seeing; a new world of ideas is in the air and affects us, though we do not see it.'[1]

Historical criticism of scripture led to paralysing doubts about the historical truth of the Bible. Various works such as the translation of Renan's *Life of Jesus* in 1863, or J. R. Seeley's *Ecce Homo* in 1865, argued that the Bible was the work of real men and not the literal word of God. Science then delivered a series of shattering blows to the revealed account of the origins of the world and the belief that each species had been specially created. Mortal damage was done to the belief in the benevolence of God and the argument for existence from design by Darwin's theory of natural selection, an account compelling to many Victorians because it conformed to their experience of a changing, progressive and highly competitive world. For many Victorians, this apparent confirmation that existence was no more than the confluence of chance, brutality, suffering and extinction changed their whole view of the universe and therefore the codes by which human beings should conduct their affairs.[2]

In 1860 *Essays and Reviews*, written by seven liberal churchmen, produced even greater shock waves than *The Origin of Species* the previous year. The essays assumed that man was a developing creature and therefore could not have been formed in Eden. Two authors, H. B. Wilson and Rowland Wilson, were tried in the church courts and saved from conviction only by appeal to the Privy Council. In 1871 Darwin published *The Descent of Man*; the novelist George Eliot and the poet Matthew Arnold were producing their masterpieces popularising Victorian doubt. The whole scheme of Christian belief was in deepening disarray.[3]

Loss of belief was the dominant theme of poems and stories. *Robert Elsmere* by Mrs Humphry Ward achieved a remarkable success for this thirty-six-year-old niece of Matthew Arnold. Her book was a plea for rational Christianity in which the hero, Robert Elsmere, says: 'The miraculous Christian story rests on a tissue of mistake ... The problem of the world at this moment is – *how to find a religion*? Some great conception which shall be once more capable, as the old were capable, of wielding societies, and keeping men's brutish elements in check.'[4]

Having lost this great conception of religion to give a meaning to existence, the Victorians found consolation instead in process rather than revelation. With God left dead or dying by Darwin, the Victorians adopted instead the evolution of man as the route to perfectibility and the principal source of optimism. Even before *The Origin of Species* was published, Herbert Spencer had created a science of evolutionary ethics, in which moral conduct was defined as that which contributed to man's better adaptation and his higher evolution from primitive to advanced levels.[5] For enlightenment to progress, thought his fellow Victorians, people of refined and deepened intellect would have to be cultivated, but these virtues were being threatened by mass education and democracy.[6] So there was a constant attempt to find ways of elevating human behaviour to a refined and morally superior level. The overwhelming anxiety that cast its giant shadow over the whole of Victorian thought was that human beings might be no different from animals, and that civilisation might crumble before the savage, animalistic instincts of the mob.

The energies released by these profound intellectual developments often resulted in the founding of an organisation or a journal. In the late 1860s the London Dialectical Society discussed freethinking subjects like Malthusianism or birth control and cremation.[7] George Bernard Shaw wrote of such societies: 'The tone was strongly individualistic, atheistic, Malthusian, evolutionary, Ingersollian, Darwinian, Herbert Spencerian.'[8] It was also markedly feminist. The Rev Charles Maurice Davies was struck by the Dialecticals' discussion of chastity: 'It was then quite a new sensation for me to hear ladies discussing these hitherto proscribed subjects, and they were not elderly *bas bleus* either, but young ladies, married and unmarried.'[9]

The anxiety about the state of humanity, allied to the growth of evangelicalism, led to an explosion of charities and good causes. There was deepening guilt at the contrast between huge wealth on the one hand and the appalling conditions of the poor on the other. The National Association for the Promotion of Social Science, founded in 1857, gave many controversial subjects a hearing.[10] But the changing nature of politics, with the considerable overlap between parliamentary reform, free trade and dissent, meant the rise of a new phenomenon: the interconnections between pressure groups, with the anti-slavery movement the guiding motif. This was the era of the moral crusade.

Itinerant lecturers such as George Thompson were hired to proselytise the country and appeal to middle-class sensibilities on the grounds of morality. Sir George Stephen, the leading chronicler of the anti-slavery campaign, wrote that the choice was between good and bad, sin and virtue.[11] The new militancy derived from the belief that slavery was a sin and so had to be abolished immediately and without regard to the consequences. This new radicalism lifted such campaigns out of ordinary, run-of-the-mill politics and turned them into a religious crusade.[12]

The anti-slavery movement had been of the greatest significance because it was at the root of so much else. It pioneered campaigning techniques based on voluntary work and private subscription and the concept of the active citizen; it displayed anti-political tendencies; it championed the provincial masses against official metropolitan sophistication and expertise. It had connections with female suffrage, women's rights, temperance and prison reform movements. These moral reformers shared many personalities, attitudes and techniques. They all used petitions, subscription lists, processions, public meetings, local branches, reforming periodicals and letters to MPs. They used publicity to gain influence and change attitudes. The temperance organisations saw themselves as pitting female dignity against male selfishness. The medical profession was attacked through libertarian bodies such as the Vigilance Association for the Defence of Personal Rights and the London Society for the Abolition of Compulsory Vaccination.[13] All these moral-reform movements pushed women into the front line of public political controversy; the campaigns in the 1880s against compulsory vaccination, vivisection and the Contagious Diseases Acts shattered the convention that it was dangerous and improper for women to speak in public on indelicate matters.[14]

The campaign against vivisection had a number of close similarities with the suffrage movement, and so it was no coincidence that some of its leading personalities were closely involved with the suffrage, too. The prototype was once again the anti-slavery movement, which was regularly invoked by anti-vivisection campaigners. They stood in spiritual affinity with the movements against compulsory vaccination and the Contagious Diseases Acts, all of which played upon hostility towards science and medicine. All three campaigns were pitched against professional solidarity, political expediency and bourgeois morality to bring issues of health and medicine into the open. All three wanted to rouse the moral instincts of lay people against arrogant scientists, doctors and legislators. All three saw themselves as battling a 'materialism which sets the body above the soul, profaning the sacred name of science'.[15] All were identified with upper-class values of moral responsibility and *noblesse oblige* against the vulgar careerism, materialism and utilitarianism of the doctors. All three had firmly in their sights a medical profession which, as it sought to carve out a new empire, appeared to be colonising the inert bodies of women, children and animals.

The practice of vivisection was negligible until the latter part of the nineteenth century. By the late 1860s foreign advances were making English medicine look inadequate. In 1870 a small group of experimentally minded physiologists was appointed to institutional positions, and guidelines for experiments on animals were produced. However, a handbook for the Physiological Laboratory published in 1873 made no reference to animal anaesthesia, which provoked widespread indignation, revived by a surge of agitation against animal experiments in Florence. In 1874 some doctors were tried on charges of cruelty to a dog.

There was a most powerful resonance between the anti-vivisection movement and feminism. Like the animals who were being physically ill-treated under the vivisector's knife, women were being surgically violated by the doctor's speculum under the Contagious Diseases Acts. A parallel was drawn between women as victims of the sadistic monsters of the medical profession and animals tortured by male scientists in vivisection experiments. Frances Newman, an activist in both the temperance and feminist movements, equated the inspection of a woman for venereal disease with a carcass laid out for dissection, and claimed that doctors were being empowered to torture women, children and animals. Elizabeth Blackwell, the feminist and anti-vivisectionist physician, thought exposure to cruel vivisectionist experiments was encouraging doctors to treat women patients with brutality. She directly attributed the gynaecologists' willingness to submit women to 'degrading' vaginal examinations to the corruption of their moral sense from 'unrestrained experiment on the lower animals'.[16] The metaphor of medical science as rape became a dominant theme in late-Victorian anti-vivisectionist literature.[17]

The passions generated by all this were marshalled and manipulated by the indomitable Anglo-Irish spinster Frances Power Cobbe, who dominated the anti-vivisection movement. Born in 1822, she was a journalist who wrote extensively on feminist, religious and philanthropic topics and founded the Society for the Protection of Animals Liable to Vivisection, the largest and most politically influential of all the anti-vivisection groups.

The great issue boiling away behind this preoccupation with animal welfare was the perceived threat to spiritual values from the rise of science, or to put it another way, the eclipse of the spiritual by the corporeal. This was why many anti-vivisectionist leaders were evangelicals. Anti-vivisection was used as a symbol of a society thought to be in the grip of an animalistic obsession with bodily health, whereas disease was a divine retribution for sin and folly. Frances Power Cobbe called this 'hygieology', and said it showed how the body was overestimated compared with the soul. In the anxiety to uphold the spiritual over the corporeal, she anthropomorphised and sentimentalised animals and ascribed to them human characteristics. In this way their psychic and spiritual continuities with man were emphasised while the physical side was played down or ignored. Indeed, Frances Power Cobbe appeared to think that the moral sensibilities of animals were higher than those of humans. She wrote of dogs' 'inner nature of thought and love', and that their eagerness, joyousness, 'transparent little wiles' and 'caressing and devoted affection' were 'more really and intensely human (in the sense in which a child is human) than the artificial, cold and selfish characters one meets too often in the guise of ladies and gentlemen'.[18]

This emphasis on the continuity between humans and animals owed much to Darwin, with whom Frances Power Cobbe was initially friendly. Darwin himself believed that animals possessed psychological and even moral characteristics. He wrote to Frances Power Cobbe in 1872 that since writing The Descent of Man, he had come more to believe that dogs might have a conscience since, when a canine offence was discovered, the dog seemed ashamed rather than afraid of its master. He had been glad to read her remarks, he wrote, about the reasoning power of dogs and 'that rather vague matter, their self-consciousness'; although he couldn't believe that dogs ever committed suicide. However, such uplifting musings with Darwin came to an abrupt end when the anti-vivisection crusade began in 1875 and Darwin insisted that animal experiments were necessary in the cause of physiology, becoming as a result the centre of an adoring clique of vivisectors.[19]

Although Darwin's influence lay behind this tendency to see animals as more moral than human beings, the real motor behind the anti-vivisection movement was the terror he had struck into the Victorian soul that human beings were really no different from animals. Anti-vivisectionists had a particular horror of the corporeal and bodily. There was a profound fear of the dark and terrible 'lower self' lurking in man which emerged with startling clarity in the practice of vivisection.[20] W. S. Lilly wrote: 'The new naturalism . . . eliminates from man all but the ape and the tiger. It leaves of him nothing but the *bête humaine*, more subtle than any beast of the field, but cursed above all beasts of the field . . . The great criterion of elevation in the order of existence is whether the higher or lower self . . . is dominant; the self of the appetites and passions, or the self of the reason and moral nature.'[21]

This was the deep and abiding trauma of the Victorian period, the appalling vista Darwin had opened up that man was not created in the image of God but was instead no more than a savage brute. The overwhelming need to defeat this terrible prospect lay behind the preoccupation of the age to transcend animal appetites through spiritual purity. It was this that galvanised the evangelicals to raise the moral condition of mankind; it was this that lay behind the developing fashion for psychic and spiritual exploration; it was this that lay behind the fear of the lower orders and savage races; and it was this that was to turn female suffrage from a simple quest for civic equality into a spiritual crusade.

It was what lay behind Josephine Butler's odyssey into the sexual underworld to bring those souls lost to prostitution up into the spiritual light. For Mrs Butler viewed the lowest social groups as subhuman, a backwards evolution towards a primitive form of existence. She wrote: 'And thus, as we descend to the poorest populations of our towns, we find, in place of marriage, loose and lawless intercourse, consciences becoming darker and more dead through the ever-accumulating weight of crime and misery which is passed on as a family heritage, and even the physical type degraded for successive generations, till finally our prisons, penitentiaries and workhouses are crowded to overflowing with worth-less, unwholesome human weeds, low-browed apes, in whom intelligence is all but extinguished, and love has perished, and the instinct of hunger and the lowest animal instincts alone remain.'[22]

It was not surprising, therefore, that Frances Power Cobbe, who thought she recognised morality in a dog, should also have been a lead-ing member of the suffragist movement. Socially very well connected, she boasted that she knew nearly all the most gifted Englishwomen of the time. A deeply conservative woman, she did not dress fashionably and intensely disliked the licentiousness of modern life, manners and morals. Yet her own life was hardly conventional. She lived with her very close friend Miss Mary Lloyd, whom she described in terms of deepest love.[23]

Introduced to the issue of women's rights by the penal reformer Mary Carpenter, Miss Cobbe did not, however, believe that women *en masse* were the intellectual equals of men. But she did think that women of high ability should have the vote, and she wrote in favour of women's suffrage as 'the natural and needful constitutional means of protection for the rights of the weaker half of the nation'.[24] During the 1860s and 1870s she threw herself into feminism, writing and lobbying for higher educa-tion for women, the franchise, entry into the professions and legal protection for the rights of married women. Like many suffragists, she believed that women, though less intelligent and physically weaker than men, were more sympathetic, direct and practical, less hypocritical, more religious and more moral. So women's mission was nothing less than the moral and spiritual regeneration of society. Women, she said, should use their superior moral qualities outside the home in any cause of humanity, 'but above all, in the cause of their own sex and the relief of the misery of their own sisters'.[25]

The whole point of the suffrage was moral elevation. If the vote did not achieve this for women, it was not worth having. She wrote: 'Greatly as I desire to see the enfranchisement and the elevation of women, I consider even that object subordinate to the moral character of each individual woman. If women were to become less dutiful by being enfranchised – less conscientious, less unselfish, less temperate, less chaste – then I should say: "For Heaven's sake, let us stay where we are! *Nothing* we can ever gain would be worth such a loss". But I have yet to learn that freedom, which is the spring of all the nobler virtues in man, will be less the ground of loftier and purer virtues in women.' Confusing emancipation with looser moral standards or unconventionality would pose 'deadly perils to the whole movement for the advancement of women', whose mission was 'to make society *more* pure, *more* free from vice, either masculine or feminine, than it has ever been before'.[26] She did not believe that the vote would cause women to abandon their responsibilities. 'The spectre of the female politician who abandons her family to neglect, for the sake of passing bills in Parliament, is just as complete an illusion of the masculine brain as the older spectre whom Sydney Smith laid by a joke; the women who would "forsake an infant for a quadratic equation".' Nevertheless, she also thought that mothers shouldn't be breadwinners, philanthropists or politicians, since they were already serving the community in the highest possible way.[27]

The demand for female suffrage was not just about equal political representation. The vote meant different things to different people; it was like a tree on whose branches was hung a bewildering array of expectations, grievances and causes, not to mention a series of contradictory views about the position of women. Were women the weaker sex who needed the added protection of a representative voice, or did they possess superior attributes which needed wider scope? Did they want equality with men in the public sphere, or did they think their superior moral qualities would bring men to heel? Did they see themselves marching shoulder to shoulder with men towards a better world, or did they want to free themselves from men altogether?

Right from the start some feminists were advocating a degree of female emancipation with which others profoundly disagreed. Helen Taylor, the stepdaughter of John Stuart Mill, put forward an argument for an advanced form of female autonomy. Women, she said, were dictated to by men, to whom they were a 'servile appendage', and unable to use their God-given powers. A woman needed to be free.

'She claims the right to belong to herself, as a self-contained individual existence – the right that every soul, stamped with the divine image, has of striving to perfect itself by the free exercise of its own faculties; the right to refuse submission to the sovereign rule of a fellow-creature, weak and erring as herself; the right to perfect liberty in fulfilling her duties to the world in accordance with nature's teachings and her own convictions; in short, her right to live up to the full measure of her capacities, to reach up to the highest and more useful standard she can attain . . .'[28] The 'right to belong to herself' was a radical position which was part of a quite different agenda from the one mapped out by the feminist advocates of equality with men.[29]

The leading advocate of equality was Millicent Fawcett. She did not deny the differences between the male and female spheres, public and private. She simply wanted to enable women's different and much more domestic concerns to be articulated in the public sphere. 'With regard to the differences between men and women, those who advocate the enfranchisement of women have no wish to disregard them or make little of them,' she wrote.

On the contrary, we base our claim to representation to a large extent on them. If men and women were exactly alike, the representation of men would represent us; but not being alike, that wherein we differ is unrepresented under the present system . . . we want the home and the domestic side of things to count for more in politics and in the administration of public affairs than they do at present. We want to know how various kinds of legislative enactments bear on the home and domestic life. And we want to force our legislators to consider the domestic as well as the political results of any legislation which many of them are advocating . . . I advocate the extension of the franchise to women because I wish to strengthen true womanliness in woman, and because I want to see the womanly and domestic side of things weigh more and count for more in all public concerns.[30]

Yet even egalitarian Mrs Fawcett believed that women were superior to men. Women, she said, had a high standard of virtue; fewer women than men were tried for serious crimes, for example, so women voters would raise the tone of public life.[31]

A simple but overwhelming perception of injustice provided a powerful stimulus for outrage. It was insufferable that women's property was not legally their own. In a society for which property had become the principal mechanism for marking out an individual's protected space in the world, the fact that women were not allowed to own their own property was regarded as a kind of state-sponsored daylight robbery. The brilliant thinker Mrs Harriet Grote was tall and robust and towered over her husband, who resembled a Dresden china figurine and to whom she had a habit of referring as 'the Historian'. She explained why she had become a suffragist. 'When I discovered that the purse in my pocket and the watch at my side were not my own but the Historian's, I felt it was time women should have the power to amend these preposterous laws.'[32]

At the same time there were many suffragists who believed that the vote would elevate women from lives of frivolity and excess which they were forced to lead because they had no role in society. Millicent's cousin Rhoda Garrett, for example, said that having a share in government would stir female responsibility and 'awaken from their lethargy those women who are now leading selfish – wickedly selfish – lives of indolence and gaiety'.[33] Mrs Bodichon agreed that the vote would transform such attitudes. At present, she observed, middle-class women occupied themselves with little beyond their families. They didn't think about the ill-treatment in workhouse infirmaries or inadequate workhouse schools; if the roads were in bad condition or the drains neglected, it didn't occur to them to put it right as they assumed that it was men's business. 'The mere fact of being called upon to enforce an opinion by a vote would have an immediate effect in awakening a healthy sense of responsibility.'[34]

The belief that the standard of public life would be raised by giving women the vote was endemic within the suffrage movement. If women were leading selfish and irresponsible lives now, it was because they had been deprived of any alternative. But what was pent up as a result was a host of virtues far superior to the characteristics of men. Giving women the vote would diffuse the virtues of the home into the wider world.

To Josephine Butler, the home was 'the nursery of all virtue, the fountain-head of all true affection and the main source of the strength of our nation'. Ingeniously, she managed to argue both that women should be liberated from the domestic sphere and that they always embodied the virtues of the home. Marriage was not the only salvation for women, she believed. And yet she claimed that 'home *is* the sphere of women', who instinctively created a home around themselves. Because they called up domestic influences wherever they were, home influence and character might be diffused among the masses if women did public work.[35] A double standard – or, at the very least, having her cake and eating it.

The outcome of such public work by women would be to replace their meddling, Lady Bountiful approach to the poor by a large infusion of home elements into workhouses, hospitals, schools, orphanages and prisons through the 'setting free of feminine powers and influence from the constraint of bad education and narrow aims and listless homes where they are at present too often a superfluity'.[36]

For Frances Power Cobbe, women needed the vote in order to combat male brutality towards their wives. She observed:

When we women of the upper ranks – constitutionally qualified by the possession of property (and, I may be permitted to add, naturally qualified by education and intelligence at least up to the level of the 'illiterate' order of voters) to exercise through the suffrage that pressure on parliament – are refused that privilege, and told year after year by smiling senators that we have no need whatever for it, that we form no 'class' and that we may absolutely and always rely on men to prove the deepest and tenderest concern for everything which concerns the welfare of women, shall we not point to these long neglected wrongs of our trampled sisters, and denounce that boast of the equal concern of men for women as – a falsehood? Were women to obtain the franchise tomorrow, it is normally certain that a Bill for the protection of wives would pass through the legislature before a session was over.[37]

It was true, she acknowledged, that the average Englishman meant well towards women and would make no small sacrifice for them. It was true that there were as many noble-hearted champions of women in and out of Parliament as wife-beating ruffians in the slums of Liverpool and London. But men simply didn't deliver justice. Nor would they until a stage further had been reached: the condemnation of male sexual licence and the adoption of chaste behaviour. 'Profoundly satisfied am I of this, that the cause of the emancipation of women is identical with that of the purification of society,' she wrote.[38] Women needed to enter the public sphere in order to sanitise the moral sewer. Sexual continence by men would only be delivered through votes for women.

Women's emancipation was therefore a project to elevate men and humanity as a whole. Women were presented as a brake on men's rash or corrupt behaviour. An anonymous author wrote in the *Westminster Review* in 1874:

> The same woman who will cheerfully destroy her own health in nursing one she loves, who will uncomplainingly share with him his involuntary poverty, or even deserved disgrace, would on the other hand discourage him with all her powers of persuasion from risking his worldly fortune or bringing on himself the world's reproach, at some call of conscience with which she has not been taught to sympathise. Again, a husband should blush before his wife for a mean public action, a vote given through self-interest or class interest, or faction, as he would for cheating his neighbour, for official falsification as he would for perjury in a court of justice, for conniving at the bribery of an elector as he would for receiving stolen goods, for taking an unfair advantage in trade as he would for picking a pocket. But we hear nothing of other desirableness of feminine influence in such matters as these.

If such feminine qualities could be applied to the wider world, the author went on, 'This change alone would in time revolutionise the whole race and man himself would grow to a greatness he denies himself whilst he ignorantly insists on stunting woman.' The emancipation of woman would be 'the beginning of a new world-era, a new revelation, a new religion to man'.[39]

This emphasis on women's superior virtues was of course the mirror image of the separate sphere of philosophy that was being invoked to prevent women from entering the public realm. Opponents of women's suffrage insisted that women should keep out of public life because they had different attributes from men. The feminists used exactly the same evidence about feminine qualities in support of precisely the opposite point of view. Julia Wedgwood wrote in 1869: 'Of course, if women are either exactly like men, or simply men minus something or other, they could add no light to that already possessed by a male constituency, but I know of no-one who seriously believes either of these things . . . The strongest opponents and the warmest advocates of women's rights would probably agree that women are distinguished from men by the predominance of that faculty which is, on the intellectual side, insight, and on the moral, sympathy; judgement or justice, according to our point of view, being the analogous faculty in the case of men.' Large and increasing areas of public life were concerned with women's issues. 'To care for the sick and poor, and to teach children, are accepted as the special duties of women when we count by units.' So women's voices needed to be heard in the debates over education or pauperism.[40]

Even while they were extolling women's virtues as guardians of the domestic sphere, however, these feminists were railing against the earth-bound nature of their dominion. Josephine Butler wrote that the emphasis on a woman's physical life as the link in the generation chain was 'common to all savages' and 'belongs properly to ages of barbarism, when the material always took precedence of the spiritual . . . it exists now, as regards women, only among the coarse and carnal-minded of both sexes . . .' It was moral nature, religious sentiment and a woman's immortal soul which were vital to both sexes. And yet at the same time the home was 'woman's proper kingdom; that all that pertains to its order, comfort and grace falls under her natural charge, and can by no means be transferred to a man; that a woman's life without such a domestic side must always be looked on as incomplete, or at best exceptional: all this is very true'. Domesticity, however, was not enough for 'habits of reason, the habits of mental order, the chastened and refined love of beauty, above all, that dignified kind of loving care which is never intrusive, never fussy, but yet ever present, calm, bright and sweet . . .' To be truly the Angel in the House, woman had to be lifted above it.[41]

Indeed, Mrs Butler even attacked marriage, which she said had been degraded by the dependency of women upon men that the institution entailed:

> What dignity can there be in the attitude of women in general, and towards men in particular, when marriage is held (and often necessarily so, being the sole means of maintenance) to be the one end of a woman's life, when it is degraded to the level of a woman's profession, when those who are soliciting a place in this profession resemble those flaccid Brazilian creepers which cannot exist without support, and which sprawl out their limp tendrils in every direction to find something – no matter what – to hang upon; when the insipidity or the material necessities of so many women's lives make them ready to accept almost any man who may offer himself? . . . I cannot believe that it is every woman's duty to marry, in this age of the world. There is abundance of work to be done which needs men and women detached from marriage ties; our unmarried women will be the greatest blessing to the community when they cease to be soured by disappointment or driven by destitution to despair . . .[42]

Independence was now the goal for some women. Maria Grey and Emily Shirreff wrote that while wives renounced their independence and had to comply with their husbands, single women retained their independence and their friends. 'Perhaps in time even mothers might be found wise enough to prefer their daughters remaining cheerful amiable old maids to becoming miserable wives,' they suggested. Women were being forced to marry for a meal ticket rather than for love. 'This error of our social system forces women too often to consider marriage not as a question of happiness but of subsistence and it would be little flattering to the vanity of men, who are apt enough to think women cannot live without them, to know how many a one has shrunk with repugnance from the ties her poverty compels her to form, and represses her warmest feelings to enable her to bear the trials of a condition she would not have entered into had she not been free.'[43]

According to Josephine Butler, women were being left stranded by the profound changes in the world of work and the loss of equilibrium in society. More women, she said, had to support themselves. The census taken in 1866 had showed that in England alone there were three and a half million women working for their subsistence, of whom two and a half million were unmarried. This did not reveal, however, how many were working for starvation wages or in prostitution: 'forced downwards to the paths of hell by the pressure from above'. The public had constantly to be reminded that: 'there is no analogy whatever among men, however miserable certain classes of men may be, to the wholesale destruction which goes on from year to year among women . . .'[44]

The vote was the pathway out of all such miseries as it would bring to an end the slavery and serfdom of half the human race. Moreover, feminists believed they were not making a new claim but were rather fighting for the restoration of civic rights they had enjoyed in earlier times. In an erudite paper on the subject Mrs Harriet McIlquham argued that the principle of no taxation without representation dated from the earliest times. Women had been burgesses in ancient boroughs, and the female burgesses of Tamworth were recorded in the Domesday Book. It was the seventeenth-century Lord Chief Justice Sir Edward Coke who had denied women the right to the parliamentary franchise. Women had done better in local franchises; until 1835 they had voted freely in municipal elections. But the 1835 Municipal Corporations Act passed by the Whig government under Lord Melbourne was framed on the 1832 Reform Act and used 'male persons' to disenfranchise women from municipal elections for the next thirty-four years until the word 'male' was removed before the word 'person' in municipal election law with no dissent whatever.[45]

Nevertheless, only unmarried women could vote in municipal elections. The Married Women's Property Act 1870 raised hopes that some married women would qualify as municipal voters. But in a case in January 1872 the courts decided that even though married women might be householders and ratepayers, they could not vote for town councillors because a married woman was not a person in the eyes of the law. The judiciary, said Mrs McIlquham, was simply ignorant of past precedent and practice. When Lady Sandhurst, who, along with Miss Cobden, was elected as a county councillor, asked the Court of Appeal to be allowed to sit, the Master of the Rolls said: 'I take it that, by neither the common law nor the constitution of this country from the beginning of the common law until now, can a woman be entitled to exercise any public function.' Yet women at that time, said the author, were acting as overseers, waywardens, churchwardens, Poor Law guardians and members of school boards – and Queen. Even more illogically, although married women could sit and vote as members of school boards and boards of guardians, their votes for members of these boards as well as for town and county councillors were frequently rejected on the grounds that they were married.[46] Such were the contradictions of an age which simply couldn't reconcile the growing participation by women in the public sphere with its attitudes towards marriage, home and family.

Indeed, marriage was an issue on which the suffragists themselves all but came to blows. For they too could not agree on whether married women should have the same rights as unmarried. Some thought they should not; some thought they should and the movement should fight for them to have such rights; some thought they should but that it was tactically unwise to antagonise the public still further over such a sensitive issue. For marriage was the great dividing line between the two spheres of home and work, public and private.

The issue was coverture, the doctrine that deprived married women of a separate legal identity from their husbands. Since property ownership was required for the right to vote, some feminists – particularly the radicals from Manchester, Richard Pankhurst, Elizabeth Wolstenholme Elmy and Jacob Bright – wanted coverture abolished and married women enfranchised. In London, however, the more conservatively minded women, including Emily Davies, Frances Power Cobbe and Mrs Fawcett, disagreed.

Mrs Fawcett wanted to enfranchise only single women and widows bearing the burden of citizenship as ratepayers and taxpayers. Her reasoning marked her out not only as an upholder of the separate spheres demarcation but even more remarkably as a supporter of the traditional role of the husband as head of the household and in command of his wife:

> If we have household suffrage, let the head of the house vote, whether that head be a man or a woman. The enfranchisement of wives is an altogether different question . . . If they were enfranchised, the effect, in ninety-nine cases out of a hundred, would be to give two votes to the husband. Wives are bound by law to obey their husbands. No other class in the community is in this position, and it seems inexpedient to allow political independence (which would only be nominal) to precede actual independence . . . We do not want women to be bad imitations of men; we neither deny nor minimise the differences between men and women. The claim of women to representation depends to a large extent on those differences. Women bring something to the service of the state different from that which can be brought by men.[47]

Since the Manchester suffragists were urging, on the contrary, that married women be included, a compromise had to be reached. Jacob Bright, who had become the movement's parliamentary leader after John Stuart Mill was defeated in the 1868 general election, put forward in 1870 the first women's suffrage bill, which proposed that women be given the vote on the same terms as men. Since only men owned property and the vote depended on a property qualification, this effectively excluded married women. But as it did not explicitly exclude them, it left open the possibility that they might be included if the property qualification was later removed.[48]

This thinnest of paper coverings had been pasted over such a deep crack, and it duly split open. After the Bright bill was defeated, Lydia Becker handed it to a new champion, the Conservative MP Mr Forsyth, adding a clause which specifically excluded married women. When he presented this bill in 1874, there was uproar. 'I am aghast at the new Women's Suffrage Bill,' wrote a correspondent to the *Women's Suffrage Journal*.

I have not the least objection to married women being without exception and even permanently *incidentally* shut out ... but it is another matter to ask parliament distinctly to enact that married women shall by the fact of their marriage be a disqualified class ... What we were asking would be the suffrage for *femmes soles* and might seem to cast a slur on wives. The [former] answer to them, namely, that there was no slur cast by the accidental want of qualification that came from laws as to the tenure of property – the necessity that the husband rather than the wife should be the householder – and so forth, was generally a sufficient answer whether to friend or foe ... This change will do little to conciliate our opponents, and will plainly alienate many of our working friends.[49]

But marriage was only one of a number of issues which were repeatedly to split the suffrage movement. It was permanently riven by factions, infighting and stormy exits. An early fissure developed in 1871 over the relationship between the suffrage organisation and the campaign to repeal the Contagious Diseases Acts. Josephine Butler's great crusade was causing apoplexy around the country, as people found the spectacle of women taking up such a subject in public shocking and outrageous. One scandalised MP fulminated: 'The agitation was a disgrace to the country, as it flooded gentlemen's breakfast tables with abominable literature, not addressed to themselves only but also to their wives and daughters.'[50] The more the Butler crusade was heard of, the more bitter opposition to the suffrage became.[51]

Most of the active workers in the suffrage movement were also prominent in the Butler campaign. This was hardly surprising, since the issue of the sexual double standard and the perceived ill-treatment of vulnerable women by a hostile or indifferent male legislature was a key driver behind the women's crusade. However, although some suffragists thought that the Butler crusade was essential to the emancipation of women, others believed it had the potential to destroy the suffrage cause. This was also not surprising. The extreme indelicacy of the subject matter, and the fact that it was being broached by the guardians of the shrine of modesty, was likely to cause such outrage and revulsion that the wider issue of women's reform would be seriously threatened. It is hard to exaggerate the potential affront to the general sense of propriety caused by women who were daring to move from the domestic to the public sphere. Women who managed to gain acceptance in public life as doctors, nurses, academics, social scientists or factory inspectors often did so only by cloaking themselves in exaggerated modesty, propriety and acceptable femininity and by specialising in corners of professions deemed suitable for women.[52] Women could only penetrate the public sphere if they reassured a deeply nervous and insecure populace that the female values which were universally considered to be an antidote to barbarism would not be sacrificed as a result.

Even though she personally strongly supported the Butler crusade, Mrs Fawcett took this cautious view and so did her London committee. However, when some seventeen prominent suffragists joined the executive of Mrs Butler's Ladies' National Association, the London suffrage society split apart from the national society and didn't reunite until 1877.

Mrs Fawcett was indeed highly conservative in attitude. Not for her the association between suffragism and emancipated sexual behaviour. It was she who told Elizabeth Wolstenholme that to be pregnant and unmarried disqualified her from being secretary to the committee on married women's property. She opposed state regulation of prostitution because it endorsed the sexual double standard, but she refused to support the Butler campaign publicly in order not to make more enemies for suffragism. Her own self-control and her conformity on family matters and appearance went far to defuse public hostility to the suffrage cause. Gladstone's private secretary wrote in 1882: 'She is a very nice, attractive, ladylike little person, and bears no trace of the "strong-minded female" about her.' On the other hand, Gladstone proved an immovable obstacle in the path of the female suffrage, and her 'don't frighten the horses' tactics did not impress everyone. 'Fawcett is all brains but utterly without *heart*, and that is why she has been 50 years getting the vote,' wrote one exasperated militant in 1909.[53]

However, Mrs Fawcett's attempt to hold the line for a conservative, step-by-step approach was already palpably slipping. In the late 1870s a scandal broke whose echoes were to resurface within two decades in the militant suffragette movement. Annie Besant, a professed atheist and republican who was estranged from her husband, was put on trial with the freethinker Charles Bradlaugh for obscene libel after they published *The Fruits of Philosophy*, a book by an American physician, Dr Charles Knowlton, which advocated the use of contraception by married couples.

In 1866 Charles Bradlaugh, a man with a magnetic personality who was anti-Queen and anti-God, had launched the National Secular Society. In 1874 he captivated the brilliant and beautiful Mrs Annie Besant. Annie's personality lent itself to passionate and unbalanced extremism. She said of herself that when young she was deeply religious and 'of the stuff from which fanatics are made . . .' Religion became for her 'too meagre, too commonplace, too little exacting, too bound up with earthly interests, too calculating in its accommodations to social conventionalities'.[54] Born Annie Wood in 1847, as a child she was mystical and imaginative, with a facility for seeing visions and dreaming dreams. In 1867 she married Frank Besant with no more idea of the marriage relation, she said, than a child of four. She didn't love him and they were ill matched from the outset. Her privations, the near death of her small daughter Mabel from whooping cough and the suffering of her beloved mother, who was defrauded by a lawyer, provoked a sense of outraged justice which led her to atheism. In 1873 her husband ordered her to take communion; she refused. He gave her an ultimatum: conformity or exclusion from the home. She chose the latter, taking her little daughter with her but leaving her son behind, and met Charles Bradlaugh.[55]

In 1877 they reissued Knowlton's birth-control pamphlet, which had been published on and off since 1833 after the original publisher, Charles Watts, pleaded guilty to selling obscene literature. The book was the first widely circulated advertisement of birth control in England. In June that year, Bradlaugh and Besant were put on trial. They were fined £200 and Bradlaugh was sentenced to six months in prison. In an address to the court which lasted for two days, Annie Besant covered the right of free speech, overcrowding, incest, infant mortality and infanticide in the slums. The charge against them was dismissed on appeal with huge attendant publicity. But Annie lost her daughter. Frank Besant used his wife's notoriety to remove Mabel from her custody on the grounds that her irreligion had undermined the proper attributes of motherhood. After the case, she remarked: 'It's a pity there isn't any God; it would do one so much good to hate Him.'[56]

The National Secular Society itself was shaken and split by the trial. Within three years, sales of the Knowlton book were getting on for a staggering 200,000 copies. Besant eventually published her own book, *The Law of Population*, and her backing for birth control revived the moribund Malthusian League (motto: Prudence after Marriage), of which she became one of fourteen vice-presidents, despite the fact that Malthus had specifically opposed birth control as a means of keeping the population down.

Her use of the criminal justice system as a theatre for sensational political propaganda was to be closely emulated by a feminist ideologue who was not yet born – Christabel Pankhurst. In 1874 Mrs Besant argued in a brilliant and prophetic pamphlet, *The Political Status of Women*, that women were being forced into extremism to obtain the vote:

> Do men think of what they are doing when they taunt the present agitators with the indifference shown by women? They are, in effect, telling us that if we are in earnest we must *force* the matter on their attention; we must agitate till every home in England rings with the subject, till mass meetings in every town compel them to hear us, till every woman has our arguments at her finger's end. You are nerving us

to a struggle which will be fiercer than you dream, forcing us into an agitation which will convulse the state. You have as yet the frivolous, the childish, the thoughtless on your side; but the cream of woman-hood is against you. We will educate women to reason and to think, and then the mass will only want a leader.[57]

She also conjured up a nirvana where elevated moral behaviour would cascade down the generations to usher in spiritual and sexual perfection. There was a danger, she acknowledged, that well-educated women would turn away from marriage. But if only the female élite were to mate with men who did not expect them to be only concerned with children and domesticity, there would be a nobler idea of marriage, with men growing more tender and pure and women more strong, brave and free, 'till at last the race shall develop into a strength and beauty at present yet unimag-ined, and men and women shall walk this fair earth hand in hand, diverse, yet truly one-set each to each – "As perfect music unto noble words"'.[58]

In Christabel Pankhurst's own speeches and writings, almost every point Annie Besant made in her pamphlet was in due course to appear once again.[59] But first a more decorous attempt was made to secure votes for women.

In 1870 Lydia Becker and Jessie Boucherett started the *Women's Suffrage Journal*. Meetings and petitions multiplied, and from 1871 sys-tematic speaking tours were organised. Women such as Caroline Ashworth Briggs, Rhoda and Agnes Garrett, Helen Blackburn and Helen Taylor, Isabella Todd, Arabella Shore, Jessie Craigen and Millicent Fawcett became semi-professional itinerant lecturers, campaigning for the suffrage around the country.[60] Women speakers were still a rarity, and people came just to see the spectacle of a woman on a political platform.

From the start of the fight for the vote, however, a political paradox was apparent. In 1870 Dr Richard Pankhurst drafted the Women's Disabilities Removal Bill, which began nearly half a century of parliamentary struggle. Later that year Jacob Bright presented to Parliament the bill, which said that the words importing the masculine gender on the right to vote should apply to women. The bill was actually passed on second reading

Mary Wollestonecraft

John Stuart Mill

MILL'S LOGIC; OR, FRANCHISE FOR FEMALES.

"PRAY CLEAR THE WAY, THERE, FOR THESE—A—PERSONS."

Punch cartoon, 1867, showing John Stuart Mill advocating votes for women

Harriet Taylor, close friend and later wife of John Stuart Mill

Millicent Fawcett, leader of the constitutional campaign for female suffrage

Henry and Millicent Fawcett

Elizabeth Blackwell, the first woman to qualify as a doctor

Emily Davies, campaigner for women's
higher education and founder of
Girton College, Cambridge

Josephine Butler, leader of the campaign
against the sexual double standard
in prostitution

Josephine Butler

Elizabeth Garrett Anderson,
pioneering woman doctor

Frances Power Cobbe, suffragist
and indefatigable campaigner
for moral causes

Teresa Billington-Greig, Woman's Social and Political Union organiser
and founder of the Women's Freedom League

Lady Constance Lytton

Annie Kenney

Emmeline Pankhurst

Sylvia, Adela and Christabel Pankhurst

Christabel Pankhurst

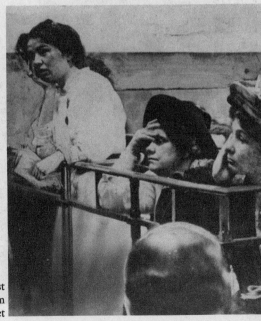

Christabel Pankhurst
addressing the court from
the dock at Bow Street

Sylvia Pankhurst

Adela Pankhurst

Sylvia Pankhurst addressing a meeting

Millicent Fawcett, President of the
National Union of Women's
Suffrage Societies

Emmeline and Frederick Pethick-Lawrence,
architects of the WSPU fighting machine

Dr Elizabeth Garrett Anderson and Emmeline Pankhurst outside
the Houses of Parliament, 1903

by a comfortable majority, 124 to 91. Liberal MPs were sympathetic to women's suffrage – but their leadership was not. Gladstone was implacably opposed, saying – when the bill was reintroduced the following year – that the intervention of women in parliamentary election proceedings would be 'a practical evil of an intolerable character'. Once Gladstone announced his opposition, his backbenchers swiftly changed sides and the Bright bill was defeated in committee.

Mrs Fawcett thought that Gladstone was 'all over the place' on women's suffrage. In 1871 he said, in a debate on divorce law in the House of Commons: 'our law in the matters where the peculiar relations of men and women are concerned . . . does less than justice to women, and great mischief, misery and scandal result from that state of things . . . and if it should be found possible to arrange a safe and well-adjusted alteration of the law as to political power, the man who shall attain that object and shall see his purpose carried forward to its consequences in a more full arrangement of the provisions of other laws bearing upon the condition and welfare of women will, in my opinion, be a real benefactor of his country'.[61]

Yet although Gladstone supported justice for women, his governing fear was that women's distinctive characteristics and their role as guardians of the sacred hearth would be imperilled if they developed a political role. His reasoning was spelled out in a letter to the anti-suffragist MP Samuel Smith, in which he described women's suffrage as a novel measure which would disadvantage married women and other women hostile to it. Gladstone wrote:

I think it impossible to deny that there have been and are women individually fit for any public office however masculine its character; just as there are persons under the age of twenty-one better fitted than many of those beyond it for the discharge of the duties of full citizenship. In neither case does the argument derived from exceptional instances seem to justify the abolition of the general rule . . . A permanent and vast difference of type has been impressed upon women and men respectively by the Maker of both . . . I am not without the fear lest beginning with the State we should eventually be found to have intruded into what is yet more fundamental and more sacred, the precinct of the family, and should dislocate, or injuriously modify, the relations of domestic life ... I have no fear lest the woman should encroach upon the power of the man. The fear I have is, lest we should invite her unwittingly to trespass upon the delicacy, the purity, the refinement, the elevation of her own nature, which are the present sources of its power.

He had no problem with women being admitted to higher education or the professions, but it appeared that it was the specific characteristics of political life which he feared would erode the special role women played in the human story.[62]

Throughout the 1870s a women's suffrage bill was introduced every year except 1875.[63] Every time it failed. Although the majority of Liberal MPs supported it, the leadership was opposed. In 1874 the Conservatives took power under Disraeli; but in a neat mirror image of the Liberals, while Disraeli supported women's suffrage most Tory MPs were hostile. Liberal leaders opposed the suffrage in part at least because they feared that most women would vote Tory.[64] The Tory leadership, which was sympathetic, never took it seriously enough to face down their own hostile backbenchers. So the stage was set for years of stalemate.

As women's suffrage bills were introduced to Parliament and lost with monotonous regularity, reaction ranged from indifference through mockery to outright hostility. As ever, the most visceral opposition was couched in the ambiguous terms of damning women with chivalric praise. The Tory MP Beresford Hope said in the debate on the Women's Disabilities Bill 1871 that he wanted to protect women 'from being forced toward the hurly-burly of party politics' since 'the very nature of women called for sympathy and protection, and for the highest and most chivalrous treatment on the part of the men . . .' Men and women, he said, were different. 'Reason predominated in the man, emotion and sympathy in the woman . . .' A woman-dominated parliament would emphasise social or philanthropic issues at the expense of 'the great constitutional and international issues which the legislature was empanelled to try'. He warned: 'We should have more wars for an idea, or hasty alliances with scheming neighbours, more class cries, permissive legislation, domestic perplexities and sentimental grievances. Our legislation would develop hysterical and spasmodic features, partaking more of the French and American system than reproducing the interest of the English parliament.'[65]

Many Liberal backbenchers supported the suffragists, but some took the same line as their leader, Gladstone. The Liberal MP Captain Maxse, for example, said that the women's vote would be injurious to society. Women were weak and dependent on men; this was a natural law and justified their government by men. Women who demanded the suffrage were exceptional and unrepresentative. Mental strength in women, he declared, was rare. 'The tendency of most women is favourable to arbitrary government and clerical supremacy. They seem to be incapable of sympathising with great causes – they have a strong predilection for personal institutions. As a rule, they are completely without interest in great national questions. Theirs is essentially the private life point of view . . .' And he articulated the real nightmare for the Liberals, that female suffrage would usher in a long period of uninterrupted Tory rule. 'Propertied widows and spinsters will possess the suffrage not on account of their sex but on account of their property, while marriage will stand out as a political disqualification . . . Under a delusive plea, it represents a class measure, for the propertied single woman exists mostly in the upper and middle classes; it will therefore operate unfairly towards the working class and afford additional means of class oppression.'[66]

The deeper objection, as ever, was the belief that women's proper sphere was the home, and that women who challenged that role were some kind of monstrous sexual hybrid. In the *Quarterly Review* in 1869, Mr M. Burrows wrote that men didn't like the 'man-woman'. Women's 'sprightly intuition' was worth far more than the reasoning faculty developed in man. 'But whatever Mr John Stuart Mill may think,' he expostulated,

England is not prepared for either female suffrage or a female parliament, for women as Poor Law guardians, attendants at vestries, public lecturers, public speakers, doctors, lawyers, clergy or even, to any greater extent than at present, as authors. The attempts of Miss Becker and her friends to prepare the country for this change simply defeat their own object. They are perceived with unmitigated disgust by all but an isolated few. The sphere of women is home. Such a cultivation as will make a really good wife, sister or daughter, to educated men, is the thing to be aimed at, and this must be something which recognises woman not as a 'fair defect of nature', something which may be brought up to the same point as men by education, and taught to be his rival; but rather as the complement of man, perfect in herself, and intended to hold an entirely different place in the world . . . We want to entice our 'golden youth' into matrimony, not by wiles and plots and match-making warfare but by the exhibition of a true, modest, retiring, useful, womanly character.[67]

At the same time, the suffragists were taunted with the fact that they would exclude married women from the vote. Conservative suffragists based their demand on the fact that limiting the vote to unmarried women who met the property qualification would reinforce a property-based electorate. This supported the prevailing concept that voters should be financially independent and that political institutions should be accountable to heads of household. However, this limitation exposed the suffragists to the (justified) accusation that they were not really interested in women's rights so much as the rights of the female members of a particular class. In 1879 Sir Henry James asked whether they really wanted a reform which would 'give power to a class who are influenced by clergymen, by friends, by husbands, by anyone whose will is stronger than their own. I cannot believe that that will be your deliberate policy.'[68]

As the campaign wore on, opposition to female suffrage grew more vocal and organised. Opponents believed that women had a different sphere of influence from men and should stay within it. Many wanted more freedom for women within the family; Mrs Eliza Lynn Linton, for example, who opposed the 'shrieking sisterhood', wanted to extend women's rights in divorce and guardianship. But all believed that separate spheres for the sexes had been ordained by God or nature. They were appalled at the way suffragists tried to blur the distinctions between the sexes, and roused themselves to fury at the thought that a man might return from work to find his wife at a political meeting and the children neglected. Earl Percy said in a 1873 debate: 'The real fact is that man in the beginning was ordained to rule over the woman and this is an Eternal decree which we have no right and no power to alter.'[69] Women had a principal duty to look after home, husband and children. Thomas Carlyle wrote in 1871: 'The true destiny of a woman . . . is to wed a man she can love and esteem and to lead noiselessly, under his protection, with all the wisdom, grace and heroism that is in her, the life presented in consequence.'[70]

They believed that women not only had a duty to stay at home, but would be intrinsically ill-fitted to the public sphere. The anti-suffragists maintained that votes counted only because they were backed by the capacity for force. So women might demand some cause unpopular with men and be unable to get it. They also feared that women would be too pacific and refuse to go to war because they were governed by their feelings. Lord Cromer thought that women's sympathy and emotion might lead from philanthropy into sentimental socialism.[71] The Empire itself might become endangered.

Biology was woman's destiny; the new science said so. Darwinian thinking held that sexual differentiation was a hallmark of advanced societies. Henry Maudsley wrote that it was fruitless to try to assimilate the female to the male mind; women would be exhausted by mental exertion and the race would be harmed:

In the first place, a proper regard to the physical nature of women means attention given, in their training, to their peculiar functions and to their fore-ordained work as mothers and nurses of children. Whatever aspirations of an intellectual kind they may have, they cannot be relieved from the performance of those offices as long as it is thought necessary that mankind should continue on earth. For it would be an ill thing, if it should so happen, that we got the advantages of a quantity of female intellectual work at the price of a puny, enfeebled and sickly race. In this relation, it must be allowed that women do not and cannot stand on the same level as men.[72]

Behind such opinions lay terror: terror of the disappearance of the remaining certainties of life, terror of the threat to male virility, terror of a loss of control. There were warnings against the 'monstrous army' and 'whirlwinds in petticoats'. *Punch* magazine campaigned against 'bloomerism' and 'strong-minded women'. Yet such opposition was not confined to men. Some educated and outspoken women signed petitions against women's suffrage, denounced the assault upon the universities and the professions and lampooned the bluestockings. Mrs Lynn Linton, for example, attacked the advanced girl who had given up the ideals of womanly womanhood: the flirtatious, shallow, vain girl, a slave to fashion, addicted to bold talk and fastness, disdainful of parents or traditional morality, and who married for money and title. 'Men are afraid of her; and with reason,' she wrote.[73]

Queen Victoria spoke of the 'mad, wicked folly of women's rights'. Some women who had championed higher education for women disowned the early suffragettes. One, the bluestocking Harriet Martineau, said that too many advocates of the women's cause spoke from personal unhappiness. Mary Wollstonecraft, said Miss Martineau, had been 'a poor victim of passion' with 'no control over her own peace, and no calmness or content except when the needs of her individual nature were satisfied'. She herself regarded her inability to vote as an absurdity; but women had to be rational and dispassionate to improve the condition of their sex:

When I see an eloquent writer insinuating to everybody who comes across her that she is the victim of her husband's carelessness and cruelty, while he never spoke in his own defence: when I see her violating all good taste by her obtrusiveness in society, and oppressing everybody about her by her epicurean selfishness every day, while raising in print an eloquent cry on behalf of the oppressed; I feel, to the bottom of my heart, that she is the worst enemy of the cause she professes to plead . . . The best friends of the cause are the happy wives and the busy, cheerful, satisfied single women who have no injuries of their own to avenge, and no painful vacuity or mortification to relieve. The best advocates are yet to come – in the persons of women who are obtaining access to real social business – the female physicians and other professors in America, the women of business and the female artists of France; and the hospital administrators, the nurses, the educators and substantially successful authors of our own country . . . whatever a woman proves herself able to do, society will be thankful to see her do – just as if she were a man.[74]

Nevertheless, in the teeth of such opposition the suffragists pressed on. A promising opportunity presented itself with the Liberal government's 1884 Reform Bill. To make female suffrage acceptable to as many MPs as possible, an amendment was narrowly drawn to enfranchise only about 100,000 wealthy property-owning women. Tories were more inclined to support it, because these women would have been Tory voters. But when Gladstone announced his opposition, 104 Liberal MPs who had declared themselves in favour promptly voted against it, causing it to be rejected by 271 votes to 135.[75]

This was an epochal event. As Mrs Fawcett later observed: 'That division probably sowed the seed of the militant movement.' It also sowed the seeds of discord between Gladstone and the Fawcett household. In that crucial vote Henry Fawcett, who was Postmaster-General, abstained. Gladstone wrote to him angrily to say that such an abstention in a critical division amounted to resignation of his office – although with a foreign crisis approaching, he was requesting him and others not to resign. It was a symptom of a prime minister losing his grip. When Henry Fawcett died later that year, Millicent received hundreds of letters of condolence but not one word from Gladstone.[76]

10

SLOUCHING TOWARDS MILITANCY

The failure to tack votes for women on to the 1884 Reform Act was a serious blow to the cause. Now, even agricultural labourers had the vote while women did not. The movement lost heart. Even though some forty per cent of men were still disenfranchised, the suffragists assumed that this was as far as democratic reform would go. Household suffrage for men had lanced the boil of the franchise agitation. Men had got what they wanted; women were now fighting alone for sex equality.

The women's suffrage societies went into eclipse. They polarised increasingly along party lines, and radicals were incensed by Lydia Becker's insistence on excluding married women from the vote and on making a tactical alliance with the Conservatives.[1] Women were actually becoming increasingly involved in politics, but as party workers. As a result of the 1883 Corrupt Practices Act, which made it illegal to employ paid agents to do canvassing and other party work, women became much in demand as volunteers. The parties formed women's auxiliary organisations: the Conservatives' Primrose League in 1883 and the Women's Liberal Federation in 1887.[2]

In 1897 Mrs Fawcett became leader of the National Union of Women's Suffrage Societies. But the NUWSS had run out of ideas. Well-bred, intellectual and civilised, it limited its attention to the vote, ignoring other avenues for reform. Its tactics were sedate; it didn't intervene at by-elections or hold outdoor meetings or appeal to the masses. Many concessions had already been made. Married women had gained their right to their earnings and now property in the Married Women's Property Act 1882.

Women came forward in increasing numbers for public positions. In 1888 Lady Sandhurst and Miss Cobden were elected to the London County Council by heavy majorities, although they were not allowed to take their seats; not until 1907 were women allowed on to county councils. In 1875 the formation of the Salvation Army was a significant influence on women's public role. Its leaders were Catherine and William Bramwell Booth, who married in 1855 and had eight children. They insisted on absolute sex equality within the organisation, which caused a storm of opposition from male officers who resented being placed under the orders of a woman. But the Booths held firm, and by liberating female energies in this way, the Salvation Army more than doubled in strength. In 1886 the Guardianship of Infants' Act gave mothers the right to become at least joint guardians of their children after a father's death. And in 1891 women's personal freedom was safeguarded by law after a notorious case in which a husband imprisoned his wife who refused to obey his order to restore conjugal rights after she had left him.[3]

As women's participation grew, the discrepancy over the vote became ever more glaring. The Boer War in 1899 would eclipse the cause. In a pamphlet of that year Dora Montefiore wrote in frustration, with reference to the question of equal rights in the Transvaal: 'If nothing but war will meet the situation, then war must be declared by women at all parliamentary elections, by making woman suffrage a test question.'[4]

Throughout the 1880s frustration provoked militant noises. Mrs Wolstenholme Elmy wrote that if Liberal leaders continued to nullify the wishes of Liberal MPs, this would lead to an agitation 'stronger even than that which forced the repeal of the CD Acts'. She protested: 'The Representation of the People Act (1884) implicitly placed the lowest male felon, by virtue of his sex privilege, above the noblest women in the land, an insult of the deepest and most cowardly kind.' In *Woman and Labour* Olive Schreiner issued her own call to arms: 'From the judge's seat to the legislator's chair; from the statesman's closet to the merchant's office; from the chemist's laboratory to the astronomer's tower . . . there is no closed door which we do not intend to force open, no fruit of the garden of knowledge which it is not our determination to eat.'[5]

Nevertheless, the movement's tactics remained unchanged for twenty years after the 1884 defeat. Mrs Fawcett and others continued to try to build support among MPs, even though it was clear that the problem lay with the government rather than with the backbenchers, many of whom were converts to the cause.

Politicians, however, were preoccupied with other matters. The 1880s was a turbulent decade. Anarchy seemed an imminent threat. There were acts of violence by anarchists and Irish terrorists. In July 1884 a crowd of five thousand were incited to riot in Hyde Park by the Social Democratic Federation firebrand John Burns. In 1886 the unemployed rioted in Pall Mall. There were fears of a socialist uprising as riots continued into 1887.[6] There was also a persistent dread of racial decline and collapse. After General Gordon's defeat at Khartoum in 1885, many thought the Empire was being undermined by racial degeneration and the rebellion of the lower races.[7]

At the same time there were desperate attempts at optimism on both left and right. In 1882 a group of freethinkers founded the Fellowship of the New Life in Chelsea, which was later to mutate into the Fabian Society. Supporters believed in communistic living to cultivate a perfect character by subordinating material to spiritual things. There was a widespread belief that a new and better order lay just round the corner. The only question was how to get there.[8]

On the other side of the political spectrum arose the cult of theosophy, brought to England during the 1880s by Madame Blavatsky, who claimed to have learned it at the knee of teachers in Tibet. Theosophy was a mystical doctrine whose cardinal principles were to echo again and again in the women's suffrage movement as its supporters became more and more extreme. It rested on the eastern belief that the universe was a harmonious whole that moved in cycles, including human reincarnation. The essence was spirituality, with the soul returning to the 'original source' after a brief residence within the body. Evolution applied on a grand scale to the whole of existence, with each person's life evolving through seven stages from the physical to the purely spiritual.

These matters had allegedly been 'dictated' to Mme Blavatsky, who had written them down in two enormous books. Never mind the whispers of 'charlatanry'; virtually all Victorian intellectuals flirted with spiritualism in one way or another. Séances and thought-reading were popular, and several such sessions were preceded by Church of England rituals. Annie Besant, who was convinced of the reality of clairvoyance and thought-reading, became a prominent theosophist. Shaw later wrote in a letter to the magazine *Freethinker*: 'Like all great public speakers she was a born actress. She was successively a Puseyite evangelical, an atheist Bible smasher, a Darwinian secularist, a Fabian socialist, a strike leader, and finally a theosophist, exactly as Mrs Siddons was Lady Macbeth, Lady Randolph, Beatrice, Rosalind, and Volumnia. She "saw herself" as a priestess above all; that was how Theosophy held her to the end.'[9]

Atheists might scoff, but theosophy was tapping into precisely the anxieties and beliefs of virtually the entire intellectual class in late-Victorian England. There was, above all, the desperate desire to believe in something beyond the self, to believe in a capacity for human perfectibility, to believe that mankind was superior to animals. And that superiority could manifest itself only through the exercise of spirituality, that preoccupation which was to unite feminists from Mary Wollstonecraft to Christabel Pankhurst in a distaste for the physical. It was no accident that theosophists believed in celibacy.

The perception that women were identifying themselves with wacky, extreme or militant attitudes fed into a growing resentment and fear of their increasingly visible push into the public sphere. Growing fears about Britain's national defence capability and her status as a world power meshed with anxieties about the changing role of women and the decline in the birth rate.[10] There was also opposition from working men to the entry of women into their preserve. Wherever women tried to improve their position by entering male fields, they merely added to the labour reserve and pulled down male rates. So men fought off the entry of unorganised women into their trades.[11]

In 1885, while the women's suffrage movement unhappily marked time, an event occurred which was a harbinger of the dramatic way in which it was to develop. Dr Richard Pankhurst, the indefatigable man of causes and the drafter of the first women's suffrage bill (presented by Jacob Bright in 1870), stood for Parliament in Rotherhithe in the general election. It was a débâcle. Condemned for his ultra-radical views on religious freedom, church disestablishment and abolition of the House of Lords, he was assaulted by the crowds. But his fate was sealed by Irish politics. Charles Stewart Parnell, the Irish nationalist leader, instructed all Irish electors to vote against the Liberal Party in order to force it to change its policy on Home Rule. The result was the return of the Conservative candidate, Colonel Hamilton.[12]

Parnell's tactics introduced into British electoral politics a new sophistication in strategic single-mindedness, an unerring instinct for manipulative pressure and a brutal adherence to the philosophy that the end justified the means – even if the means involved the defeat of candidates from the party that was most sympathetic to the cause. These tactics made a particularly deep impression on Dr Pankhurst's wife, Emmeline, who wept inconsolably at her husband's defeat.[13] It was Dr Pankhurst who drove home the lesson to be learned from Parnell's tactics, which his wife never forgot. 'With his small party,' she wrote, 'he could not hope to win Home Rule from a hostile majority, but by constant obstruction he could in time wear out the government and force it to surrender. That was a valuable political lesson, one that years later I was destined to put into practice.'[14]

There was an unpleasant aftermath to the campaign. Dr Pankhurst sued Colonel Hamilton for libel after the colonel condemned him as an atheist. The case was thrown out by the judge, himself a failed Tory candidate, who commented that it was understandable if people felt unwilling to vote for someone with Pankhurst's views. Mrs Pankhurst promptly wrote an insulting letter to the judge, which placed her in danger of committing contempt of court. Her reaction was highly prescient. 'Let him send me to prison!' she exclaimed. 'I want to go to prison for contempt of court!'[15] She had instinctively grasped not just the implications of Parnell's tactics, but also the use of martyrdom as a political weapon. These were lessons that were shortly to transform the entire nature and course of women's campaign for the vote.

They were also to propel to the forefront of British politics the extraordinary Pankhurst family, whose own psychodrama was to be played out in the theatre of women's suffrage over the next three decades.

Rebellion was in Emmeline's blood. Her grandfather had narrowly escaped with his life at the 'Peterloo' massacre of franchise demonstrators on St Peter's Fields, Manchester, in 1819; her grandmother had been a member of the Anti-Corn Law League. Her father, Robert Goulden, who managed a cotton printing factory, was an amateur actor and supporter of radical causes: he served on the Manchester committee to welcome Henry Ward Beecher, the apostle of Negro emancipation. Born in 1858, Emmeline was the apple of her father's eye. Intellectually precocious, she read at three and was always drawn to adventure and excitement. 'She should have been a lad,' said her father; he meant it as the highest compliment but 'she heard him with rebellion in her heart'.[16]

Slavery and Ireland figured as large issues in the young Emmeline's development. At five years old she was collecting for a fund to relieve the poverty of Negro slaves. When she was nine there was a Fenian riot in Manchester. Two of the Irish leaders were arrested, but an attempt to free them from the prison van led to a policeman being shot. Three men were tried for murder and hanged. Emmeline saw the place where the gallows had been and was transfixed with horror. 'It was my awakening to one of the most terrible facts of life – that justice and judgement lie often a world apart,' she later wrote.[17]

Since Manchester was the centre of the women's emancipation movement, the young Emmeline grew up in a household where all the talk was of the initiatives by Dr Pankhurst and Jacob Bright for women's suffrage.

When she was twelve she began to attend suffrage meetings with her mother and heard Lydia Becker speak.

After pestering her father for a good education she was sent to the École Normale in Paris, which taught girls science and bookkeeping. With her health considered too delicate for prolonged school work, she spent much of her time exploring Paris, reading French novels and becoming a fashionable and elegant young woman. She was very attractive, with black hair, violet eyes, high cheekbones and a beautiful skin with 'a kind of velvety bloom'. At twenty she decided to marry a French suitor, who expected a dowry. Her father, however, was outraged at the idea of 'selling' his daughter and refused, prompting an altercation with his overindulged and headstrong offspring. Emmeline's daughter, Sylvia, was later to write that her mother had been influenced by current debates about women having their own income and had been anxious to be financially independent. Whether or not this was true, the episode revealed that Emmeline was impetuous, and did not like to be thwarted in any way.[18]

The same qualities were to emerge in her choice of the man she was eventually to marry. Richard Pankhurst may have been the darling of radical Manchester, but he was hardly a conventional catch. He was, in fact, something of a personal and political failure. Having neglected his career as a barrister, preferring to spend his time on causes, he failed to win a seat in Parliament because he was unable to connect with ordinary voters. Gentle and childlike, he read Shelley and Whitman aloud in his bath in the mornings.[19] His hands and feet were slender and sensitive; the nails curved over the tips of his fingers.[20] The impression he gave of being an intellectual zealot was compounded by his untidy dress, pointed red beard, squeaky voice and small, penetrating eyes. An advanced radical, he held republican views that were too much even for his own liberal party to stomach.[21]

Robert Goulden, however, was a fan. On 31 April 1878 he went with the twenty-year-old Emmeline to hear Richard campaign against Disraeli's jingoism at a rally in Manchester's Free Trade Hall. Emmeline was smitten. 'I was charmed with him; he was so eloquent,' she wrote.[22] But why was such an attractive girl so enchanted by such an unprepossessing figure? The answer almost certainly lay in her single-minded character. She wanted to marry an important man. She thought Richard was a fast-rising public figure and she wanted to be his partner in the inevitable triumph. An early marriage to him was a ticket not to domesticity but to a public and political role for herself.[23] As her daughter Christabel was later to observe: 'Mother's career began with her marriage.'[24]

Her beloved, however, had to be wooed. Still living with his parents in his forties, he was settled in his bachelor ways. But as Emmeline's mother remarked, her daughter threw herself at him and he could not fail to be charmed – in his own way. Moreover, since his parents happened to die around this time, the brutal fact is that he needed to find an alternative home.

His courtship was entirely in character. Not for him the inconsequential endearments of romantic love. This was a mutual attraction of causes, and his love letters were as a consequence meaningful tracts. 'Dear Miss Goulden,' he wrote, 'There is as you know now in action an important movement for the higher education of women. As one of the party of progress you must be interested in this.' Even as they became more familiar, his expressions of tenderness remained appropriately elevated. 'Dearest Treasure, I received with greatest joy your charming likeness . . . In all my happiness with you I feel most deeply the responsibilities that are gathering round us . . . Every struggling cause shall be ours . . .'[25]

Not to be outdone, Emmeline was keen to make their union into a political statement. To show solidarity with the sufferings of unhappy wives, highlighted by the agitation for the Married Women's Property Act 1882, she suggested they dispense with the legal formalities of marriage, following the example of Elizabeth Wolstenholme and Ben Elmy. This was a step too far even for radical Richard. He explained to her that reformers who flouted current morality were hampered in their work for humanity. Emmeline accepted his logic: a victory which, as David Mitchell has observed, was almost the last point he was ever to gain over his wife in nineteen years of marriage.[26]

Robert Goulden, who had been the unwitting catalyst for the relationship between Emmeline and Richard, nevertheless thought her choice of husband was grotesque.[27]

The marriage was, however, a success, founded on mutual admiration and dedication to common ideals.[28] Richard, who had never known the responsibilities of independent adult life, handed over to Emmeline the entire management of the household. Indeed, he would frequently remark: 'I am a helpless creature!' and even handed to his wife the task of carving the family joint.[29] Instead, he devoted his attention to his causes. According to his daughter Sylvia's account, he was 'a standard bearer of every forlorn hope, every unpopular yet worthy cause then conceived for the uplifting of oppressed and suffering humanity'. Her mother was the most zealous of his disciples, 'having no dearer wish than to emulate him in the extremity of his ideas'.[30] When it came to the issue of the suffrage, the good doctor was suffused with chagrin over the obduracy of his own sex, going so far as to exclaim on one occasion to his wife and daughters: 'Why are women so patient? Why don't you force us to give you the vote? Why don't you scratch our eyes out?'[31]

Children were born to the Pankhursts in quick succession. Christabel was born in 1880, Sylvia in 1882, Frank in 1884 (he died four years later), Adela in 1885 and Harry in 1889. Emmeline was never an involved mother, and both Sylvia and Adela grew up feeling neglected. Christabel was her mother's favourite; Richard was fond of Sylvia, who was constantly trying to win her mother's affection; and Adela felt that neither parent cared for her. The feuds between the siblings were later to play themselves out in vicious political in-fighting and rival biographical accounts.

Emmeline, who breastfed Christabel but handed her other children over to a nurse, viewed her children as adults rather than as dependants, as did Richard.[32] She inflicted upon them eccentric ideas; her reluctance to accept any kind of weakness led to her refusal to allow Sylvia and Harry, who both had poor eyesight, to wear spectacles, as a result of which Sylvia endured migraines for years.[33]

The children were saturated in an atmosphere of what their father called 'noble endeavour'. He told them daily to be 'workers for social betterment', because if they didn't work for other people they would 'not have been worth the upbringing'. So the children were effectively forced to prove to their father the worth of their own existence. He brought them home every night books on history, astronomy, botany, as well as novels, and exhorted them to 'Drudge and drill! Drudge and drill!'[34] If they loved him, he said, they should act on his favourite slogan: 'To do, to be and to suffer!'[35] An ordinary childhood this was not. The children seldom played games, while Emmeline, a rigid disciplinarian, demanded implicit obedience and tolerated no likes or dislikes.

Richard was losing clients and money because of his political views, and was away a lot on legal business. Meanwhile Emmeline presided over a whirl of social activity as a glamorous political hostess.[36] Their London house in Russell Square became a salon for socialists, Fabians, anarchists, suffragists, freethinkers, radicals and humanitarians. Discussions included trade unionism and socialism, the prophecies of Kropotkin, and theosophy: at one of these sessions, it was said, Mme Blavatsky had been seen to extend her arm to an abnormal length to light her cigarette at the gas jet in the ceiling.[37] In Manchester, where the children spent part of their childhood as the family moved back and forth from London, the house was a less cosmopolitan version of Russell Square, hosting assorted vegetarians, pacifists, teetotallers, freethinkers, radicals, republicans, Catholics and nonconformists, all united by the desire to lift the masses above capitalist greed.[38]

The younger children, meanwhile, often felt neglected and abused. Christabel, the eldest and the favourite, showed less jealousy and insecurity than her siblings. Clever and well aware of her importance in the family, she was confident and mature, basking in the adult approval she obtained.[39] Although the later, embittered accounts by the younger siblings should not be accepted at face value, Sylvia and Adela were plainly psychological casualties. While Christabel was indulged, Mrs Pankhurst tended to punish Sylvia and Adela. Adela was small and sickly and for her first six years walked with the aid of splints. Jealous of both Sylvia and Harry, she was a more instinctive rebel than Christabel. When Richard pushed his children towards atheism, it was Adela who had the character to resist such pressure whereas Christabel accepted her father's views. As Martin Pugh comments, this underlined her strong desire to conform, to respect authority and to use it, characteristics which were to reveal themselves both in her strategy for the suffragette movement in seeking the backing of the élite she was attacking, and in her support for the establishment during the First World War.[40]

Sylvia was hypersensitive and from childhood subject to migraines and fainting fits. According to her own account, she was punished for refusing to eat lumpy cold porridge and was tied to her bed all day for refusing to take cod-liver oil. After such incidents she would be on her knees to her mother, imploring her: 'Help me to be good!'[41] When little Frank died of diphtheria, Emmeline said of her lost son: 'He had much finer eyes than any of these children.' Sylvia was to write of this shattering remark: 'The words fell like a stone upon my heart. I longed to have died instead of Frank. He was the only boy; there were three girls; one of us could better have been spared; I was considered not strong; I had weak eyes and headaches and light hair Mother had called insipid; surely it would have been better for me to die instead of Frank! For years that thought would recur with a deep anguish.'[42]

In due course the Pankhurst family drama was to play itself out in suffrage politics. But in the 1880s and 1890s the movement was in the doldrums. It wasn't going anywhere, and the strain began to show. Between 1886 and 1892 the House of Commons didn't debate women's suffrage. Rows over whether or not to support the campaign against the Contagious Diseases Acts caused the National Society for Women's Suffrage to split in two.

There were two further schisms in the movement. Many Liberal women were bitterly disillusioned by Gladstone's obduracy, but others wanted to ally party loyalty with the suffrage cause, causing the suffrage societies to wage fierce battles at agitated tea parties, prolonged meetings and in swarms of confidential correspondence. When Liberal Party women affiliated to the NSWS, Mrs Fawcett, Lydia Becker and others withdrew to form a rival organisation, the Central Committee of the National Society for Women's Suffrage, on the grounds that women and morality were greater than party. Although Mrs Fawcett remained a Liberal, she opposed Gladstone's sudden conversion to Home Rule, which she thought was merely an expedient manoeuvre to control his small majority. She thought it was wrong to give in to violence and betray the Irish loyalists. So she joined the new Liberal Unionists, visiting Ireland repeatedly and speaking against Home Rule.[43]

In addition to the rows over party affiliation, there were continuing divisions over the Central Committee's insistence that married women should not get the vote. In 1889 Elizabeth Wolstenholme Elmy founded the Women's Franchise League, which was committed to votes for married women, developed links with the working class and became the voice of ultra-radical suffragism. The new group was formed at Mrs Pankhurst's home in Russell Square. Its council included the Pankhursts, the Brights, the Elmys, Josephine Butler, Mrs Cunninghame Graham, the apostle of Negro emancipation William Lloyd Garrison, the American suffrage pioneer Elizabeth Cady Stanton, Jane Cobden, Lady Sandhurst and Mrs Harriet Taylor (wife of Peter Taylor), the last of whom had convened London's first-ever women's suffrage committee.[44]

The League worked for equality of women in divorce, inheritance and custody cases and over the guardianship of children. Its members held other advanced views, advocating for example co-education, trade unionism, internationalism, the defence of oppressed races and the abolition of the House of Lords – the pet causes of Richard Pankhurst. Their treasurer, Mrs Alice Cliff Scatcherd, a wealthy woman from Yorkshire, repudiated as badges of slavery the middle-class dress code of wedding ring and veil (Mrs Pankhurst never went out without a veil); as a result, hotels would refuse to accept her when she arrived to stay with her husband, even though she was respectably – even stodgily – dressed.[45] The League contemptuously referred to Mrs Fawcett's more conservative faction as the 'spinster Suffrage Party' which was pursuing a 'cowardly policy'. By 1893, however, the League was extinct.[46]

But the argument over married women was a deep and bitter one. Mrs Fenwick Miller, for example, wrote that restricting the vote to unmarried women was 'grotesque'. Giving the vote to widows would mean that if a bereaved woman married again she would lose her right to vote, a disincentive to getting married. As for the argument that the suffrage campaign should proceed cautiously 'step by step', she raged, this was like getting a living body halfway through a door and allowing the door to be shut on it, squeezing it to death. Moreover, the conservative suffragists were putting forward contradictory arguments that cancelled each other out. They were claiming both that wives would vote as their husbands told them, *and* that allowing married women to have separate opinions would introduce discord into families.[47]

On the other side of this argument, Mrs Fawcett's innate conservatism and caution were bolstered by the more idiosyncratic prejudices of the veteran suffragist warhorse Lydia Becker. She was later to remark to Mrs Pankhurst: 'Married women have all the plums in life.' To the radicals, Lydia Becker was an embittered wrecker. According to Sylvia Pankhurst, the socialist who was to become an ardent proponent of universal suffrage, Miss Becker's hostility to married women drove away many early suffrage pioneers. As far as this confirmed spinster was concerned, it was unmarried women who were looked down on and needed protection.

Sylvia Pankhurst was later to lump this attitude in with the innate conservatism and caution of much of the suffrage movement. It was 'honeycombed', she said, with people who would go only a small part of the way towards real social equality for women and who were prominent in the campaign only because they had money and leisure. So Helen Blackburn, in the periodical *Record of Women's Suffrage*, had argued that electing women to office 'forms no part of the women's suffrage question. The right to vote is the symbol of that freedom from which no human being should be debarred . . . eligibility for office is a question of individual adaptability for the performance of special duties'. For Sylvia, this epitomised the timidity of the movement. 'Its opponents were prejudiced; many of its protagonists only less prejudiced,' she bitingly concluded.[48]

Nevertheless, despite the many rows and fissures in the suffrage movement during this dispiriting period, opinion was consolidating and
hardening. A sense of inevitability was developing about the women's
franchise. In 1890 the sex researcher Havelock Ellis said in *The New
Spirit* that the march of science, democracy and women was irresistible.[49]
Women were continuing to develop a sense of solidarity and injustice.
They still cast themselves as slaves, men as their slave masters and marriage as their bond of oppression; and only parliamentary representation
could free them. Mrs Fenwick Miller told an audience at the National
Liberal Club that since the fruit of a slave's labours could be taken by
force and with the sanction of law to enrich another person, English
wives were indeed slaves. 'There was no protection from the law for
women except it was invoked by the men who owned them, while it was
the most cruel fact in many a woman's lot that in her master she found
her sternest enemy, her most heartless oppressor,' she said. A woman
could get maintenance for her children if her husband had deserted her
only if she went into the workhouse. A woman's character could be
taken away in court without her saying a word. Divorce was granted to
men rich enough to pay for it, but refused to women under almost all circumstances. Mothers had no rights to their children, a situation of gross
injustice that Mrs Miller would not abolish but rather reverse, to do
exactly the same to men. 'The claims of the mother to the custody of the
young child so absolutely outweigh those of the father that really the
father ought not to come into the question as such at all.' Only the vote
could begin to remedy all this, she concluded. Even the poorest men
could improve on bad laws that affected them by sending representatives
of their own interests to Parliament and giving them power over their
own position.[50]

Yet during the late 1880s opinion was hardening against women's suffrage too. An organised anti-suffrage movement began to emerge. In
1889 a 'Solemn Protest Against Women's Suffrage', signed by the popular novelist Mrs Mary Humphry Ward and others, appeared in *The
Nineteenth Century* magazine, which declared: 'We believe the emancipating process has now reached the limits fixed by the physical

constitution of women.'[51] Mrs Humphry Ward was by no means against advancement for women. She had helped pioneer women's education at Oxford, choosing the name for Somerville women's college. She approved of women becoming members of school boards or boards of guardians. But the physical constitution of women placed limits on the emancipating process. While wanting the fullest development of women's powers, energies and education, she said, she believed that their responsibilities towards the state were different from those of men. Parliamentary legislation, for example, exhausting labour in the administration of national resources and powers, relations with the external world, the workings of the army and navy and industries such as mines, metals and railways, supervision of commerce, management of finance, or the service of the merchant fleet – in all these, women's direct participation was impossible because of the disabilities of their sex or because of strong habits and custom resting on the physical difference from men.[52]

She wanted increasing activity by women in areas resting on thought, conscience and moral influence, but no admission to direct power in the state which rested on force. Citizenship, she said, was not dependent on the suffrage but lay rather in individual participation for the good of the community. Furthermore, women's moral influence 'depends largely on qualities which the natural position and functions of women as they are at present tend to develop, and which might be seriously impaired by their admission to the turmoil of active political life. These qualities are, above all, sympathy and disinterestedness.' These were difficult to retain in the heat of party struggle, not least because women's temper would make them hotter partisans than men. Women were more emotional. 'The quickness to feel, the willingness to lay aside prudential considerations in a right cause which are amongst the peculiar excellencies of women, are in their right place when they are used to influence the more highly trained and developed judgment of men. But if this quickness of feeling could be immediately and directly translated into public action, in matters of vast and complicated political import, the risks of politics would be enormously increased, and what is now a national blessing might easily become a national calamity . . .'[53]

If the vote was given to women on the same terms as to men, 'large numbers of women leading immoral lives will be enfranchised on the one hand, while married women who, as a rule, have passed through more of the practical experiences of life than the unmarried, will be excluded'. Admitting married women with the requisite property qualification would introduce enormous changes in family life and the English conception of the household.[54]

It was of course an irony – one bitterly remarked upon by Mrs Fawcett – that Mrs Humphry Ward, who claimed that women were unfit to take part in public life, herself wrote and spoke on political platforms, canvassed electors, published election literature and trained women in public speaking so that they could proclaim that 'woman's place is home'.[55]

However, the core of the opposition was a view of women that was in fact shared by the suffragists themselves. Both sides believed passionately that women were the embodiment of morality. The suffragists wanted to introduce female morality, and the virtues of the home from which it sprang, into the political sphere. The anti-suffragists feared that emancipation would weaken women's moral influence by distracting their attention or coarsening women's nature. It was this common view of women's moral strength that led about a hundred intelligent women to sign Mrs Humphry Ward's petition, including Beatrice Webb, Mrs Lynn Linton, Mrs T. H. Huxley, Mrs Leslie Stephen, Mrs Matthew Arnold, Mrs Walter Bagehot and Mrs Arnold Toynbee – although Beatrice Webb came later to regret it.

It was this deep anxiety about the erosion of the vital moral influence of women that lay behind the wide hostility to emancipation from both liberals and conservatives. Sensibility was considered a vital partner to sense; but the former belonged to women, and the latter belonged to men. In his novel *Yeast* Lancelot Smith wanted to assert mental superiority over his heroine Argemone but also to look up to her as 'infallible and inspired' on all 'questions of morality, of taste, of feeling', longing to teach her 'where her true kingdom lay – that the heart, and not the brain, enshrines the priceless pearl of womanhood'. Edwin Hood gave the title 'Woman the Reformer' to a chapter of his book *The Age and Its Architects*, and began by announcing: 'The hope of society is in woman! The hope of the age is in woman! On her depends mainly the righting of wrongs, the correcting of sins, and the success of all missions.' The sins to be corrected were revolution, prostitution and atheism. It was, therefore, a terrible mistake to encourage women instead to enter professional and political careers.[56]

Political opinions on women's suffrage, however, did not divide neatly. The same middle-class, temperance-supporting, provincial nonconformity that was the mainstay of Gladstonian liberalism gave rise to some of the most implacable opponents of the suffrage: for example, the future Liberal Prime Minister, Herbert Asquith. Male opposition was rooted in personal temperament, bachelor lifestyles, old-boy networks and masculine clubland more than in any social or political group.[57]

Opinions were also distorted by crude electoral calculations. Liberal MPs were broadly in favour, but their leaders were hostile for fear the women would vote Tory. The Conservative rank and file may have been dyed-in-the-wool opponents, but several Tory leaders were sympathetic. Benjamin Disraeli said in 1866: 'I have always been of the opinion that, if there is to be universal suffrage, women have as much right to vote as men. And, more than that, a woman now ought to have a vote in a country in which she may hold manorial courts and sometimes act as churchwardess.'

Lord John Manners, later Duke of Rutland, agreed, saying that female farmers had shown themselves fit to vote. He quoted a well-known man in Lincolnshire and Leicestershire, Mr Wilders, who said: 'To my mind the greatest injustice is that the female ratepayer and owner should not be allowed to vote. Fancy a woman farming five hundred acres of land and paying the usual contributions to the taxes of the country, having no voice in the representation of the country, while her own labourers have. If any man disputes the business capabilities of women, let him begin an important business transaction with her, and I will answer for it that he will come off second best.'

Lord Salisbury, who was to be a Conservative Prime Minister from 1885 to 1902, said in 1888: 'I earnestly hope that the day is not far distant when women will also bear their share in voting for members of Parliament and in determining the policy of the country. I can conceive no argument by which they are excluded. It is obvious that they are abundantly as well fitted as many who now possess the suffrage, by knowledge, by training and by character, and that their influence is likely to weigh in a direction which, in an age so material as ours, is exceedingly valuable – namely, in the direction of morality and religion.'[58]

In 1898 the looming Boer War reintroduced talk of political rights. If England was fighting for the representation of the Uitlanders against the Boers, denial of rights to women was even harder to defend. The Independent Labour Party, which was growing in the north, attracted many feminists. But its leaders were less keen; some opposed women's suffrage altogether, while others wanted full adult suffrage regardless of sex.[59] They also feared wage reductions through women's employment, and, like the Liberals, worried that the vote would deliver election victory to the Conservatives.

In 1890 Lydia Becker, that implacable foe of votes for married women, died. As the century wore towards its end, and the implications of widening the democratic settlement sunk in, the realisation grew that limiting women's franchise to property holders was no longer tenable.[60] The vote had always been tied to property ownership, since property owners were held to represent the whole community. At the beginning, demanding the women's vote merely for equivalent female property owners was adopted as a tactic not to frighten people. Helen Taylor, John Stuart Mill's stepdaughter, had written in 1866:

I think the most important thing is to make a demand and commence the first humble beginnings of an agitation for which reasons can be given that are in harmony with the political ideas of English people in general. No idea is so universally accepted and acceptable in England as that taxation and representation ought to go together, and people in general will be much more willing to listen to the assertion that single women and widows of property have been unjustly overlooked, and left out of the privileges to which their property entitles them, than to the much more startling general proposition that sex is not a proper ground of distinction in political rights.[61]

In other words, the cause was not about equality between the sexes but rather equality of class within the sexes. But the cry of 'one man one vote' was growing – and with it the view that all women, not just those who owned property, should be similarly enfranchised.

Mrs Fawcett, however, made it very plain that the suffragists' aim was not a universal franchise. The conventions in favour of property and against married women would remain unchallenged. She was not interested in anything so radical as universalism. In 1892 she tried to scotch the nightmare of wives voting against their husbands, or neglecting their families to attend clubs and political meetings. All that was being requested, she said, was to enfranchise one million women who for twenty-two years had held local franchises. Universal womanhood suffrage might be a logical extension but this was for Parliament to decide. 'We are not asking Parliament to give legislative expression to any theory or doctrine of equality between the sexes,' she wrote, 'but we ask Parliament to weigh the practical expediency of giving parliamentary representation to a certain class of women who, as heads of households and ratepayers, have already had experience of voting in other elections, where much good and no harm whatever has resulted from including them in the lists of persons entitled to vote.'[62]

In 1892 another attempt was made to translate this into law. Sir Albert Kaye Rollit, the MP for Islington South, made a roistering speech in support of his parliamentary bill extending the existing franchise to widows and spinsters. This, he declared, was the age of successive and successful franchises. Women's suffrage was not a party matter, and its opponents' arguments were contradictory.

Among the MPs who opposed Sir Albert's bill was the Liberal MP Herbert Asquith. There was nothing democratic, he declared, about the attempt to blur natural distinctions. 'The inequalities which democracy requires we should fight against and remove are the unearned privileges and the artificial distinction which man has made, and which man can unmake. They are not those indelible differences of faculty and function by which nature herself has given diversity and richness to human society.'[63] His personal intervention in the debate was a harbinger of what was later to develop into the most deadly and desperate battle of wills of the entire suffrage campaign.

Sir Albert's bill was lost by twenty-three votes. But the campaign was reinvigorated. The suffragists could see that all but a small minority of MPs were now committed to the cause. The problem lay in their leaders. Women were now heavily involved in politics and the issue of women's suffrage figured on the programme of many societies.[64] The issue was achieving critical mass.

In 1894 a very significant development occurred. The Local Government Act at last gave married women the equal right to vote for and sit on municipal councils.[65] From this point on, the argument that the parliamentary franchise should be restricted to spinsters and widows was discarded for ever.[66]

It also helped repair the fissure in the suffrage movement. In 1897 the two national suffrage societies – which had split in 1888 over the issue of affiliation to the Liberal Party – were reunited to form the National Union of Women's Suffrage Societies, presided over by Mrs Fawcett. Its only purpose was to seek votes for women 'on the same terms as it is, or may be granted to men'. This disappointed those who wanted it to campaign for other reforms. The NUWSS believed in painstakingly building up support among MPs by lobbying, petitions, pamphlets, speeches and articles.

In 1874 Mrs Fawcett had noted that women had now been admitted to municipal and school boards, were active in social and moral regeneration, worked as Poor Law guardians, and were achieving success in higher education. Political parties were vying to get women to work for them. 'I think there is no doubt,' she ventured, 'that the glacial drift of English public opinion has moved and is moving in the direction of the active participation of women in politics.'[67]

It was true; Mrs Fawcett's careful work began to pay off. From 1897 the Commons began to vote consistently in favour of women's suffrage.

Yet MPs did not regard the issue as of pressing importance, largely because they associated the vote with middle-class women who they thought didn't need it or with unmarried women who seemed atypical of their sex.[68] So the issue was deadlocked. But now another, more explosive group of characters was about to take the struggle in a dramatically new direction.

Emmeline Pankhurst had so far taken very little interest in the campaign for women's suffrage. In 1893 Richard Pankhurst's health collapsed under financial pressures and the family moved back to Manchester. Six months later the Pankhursts joined the Independent Labour Party (ILP). Poor Richard was still trying fruitlessly to become an MP. In 1895 he stood again, this time for the ILP, at Gorton and narrowly lost. His wife's reaction illustrated the extent of her arrogance and capacity for self-delusion. She thought that because of the prestige her husband had brought to the ILP, the party's leader, Keir Hardie, should resign and give the leadership to Richard instead. Her family seemed to exist for the furtherance of her own glory, and she could not acknowledge failure by any of them. As David Mitchell has remarked, her marriage had to be splendid, her husband a Galahad, her daughter a genius. Criticism of them meant criticism of her. All of them shared a sense of self-importance and moral superiority, but Mrs Pankhurst and her daughter Christabel in particular were very bad losers.[69]

In 1894 Mrs Pankhurst was elected to the Chorlton Board of Poor Law Guardians. Her experiences here opened her eyes to the desperate poverty of women. Most who came her way were paid starvation wages, and when they could no longer work they often ended in the workhouse. Pregnant women or mothers with babies were treated abominably when they applied for out-relief, and she began to see the vote not as a right but as a 'desperate necessity'. She used to say: 'When women have the vote they will see that mothers *can* stay at home and care for their children. You men have made it impossible for these mothers to do that.' She became a dominant voice on the board, attracting admiration for her statesmanlike powers of analysis and her exposure of corruption and incompetence among the workhouse staff.[70]

In 1896 an affair blew up which was to prove important in the political development of both Mrs Pankhurst and Christabel. The Manchester parks committee banned the ILP from Sunday meetings in an area known as Boggart Hole Clough. Two men and Mrs Pankhurst repeatedly defied the ban. The row drew huge crowds to the Clough. The three were arrested, but only the men were jailed. Mrs Pankhurst told the magistrate that if she was convicted she wouldn't pay the fine and was prepared to spend the night in Strangeways. She was not jailed, almost certainly because she was the wife of a prominent member of the northern circuit. Eventually all summonses were withdrawn, the council backed down and the Pankhursts were treated as local heroes, driving through the streets with Keir Hardie in an open carriage.

This episode taught Mrs Pankhurst some very important lessons. She saw the political power of the theatrical gesture. She saw how male authority backed down when confronted by a middle-class woman. She saw the capacity for martyrdom and propaganda when a woman confronted the power of the state and faced the threat of imprisonment for a principle. And she saw how she could manipulate all these things for political advantage. All these lessons would be used in due course in the militant suffragette campaign that she and Christabel were to lead.[71]

On 5 July 1898, at the age of sixty-four, after ill health and financial difficulties, Dr Richard Pankhurst died of a perforated ulcer. Emmeline, distracted by grief, lost heart in public work and for two years took no part in politics.

Meanwhile Christabel was drifting through life, showing no interest in politics or women's suffrage, nor in achieving an education, a career or a marriage. At seventeen, she had shocked Sylvia by saying that all she wanted was to find an easy job which would occupy her from ten until four each day. She appeared to hanker for a life of social activities, visits and entertainments, as opposed to her parents' home, which was filled with 'nothing but politics and silly old women's suffrage'. She showed no interest in any of the young men from the ILP who adored her; nor did she want to pursue her education.[72]

But in 1901 all this was to change. Christabel fell under the spell of Eva Gore-Booth and Esther Roper, who were the mainstays of the North of England Society for Women's Suffrage. They were both remarkable women. Esther Roper, who was thirty-two when Christabel met her, was the daughter of a missionary and one of the first women to gain a degree – in history – from the Victoria University in Manchester. In 1893 she had taken over the Manchester suffrage campaign and targeted it at local factory women. In 1896 she struck up a close relationship with the Irish poet Eva Gore-Booth, whom she met on holiday in Italy. Eva Gore-Booth, who was twenty-one, came from the Anglo-Irish gentry and was a tall, slender, delicate woman with a mass of beautiful golden hair. She felt repelled by masculinity, which for her was characterised by possessiveness, domination, materialism and pride.[73]

At the age of twenty-one Christabel met both of these women and became a frequent visitor to their house in Manchester's Victoria Park. Suddenly a new world opened up to her. Encouraged by Esther Roper, she enrolled to read law at Manchester University, from where she graduated in 1906 with a first-class degree. She was immediately drawn into the suffrage society. Indeed, she discovered that women's suffrage gave her life new purpose. Before long Emmeline began to complain that Christabel was never at home because she was always with Esther and Eva. Christabel adored Eva and would sit with her for hours massaging her forehead whenever Eva had neuralgia.[74]

Were these lesbian relationships? As several commentators have observed, the question is probably unanswerable. Women of this time often had very deep and intense friendships with one another in which sex was not necessarily an issue. The fact was that Christabel, who was in time to inspire hysterical devotion among her followers, was a detached individual. 'Christabel is not like other women,' said her mother. 'She will never be led away by her affections.'[75] Helena Swanwick, the wife of a Manchester lecturer, who knew Christabel, remembered her as a 'lonely person; with all her capacity for winning adorers (women and men), with all the brightness of her lips and cheeks and eyes, she was unlike her sisters, cynical and cold at heart. She gave me the impression of fitful and impulsive ambition and of quite ruthless love of domination.'[76]

By the summer of 1902 Christabel was speaking on women's suffrage, and adopting Esther's line that the best way of winning the vote was to put pressure on Labour MPs through raising the consciousness of the Lancashire women textile workers.

By 1903 she was beginning to rebel against the ILP. In a letter to the *Labour Leader* in response to criticism of her efforts to damage John Hodge, the ILP candidate in Preston, her remarks were revealing. 'Can Mr Hodge expect those who are working for the enfranchisement of women to be satisfied with that degree of friendship which allows of him not even referring to it in a speech or an election address? There is, after all, little to choose between an enemy and a friend who does nothing ... a majority of the Commons is "in favour" of giving political rights to women, but with no result.'[77] The reclassification of her friends as her enemies if they did not deliver the suffrage was to be a hallmark of Christabel's militant campaign. To her mother, she said: 'How long you women have been trying for the vote! For my part I mean to get it.'[78]

In August 1903 Sylvia Pankhurst received a personal affront. Commissioned to decorate the Dr Pankhurst Memorial Hall in Salford, she learned that women were not to be allowed to use it as it was to be a social club only for men attached to the ILP branch. Within a week of the hall opening, the Women's Social and Political Union (WSPU) was formed. 'We must have an independent women's movement!' Mrs Pankhurst reportedly told her friends. 'Come to my house tomorrow and we will arrange it!'[79]

According to Sylvia, Mrs Pankhurst had become intensely jealous of Christabel's involvement with Esther and Eva, and this was why she set up the WSPU.[80] However, Martin Pugh is surely correct to find this implausible, not least because when the WSPU was set up Christabel did not even bother to turn up to the first meeting and took time before she devoted herself to it fully.[81]

The WSPU was set up against a public mood of fragmentation and decadence. Liberalism was rudderless and anxious. The Liberal Lord

Macaulay viewed the expanding suffrage with 'dread and aversion' because it was 'incompatible with property and . . . consequently incompatible with civilisation'.[82] In 1885 Mark Rutherford wrote that civilisation was 'nothing but a thin film or crust lying over a volcanic pit' and wondered whether 'some day the pit would not break up through it and destroy us all'.[83]

Moreover, direct action was in the air. Since the 1880s terrorist methods had played an important role in attacking the Tsarist autocracy in Russia. In the 1890s a wave of anarchist bombings hit Europe. Anarcho-syndicalism, the theory of mass direct action by industrial workers to fashion and control a new radically egalitarian society, spread from France and Spain to the USA.

In Britain, militancy, and ultimately terrorism, were about to be waged by the militant suffragettes under the leadership genius of Mrs Pankhurst and her extraordinary daughter Christabel.

II

THE WOMEN'S NAPOLEON

When Emmeline Pankhurst started the Women's Social and Political Union in Manchester in 1903 there was an immediate indication that it might be different from the existing suffrage societies. Her aim was to persuade the new Independent Labour Party to support votes for women on the same terms as the male franchise. She invited a number of working-class women, most of them the wives of ILP members, to be part of a new organisation whose motto was 'Deeds, not words'.[1] That motto was an augury of what was to come. As Ray Strachey was to write, 'What they believed in was moral violence.'[2] While Mrs Fawcett's suffragists patiently pursued reform by constitutional means, the WSPU was soon to embrace militancy, intimidation and violence. The *Daily Mail* coined a derogatory term for these new women's activists. It called them 'suffragettes'.

At first Mrs Pankhurst, who always maintained that she was a law-abiding individual, campaigned in conventional fashion by attempting to influence politicians. So she attended ILP annual conferences, where she spoke on education as well as votes for women.[3]

The Labour movement, however, was divided over women's suffrage. Many members were deeply suspicious of the emancipation of women, believing that they would vote Tory or Liberal and also that their mass entry into the workplace would drive down wages. Others thought that votes for women was a divisive platform, and wanted to press instead for full adult suffrage since they thought that wives in particular would not vote Labour. But the WSPU wanted a much more limited franchise, not just for women but only for unmarried women who could qualify as heads of households. The franchise was still, after all, well short of full democracy. Under a third of all adults were registered voters; electors were heads of households, some lodgers, owners of property and graduates.[4]

The edgy relationship between the WSPU and the ILP was not helped by serious personality clashes between the men of the Labour movement and Mrs Pankhurst and Christabel. Here were two aggressive, patronising, upper-middle-class women presuming to lay down the law to a working-class political party. It did not go down well.

Bruce Glasier, the editor of *Labour Leader*, found himself being harangued by the Pankhurst women over the party's neglect of the woman question. He wrote in his diary in February 1904: 'At last get roused and speak with something like scorn of their miserable individualist sexism, and virtually tell them that the ILP will not stir a finger more than it has done for all the women suffragists in creation. Really the pair are not seeking democratic freedom but self-importance ... Christabel paints her eyebrows grossly and looks selfish, lazy and wilful. They want to be ladies and lack the humility of real heroines.'[5] Glasier had decided instinctively that the two of them were not so much radical reformers as using the suffrage to act out some personal character deficiencies.

He was not alone. Some thought that, since her husband's death, Mrs Pankhurst had changed from a sweet and gentle person into a domineering harridan. Philip Snowden, another ILP luminary, wrote that he could not help thinking that 'the development of Mrs Pankhurst into a law-breaking militant was due to the influence of her daughter Christabel, whom she worshipped fanatically. Christabel was a very strong-minded young woman with a dictatorial manner ... she had a profound belief that all politicians were insincere, that not one of them was to be trusted to keep his pledged word, and that they never gave a reform from conviction of its justice but only under the compulsion of force.'[6]

The ILP leader, Keir Hardie, however, became a devoted friend of the Pankhursts and was deeply sympathetic to women's suffrage. Like Richard Pankhurst, he had a quixotic attraction to good causes and was less inhibited than his colleagues about collaborating with middle-class radicals.[7] Under his encouragement the ILP published Christabel's pamphlet *The Citizenship of Women: A Plea for Women's Suffrage.* Here she set out her highly tactical case for limiting the women's vote. A 'wedge' bill, she wrote, would immediately lift 1,250,000 women from being classified along with paupers, idiots and lunatics and would open the door for eventual full adult suffrage. It was all a question of softening up public opinion. Resistance to anything more radical would be even stronger. Since men didn't think their wives were their equals, they would not want them to have the vote; but if women householders had the vote, this would gradually accustom men to the idea that all women should have it. And she set out the key WSPU tactic. Although women's suffrage was not a party issue, women should make it a test question at elections and refuse to work with any candidate who opposed them.[8]

This divisive approach horrified men like Glasier and Snowden. They complained that Keir Hardie was obsessed by women's suffrage and that his already messianic self-importance was deepened by his association with the Pankhursts. Unlike his colleagues, Hardie never felt threatened or patronised by the socially confident women who were its proponents.[9] Glasier wrote: 'All through, I fancy I can detect a conscious desire on his part to figure in history as the women's champion. What I object to is that his power to champion them is derived from us – our work and cohesion – but that we must all serve and be sacrificed as reactionaries on this question, all to enable him to triumph.'[10]

In 1905 Hardie tried to win a place in the parliamentary ballot for a bill proposing the suffrage for women householders. According to Sylvia Pankhurst, Emmeline had worked herself into a frenzy. Since the Liberals, who were expected to win the next election, were thought to be backing full manhood suffrage, Mrs Pankhurst thought that if women didn't get the vote now the issue would be closed for another twenty years.[11] When Hardie failed to win a place in the ballot, a liberal MP called Bamford Slack took it up at the urging of his wife; but it was insultingly talked out. The watching women were inflamed. Isabella Ford wrote: 'In the heart of each woman there the seed of discontent and revolution is now too deeply implanted for us to fear for the future. The future is ours.'[12]

Christabel, meanwhile, remained semi-detached from the WSPU and its pedestrian and fruitless attempts to turn the parliamentary process to its advantage. She began to entertain other, more dramatic ideas. In 1904 Winston Churchill MP, who had attracted attention to himself by leaving the Conservative Party and recasting himself as a Liberal, was speaking in Manchester, at the Free Trade Hall. He had just started proposing a motion in favour of free trade when, from the audience, Christabel interrupted by suggesting that women's suffrage be added to the proposal. Not surprisingly, the chairman refused and Christabel backed down, but not before an argument took place and attention successfully diverted from Churchill to Christabel. Later she was to write that this 'first militant step . . . was the most difficult thing I (had) ever done'.[13]

Both Christabel and her mother were deeply influenced by the militant and brilliantly manipulative tactics of Charles Stuart Parnell. Parnell ran an army, disciplined, ruthless and single-minded, and his tactics had converted Gladstone to Home Rule. The Pankhursts determined to do likewise. 'The WSPU is simply a suffrage army in the field,' wrote Mrs Pankhurst. 'It is purely a volunteer army and no-one is obliged to remain in it. Indeed, we don't want anybody to remain in it who does not ardently believe in the policy of the army.'[14] That policy was to oppose any government in power if didn't support the suffrage. That meant opposing even the Liberals, who were most sympathetic, if their leaders wouldn't give women the vote – just as Parnell had fought every Liberal candidate, including those who personally supported Home Rule, in order to put pressure on the government. If any member lost faith in

WSPU policy, suggested another or tried to add one on, stated Mrs Pankhurst bleakly, that woman would simply stop being a member. She admitted that this was autocratic, but it was necessary since ordinary suffrage organisation was simply not effective.[15] This campaign was to be run like a war.

Teresa Billington-Greig, who, like Mrs Pethick-Lawrence, helped run the WSPU until she broke with the Pankhursts, was later to map the similarities between the WSPU and Parnell's campaign. Parnell, she observed, believed in angering and shocking the enemy and rejoiced to think he was hated by the English; the Pankhursts' policy was to awaken hatred of the Liberals. Both wanted to inflict retribution as well as bring about reform. Parnell was reported as saying that they would punish the English, who would soon get afraid of punishment. Christabel similarly said: 'We will bring the government to its knees' and 'the government will be harassed in every possible way'. Parnell skirted on the edge of treason; the Pankhursts chose the next best course, talking revolution and flirting with sedition, courting both protest and propriety. Like Parnell, they played off one set of people against another, and copied his unscrupulousness about the means they employed. Christabel, she added, seemed to have copied Parnell's personal qualities too, displaying a similar reticence and aloofness. Like him, she never explained policy but applied it and justified it after the event, thrusting colleagues into new situations with only hazy hints about the policy being followed, thus stifling any opportunity for criticism.

But there were also some key differences. Parnell, who had determined to wage a relentless war on government, nevertheless had good judgement, knowing when and when not to strike. The Pankhursts, by contrast, were to strike indiscriminately. Parnell knew how to trust his men; the Pankhursts did not trust their women. Parnell knew when war was over and it was time to negotiate; the Pankhursts were to reject negotiation. Mrs Billington-Greig's conclusion was caustic: 'He was the leader, the natural chief, the chosen, the master of circumstance; they are the autocrats self-made, the artificially created dictators. He deserved to win. I dare not ask, "Do they?"'[16]

But this bitter criticism was for the future. In the early days Teresa Billington was a key player. Of the five main platform speakers for the WSPU, four were Pankhursts – Emmeline, Christabel, Sylvia and the youngest sister, Adela – and the fifth was Teresa. Like so many of the most committed suffragettes, she came from a tumultuous background. Born in 1877 above her parents' shop in Preston, she ran away from home at seventeen. Her father beat her brother, although she and her two sisters were protected by their mother, a devout Catholic. A striking woman with auburn hair, green eyes and a domineering manner, Teresa became an agnostic and a schoolteacher, and developed considerable organising skills as the secretary of a university settlement which worked with poor children. In 1903, when she sought to be exempted as a matter of conscience from teaching religion, she was referred to Mrs Pankhurst, who was a member of the school board. Teresa went to see her in the 'arty crafty' shop she ran to supplement her income as a registrar of births and deaths. Mrs Pankhurst, however, brushed her request aside. She was, wrote Teresa much later, 'as gracious, lovely and dominant as she was always to be'.[17]

In 1905 the WSPU recruited two more key activists, both women from troubled backgrounds. Hannah Mitchell, born Hannah Webster in 1871, grew up on a farm. Her mother, who hated farm life, was deeply embittered and angry, obsessive about cleanliness and beat Hannah to do the chores, mocking her desire for education. Hannah was to write about her girl friends falling victim to 'the primitive passions of the farm lads, who in many cases were scarcely more intelligent, and not so decent, as the animals they tended'. This produced a kind of 'anti-male complex' in her mind. However, under the influence of socialist ideas about marriage as comradeship rather than a state of subservience for women, she married Gibbon Mitchell to get a home of her own.[18]

It was a move she came to regret. Soon, she concluded bitterly that 'a lot of the Socialist talk about freedom was only talk and these Socialist young men expected Sunday dinners and huge teas with home-made cakes, potted meat and pies, exactly like their reactionary fellows . . . They expected that the girl who had shared their week-end cycling or rambling, summer games or winter dances, would change all her ways with her marriage ring and begin where their mothers left off.' When she realised she was pregnant, she became desperate. There would now be no time at all to read and improve herself, enjoy the fresh air or walks in the country. She had one child after a painful labour, a baby she was too poor to feed properly. Her husband's wages were fixed and she couldn't get him to understand that money was not elastic. He was happy with his comfortable chair and the fire, and was extravagant with coals and light, making Hannah nearly frantic. She wrote later: 'Perhaps if I had really understood myself, as I did later, I should not have married. I soon realised that married life, as men understand it, calls for a degree of self-abnegation on the part of women which was impossible for me. I needed solitude, time for study and the opportunity for a wider life.'[19] Bitterly resentful at the inequality of the sexes, she was drawn into the WSPU, having met Emmeline after standing for election to the Ashton Board of Guardians in 1904.

The second key figure was Annie Kenney, a very different character. Annie, the child of a textile worker, had grown up in poverty. She was eager and impulsive, with a thin, haggard face and restless, knotted hands with a finger torn off by an accident in the cotton mill. She had had a less harsh childhood than Hannah Mitchell, but her mother ruled the family; her father was a kindly man dominated by his wife. Annie later wrote: 'Father never seemed to have any confidence in his children, and he had very little in himself. Had he possessed this essential quality, perhaps the whole course of our lives would have been changed. My mother always said she ought to have been the man and Father the woman.'[20]

During her adolescence, Annie was a childlike creature, still playing with dolls at fourteen; as a young woman she lacked interest in men her own age, dreaming instead of God and kings. When her mother died, Annie went in search of a substitute family and at the age of twenty-six found it in the Pankhursts. She developed a number of very close friendships within the movement, but above all she gave uncritical devotion to Christabel. Annie's vulnerability guaranteed that she would become

Christabel's slave. As the WSPU's treasurer, Mrs Pethick-Lawrence, was to write, Christabel was 'lit up with a spiritual flame'; she neither gave nor looked for personal tenderness, but devotion to her took the form of unquestioning faith and absolute obedience. This found its perfect object in Annie Kenney, whose needy character lent itself to a complete surrender of mind, soul and body to a single idea and to the incarnation of that idea in a single person. Sylvia observed: 'Her lack of perspective, her very intellectual limitations, lent her a certain directness of purpose when she became the instrument of a more powerful mind. Her obedience to instructions ignored all difficulties.'[21] Annie knew that Christabel was an autocrat, but she didn't mind. Autocracy, she said, suited her 'conservative, liberty loving nature', because she liked to be either told what to do by someone she respected or left alone.[22]

During the initial months the WSPU existed on a shoestring and operated like a collective. Teresa Billington described its headquarters at the Pankhurst house as 'a home of love, unity and confusion'. She also described the extraordinary atmosphere of manipulative mind-control. 'To work alongside of [Emmeline] day by day was to run the risk of losing yourself. She was as ruthless in using the followers she gathered around her as she was ruthless to herself.'[23]

Such was Emmeline's personal magnetism that followers flocked round her like bees to honey. To discontented women who were looking for excitement and purpose in their lives, the Pankhursts were deeply romantic and mesmerising figures. The movement which took off was fraught with far deeper issues than the public life of the country. 'It meant to women,' wrote Mrs Pethick-Lawrence, 'the discovery of their own identity, that source within of power, purpose and will . . .' There was also a wealth of spiritual sympathy, loyalty and affection in such comradeship in a common cause. 'Gone was the age-old sense of inferiority, gone the intolerable weight of helplessness in the face of material oppression, gone the necessity of conforming to conventional standards of behaviour, gone all fear of Mrs Grundy. And taking the place of the old inhibitions was the release of powers that we had never dreamed of.'[24] It was, in short, both a liberation and a revolutionary sense of destiny. 'We young people find a world run on ideas entirely contrary to our own,' declared Christabel. 'We mean to mould a new world to our will!'[25]

The Pankhursts were a force of nature. Teresa Billington-Greig wrote that the family, united by a single mission, was reformist, rebellious and revolutionary. The Pankhurst home was 'a house which was inevitably to produce martyrs, missionaries, fanatics, politicians, publicists, saints and dictators'. Mrs Pankhurst was 'very wonderful, very beautiful, very gracious, very persuasive' – but utterly ruthless. 'She was a most acute statesman, a skilled politician, a self-dedicated re-shaper of the world – and a dictator without mercy.'[26] Emmeline was later to explain her leadership of the WSPU in typically arrogant manner: 'My daughter and I took a leading part, naturally, because we thought the thing out and, to a certain extent, because we were of better social position than most of our members, and we felt a sense of responsibility.'[27]

The fact was that she and Christabel had an extraordinarily unhealthy effect upon the women whom they recruited to the sex war. It was an uneasy precursor, in a minor key, of the demagoguery and dictatorships that were to disfigure the century that was just beginning. For the two of them became, in the eyes of their worshippers, almost superhuman, all powerful and without flaw. The effect resulted from the combination of their personalities and the heroic mould in which they cast themselves. Forty-one-year-old Lady Constance Lytton, an aristocrat given to wearing long, flowing robes (and great-granddaughter of the early feminist Anna Wheeler) first saw Mrs Pankhurst in the prison cells, which she likened to an animal's den. In the midst of this nightmare vision was a woman 'whose appearance struck awe into every fibre of my being'. It was a moment which transformed Lady Constance's life:

> From that moment I recognised in her, and I have held the vision undimmed ever since, the guardian protector of this amazing woman's movement, conscious not only of the thousands that follow her lead today but of the martyred generations of the past and of the women of the future whose welfare depends on the path hewn out for them

today. I seemed to grasp prophetically and all at once the characteristic qualities which I learnt later on by closer observation and experience. I saw that the quality of sternness, which presented so unyielding a front to every opponent and every obstacle, drew its force from deep fountains of understanding, of sympathy and of love.

If Mrs Pankhurst provoked adulation, her daughter was an elemental force. 'Christabel Pankhurst was the sunrise of the woman's movement. I cannot describe her in any other way. The glow of her great vitality and the joy of her being took hold of the movement and made it gladness. Yet, her nature being so essentially a woman's, there was a vein of tenderness throughout her speech, and her strength lay in her steadfast, resourceful and brilliant intellect.'[28]

Lady Constance, like so many others who fell under Christabel's spell, was naïve. For Christabel, the means of revolt were always more important than the cause itself. 'Christabel cared less for the political vote itself than for the dignity of her sex,' wrote Mrs Pethick-Lawrence, 'and she denounced the false dignity earned by submission and extolled the true dignity accorded by revolt. She never made any secret of the fact that to her the means were even more important than the end. Militancy to her meant the putting off of the slave spirit.' Her mother knew she was cast for a great role and had a temperament 'akin to genius'. 'She could have been a queen on the stage or in the salon,' she wrote. 'Circumstances had baulked her in the fulfilment of her destiny.'[29]

And so it was Christabel who conceived and launched the militant suffragette campaign, and took the cause into its most savage and controversial period. She noted that, after a meeting on unemployment in Manchester which was dispersed by the police and subsequently described as a riot, an unemployment bill which had been shelved was promptly brought down off the shelf and passed. Christabel decided that this offered a lesson women had to learn. 'Militancy by the unemployed, militancy that was only thought to have happened, moved the government to do what before they could not or would not do!' she wrote. And did not women have greater justification for militant methods, since unlike men they had no constitutional means?[30]

So Christabel decided to go to prison, and – ever mindful of the politics of propaganda – to take the rebel mill girl Annie Kenney with her in order to appeal across the social classes. In October 1905 the Conservative government was on the brink of defeat. A big Liberal demonstration was arranged for the Free Trade Hall, where Sir Edward Grey, later Viscount Grey of Falloden, was the principal speaker. Christabel and Annie went along. Before setting out for the meeting, Christabel told her mother gaily: 'We shall sleep in prison tonight.'[31]

Their tactic was to interrupt the meeting with a question: 'Will the Liberal government give the vote to working women?' As soon as they spoke, chaos broke out, with some attempting to make them sit down and shut up and others demanding that they be allowed to speak. Grey said he was in favour of women's suffrage but as it was not a party question it was not a fitting subject for the meeting. Christabel and Annie were duly thrown out of the meeting.[32] But their task was not yet accomplished.

'What we had done must be made a decisive act of lasting import,' wrote Christabel. 'We must, in fact, bring the matter into court, into prison. For simply disturbing the meeting I should not be imprisoned. I must use the infallible means of getting arrested, I must "assault the police".' So, in order to commit a technical assault, she spat at a policeman.[33] The following day Christabel and Annie were charged with assault and obstruction. Christabel used the court appearance to argue that women were deprived of the means of orderly protest, until the magistrates stopped her from speaking. The pair were fined, prompting Mrs Pankhurst to plead with her daughter to let her pay their fines and take them home. But Christabel retorted: 'Mother, if you pay my fine I will never go home.'[34] Winston Churchill, who understood well what was at stake, had also tried unsuccessfully to pay the fines for fear of the adverse effect their jailing would have in his constituency.[35] Having refused to pay or have their fines paid for them, the two were taken to Strangeways.

When they emerged from prison a few days later, the women's suffrage campaign was changed for ever. Nearly a thousand people had gathered on the day of the hearing to listen to speeches by Emmeline, Teresa Billington and Hannah Mitchell protesting at their treatment. When Christabel and Annie were released, there were more big meetings, bouquets, a speech from Keir Hardie. The press was full of public sympathy; opponents of women's suffrage were enraged. Hardie telegraphed: 'The thing is a dastardly outrage, but do not worry, it will do immense good to the Cause.'[36] The women's suffrage movement had found its best recruiting sergeant – martyrdom by law, affording the opportunity to wrong-foot the authorities utterly through expert manipulation, speech-making and propaganda. 'Twenty years of peaceful propaganda had not produced such an effect,' wrote Hannah Mitchell.[37]

One suffragette, Margaret Wynne Nevinson, saw the event in epochal terms. When Christabel and Annie were arrested at the Free Trade Hall, she wrote, the great liberal slogan of no taxation without representation was betrayed and from that day the Liberal Party decayed. 'That day, those two girls lit up a candle in England.'[38] Mrs Helena Swanwick, a Newnham graduate and the wife of a professor of mathematics in Manchester, who had refused to commit herself to the cause, changed direction abruptly with the jailing of Christabel and Annie. 'Their challenge had this effect on me, (as it had on countless other women) that I could not keep out of this struggle . . . It did not attract me; it bludgeoned my conscience. I could do no other than become one of those who were heaving the wheel of reform out of its rut . . . Let there be no mistake about it – this movement was not primarily political, it was social, moral, psychological and profoundly religious.'[39]

But not all suffragists were so impressed. Moderates condemned what had happened, and were furious with Mrs Fawcett for refusing to do so. Margaret Ashton of the Women's National Liberal Association wrote to her to deplore her failure to 'condemn the action of these few violent women who have so much injured the reputation of women politicians in Manchester . . . It has been deplorable from all points of view and has made it more difficult to approach the government with dignity than ever before.'[40] The Pethick-Lawrences, who at that stage were in South Africa, read about these dramatic events and were intrigued, as was a woman they befriended on the ship back to England, the politically naïve Mabel Tuke, who joined the WSPU and whose excessive femininity and charm were to be a great asset in reassuring people about the movement's respectability. Others, though, were already getting worried. Eva Gore-Booth, Christabel's erstwhile close friend, took a very dim view indeed. She grabbed Teresa Billington one evening after a meeting and said she should tell Christabel she must not fit her explanation of the Free Trade Hall events to the preconceptions of her audience. 'She either deliberately invited imprisonment or she was a victim; she either spat at the policeman or she did not,' she said. 'She can't tell one tale in Manchester and another in Oldham.'[41] But Christabel could, and did; and the deliberate courting of martyrdom in order to win the propaganda war became the key motif of her militant strategy.

Not for her the patient, painstaking suffragist strategy of appealing to MPs. There was now, after all, a majority of MPs in favour of women's suffrage. The enemy to be defeated was the government. As Margaret Wynne Nevinson observed: 'To strike at the heart was her Napoleonic strategy, and in other ways she followed the Napoleonic maxim of war: "Never do what you know the enemy wants you to do".' There was something beyond comprehension, she wrote, in Christabel's nature. 'In spite of her charm and feminine attraction, there was in her soul a core hard and brilliant as steel, and I sometimes thought as pitiless. But indeed she was possessed by that incalculable force which Goethe called "daimonic". She seemed to me like one of nature's forces, driving blindly, irresistibly and unconsciously forward. I doubt whether with all her wits she quite realised the revolution she was accomplishing.'[42]

The WSPU duly set about harassing and intimidating Liberal politicians wherever possible. During the 1906 general election it organised widespread heckling. Women's suffrage, though, was not an issue. The Conservatives were indifferent, the Liberals were ambivalent and the new Labour Party was hostile.[43]

12

THE THEATRE OF VIOLENCE

The Liberals won the 1906 general election with a large majority. The King's Speech promised to democratise the men's franchise but said nothing about women. Keir Hardie denounced the 'scandal and disgrace' of treating women no better than criminals or the insane. But his party didn't support him; had it done so, the Liberals might have listened since they were nervous of rising Labour competition. Mrs Pankhurst was torn between affection for Keir Hardie and the growing influence of Christabel, who wanted to cut the WSPU free of Labour altogether. She believed that the Tories would deliver votes for women, just as they had given household suffrage to men in 1867 in order to dish the Liberals.[1]

In 1906 the WSPU moved from Manchester to London, reinforcing the distance it had travelled from its claim to working-class support. Christabel's severing of her links with the ILP made it safe for upper-class women to join, so much so that it became known derisively as 'the Social Women's Political Union'. Alice Milne, secretary of the Manchester branch, wrote in her diary after visiting London in October 1906 that she had 'found the place full of fashionable ladies in silks and satins . . . It struck me then that if our "adult suffrage" Socialist friend [probably Snowden] could have looked in that room he would have said more than ever that ours was a movement for the middle and upper classes.'[2] But Christabel believed that the government would take more notice of the feminine bourgeoisie than the proletariat.

The WSPU strategy of aggressive picketing, noisy interruptions and causing maximum public nuisance provoked much opposition, not least within the women's movement itself. In May 1906 the NUWSS organised a big deputation to the new Prime Minister, Henry Campbell-Bannerman. Many bodies refused to take part because the WSPU was included. The deputation led by Emily Davies made a case which Campbell-Bannerman said was 'conclusive and irrefutable', but nevertheless he could do nothing about it. Because of differences of opinion in Cabinet and in the Liberal Party, he said, his hands were tied and all he could advise was 'go on pestering' and exercise 'the virtue of patience'. This provoked Annie Kenney to jump on a chair and cry, 'Sir, we are not satisfied!'[3]

From that point onwards, as Mrs Fawcett recorded, the whole country rang with the doings of the militant suffragettes. But for the first five years, while they suffered extraordinary acts of violence they used none; 'and all through, from beginning to end of their campaign, they took no life and shed no blood, either of man or beast'. The suffragettes caused a tremendous sensation, towards which Mrs Fawcett was notably ambivalent. Unlike other moderate suffragists, she did not condemn the WSPU – or not yet. For the moment she saw that the attention they were drawing to the cause was attracting a wave of recruits and radicalising women as never before. And much of what they were doing was sheer, audacious spectacle. Public meetings were forbidden within one mile of Parliament; on one occasion, half a dozen large vans got to the House of Lords when their doors flew open and out stepped from each van some ten to dozen 'daintily clad suffragettes who immediately began to hold a meeting'. All of London, apart from perhaps the Home Office, laughed.[4]

If the WSPU in its early days was a shoestring collective, this was about to change. It recruited Emmeline Pethick-Lawrence as treasurer and was transformed into an efficient, focused and solvent fighting machine. Emmeline Pethick was born in October 1867, the second of thirteen children. She received little attention from her semi-invalid mother, and was cared for by a succession of nursemaids. Her father was a born rebel, inspiring in her a hatred of social injustice. She was sent to harsh boarding schools; at one Quaker establishment she was accused of 'corrupting the mind' of a younger girl when she expressed curiosity about birth. 'The result was,' she wrote, 'that for many years I tried to put the whole subject of sex completely out of my mind.'5 She developed a deep concern for social reform and was uninterested in marriage. However, in 1899 she met Frederick Lawrence, a barrister and Liberal Unionist. Despite her reservations about their differences in politics and her fears that a conventional marriage would stifle her hopes of self-fulfilment, they married in 1901.6

When she and Fred read about the furore over the jailing of Christabel and Annie, she was curious to meet these women. After the Pethick-Lawrences returned to Britain from their South African tour in 1906, Mrs Pankhurst asked her to develop the WSPU in London, but at first she declined. It was Annie Kenney who broke down her reluctance; touched by Annie's eagerness and vulnerability, Mrs Pethick-Lawrence was drawn in against her better judgement. 'To tell the truth,' she wrote, 'I had no fancy to be drawn into a small group of brave and reckless and quite helpless people who were prepared to dash themselves against the oldest tradition of human civilisation as well as one of the strongest governments of modern times.'7

Both the Pethick-Lawrences then moved in to sort out the WSPU's organisation. When they arrived, they found no office, organisation, funds or even postage stamps. Teresa Billington-Greig wrote later that the inner circle of WSPU were hopeful that the arrival of the Pethick-Lawrences would act as a counterbalance to the power of the Pankhursts.8 What the Pethick-Lawrences possessed in great measure was method, a vital complement to the temperamental and intuitive Pankhursts. Mrs Pethick-Lawrence loved pageantry, colour and music, which she introduced and thereby immeasurably popularised the cause. She was a gifted communicator, born for national executive work; her powers of deep reflection and imagination helped build the movement. For his part, Mr Pethick-Lawrence ran and organised the staff and the office and produced regularity and order; he mapped out and planned the demonstrations, understood the detail of big schemes and conceived the organisation's newspaper, *Votes for Women*.

The two of them turned the movement into one of the most highly organised societies in the country. But it was still not democratic. 'The true and inner secret of the militant movement was that we were an autocracy,' said Mrs Pethick-Lawrence; and the autocrat was Christabel Pankhurst.[9]

It wasn't long before the WSPU was putting into widespread practice the strategy that Christabel had tried out with such success in Manchester. This was to use the courts as theatre and prison as martyrdom.

The WSPU began the regular heckling of anti-suffragist Cabinet ministers. Herbert Asquith, the Chancellor of the Exchequer and an implacable foe, was a prime target. In June 1906 police struck out at women on a protest near Asquith's house in Cavendish Square. When Teresa Billington objected, she was herself seized, struck and throttled. When she slapped and kicked the officer in turn, she was arrested and brought to court. She refused to testify; the court, she said, had no jurisdiction since women were not represented in making laws. Accordingly, she became the first suffragette to go to Holloway prison, although she was released against her will when the *Daily Mirror* paid her fine.[10] Two days after Teresa was sent to prison, Adela Pankhurst and Hannah Mitchell were jailed after refusing to pay fines for obstruction at a meeting in Manchester addressed by Churchill and Lloyd George.[11]

Teresa Billington was fighting for more than the vote. She believed that if people were educated to reason, individual liberty would produce the best possible world. She wrote: 'I seek [woman's] . . . emancipation from all shackles of law and custom, from all chains of sentiment and superstition, from all outer imposed disabilities and cherished inner bondages which unite to shut off liberty from the human soul borne in her body.'[12] She wanted not just equal rights in the workplace but a transformation of women's dependent role, with the elimination of traditional marriage customs, rejection of the family as the unit of society, changes in attitude towards prostitution and 'unrecognised sex relations', and motherhood by choice. She lashed out at the double standard of morality, and at unfair marriage, divorce, parentage and prostitution laws.[13]

In a manuscript written in Holloway prison that year, Teresa wrote that the nature of agitators had changed. Older suffragists believed in argument, politeness and reason. The young ones thought differently because the history of their movement was a scandalous series of betrayals, despicable tactics and broken pledges. Such a contemptuous refusal to enfranchise women could never have happened, she wrote, had women suffragists made MPs fear their influence. Since women were denied the rights of citizenship, logically they had to be outlaws and rebels. Parliament had meaning and sanctity for men. 'But to women it only bears the relation that the Czar bears to his people.' The old, quiet methods were absolutely useless. What she advocated instead was provoking a reaction, however strong or savage, since this was the only way to attract public attention and gain popular sympathy – the classic rationale of terrorism. She wrote:

Strange as it may sound, we want the bitter, prejudiced and unreasoning opponents to be ruffled into speech and action. He is a strong if unknowing ally who allows his bigotry and abuse to escape him. The dramatic protests which occasion his outspoken opposition startle the unconscious opponent into thought. In this newly awakened condition of mind he is eager for argument and information. Then it is that the irrational masculine bigot quickens or completes his conversion. Thus the man in the street is reached and popular support gained. Only by methods which break through the indifference and carelessness of the public which sets the opponents condemning, and the ignorant questioning, can apathy be turned into sympathy and a popular demand be created. This element has long been wanting for the women's movement.[14]

She accordingly justified violence itself. The treatment of protesting women by the stewards at public meetings was getting steadily worse. It was violent, humiliating and sexual. Women came away shocked, weeping and shuddering. This, Teresa felt, called for retaliation and punishment. So she carried a dog whip to a meeting in Northampton, defending her actions in a defiant statement that the treatment of women was brutal and criminal and could only be promulgated by curs, for which the dog whip was fitting punishment. Touch the primal passions of the blind prejudiced brute, she said, and he stands revealed as a semi-savage. The unfair marriage, divorce and separation laws, the laws of parentage and of criminal offences were not only immoral and unjust but formed an evil environment in which both men and women were degraded. But legislation for equal morality, which meant raising women's status, would never come until women became lawmakers. 'So, for the sake of uplifting the men and women of our race from this cesspool of vice, for the sake of purifying our human and sex relations, for the sake of bringing salvation to the soiled and tainted children of humanity born with poisoned life-blood and an inheritance of evil, women must win and use those powers of citizenship which the vote alone can bring.'[15]

Such exaggerated language and the depiction of men as dogs indicated that militant suffragism was nothing less than a sex war. As Mrs Pethick-Lawrence said in 1906: 'The struggle has begun. It is a life and death struggle . . . What we are going to get is a great revolt of the women against their subjection of body and mind to men.'[16] Mrs Fawcett's societies, by contrast, saw their work not as an attack on men but seeking reform for the good of all and as the next step in human progress. Mrs Fawcett actually rebuked a woman speaker in Yorkshire who was holding forth on the virtues of women and their great superiority to men. Not so, said the leader of the NUWSS. 'I think that the same spirit which brought women into the profession, the spirit of generosity in men and of enterprise in women, was the spirit which brings progress.'[17]

Four months later an event occurred which marked a step-change in the spiral of militancy and reaction. At the state opening of Parliament on 25 October a group of women got into the central lobby of the House of Commons and waved flags and stood on seats making speeches. Ten were arrested for a breach of the peace, and chose to go to prison rather than be bound over. But these were women of title or social position: Mrs Anne Cobden Sanderson, the daughter of Richard Cobden; Mrs Pethick-Lawrence, Adela Pankhurst, Mary Gawthorpe. Only one woman among them, Mrs Baldock, was working-class. The jailing of such distinguished company provoked widespread uproar. The suffragist Mrs Florence Fenwick Miller said: 'You have taken, and are treating as a felon, a daughter of the great Cobden, the man who gave you the cheap loaf.'[18]

The juxtaposition of good breeding and jail conditions was a toxic propaganda weapon. Asquith understood this well, and sensing the trap into which the government was walking had already criticised the six-week prison sentences given to Teresa Billington and Annie Kenney after Cavendish Square, writing to the Home Secretary, Herbert Gladstone, that he deplored 'the prosecution of these silly women' and hoping that their sentence could be reduced or annulled.[19]

Mrs Pethick-Lawrence had a nervous collapse in prison and was released early. Her husband gave the *Labour Record* the approved line: 'They did not go to prison because they sought notoriety; they are women who never courted observation.'[20] But the controversy and the publicity brought donations and volunteers rolling into the WSPU. When the prisoners were released, they were treated as heroes. Respectable social circles invited them in, and well-known writers endorsed their claims. From being viewed as cranky and irritating self-publicists, they were now being treated with unhealthy hero worship and exaggerated devotion. Teresa Billington-Greig later wrote: '"These militant suffragettes are actually ladies!" was the gasping cry; and straightaway most of us were ladies again, and the rebel woman was veneered over or given hasty burial.'[21]

Mrs Fawcett was also enraged. She visited her friend Mrs Cobden Sanderson in prison and described conditions there: not even a chair to sit on, and only three potatoes for supper as she was a vegetarian. Mrs Fawcett could not believe the police claims that Mrs Cobden Sanderson had bitten and scratched and screamed. The NUWSS leader said she wanted above all to make a point about the 'unscrupulous abuse and misrepresentation' to which the ten had been subjected in the press.[22] So she wrote to *The Times* that she hoped the more old-fashioned suffragists would stand by the suffragettes, since 'far from having injured the movement, they have done more during the last twelve months to bring it within the region of practical politics than we have been able to accomplish in the same number of years'. She went further and held a banquet in their honour, at which she told that the ten had broken 'not a moral law but a rule of etiquette'.[23] None of the Pankhursts was present at this dinner. Adela was unable to attend, Mrs Pankhurst and Christabel hadn't been among the imprisoned and Sylvia wasn't invited. Christabel was later to write an acidly double-edged acknowledgement of this gesture: 'One day the non-militants gave a dinner to our prisoners. We highly appreciated this act of solidarity and moral support. Had they shared our fare in prison it would have meant still more.'[24]

Christabel milked the reaction for all it was worth by rushing some of the ex-prisoners to campaign in the Huddersfield by-election. The *Daily Mirror* commented admiringly: 'When the suffragettes began the campaign, they were mistaken for notoriety hunters, featherheads, flibbertigibbets . . . Now that they have proved they are in earnest, they have frightened the government, they have broken through the law, they have made votes for women practical politics.'[25]

But working-class suffragists recoiled from such upper-class histrionics, which seemed to them utterly self-indulgent. Eva Gore-Booth wrote to Mrs Fawcett:

There is no class in the community who has such good reason for objecting and does so strongly object to shrieking and throwing yourself on the floor and struggling and kicking as the average working woman, whose human dignity is very real to her. We feel we must tell you this for this reason that we are in great difficulties because our members in all parts of the country are so outraged at the idea of taking part in such proceedings, that everywhere for the first time they are shrinking from public demonstrations. It is not the fact of demonstrations or even violence that is offensive to them, it is being mixed up and held accountable as a class for educated and upper class women who kick, shriek, bite and spit. As far as importance in the eyes of government goes, where shall we be if working women do not support us? . . . It is not the rioting but the *kind* of rioting.[26]

Christabel disagreed. She grasped that social class was the key to provoking that all-important reaction. It was the sight of the symbols of bourgeois ultra-respectability taking to the streets which would get under the government's skin like nothing else. She wrote: 'It was evident that the House of Commons, and even its Labour members, were more impressed by the demonstrations of the feminine bourgeoisie than of the female proletariat.'[27] So she turned the WSPU into an upper-class and bourgeois organisation. This was not just an argument over tactics. Her aims were, in fact, radically different from the aims of the radical, working-class suffragists. They wanted the vote to achieve a wide range of reforms for women in the fields of employment, marriage, divorce, child care, education and so on. Christabel was interested in none of these things on the feminist agenda. She wasn't interested in democracy or social reform. Her aim was far more narrowly focused. 'Another mistake people make,' she wrote to a supporter in 1913, 'is to suppose that we want the vote only or chiefly because of its political value. We want [it] far more because of its symbolic value – the recognition of our human equality that it would involve.'[28]

The militancy and drama intensified. Huge sums of money came in from supporters and went out again on flags, banners, leaflets, organisers and meetings. There seemed no limit to the suffragettes' ingenuity. They would arrive in disguise as messenger boys or waitresses; they chained themselves to the railings in Downing Street or to statues in the lobby of the House of Commons; they materialised out of organ lofts, furniture vans or on station platforms.[29] In scuffles when they were turned back by the police, women were injured – and were then able to point to the undoubted violence of the authorities. Suffragettes who interrupted meetings were frequently assaulted by men in the audience and handled roughly by stewards. Outside London especially, bands of young men disrupted suffragette meetings, and the police refused to intervene.[30]

In February 1907 the WSPU organised the first 'women's Parliament' at Caxton Hall, in Westminster. At the end a number of deputations set off for the Commons but were confronted by mounted police, dubbed 'the Cossacks' by the press. This prompted Mrs Pankhurst to declare melodramatically that she would not 'shrink from death if necessary for the success of the Movement . . . If the government brings out the Horse Guards and fires on us, we will not flinch.'[31] There was a fracas; fifty-eight women were brought to court and most got two to three weeks in Holloway, among them Christabel and Sylvia Pankhurst.[32]

Sylvia noted that non-socialist women simply cast respect for authority to the winds. She observed: 'Women brought up in Conservative traditions, and those who had hitherto taken no interest in political theory, were often most vehement in this militancy, which was primarily a vindication of their status as women.'[33] The demonstrations got larger and larger. In February 1907 the NUWSS – which was reaping the harvest sown by the WSPU's militancy – held a 'Mud March' in a downpour, attended by three thousand women.

The meetings, which were multiplying, had a missionary fervour and brought new converts.[34] The stage manager Emmeline Pethick-Lawrence invented the suffragette costume: white for 'purity in private as well as public life', purple for dignity and green for hope. The spectacle of so many women dressed in such a striking way was beautiful, moving and impressive. But taking part was still an act of courage. Ray Strachey of the NUWSS later wrote that processions still felt dreadful and the participants felt like martyrs. Worst of all was that people laughed at them. The suffragettes braved convention to stand at street corners to address passers-by. They chalked pavements, sold papers in the streets, carried sandwich boards and went canvassing house to house. Sometimes pepper, mice, rotten eggs, fish, oranges and other missiles were hurled at speakers.[35] Despite all this, Helen Fraser, the WSPU organiser in Scotland, later wrote: 'It seemed to me, however, that the vast mass of people were simply curious – not sympathetic – not opposed. Simply indifferent.'[36]

But support was nevertheless growing as more and more women were being arrested and jailed. The writer Israel Zangwill said: 'In politics, force only counts'; while Keir Hardie remarked: 'If your cause is advanced today, you have to thank the militant tactics of the fighting brigade . . .' Another writer, Brougham Villiers, wrote that 'in less than three years the movement for the enfranchisement of women has made greater strides than in the century before, and the seed sown by Mary Wollstonecraft seems at last likely to bear fruit'.[37]

The jailings were essential. 'Every prisoner means a harvest of converts,' said Mrs Pethick-Lawrence.[38] She organised events after each release with all the panache of a modern public-relations executive. Breakfast meetings with the released prisoners were a goldmine. 'A very great effort should be made,' she wrote, 'by every one of the members to push the sale of breakfast tickets amongst their friends, for no better opportunity could possibly be afforded for making converts and enthusiastic adherents to our cause. Of all our meetings the breakfast party is the most significant. The sight of the women who have suffered so bravely, and their words of greeting to the world as they come back to it, must go straight to the heart of everyone present, whether previously friend or foe to the women's movement.'[39] Far from killing off the suffrage, militancy brought a huge surge of support and applications for membership, not just of the WSPU but also of the older suffrage societies. Women's suffrage was the topic of conversation in every household and at every social gathering. One of Mrs Fawcett's own relatives acknowledged: 'I was lukewarm; now I am boiling.'[40]

Yet politically the suffragettes were still getting nowhere. In October 1907 Arthur Balfour, the Conservative leader, wrote to Christabel that he was not convinced that most women wanted the vote. The meetings and marches were designed to prove this wrong. The WSPU claimed that during 1907 and 1908 they held more than five thousand meetings, four hundred of which drew more than a thousand people.⁴¹

In 1907 the Labour Party conference again rejected anything but full adult suffrage. Labour thought the slogan 'Votes for Women' was dishonest, since the movement's demands would still leave working-class women disenfranchised.⁴² But Christabel saw adult suffrage as a trap to produce universal male suffrage and an anti-feminist majority. At the ILP conference in Derby in April 1907 Mrs Pankhurst said: 'We are not going to wait until the Labour Party can give us the vote. It is by putting pressure on the government that we shall get it. We have opposed nobody but government nominees and in that we have followed the tactics of the Irish party . . .'⁴³ The WSPU revealed a new ruthlessness when it campaigned against the Liberal candidate in the 1906 Cockermouth by-election, ensuring a Conservative victory over the Labour candidate. At the Huddersfield by-election a few months later, the WSPU adopted the same strategy even though the Labour candidate was a supporter of women's suffrage.⁴⁴

Mrs Charlotte Despard, the WSPU's secretary and a socialist, objected strongly to this strategy. With her long, pale, aquiline face and snowy hair topped by a black mantilla, her tall, thin body clad in a flowing black gown and her feet in low-heeled leather sandals, she cut an eccentric figure.⁴⁵ After her husband died in 1890 she had a nervous collapse and tried to communicate with him through spiritualism.⁴⁶ Now she declared that she would never again help in an election unless it was to support the Labour Party. She was ignored, like everyone else. In 1907 the WSPU finally severed its link with the Labour movement.

Desperate at the political impasse, the WSPU then turned up the temperature. In 1908 the form of militancy changed. Civil disobedience gave way to threats to public order, with destruction of property such as window-breaking and occasional violence against members of the government. When Mrs Pankhurst and a group of elderly suffragists were evicted from the Commons while delivering a petition, women smashed windows at the Privy Council, Treasury and Home Office in protest.⁴⁷

However, all was not well within the WSPU. With no democratic internal procedures, it was run as autocratically as an army. Sylvia Pankhurst wrote: 'It was made a point of honour to give unquestioning assent to the decisions of the leaders, and to obey the command of the officials, paid or unpaid, whom they had seen fit to place over one. Processions and pageantry were a prominent feature of the work, and these, in their precision, their regalia, their marshals and captains, had a decided military flavour. Flora Drummond was called the General and rode at the head of processions with an officer's cap and epaulettes.'[48]

The Pankhursts' despotic style and the increasing violence were breeding revolt within – but under no circumstances would dissent be tolerated by Christabel or her mother. The first casualty was Dora Montefiore, who had been largely responsible for developing the WSPU in London and had been trying to expand its working-class membership. She confronted Christabel over her election policy, asked for the publication of detailed accounts and complained about the lack of internal democracy. For her pains, she was effectively thrown out.

Few realised that Mrs Pankhurst was merely the organisation's figurehead and that the real power resided in Christabel, to whom her mother constantly deferred. It was Christabel who was the chief strategist and whose writ ran without challenge. 'It was all destructive,' wrote a very critical and embittered Sylvia, 'but how much easier to win applause by destructive condemnation than for any constructive scheme, however brilliant, however beneficent!'[49] Christabel mesmerised people through her extraordinary appeal as a platform speaker. While her mother had a talent for moving her audiences and arousing their protective instinct, Christabel dazzled. Her intellectual skills, her marshalling of facts and logic and her witty and devastating repartee left audiences in awe.

But this alone would not have made such an impact. She was a pinup – slender and young, with 'the flawless colouring of a briar rose' and an easy grace; but the real secret of her attraction, wrote Sylvia, was her fluent, gay audacity. She had the admiration of a multitude: hundreds, perhaps thousands, of young women adored her to distraction and longed to be and to do likewise. Mrs Pankhurst upheld her as an oracle; the Pethick-Lawrences lauded her to all comers. 'As for me,' wrote her jealous and wounded sister, 'I detested her incipient Toryism; I was wounded by her frequent ruthless casting-out of trusty friends for a mere hair's-breadth difference of view; I often considered her policy mistaken, either in conception or application; but her speaking always delighted me; her gestures, her tones, her crisply-phrased audacity.'[50]

By 1907 the WSPU had expanded rapidly. There were branches, especially in the north of England, that were still close to Labour. Christabel was aware that there was likely to be a challenge to her at the WSPU's annual conference. Teresa Billington-Greig – who had married earlier in the year – drafted a constitution to be ratified by conference, which would introduce internal democracy and cut the Pankhursts down to size. Christabel reacted emotionally, calling Mrs Billington-Greig 'a wrecker'; but this time her mother asserted control. She tore up the constitution, cancelled the conference and formed a new committee on the spot with Mabel Tuke, Mrs Wolstenholme Elmy, Mrs Pethick-Lawrence, Annie Kenney, Mary Gawthorpe, Mary Neal and Elizabeth Robins. Members were informed they were in the ranks of an army of which Mrs Pankhurst was the permanent commander-in-chief. A letter declared: 'We are not playing experiments with representative government. We are not a school for teaching women how to use the vote. We are a militant movement and have to get the vote next session.'[51] Mrs Pankhurst said that no one was obliged to remain in her 'army'.[52]

She was taken at her word and the WSPU split – the first of seven splits provoked by Christabel before the war. Dissidents gathered around Mrs Billington-Greig and the socialist Mrs Charlotte Despard and formed the Women's Freedom League (WFL), which worked closely with labour organisations and which, although militant, tried to devise forms of militancy which were not violent. It was also committed to democracy. As Mrs Billington-Greig observed: 'If we are fighting against the subjection of woman to man, we cannot honestly submit to the subjection of woman to woman.'[53]

Mrs Billington-Greig wanted the women's movement to fight for reform on a wide front. She wrote of the WSPU that its radical tactics masked a profoundly reactionary position. 'Daring to advertise in an unconventional way, the movement has dared nothing more. It has cut down its demand from one of sex equality to one of votes on a limited basis. It has suppressed free speech on fundamental issues. It has gradually edged the working class element out of the ranks. It has become socially exclusive, punctiliously correct, gracefully fashionable, ultra-respectable and narrowly religious.'[54]

By contrast, she saw the WFL as a movement for women's freedom. She told its first conference: 'Our cause is not only votes for women, but the binding together of all womanhood with human rights.' For her, feminism was based on the importance of self-discovery. When sweated women workers forging iron chains went on strike in 1910 for higher pay, she urged the WFL to support them because they were symbolically breaking the chains 'which woman has forged round her own consciousness from the moment she permitted herself to be the instrument of man's pleasure'.[55]

Yet, despite her commitment to democracy, she did not support adult suffrage. In 1907 she debated the issue with Margaret Bondfield, assistant secretary of the Shop Assistants' Union and President of the Adult Suffrage Society. Miss Bondfield pointed out that there could be no real equality if married women were not enfranchised, and that adult suffrage was the quickest way to establish real sex equality.[56] But Mrs Billington-Greig argued that the most far-reaching anomaly was the lack of votes for women, and the priority should be for women to vote on the same basis as men. Women would then be recognised immediately as the equals of men. The only way to achieve women's suffrage was gradually to educate people into the principle of sex equality through an immediate franchise. Adult suffrage would simply unite the opposition.[57]

However, the cause was about to meet its most obdurate opponent. Asquith, the new Liberal leader, was implacably hostile to giving women the vote. In October 1907 he said that women's suffrage would do 'more harm than good' and that Parliament was not elected on the basis of universal suffrage as 'children are not represented there'.[58] His long-standing opposition to votes for women was reinforced by his wife Margot's loathing for suffragist puritans; she had been severely rebuked by Mrs Fawcett for talking during a concert. Margot enjoyed offending bourgeois convention by smoking in public and talking to shock. Asquith disliked feminist puritans too; he liked to drink and found the discreet lechery of the smart set very agreeable. Lytton Strachey described him as 'a fleshy, sanguine, wine-bibbing medieval abbot of a personage – a gluttonous, lecherous, cynical old fellow'. It was fitting, therefore, that Asquith should believe that the natural sphere of women was not in the turmoil and dust of politics but in the circle of social and domestic life. After becoming Prime Minister he announced that he would bring in a reform bill widening the male franchise, with an opportunity to move an amendment on votes for women. This was dismissed by Christabel as an insult.[59] Which it certainly was.

Before Asquith became Prime Minister he remarked that he would abandon his opposition to women's suffrage if it could be proved that most women wanted the vote and that this would benefit society. In response Christabel organised a mass demonstration. On 21 June 1908 seven processions wearing the WSPU colours of white, purple and green, a crowd of an estimated 250,000, marched to Hyde Park. Asquith simply brushed this aside. Christabel concluded that peaceful agitation was useless, and militancy took off again in even more violent form.[60]

That same month suffragettes were roughed up sexually at a demonstration in Parliament Square. Following this, Mary Leigh and Edith New took a cab to Downing Street and flung two stones through the windows of No. 10.[61] 'It will be a bomb next time,' Mrs Leigh reportedly declared.[62]

The disorder increased as feelings boiled over on both sides. In October there were violent scenes in Parliament Square, witnessed by several Cabinet ministers, following which Mrs Pankhurst, Mrs Drummond and Christabel were put on trial charged with incitement to rush the House of Commons. Christabel defended herself and turned the situation into a *coup de théâtre*, calling the Chancellor of the Exchequer, Lloyd George, and the Home Secretary, Herbert Gladstone, in evidence and captivating onlookers by her manner. Max Beerbohm wrote of the scene in court: 'She is a most accomplished comedian . . . She has all the qualities an actress needs . . . Her whole body is alive with her every meaning . . . With her head merrily inclined to one side, trilling her questions to the Chancellor of the Exchequer, she was like nothing so much as a little singing-bird, born in captivity.'[63]

After trouncing the government from the dock at Bow Street, however, Christabel was jailed, along with her mother, for her third and longest sentence, from October to December 1908. When they were released, the two stood in an open landau filled with flowers drawn by four white horses along Holborn and Oxford Street. The experience of prison appeared to have inflamed Christabel's self-aggrandisement to epic proportions, for in a speech she said that the country failed to see that the Christ story was being acted out by the WSPU, albeit on a smaller and humbler scale. There was honour only in militancy. To 'women who want the vote but don't agree with our methods', she said, revolt was a 'great and glorious thing' and women who appealed for the vote without fighting for it dishonoured themselves. 'How simple it all is! Can't you understand that the government have brought these troubles down upon their own heads? We are not responsible for it – they are responsible. Do not waste your sympathy upon them, my friends. It is all their own fault. If they would give us the vote they would have no more trouble from us.'[64] The *Daily News* described it as 'a night of hero worship'.[65]

When they emerged from jail, wrote Sylvia, Mrs Pankhurst, who had realised that rendering the prison ordeal so terrible would make it a compelling weapon in the winning of the vote, was resolved to return to prison in the new year to begin this struggle; while Christabel was determined never to go to prison again.[66]

Once again, the juxtaposition of the horror of jail with the incandescence of Christabel's personality won yet more women to the cause. It was more than hero worship; Christabel became the object of a kind of quasi-religious fervour, with her face reproduced on postcards, badges and photographs issued by the WSPU. She even had a waxwork in Madame Tussaud's. Mrs Pethick-Lawrence called her the 'maiden warrior'; men found her fascinating and physically enchanting. Annie Kenney said that if all the world were on one side and Christabel on the other she would walk over to Christabel.[67]

But not all suffragists were so enamoured. Henry Nevinson, for example, wrote coolly that the appeal to the press and public of Christabel and Mrs Pankhurst lay in the fact that 'they gave a more satisfying sensation of blood, of vicarious danger . . . The more violent and dangerous the proposals for others, the more vehemently they applauded, just as Spanish spectators applaud most when a horse is disembowelled and man or bull drips blood.'[68] And Mrs Swanwick, who had been converted to the cause by the jailing of Christabel and Annie Kenney in 1905, but who had joined the NUWSS, wrote: 'She gave me the impression of fitful and impulsive ambition and of a quite ruthless love of domination. I used to find many of her speeches silly: heaven was to come down to earth, sweating to be abandoned, venereal diseases to disappear, eternal peace to reign' when women got the vote.[69]

One of the most savage dissections of the Pankhursts' tactics, however, was performed by Teresa Billington-Greig, their renegade former mainstay. With brutal directness she accused them of moral and mental duplicity in assuming a pose of martyrdom as a deliberate ploy. She revealed that they engineered the militancy and violence in order to provoke the authorities into jailing them so that they could then assume the mantle of innocent victims and arouse public anger on their behalf. 'If we had frankly and strongly stated that we had set out to make the government imprison us, that we had deliberately chosen just those lines of protest and disorder that would irritate those in authority into foolish retaliation, if we had told the truth, the very proper persons who became our champions would have spent many weary months and years in condemning us before they had finally realised the value and intention of our efforts,' she observed.

The WSPU campaign was therefore based on dishonesty, hypocrisy and cynicism. In time, wrote Mrs Billington-Greig, it became conventional and narrow. Social evils were pushed aside in favour of technical, legal and political grievances; advocacy of reforms in sexual relations was reduced to the vaguest generalities; working-class women were dropped without hesitation; 'advanced' women were even more speedily driven out or silenced. Decisions were made in private by the Pankhursts and the Pethick-Lawrences and then rubber-stamped or just announced. Public praise was diverted to bolster just this inner core. 'The arts of skilled social intrigue were employed and personal devotion was sedulously cultivated', along with methods of evasion, manipulation and exaggeration.

There grew up an admitted policy of playing purely for effect, to excite the public curiosity, to fill the treasury. Tactics were adopted which seemed to indicate that militancy would be degraded to the purposes of advertisement and the movement reduced to the level of a spectacular suffrage show . . . under the cover of this emotional condition the will of the leaders rapidly came to be substituted for the will of the members; free choice and personal liberty dwindled into insignificance; the subtle tyranny of affectional appeal showed itself as a serious danger. Women were being carried into protests and positions of danger by the misuse of their emotions; and the steady setting up of agencies of influence showed that this was becoming a deliberate plan of action.[70]

As a portrait of unscrupulousness, this could scarcely have been more damning.

The WSPU's embrace of violence left Mrs Fawcett with no alternative but to distance the NUWSS. It published protests against the WSPU's stone-throwing, window-breaking and other forms of violence, and also excluded the militant suffragists from membership of NUWSS societies. 'To put the whole matter in a sentence,' wrote Mrs Fawcett, 'we were convinced that our job was to win the hearts and minds of our countrymen to the justice of our cause, and that this could never be done by force and violence . . . We had seen force ever leading to more and more violent force in Ireland, in Russia and other places, and felt certain that our movement would be no exception to this rule.'[71] Nevertheless, Mrs Fawcett still tried to use the WSPU's tactics to serve her own ends. She deputed Lady Frances Balfour to use the 'menace' of militancy to put pressure on Herbert Gladstone, the Home Secretary. Lady Frances accordingly wrote to him: 'Militarism in various forms is such a spreading force and many of our members wish to rush us into adopting the extreme line . . . If we are to keep the whole thing constitutional among thousands of women, we must have some help.'[72] But, she said, Gladstone had no power in the Cabinet and Asquith was uninterested.[73]

The Liberal government had more things on its mind than votes for women. It was in real difficulties over its radical programme. It was challenging the veto power of the Conservative-controlled Lords; it was pushing against Tory resistance over its proposed social reforms; it was facing violent agitation for Irish Home Rule as well as independence in Ulster; and in addition, an international crisis was threatening, with a worsening balance of trade and industrial unrest.[74] And both the Tories and the Liberals feared that votes for women would deliver power to the other party. In these circumstances the government was in no mood to pay serious attention to stone-throwing, hysterical, hooligan women (as they saw them). The Liberal MP R. A. Hudson wrote in exasperation to the suffragette Evelyn Sharp in February 1907:

You want any private influence which you can command to be exerted to get the government to show favour to the woman suffrage bill. But you can't have it both ways. You antagonise a large number of our people in and out of Parliament by seeking whenever occasion offers to let in a Tory (as the only means open to you to keep out a Liberal). Having done this you think the government should grant you the highest favour known in assisting a private member's bill . . . but governments, being made up of men, are only human: very human . . . Fight our folk, or be friends with them. A blend of the two is hopeless.

You had a friendly parliament and you decided to threaten it. With the strong and sensible men in the House, this did no harm. But with the weak and foolish ones it did your case much injury. And there are many weak and foolish MPs . . . You will gain your end, but it will be in spite of the means which you have employed.[75]

In 1908 Mrs Humphry Ward started the Women's National Anti-Suffrage League, whose aims were to resist the parliamentary franchise but maintain women's representation on municipal and other bodies concerned with domestic and social affairs of community. This was a serious blow to the suffragettes, because it showed that a number of women did not want the vote, thus appearing to confirm the jibe by Asquith and others that the suffrage was desired only by a small number of unrepresentative women. The next year the Men's League for Opposing Women's Suffrage was formed, with Lords Curzon and Cromer as dominant members; and in 1910, they joined the women to form the National League for Opposing Women's Suffrage, which at one point had ninety-seven branches. Now there were new pamphlets protesting 'The Natural Right of Man to Sovereign Authority over Women' and 'Against Female Suffrage—the Unsexing of Women', which told women that if they joined the suffragettes they would become 'thinner, dark featured, lank and dry'.[76]

Supporters also tried to discredit the suffragists by a dirty-tricks campaign. There were hints that proposals being made at suffrage meetings were licentious and immoral, and claims that suffragists of all shades were welcoming the appearance of an obscure little periodical, The Freewoman, which advocated free love. Mrs Fawcett, who had gone to huge lengths to distance suffragism from any sexual scandal, said when she saw The Freewoman she thought it 'objectionable and mischievous, and tore it up into small pieces'. In another smear, an MP asked the Home Office to prevent the NUWSS selling an 'obscene' pamphlet by a woman doctor on VD and prostitution. The Home Office had no powers to act in this way, but the MP kept repeating the question, thus making sure that the imputation of loose morals sank in.[77]

Mrs Fawcett understandably was furious at such tactics, which were indeed a very underhand blow. But it was no surprise that sexual suggestiveness was lurking so near the surface of the struggle over women's suffrage. For the sexual relationship between men and women was the ever-present subtext of the fight for the vote, and was indeed to surface with unprecedented ferocity as the campaign neared its climax.

13

THE DAMNATION OF MEN

Moralists were now setting the pace for sexual politics. What ran like a thread through the movement and united both constitutionalists and militants was the belief that the vote was a tool with which to reconstruct society in accordance with female values. Opponents of women's suffrage who feared the destruction of femininity had missed the point. Once women penetrated the male citadel, the values they brought with them of the home, of motherhood and of femininity would civilise the brutal and animalistic public world of men.

The constitutional suffragists did not present this in a confrontational or man-hating way. They wanted merely to open up the public sphere to equal representation by women in order to bring to it qualities which it lacked through their absence. Mrs Fawcett wrote in 1905: 'I advocate the extension of the franchise to women because I wish to strengthen true womanliness in woman, and because I want to see the womanly and domestic side of things weigh more and count for more in all public concerns.' The claim to the suffrage, she said, was based not on similarities but on the differences between men and women. Indeed, she stood the separate spheres argument on its head. 'If men and women were exactly alike, the representation of men would represent us; but not being alike, that wherein we differ is unrepresented under the present system.'[1]

However, it was implicit in what she wrote that the values that women would bring to the public sphere were superior to men's. Women had a higher standard of virtue, illustrated by the fact that fewer women than men were tried for serious criminal offences. Womanliness, love for children, care for the sick, gentleness, self-control, obedience to love and duty were all terribly wanted in politics. She wanted women to devote themselves to the law as it affected children, as well as 'to the example set by the higher classes to the lower, to the housing of the poor, to the provision of open spaces and recreation grounds, to the temperance question, to laws relating to health and morals, and the bearing of all these things and many others upon the home, and upon the virtue and purity of the domestic life of our nation'.[2]

The militant suffragettes took this assumption of moral superiority much further. Instead of arguing for female values to share the public platform with male virtues, the militants attacked men, masculinity and marriage as the fount of society's ills and declared that only women could raise humankind from the degradation to which men had brought it. And the proof of men's primitive savagery, the issue that had to be challenged and tamed and indeed transfigured by female control to which the vote was the key, was male sexuality. It was through sexual relations that men held women in their power both in and out of marriage, wounding and abusing them and keeping them enslaved.

The antidote was sexual separatism: celibacy, chastity and lesbianism. The principal battleground on which women would go to war against male carnality and the sexual double standard was invariably prostitution. By the turn of the century the suffrage movement had become indelibly stamped with the motif of sexual purity. And the moment at which it had turned into an overt crusade against vice had occurred some twenty years previously.

The late nineteenth century had seen a massive campaign to transform male sexual behaviour and protect women from male sexuality.

Against a background of worsening economic conditions, this campaign coincided with a new panic in the 1880s over the urban poor. Eighteen eighty-three saw the publication of *The Bitter Cry of Outcast London* by the Congregationalist minister Andrew Mearns, which exposed a vast mass of moral corruption and godlessness. In 1884 the *Report of the Royal Commission on the Housing of the Working Classes* was an extensive moral survey which connected overcrowding with incest and showed how immorality was spreading to ensnare the upright.[3]

Josephine Butler and her Ladies' National Association had been campaigning against the Contagious Diseases Acts throughout the 1870s, and in the early 1880s their pressure had finally paid off. The first breakthrough was made in 1883, when Parliament was finally persuaded to suspend operation of the Acts. On the night of the division Mrs Butler and her co-workers kept up a continuous prayer meeting in a room off Palace Yard, beside the Houses of Parliament. Even so, she had achieved only a partial triumph. The police may have been withdrawn and the compulsory examination of women been suspended. But the Acts were still on the statute book. Despite the fact that the family of the Prime Minister, William Gladstone, supported repeal, he had more important things on his mind, such as the accelerating crisis over Irish Home Rule. Many Liberals regarded the repealers as cranks and the issue as a fad.[4]

The repeal campaign was overtaken, however, by a more sensational issue. One of the repealers, Alfred Dyer, had stumbled across the scandal of 'white slavery'. Dyer was a puritan fanatic with an obsessive fear of sex. In 1879 he had been told about a young English girl who was forcibly confined in a licenced brothel in Brussels and who was contemplating suicide. He then discovered a significant trade in gullible girls who, through their prudishness and ignorance of the world, were easy prey to commercial sexual predators. He travelled to Brussels to rescue such girls but failed, and on his return formed a campaigning committee in London. An inflamed Josephine Butler wrote an emotional attack on white slavery and child prostitution, which was published in *The Shield*

in 1880 and which claimed that children aged between twelve and fourteen were being immured in Belgian brothels. As a result the Brussels
brothel owners were investigated and prosecuted.[5]

This was thought to be the tip of a monstrous iceberg of male paedophilia
and sadistic sexual violence. Virginity, particularly pre-pubescent virginity,
was the basic commodity being traded. West End club men would pay up
to twenty-five guineas for a teenage virgin and up to a hundred for
raping or tormenting a child. One house in ultra-fashionable Half Moon
Street, off Piccadilly, specialised in the flagellation and rape of children
imprisoned in soundproofed rooms. Girls in strait-jackets were strapped
to beds or held down. Children aged between ten and sixteen were
chloroformed, drugged or gagged. Girls often died from shock or suffo-
cation. Children were bought from drunken parents or kidnapped;
babies were kept until they were old enough to practise fellatio; at the age
of four or five, they were penetrated and discarded. Older girls were
lured by procuresses dressed as nuns, charity workers, or charwomen
recommending good positions.[6]

The extent of such baroque practices is a subject of dispute. Some his-
torians have claimed that there was only a small handful of such cases
and that the number was exaggerated by hysterical or unscrupulous
puritan campaigners. Nevertheless, there was clearly enough of a trade to
cause alarm and fury, not least because the men involved included some
of the most powerful in the land. One notorious case illustrated the
point. Mrs Mary Jeffries was a brothel keeper who kept houses specialising in flagellation, sodomising under-age girls, and acting as an entrepôt
for the continental trade in virgins. Magistrates and senior police officers
refused to prosecute her because of her long list of distinguished clients.
When a single-minded policeman, Jeremiah Minahan, was blocked in his
attempt to prosecute her, he resigned and took his dossier to Alfred Dyer.
By March 1885, campaigners had enough evidence to mount a prosecution and a trial took place. But the Crown took over the prosecution, and
to protect the powerful men who had been using Mrs Jeffries's services,
they persuaded her to plead guilty, for which she was merely fined and
bound over to keep the peace.[7]

The press roundly attacked the sentence. Nevertheless, attempts in Parliament to raise the age of consent and make procuring for foreign brothels an offence were blocked. The temperature among anti-vice campaigners rose. To force the government's hand, they sought the help of W. T. Stead, editor of the *Pall Mall Gazette*.

Stead was a crusading, scandal-mongering editor with a deep sense of social injustice. He was, however, initially reluctant to get involved until he realised that what he was being told was true. The head of the CID, Sir Howard Vincent, confirmed to him that thirteen-year-old girls were indeed being sold into prostitution by their parents. 'It is enough to rouse Hell,' Stead burst out, to which Sir Howard replied: 'It does not even rouse the neighbours.' Stead riposted: 'If I can prove that this thing can be done for me, it will not raise the neighbours but it will raise all England.'[8]

His initial wariness turned to incandescent fury when the National Society for the Prevention of Cruelty to Children showed him two children who had recently been picked up by its inspectors. One, aged seven, had been abducted and raped in a fashionable brothel; the other, aged four and a half, had been lured into a brothel and raped twelve times in succession. When the child became hysterical at Stead's approach, he broke down crying: 'I'll turn my paper into a tub! I'll turn stump orator! I'll damn and damn and damn!'[9]

And he did. He decided that the only way to prove what was happening was to turn agent provocateur and do the deed himself. Josephine Butler found an ideal person for the plot, a reformed brothel keeper called Rebecca Jarrett. She was to act as a procurer and purchase a thirteen-year-old girl, Eliza Armstrong, from her parents for £5. Rebecca Jarrett took Eliza to a house in Poland Street where she undressed her, tried (unsuccessfully) to chloroform her and put her to bed. Stead then entered the room, Rebecca Jarrett 'rescued' Eliza and everyone then went to a Harley Street doctor who certified the child was still a virgin.

On 6 July 1885 Stead duly reported this escapade in a series of four articles entitled 'The Maiden Tribute of Modern Babylon'. Using highly sensational and inflammatory language, he plunged the face of respectable Victorian Britain into the moral sewer of its society: 'London's lust annually uses up many thousands of women . . . If the daughters of the people must be served up as dainty morsels to the passions of the rich, let them at least attain an age when they can understand the nature of the sacrifice which they are asked to make. And if we are to cast maidens . . . nightly into the jaws of vice, let us at least see to it that they consent to their own immolation, and are not unwilling sacrifices procured by force or fraud.'[10]

The articles caused a sensation, not least because Stead, under threat of prosecution for the abduction of Eliza, then threatened to name prominent men involved in the child prostitution trade. To stop him, the government rushed into law the Criminal Law Amendment Act, which raised the age of consent to sixteen and outlawed procuring for foreign brothels. It was a singular triumph; this Act had been blocked by the government for several years. But Stead and Rebecca Jarrett went to prison.[11]

The Contagious Diseases Acts were finally repealed the following year, and then almost by chance. The repealer James Stansfield MP had been earmarked by Gladstone as a likely replacement for Joseph Chamberlain if he were to resign in opposition to Irish Home Rule. Stansfield, however, refused promotion unless the Contagious Diseases Acts were repealed, which duly occurred. The Acts were brought to an end, therefore, as a result of a parliamentary manoeuvre unrelated to the campaign. Nevertheless, the climate had shifted profoundly. The Maiden Tribute affair and the subsequent change in the law marked a decisive breakthrough in the struggle to regulate sexual morality.[12] The purity campaigners were now on a roll. From this point on, puritanism was to dominate late-Victorian and Edwardian politics – and the campaign for women's suffrage.

It is hard to overestimate the importance of Mrs Butler's crusade to the emerging women's movement. Mrs Fawcett, who had thrown herself into Stead's defence, called Mrs Butler 'one of the very great people of the world'.[13] Her portrait was regularly sold at suffrage meetings. The campaign against the Acts provided later feminists with important lessons in militancy and feminist political leadership. Edwardian suffragettes took note of the militant by-election campaign tactics, the effectiveness of the repealers' extra-parliamentary activities and the need for feminists to operate outside both political parties.[14]

But Mrs Butler did far more than teach a tactical lesson. To later feminists the Ladies' National Association embodied the ideals of sisterhood and female solidarity – and the anti-vice campaign demonstrated in the most lurid of terms the iniquity of male sexuality. As a result it ingrained upon feminist consciousness the theme of sexual wrongs perpetrated by men upon women, and committed later feminists to redouble the attack on the sexual double standard and male vice. Mrs Fawcett, that most circumspect conservative, who had taken such care to distance the suffrage campaign from the controversy over prostitution, nevertheless attacked the sexual double standard and the conspiracy of silence over it. In 1885 she said of the argument that legislation was an inappropriate antidote to sexual immorality: 'We are told ad nauseam "that we cannot make men moral by Act of Parliament". But the Criminal Law Amendment Bill was an attempt, not to make men moral by Act of Parliament but to protect the young from becoming victims of their immorality.'[15]

The purity movement was, however, split within itself. Buoyed by the success of the anti-vice campaign, the National Vigilance Association (NVA) was started in 1885. This was a divisive organisation. Rather than a broad alliance against upper-class vice and the economic forces behind prostitution, it focused instead on pornography, popular entertainments and the need for laws to clear the streets of visible vice. In 1894 Mrs Laura Ormiston Chant, backed by the British Temperance Association, tried to shut down the Empire music hall in London on the grounds of indecency on the stage and disorderliness in the auditorium. As a result of such deeply unpopular activities, working-class support for the purity campaigners diminished, the Fabians withdrew their backing – and so, crucially, did Josephine Butler.

Mrs Butler's position confused many who assumed she would take a hard line against the practice of vice. This was to misunderstand her. Her instincts were not so much moralising as maternal. Her aim was to protect vulnerable women from exploitation and harm and to reform them, but she did not want to suppress prostitution and close down the brothels. She was above all a defender of liberty, and of the rights of prostitutes and of women generally. Moreover, since she had herself founded in 1871 the National Vigilance Association for the Defence of Personal Rights, she was furious when the first part of this name was filched by the puritans to describe completely different aims.[16] When the pious ladies of Winchester asked her to sign their Vigilance Society petition to close down a theatre that was notorious as the haunt of prostitutes, Mrs Butler astonished them by refusing. She told them: 'My principle has always been to let individuals alone, not to pursue them with any punishment, nor drive them out of any place so long as they behave decently, but to attack organised prostitution, that is when a third party, actuated by the desire of making money, sets up a house in which women are sold to men.'[17]

Most of the anti-vice movement, however, was repressive in character. Reformers were trying to curb prostitution itself, eliminate child sexual abuse, make men chaste and improve common morality. Purity workers and London councils caused many brothels to close, which forced more prostitutes into the open and the number of women charged with public indecency to rise dramatically.[18] In 1901 the NVA and the Watch Committee of the London Public Morality Council, backed by Westminster City Council, recommended to the Home Secretary the vigorous clearing of prostitutes from the streets. This Watch Committee included feminists such as Lady Isobel Somerset, President of the British Women's Temperance Association, Mrs Fawcett and Salvationist Mrs Florence Booth.

The Personal Rights Association, as Mrs Butler's organisation had been forced to rename itself, called such activists 'vigilant stampers upon the feeble'. One of the most pilloried of these 'stampers' was Laura Ormiston Chant. Mrs Chant was a prominent character who was involved in the campaign for women's suffrage, the temperance movement and Liberal politics. She campaigned against indecent music halls, and wanted the regulation and censoring of all public 'temptations to vice', with inspectors of both sexes supervising the moral conduct of streets and public places. *Punch* lampooned her in a cartoon as Mrs Prowlina Pry.[19] All this helped reinforce in the public mind the image of suffrage campaigners as joyless, interfering puritans who wanted to shut down popular pleasure.

Ellice Hopkins was another leading example of this moralising feminism. Born in 1836, she idolised her father, a Cambridge maths tutor, who trained her mind. She showed an early aptitude for preaching Christianity to poor working men, on one occasion reducing four hundred rough working men to sobbing like children over their sins as she talked to them about their problems. Her father's physical and mental breakdown led to a breakdown in her own health and she was always frail, although witty, a powerful speaker and with a gift for writing. After her father's death, she and her widowed mother settled in Brighton, where she first came into contact with 'fallen' girls.[20]

In 1872 she came under the unhealthy influence of someone who was to change her life. Dr James Hinton laid upon her an obligation to rouse the world to a hatred of immorality. Hinton's mind was unhinged by a passionate desire to redeem women; he wept heartbrokenly over the degradation of womanhood that he had seen. He himself said: 'If I am remembered at all, I want to be remembered as a man who went mad over the wrongs of women.' Only the promise by Ellice Hopkins to devote herself to fighting it assuaged his anguish. He wanted her to rouse educated women and, through them, their husbands and sons to their duty to fight this social evil. Pain, he wrote, was good when it was willingly borne for others' sake. His call to martyrdom set Ellice Hopkins single-mindedly on a life of self-sacrifice in which she set aside everything, including her own deep desire for domestic happiness, to fight immorality.[21]

She founded a network of Associations for the Care of Friendless Girls and then the White Cross League, which aimed to strike at the root of impurity by reforming men, educating them to treat women with respect, to stop indecent language and coarseness, and to uphold purity for men and women.[22] She fell out badly with Josephine Butler over her general approach, the fact that she worked so closely with the police in cracking down on prostitution, and over the specific issue of the children of prostitutes. Ellice Hopkins passionately supported the Industrial Schools Amendment Act, which said that children who lived with a prostitute should be removed to an industrial school. She recounted horrific tales of prostitutes' children who were starved, neglected, beaten or sold for defloration.[23] To Mrs Butler, however, removing a child from its mother was simply anathema. Her Vigilance Association for the Defence of Personal Rights counter-attacked, saying: 'Miss Hopkins . . . is at present . . . crying for the wholesale kidnapping of little girls who may not have perfect domestic surroundings and their consignment to large prison schools.'[24]

Whatever the differences between the anti-vice campaigners, the fact was that their success in changing the law marked a watershed in the women's movement and the fight for the suffrage. As one writer put it, after the repeal of the Contagious Diseases Acts the women's cause became 'a revolt that is puritan and not bohemian. It is an uprising against the tyranny of organised intemperance, impurity, mammonism and selfish motives.'[25] And the principal target of the purity crusade was the bestial sexuality of men, demonstrated by the phenomenon of prostitution. Prostitution was thought to humiliate all women since 'the man who enslaves one woman implicitly tells every other woman that she is entitled only by accident, not by right, to be spared the same degradation'.[26] So men were judged guilty of the moral ruin of women and of buying 'the sacrifice of bodily honour and spiritual life from others . . . with them lies the responsibility for the social degradation of prostitutes'.[27]

The change of emphasis was critical. Women had always been regarded as the pivot of sexual virtue. Those who were chaste wives and mothers were regarded as saintly guardians of the domestic shrine; those who had loose morals were viewed as the source of corruption of men. But now feminists were demanding to have it both ways. Women were still the fount of domestic virtue; but if they 'fell' into prostitution, it was because they had been corrupted by men. It was men who were responsible for prostitution, by creating the demand that resulted in the supply. Women were the active promoters of sexual virtue; but men were the active promoters of sexual vice.

This damnation of a whole sex caused some progressive men to don a hair shirt over the double standard of which they stood accused. The Bishop of Durham urged: 'We must strike at the root of the evil . . . Not until it is generally recognised that the man who has wrought a woman's degradation is at least as great an offender against society as the man who has robbed a till or the man who has forged a cheque . . . So long as the violation of purity is condoned in the one sex and visited with shame in the other, our unrighteousness and unmanliness must continue to work out its own terrible retribution.'[28]

But the feminists went much further. Prostitution was no longer the Manichean alternative to the purity of marriage. For some, both marriage and prostitution were about the purchase of women, and the remedy was the economic independence of women and the transformation of marriage.

Mrs Mona Caird was a key exponent of this view. A journalist and writer, freethinker, anti-vivisectionist and member of the Personal Rights Association, influenced by Mill, Shelley, Herbert Spencer, T. H. Huxley and Darwin, she was rooted in radical individualism. The writer Olive Schreiner described her as 'a narrow, one-sided woman, violently prejudiced against men'.[29] To Mrs Caird, marriage and prostitution were 'the two sides of the same shield'. She wanted a new form of marriage based on women's self-possession, economic independence, equalisation of parental rights and divorce law reform.[30]

There was still considerable resentment over divorce and custody laws. True, as the century wore on the law had slowly been reformed. The Infant Custody Acts 1873 and 1886 gave mothers certain rights to appeal for custody; the Married Women's Property Acts 1870 and 1882 gave married women the same rights over property as unmarried women by retaining their own wages, possessions and capital; the Matrimonial Causes Act 1878 enabled women beaten by husbands – it was extended in 1886 to include desertion – to obtain separation orders with custody of children under ten. But the detested coverture – the assumption that women were under the legal protection of husbands and had no legal personality of their own – remained.

Since 1857 divorce had been available in England and Wales to a husband on the grounds of his wife's adultery, but to a wife on the grounds of her husband's adultery only if this was accompanied by cruelty, desertion or bestiality. So husbands were free to engage in extramarital sex, a double standard which enraged feminists. But not all wanted easier divorce as they feared this would prove a bad option for economically dependent wives. A few wanted divorce by mutual consent but others, like Mrs Fawcett, wanted to retain the concept of fault. All wanted to equalise the divorce law to raise moral standards through raising the status of women. They wanted the relationship between the sexes to be based on love, sympathy, companionship, mutual attraction, monogamy, fidelity, permanence, mutual responsibility, equality and female autonomy.[31] They did not think marriage currently fitted the bill.

In 1911 Olive Schreiner, in *Woman and Labour*, portrayed man as the 'lofty theorist' standing before the drawing-room fire, holding forth about women as divine child-bearers while expecting his tea to be made and his boots cleaned by some woman acting as an 'elderly house drudge'.[32] There was much talk about new forms of marriage: communes, trial marriage and, from Cicely Hamilton, about bargaining within marriage and wages for housework. Most advanced marriage manuals talked of 'marriage on approval' and advocated not only that women should sow their wild oats, just like men, but that infidelity in marriage should be treated in a 'philosophical spirit' and that married women should deliberately foster male friendships. The husband should be packed off to his club to let his wife 'go out on her own account and do a little dinner and theatre with a discreet admirer'.[33] Nevertheless, despite this blind eye to female misdemeanours, husbands were asked to take their own marital roles more seriously.[34]

Mrs Caird, however, was vindictive in her dislike of marriage and her desire to undermine it. For her, even happy marriages were wholly destructive and joyless. Each spouse, she wrote, had to suppress his or her own wants, to go to the theatre or to travel, in deference to the feelings of the other, 'who becomes a sort of amiable vampire draining the blood from its willing prey. This process of mutual injury is carried on in most marriages that are called happy.' Indeed, it followed that happy marriages of this kind were even more disastrous than unhappy ones as they stunted the spouses' potential. If a man and woman were united, she thought, no bonds should be necessary to hold them together, and when affection and friendship between them ceased the tie became intolerable.

Disobedience was a woman's first duty, and smiles, wiles and womanly devices were the power of a favourite slave. Anticipating the situation that was to develop nearly a century later, she wrote: 'In a still distant condition of society, it is probable that unions may exist outside the law but inside society; men and women caring only for the real bond between them, and treating as of quite minor importance the artificial or legal tie. So that gradually the state may come to have very little part in marriage. The tendency will be gradually to substitute internal for external law; social sentiment for anti-social licence.' It never seemed to occur to her that wives and mothers might be deserted; to her, independence from men was all. Dependence was the curse of marriages, homes and children. She wanted women to be independent of men; and yet she still added: 'It is easy indeed to see the peril to the well-being of the race that lies in the labour of women outside the home – that peril can scarcely be exaggerated.'[35]

Indeed, other feminists were also caught up in the same contradiction. They wanted women to be independent of men; and yet they could not reconcile such economic independence with the demands of motherhood. Having children was then, just like now, the point at which feminist individualism became impaled on a dilemma it could not resolve. Helena Swanwick wrote of the prospect of working mothers: 'Such proposals depend on the evolution of a race of superwomen unlike any the world has seen, and no one has demonstrated, or even suggested, how such a race is to be formed.' She agreed that women's work was less efficient than men's because of sickness or the expectation of matrimony which made their work less constant; and also – remarkably – that they had other sources of income (prostitution) and so took lower pay than men. And yet, she said, women were in economic slavery, and the trades and professions should be opened up to women.[36]

The issue driving the need for female independence was the behaviour of men. Whatever the contradictions and impossible burdens of economic independence for women, feminists believed that women had to be liberated from men who were perceived as akin to slave owners. It was safer for a working woman, wrote Helena Swanwick, not to be married to the man she lived with. A man had power over his wife since she had no money of her own unless she had earned it. He could enforce marital rights and insist on his wife's faithfulness while enjoying his own licence. He could refuse to maintain her with no redress, forcing her to become a pauper in order to qualify for maintenance; if she received maintenance, the recovery of such money was difficult and if he absconded no one need find him unless the woman again became a pauper. He could prevent his wife from earning and could keep any money that didn't go on housekeeping. He could bring up his children as he pleased, and control them even after his death. He could leave his wife and children destitute in his will. 'Flogging a wife till she is covered with bruises, driving her out of the house on a winter's night in her nightgown, kicking her when she is with child and other assaults too abominable to mention have been held insufficient to entitle the wife to a separation,' she wrote.[37]

All this was true, in principle; and some men undoubtedly behaved atrociously to their wives. But as Helena Swanwick also observed, the vast majority did not. Most men, she conceded, did not do what the law allowed them to do but were kind, toiling and fond husbands and fathers.

But marriage was charged with doing even more grievous damage to a woman's very sense of her self. The militant spinster Cicely Hamilton made the demonstrably untrue claim that married women were actually

forbidden to cultivate their intellects. 'For her the eleventh command-
ment was an insult – "Thou shalt not think"; and the most iniquitous
condition of her marriage bargain this – that her husband, from the
height of his self-satisfaction, should be permitted to esteem her a fool,'
she wrote. The insistent and deliberate stunting of women's intellectual
growth was proof of their servile position in the household. Women
were debarred not just from material possessions but from things of the
spirit. Miss Hamilton wrote of a husband's attitude to his wife: 'His use
for her was the gratification of his own desire, the menial services she
rendered without payment; his pleasure was in her flesh, not her spirit;
therefore the things of the spirit were not for her.'[38] Having made such
lurid claims, she then promptly contradicted herself, making exceptions
for professional women, whose intellects, she conceded, were not
swamped, and for 'sharp' working women who managed the household
and its finances. Her guns were trained instead on 'the women of the
"comfortable" class, with narrow duties and a few petty responsibilities',
who conformed to the servile imitation of manners and morals, sank into
the pattern of a nonentity or busybody and did her best to justify her husband's contempt for her mental capacity.[39] With this caricature of a
particular type of woman, both the institution of marriage and the male
sex were damned.

The assault on men was fundamental. It was based on a particular
anthropological view of the history of sexual relations, a view which
was influential in the Victorian and Edwardian era but which was later
to be shown to be false. This held that, in the earliest period of human
history, women had ruled over men, but subsequently their place had
been usurped by men, who had then held them in slavery through marriage. This was a theory reproduced by Frederick Engels in 1884 in his
Origin of the Family, Private Property and the State, a text which was
to be profoundly influential on feminism. Engels described 'the world
historic defeat of the female sex' deriving from the development of private property. He wrote: 'The overthrow of the mother-right was the
world historical defeat of the female sex. The man took command in the
home also; the woman was degraded and reduced to servitude; she

became the slave of his lust and a mere instrument for the production of children.'[40]

Engels was echoing the theories of nineteenth-century Darwinian evolutionary anthropologists such as Johann Jacob Bachofen and Lewis Morgan, who were later derided as 'armchair theorists' because they knew so little. Their theories indeed were merely pseudo-scientific extrapolations backwards into history of the predominant Victorian belief in separate spheres and innate female characteristics. They claimed, for example, that in primitive society it was women who were the repositories of culture, and that there had been a stage of matriarchy which led society out of barbarism. At the darkest stage of human existence, they said, mother-child love was the only light in the moral darkness. Women were more altruistic than men because of their maternal instincts and more virtuous because of their weaker sex drives, all of which gave women a special mission to rescue society from destruction, competitiveness and violence created by men upholding unchallenged dominance.[41]

Their theories – challenged, in fact, by Darwin – were later to be disproved by anthropologists who established that women had never had power over men. Even in most matrilineal societies, male relatives had always controlled economic and family decisions, a fact that has been acknowledged today even by some leading feminists.[42] But in the nineteenth century, a view of human history which gave a scientific and evolutionary gloss to a deeply entrenched view of female virtue and moral superiority was, of course, deeply persuasive. What was more, it provided feminists with 'proof' not just that men were an intrinsic danger to women but that female slavery through the institution of marriage amounted to a historic wrong and an inversion of the natural order.

This provided incendiary ammunition for an extreme, man-hating agenda to develop within the nineteenth-century women's movement. In essays published in the *Westminster Review* in 1888 and 1894, Mona Caird wrote that their purpose was to prove that the greatest evils of modern society had their origin thousands of years previously in the 'dominant abuse of patriarchal life: the custom of woman purchase', which was the foundation of marriage and was holding back the development of the race. Primitive cultures, she asserted, never saw women as inferior; 'the notion is probably confined to those communities that we call civilised'.[43]

She had some difficulty reconciling her view that woman had been 'the pioneer of all civilisation' with the claim that women had somehow become subservient to men, and that female values were a kind of male appendage. Notwithstanding some heroically tortuous logic, she concluded that the position of English women was comparable with the situation in Mongolia, where prisoners starved to death in cages in the market place. 'In reading the history of the past, and the literature of our own day, it is difficult to avoid seeing in that Mongolian market place a symbol of our own society, with its iron cage wherein women are held in bondage, suffering moral starvation, while the thoughtless gather round to taunt their lingering misery.' This apparently justified a vindictive attitude towards men. 'We are now reaping the consequences,' she wrote, 'of the wrong that has been done to our mothers and grandmothers, and the more closely one studies sociology and observes life, the more obvious it becomes that man is called upon to suffer, inch by inch and pang by pang, for that which he has inflicted.'[44]

This man-hating agenda provided an argument in favour of spinsterdom, or the separation of women from men altogether. It was a neat inversion of the popular derision and hostility of the times that was expressed against unmarried women. 'So far as I can see,' Cicely Hamilton wrote,

the average husband, actual or to be, still entertains the conviction that the word helpmeet, being interpreted, means second fiddle; and acts in accordance with that honest conviction. He still feels that it is the duty of his wife to respect him on the ground that he did not happen to be born a woman; he still considers it desirable that the mother of his children should not be over wise. He still clings to the idea that a wife is a creature to be patronised; with kindness, of course – patted on the head – but still patronised . . . And it is obvious that human beings, men or women, who consider themselves fit subjects for patronage are not those who make for progress or any very great power of improving their own status.

By contrast, as spinsters improved their own position they awakened the envy of married women, steadily destroying the prestige of marriage.[45]Spinsters were the backbone of the turn-of-the-century women's movement. By 1913 sixty-three per cent of the Women's Social and Political Union were spinsters and many of the rest were widowed. Bessie Rayner Parkes thought the economic position of single women was the material basis for the emerging woman's movement. Frances Power Cobbe said that celibacy was preferable to marriage and male domination. The spinster, she enthused, was 'an exceedingly cheery personage, running about untrammelled by husband or children; now visiting her relatives' country houses, now taking her month in town, now off to a favourite *pension* on Lake Geneva, now scaling Vesuvius or the Pyramids.'

Hatred of spinsters, however, was widespread and was a significant influence behind the anti-suffrage movement. As more single women were seen in the public arena, feminism came to seem more of a threat, particularly since women were being urged to breed healthy children to run the Empire. But the hostility was not confined to the enemies of women's suffrage. A growing number of feminists agreed that chastity was harmful to women. One, on entering a railway carriage, remarked of the passengers that 'the face of the mated woman bears a look of quiet rest, in contrast to the . . . unmated woman who glances inquiringly at each male figure . . . with a dull sense of despair.'[46]

Even men who supported women's rights attacked spinsters. Walter Gallichan, who was married to the feminist Mrs Gasquoigne-Hartley, wrote: 'Among the great army of sex, the regiment of aggressively man-hating women is full of strength, and signs of the times show that it is steadily being recruited. On its banner is emblazoned "Woe to Man" and its call to arms is shrill and loud. These are the women who are "independent of men", a motley host, pathetic in their defiance of the first principle of Nature, but of no serious account in the biological or social sense.'[47] Mrs Gasquoigne-Hartley herself wrote that the true feminist motto should be 'Free *with* Man!' and gave a lecture saying woman should merge herself with man and that the assertion of individuality was not of supreme importance to women.[48]

Many spinsters were what we would consider today to be lesbians. This was not recognised at the time, since sexuality, whose function was identified as reproductive, was assumed to be heterosexual. Same-sex relationships only became transgressive around the turn of the century, when the understanding of sexuality itself shifted. But in the nineteenth century, same-sex relationships between women were thought normal. Many leading feminists had close emotional ties with other women, including passionate declarations, explicit pronouncements of love in letters and diaries, and maybe kissing, fondling and sharing a bed. Maria Sharpe's friend Lina Eckenstein, for example, wrote to her like a lover and when Maria married Karl Pearson, Lina wrote to him of 'my darling who is now yours'.[49]

The dislike of the spinster was undoubtedly linked to her ostensible repudiation of sexual relations with men. As Cicely Hamilton observed: 'That active and savage dislike must have had its origin in the consciousness that the perpetual virgin was a witness, however reluctantly, to the unpalatable fact that sexual intercourse was not for every woman an absolute necessity . . .'[50]

From holding that sexual relations were not an absolute necessity for women, feminists then made the leap to the proposition that sexual relations should not be practised by men. Sexuality was an expression of the bestial and lowering side of human nature which had to be suppressed for the benefit of all. This meant that men had to restrain themselves, since it was male sexuality that was animalistic and dehumanising; even worse, that it threatened the very existence of the nation and the race.

The view was commonly held that the male sexual instinct was far greater than the female. Women were defined by their sexual function in that their reproductive system was thought to be the seat of innumerable psychological and emotional characteristics. But their sexuality was in turn thought to be defined by its reproductive purpose; its only expression was in motherhood. The sexual drive and the fulfilment of sexual pleasure were thought to be the prerogative of men. However, from the late 1880s the view of female sexuality started to change. In a celebrated case in 1886 a Liverpool gynaecologist, Francis Imlach, was sued by his patient, Mrs Casey, for having removed her inflamed ovaries and Fallopian tubes. A famous surgeon, Robert Lawson Tait, gave evidence at the trial that ovariotomy did not affect a woman's sexual feelings. Of seven husbands married to women without ovaries, he said, two reported a 'distinctly aggressive' sexual appetite in their wives, three said it was 'perfectly satisfactory' or 'well-developed', two said it was 'satisfactory' and only one reported little desire for intercourse. During discussion of Tait's paper one gynaecologist suggested that women might simulate orgasms out of a natural desire to retain the affections of their husbands.[51]

Not only did this show that female sexuality was independent of the reproductive organs; it confirmed the fact that, in the nineteenth century, female sexual pleasure was extremely important to both women and their husbands. For the feminist pioneer Dr Elizabeth Blackwell it was essential to correct the false assumption behind the sexual double standard that the sexual instinct was so much stronger in men than in women that restraint and continence were impossible. She wrote: 'The radical physiological error, which underlies ordinary thought and action in relation to the evils of sex, is the very grave error that men are much more powerfully swayed by this instinct of sex than are women. From this radical error are drawn the false deductions that men are less able to resist that instinct; that they are more injured by abstinence from its satisfaction; and that they require a licence in action which forbids the laying down of the same moral law for men and women.'[52]

This 'licence in action' lay behind Dr Blackwell's argument that it was men who created the demand for prostitution. It was only if men restrained themselves, therefore, that this evil would be tackled. The truth that women should spread was 'the necessity that every man should

be chaste. This is the truth so long unrecognised, but at last discovered as
the solution of the great social problem. Without male chastity, female
chastity is impossible.'[53]

Sexual continence, in the form of both chastity and celibacy, was now
a dominant motif of the women's crusade. The perception that sexuality
was the mark of the beast reflected a view that was absolutely central to
the unshakeable liberal belief in human progress that had been the defining characteristic of Western thinking since the Enlightenment. It had
surfaced in the thinking of Mary Wollstonecraft and William Godwin; it
had also been echoed by John Stuart Mill, who believed that the force of
civilisation and a mark of progress would be the diminution of sexuality.
'I think it most probable,' Mill had written in 1870,

> that this particular passion will become with men, as it is already with
> a large number of women, completely under the control of the reason.
> It has become so with women because its becoming so has been the
> condition upon which women hoped to obtain the strongest love and
> admiration of men. The gratification of this passion in its highest form,
> therefore, has been, with women, conditional upon their restraining it
> in its lowest. It has not yet been tried what the same conditions will do
> for men. I believe that they will do all that we wish, nor am I alone in
> thinking that men are by nature capable of as thorough a control over
> these passions as women are. I have known eminent medical men, and
> lawyers of logical kind, of the same opinion.[54]

Sexual restraint was now seen as a precondition of progress. Sexual
abstinence outside marriage and temperance inside now became the goal
of feminist reformers. Patrick Geddes and J. Arthur Thompson, authors
of an influential book about sexuality, argued:

> It seems to us, however, essential to recognise that the ideal to be
> sought after is not merely a controlled rate of increase but regulated
> married lives . . . We would urge, in fact, the necessity of an ethical
> rather than of a mechanical 'prudence after marriage' of a temperance

recognised to be as binding on husband and wife as chastity on the
unmarried . . . Just as we would protest against the dictum of false
physicians who preach indulgence rather than restraint, so we must
protest against regarding artificial means of preventing fertilisation as
adequate solutions of sexual responsibility. After all, the solution is primarily one of temperance. It is no new or unattainable ideal to retain,
throughout married life, a large measure of that self-control which
must always form the organic basis of the enthusiasm and idealism of
lovers.[55]

Some feminists argued that sexual intercourse should take place only in
order to procreate. Elizabeth Wolstenholme Elmy, the veteran suffragist
and sexual radical who had been forced to marry when she became pregnant, argued that men had misused women throughout history by
'positive physical oppression and excess'. Women had been reduced by
men's obsession with physical love. The aim should be instead to promote sexual self-control and free women from the 'degradation of her
temple to solely animal uses' so that she could take full part in the areas
arrogated to man.[56]

Mrs Wolstenholme Elmy saw a continuity between prostitution and
the sexual slavery of marriage. She wrote in 1897 that the Contagious
Diseases Acts 'tend to intensify in the minds of men the horrible notion
that woman is merely an appendage to man for the purpose of the gratification of his basest sensuality'.[57] But in her attribution to men of all the
ills of womanhood, she also believed that menstruation was the result of
men's sexual abuse of women. 'Revolting was the shock to the writer,'
she recalled, 'coming, some years ago, with unprejudiced and ingenuous
mind, to the study of the so-called "diseases of woman", on finding that
nearly the whole of these special "diseases", including menstruation,
were due, directly or collaterally, to one form or other of masculine
excess or abuse.'[58]

Instead she urged the realisation of 'psychic love', which was only possible in those bred to a 'realisation of justice, equality and sympathy between
the sexes'.[59] Only the wife's physical inviolability could safeguard this

psychic element, which was all too often shattered by the boorishness of the husband and the disillusionment of the wife, when all semblance of companionship withered and the marriage became a living tomb rather than a temple of consecrated love. But purer conditions for marriage were approaching. What was needed was temperance and self-control after marriage and control of the 'lower passion' by a 'higher purpose'.[60]

This was the key idea. Mankind was capable of a higher purpose. Evolution meant that humanity was impelled to ascend to a superior plane. Carnality belonged to the animal kingdom; spirituality was what distinguished humans from animals. So if the human race was to progress, it had to move from the animal, or sexual, to the spiritual. It was a key claim of the women's movement that it was the role of women to bring this about. It was women who would raise men from the savage to the spiritual. Women were to be the redeemers of mankind. And they were to do this by turning the sexual double standard on its head.

Ellice Hopkins articulated particularly clearly the belief that had been implicit in the women's movement from the beginning and which had been reinforced so vividly by the great campaign against both prostitution and its repressive laws. This was not only the deep iniquity of men, but the mission of women to rescue both them and the world from base and animalistic masculinity. In her last book, *The Power of Womanhood*, Hopkins wrote of her years in rescue work:

> But in those ten years the one truth that was burnt into my very soul
> was the truth enunciated by Ibsen, that it is to the woman that we must
> look for the solution of the deepest moral problems of humanity, and
> that the key of those problems lies in the hands of the mothers of our
> race. They, and they alone, can unlock the door to a purer and stronger
> life . . . No-one recognises more thankfully than I do the progress that
> the woman's movement has made during what have been to me years
> of inaction and suffering. The ever-increasing activity in all agencies for
> the elevation of women; the multiplication of preventive institutions
> and rescue societies; above all, that new sense of a common woman-
> hood, that *esprit de corps* in which hitherto we have been so grievously

lacking, and which is now beginning to bind all our efforts in to one great whole – these I thankfully recognise ... I say again I do not think, I simply *know*, by my own experience, that men will rise to any standard which women choose to set them.[61]

In her vision, women were to take over men's minds and drag their values upwards to meet women's own standards. 'You fancy, perhaps, as you have been told so often, that a wife's rule should only be over her husband's house, not over his mind. Ah no! the true role is just the reverse of that: a true wife, in her husband's house, is his servant; it is in his heart that she is queen. Whatever of best he can conceive, it is her part to be; whatever of highest he can hope, it is hers to promise. All that is dark in him she must purge into purity; all that is failing in him she must strengthen into truth; from her, through all the world's clamour, he must win his praise; in her, through all the world's warfare, he must find his peace.'[62]

She even compared the redemptive power of women over men to Christ on the cross:

Do you think it cost the women of that day nothing to bear all this on their tender hearts? Yet what was it that made them draw nearer and nearer, till the women who at first 'stood afar off, beholding these things', we are told, at last 'stood by the cross of Jesus'; and when all men forsook him and fled, placed themselves heart to heart with the Divine Love bearing the sins of the world, and casting them into the abysmal depths of its own being, deeper even than the depths of man's sin? ... Shall we obey the divine call, enduring the cross, and, like the women of old, win for ourselves, by faithfulness unto death, the joy of being made the messengers of a higher and risen life to the world?[63]

The campaign to expose male responsibility for prostitution was, at root, an attack on the double standard, which held that although sexual immorality was a source of blame for women, it was excused among men. But in effect, the feminists were merely reversing this double standard.

What was reprehensible among men, they said, was now to be excused among women. Moreover, not only did the focus of iniquity shift on to men, but women became transformed into the means of male redemption – by asserting their moral superiority. And for this purpose, the vote was crucial. Once women had the vote, they thought, they would be able to bring about the introduction of measures to tackle male immorality and sexual excess. The vote was not merely considered essential to bring about justice for women. It was also seen as the means to deliver chastity for men.

This sense of moral mission and the extremity of these views about male viciousness and female victimhood were to fuel the violent scenes that the militant suffragettes were now to play out on the streets, in pursuit of a franchise that would curb male sexuality once and for all.

14

MARTYRS AND HYPOCRITES

As acts of violence by the Women's Social and Political Union grew in number and ferocity, tensions between militant suffragettes and constitutional suffragists increased. In the early days of militancy, Mrs Fawcett believed that the propaganda effects of martyrdom were gaining many recruits to the cause and arousing public sympathy. But when the WSPU shifted its tactics to start attacking property, her attitude altered sharply and in November 1908 she made her position plain by sending a letter to MPs and to the press expressing the 'strong objection' by the National Union of Women's Suffrage Societies to the use of violence. It was not merely a question of tactical difference. Mrs Fawcett believed that since the women's suffrage movement was a protest against government by physical force, the WSPU's tactics undermined the movement's central claim to moral superiority.[1]

That claim was to become ever more seriously challenged over the next six years. The WSPU had realised that the image of women being violated by the forces of the state affronted some of the deepest instincts within society concerning the sanctity and vulnerability of the female person. The propaganda impact of such images was enormous. As a result, the WSPU sought out violence in order to present themselves as martyrs to the cause. The more this happened – and there were many occasions when suffragettes were badly roughed up and even sexually assaulted – the more a climate of self-righteousness, embattlement, comradeship and even hysteria increased among the suffragettes, propelling them to yet more outrageous acts of provocation and trapping the state in a spiral of ever-more excessive reaction.

On 29 June 1909, after suffragettes marched on Parliament, 108 women and fourteen men were arrested after windows were smashed at the Home Office, Treasury and Privy Council. Mrs Pankhurst struck a policeman in order to get arrested, and expressed a wish to be tried for sedition. In July the WFL began a fifteen-week picket of the House of Commons and, when Asquith refused to see them, poured ink and chemicals into a ballot box at the Bermondsey by-election, defacing the papers and temporarily blinding the returning officer, who was splashed.

But it was the rank and file who propelled the tactic of emotional manipulation to new levels of sensationalism.[2] On 24 June 1909 Miss Marion Wallace Dunlop, an artist, was jailed for printing an extract from the Bill of Rights in indelible ink on the wall of St Stephen's Hall, Westminster. Unbidden by the WSPU leadership, she went on hunger strike, followed by fourteen more suffragette prisoners. For the next six years, wave after wave of suffragettes were to subject themselves to a high degree of bodily suffering by repeated hunger strikes while in jail for public-order offences, in order to unnerve the Cabinet still further.[3]

Christabel Pankhurst, as quick as ever to associate herself with such a spectacularly manipulative tactic, inspired women to feats of ever greater daring. So they assaulted Asquith and Gladstone on a golf course and hurled roof slates at the Prime Minister's car. Gladstone was locked into the spiral of outrage and reaction still further by King Edward VII, who wondered why the hunger strikers were not being forcibly fed. So forced feeding started.

This ghastly procedure, which involved women being held down by several prison warders while tubes were inserted through their nasal passages and down their throats, resulted in scene after scene of incontestably heroic endurance which created an unrivalled martyrology.

For many suffragettes, the suffering caused by the jail sentences, hunger strikes and forced feeding boosted their morale. Christabel said, 'This is war', and the palpable suffering of the jailed women turned such hyperbole into a potent call to arms. The government seemed incapable of understanding the propaganda weapon it was handing the suffragettes every time they were forcibly fed.[4]

Those who recognised the trap into which the government had walked advised that the women should be released after arrest. Gladstone, however, had heard from the police that the Women's Freedom League were practising with revolvers; he feared that Asquith might be assassinated. 'My duty is unpleasant and distasteful enough, but that is no reason why I should shirk it,' he said. 'I admire the gallantry of many of these girls as strongly as I detest the unscrupulous use which is being made of their qualities by older women who should know better. Women's franchise will come, but it will come not through violent actions and not through sentimental or cowardly surrender to them.' Forced feeding, he insisted, was not a punishment since 'to let women starve would not only be inhuman but in the event of death would expose all concerned to a charge of manslaughter'.[5]

As the violence, the jailings, the hunger strikes and the forced feeding escalated, Mrs Pankhurst was in her element. Her personal heroism in repeatedly going to jail and enduring hunger strikes did not detract from the fact that this was a psycho-drama in which, at centre stage, she could believe herself to embody the destiny of the whole of womanhood and indeed the human race. A later age would come to identify such qualities in a leader as megalomania. At the time, the mounting suffering of the women she was leading merely cloaked Mrs Pankhurst's ruthlessness in a mantle of self-righteousness.

If there was ever any doubt of this, a personal drama which was played out just as the excitement was mounting provided the most telling and dismaying evidence. Harry Pankhurst, Emmeline's son, was delicate, gentle and sensitive, so much so that surrounded as he was by such women he was known as 'the only girl in the family'. Patchily educated and drifting from job to job, he tried to prove himself a true Pankhurst by chalking pavements and speaking at street corners.[6] He eventually went to work on a farm, but in 1909 he was suddenly taken ill with polio and was advised not to return.

Mrs Pankhurst was due to sail to the United States on a lecture tour to raise money for the WSPU. She insisted that Harry was not delicate. As her daughter Sylvia later bitterly observed, she had no time to seek other employment for him. The movement needed her; she had so many engagements; young people must learn to face difficulties. Her mission had to come first, and anyway the fees from her lectures would help pay for his needs. At Carnegie Hall she declared: 'I am what you call a hooligan!' and, buoyed by the adoration of an enchanted public, returned to Britain.[7] Sylvia was later to write: 'So ruthless was the inner call to action that, finding her son thus stricken, she persevered with her intention ... there was never a moment of doubt as to where she should be substituted – on the platform or by the bedside of her son. The movement was paramount.' On her return from America Mrs Pankhurst found Harry paralysed. It was Sylvia who sought out Helen, the girl he loved, who came to his bedside. Mrs Pankhurst, jealous of the girl who had replaced her in her son's hour of need, reproached Sylvia for acting without consulting her. But Harry was mortally ill and within a few weeks was dead. After he died Mrs Pankhurst appeared broken.[8] But she and Christabel nevertheless resumed their speaking tours without interruption.[9]

The campaign was driving onwards. In January 1910 the WSPU pulled off another sensational coup. Lady Constance Lytton was one of the movement's true aristocrats. She had originally wanted to study music and later to become a journalist, but had repressed such aspirations since her parents had disapproved. She wrote of herself as 'one of that numerous gang of upper-class, leisured-class spinsters, unemployed, unpropertied, unendowed, uneducated ... economically dependent entirely upon others ... A maiming subserviency is so conditional to their very existence that it becomes an aim in itself, an ideal. Driven through life with blinkers on, they are unresentful of the bridle.' At the age of thirty-nine she had joined the WSPU because she hoped that by

Emmeline Pankhurst, arrested in Victoria Street, London, February 1908

Emmeline and Christabel Pankhurst in prison dress, 1908

Suffragette poster created
by artist Emily Ford, 1908

One of the seven processions
to the suffragette
demonstration in Hyde Park,
London, June 1908

Suffragette demonstration, Hyde Park, June 1908

London suffragettes demonstrating, 1910

Suffragettes parade through London, 1911

The inner office at the suffragette headquarters,
run by Miss Kerr (back, right), Clement's Inn,
London, September 1911

Christabel Pankhurst in Paris,
September 1912

Suffragettes smashing
windows in Oxford Street,
London, March 1912

Wrecked shop
windows in Oxford
Street, March 1912

Suffragettes tackling
Prime Minister
Herbert Asquith, 1913

Suffragette
disturbances, 1913

Mabel Tuke, joint Honorary Secretary
of the WSPU

Emily Wilding Davison throws herself
under the King's horse at the Derby,
June 1913

Mrs Pankhurst,
arrested outside
Buckingham Palace, 1914

Mrs Pankhurst campaigning for the British war effort

Women war workers in an engineering shop

The Ladies' Fire Brigade, 1916

Emmeline Pankhurst, on adoption as
prospective Conservative parliamentary
candidate for Whitechapel and
St George's, London, February 1927

Christabel Pankhurst (right) with Sylvia
and Adela at their mother's funeral, 1928

taking part in its protests she might be jailed and thus help the cause of prison reform, which, along with the prevention of cruelty to animals, was her strongest interest.[10]

If ever there were a case of the repressive tail wagging the protesting dog, this was surely it. Lady Constance had indeed been jailed in October 1909, but as she was titled she was treated well in the First Division, the most comfortable accommodation in the hierarchical prison system. This was not at all what was intended. So on a protest outside Walton jail, Liverpool, she disguised herself as a common woman, Jane Warton, and as such got herself sentenced to fourteen days with hard labour in the Third Division. She was then force-fed eight times despite having an undiagnosed heart condition. Eventually she was released in a state of exhaustion, and her health was permanently crippled until her early death in 1923. Christabel, however, was utterly triumphant to have exposed Gladstone's hypocrisy in such a dramatic way.[11]

Adela Pankhurst reacted rather differently to the ordeal in jail. As Martin Pugh has noted, the hunger strikes and forced feeding exacerbated the depression and inner turmoil which seemed to be rooted in her unsuccessful attempt to be noticed and esteemed by her mother. Adela had noted that her mother had grown particularly close to Annie Kenney, and remarked bitterly: 'My mother loved her as her own child.'[12] For the Pankhursts, politics and personal feelings were inextricably linked. The mental and physical suffering caused by the combination of hunger strikes, forced feeding and maternal indifference pushed Adela into nervous and physical collapse.

January 1910 saw a political earthquake. After the first of that year's two general elections the Liberals' huge majority was wiped out, and although they were returned to government, they found themselves dependent upon the Irish nationalists. The King's Speech after that election contained only one legislative proposal, the restriction of the House of Lords' veto.[13]

Mrs Fawcett met Lloyd George, the Chancellor of the Exchequer, in Downing Street. She pressed upon him the absolute necessity of government support for a reasonable measure of women's franchise. He said this was impossible because of the suffragette militancy and asked her to put a stop to it. She replied that this was impossible and that even the government couldn't stop it. He claimed that the militancy had alienated even his wife who had previously supported women's suffrage. She riposted that she had seen Conservative Club windows in his Caernarfon constituency smashed to pieces by Liberals after the election but the magistrates had 'made allowances for political excitement'. So why should such indulgence be extended to men but not women? Lloyd George didn't answer this, but told her instead that he wanted to introduce her to his wife.[14]

Mrs Fawcett's growing disillusionment with the Liberals now began to push the NUWSS in the opposite political direction to the WSPU. The Pankhursts' membership base was narrowing and becoming increasingly Conservative, while the NUWSS, which expanded dramatically between 1910 and 1914, was turning into a mass movement which would eventually develop formal ties to the Labour Party. By 1910, a majority of the House of Commons supported women's suffrage but party differences about the form it should take blocked legislation. The Conservatives supported equal voting rights for women on the basis of the existing suffrage criteria, but the Liberals opposed this because they feared that such enfranchised women would be propertied and vote Conservative. By contrast, the Liberals wanted to include women in an expanded male franchise but the Conservatives feared that these new voters would be mainly Labour or Liberal.[15] So the cause was stuck fast in a party-political impasse.

The women themselves were divided by the controversy over expanding the franchise to universal adult suffrage. In 1909, to test the political water, Geoffrey Howard MP put forward a bill giving both manhood and womanhood suffrage on three months' residential qualification. His bill was carried on its Second Reading by thirty-five votes before being talked out.[16] It drew scorn from both Mrs Fawcett and Christabel Pankhurst. Mrs Fawcett said that adult suffrage was 'an altogether unpractical solution' with 'no demand for it at all in the country'.[17] The suffragists were always suspicious that adult suffrage, which they thought had no chance of being implemented, was being proposed as a cynical manoeuvre to ensure that women would never get the vote. Nevertheless, their hostility to adult suffrage placed them squarely on the wrong side of the democracy argument. It is possible, moreover, that the Howard bill had been encouraged by the government to smoke out the intrinsically undemocratic nature of the suffragist campaign. If so, this succeeded. Sylvia Pankhurst, a committed adult suffragist, was to write: 'Again was witnessed the strange spectacle of the suffrage societies passionately struggling for the enfranchisement of their sex, but with equal insistence limiting the demand to a small minority.'[18] *The Nation*, a leading Liberal journal, said that while the WSPU's attitude might be excused on the grounds of youthfulness, Mrs Fawcett should know better and that the House of Commons would not accept a limited suffrage bill.[19]

To resolve the political stalemate, an all-party approach became inevitable. The MP H. N. Brailsford took the lead in forming a conciliation committee to produce a limited bill for women's franchise. The WSPU called a truce. Brailsford's committee came up with a proposal to enfranchise women householders, and business occupiers with a rateable value of over £10 a year. Marriage would not be an automatic disqualification, although husband and wife might not vote on the basis of the same property. As befitted any such attempt at a compromise, the bill was denounced from all sides. It was attacked for giving the vote to only about one million women, mainly elderly widows and spinsters, excluding several classes among which men were by then enfranchised.[20] At a meeting with Asquith and Lloyd George, Christabel dismissed the Conciliation Bill as worthless and demanded womanhood suffrage. In the Second Reading debate in July 1910, Asquith and Austen Chamberlain made hostile speeches of complete opposition to women's suffrage, and Lloyd George and Winston Churchill made hostile speeches on the grounds that the bill didn't go far enough. *The Times* carried hostile articles every day for a fortnight. Nevertheless, on its Second Reading the bill achieved a majority of 110.[21]

But Asquith's Cabinet was divided over women's suffrage, and he was implacably opposed. The bill was consequently choked off. Now, a wave of strikes gained more attention. Two Russian anarchists died after a siege in Sidney Street, in London's East End, in a military bombardment supervised by Churchill as Home Secretary. Despite her own militancy, Christabel proclaimed that it was scandalous that men should use such childish, uncivilised methods which depreciated the value of the vote for which women were struggling. This went down well with Tory feminists, but others found it merely embarrassing.

On 18 November Asquith said Parliament was to be dissolved as discussion with the House of Lords had broken down. Government business would take priority until the dissolution.[22] Women's suffrage was once again booted unceremoniously off the government's agenda.

That day, after Asquith had announced the dissolution, there was a riot in Parliament Square. Some three hundred women had assembled and were handled with extreme violence by the police. Several of these attacks were sexual in nature, and three women later died from their injuries or from heart failure. A total of 115 women and two men were arrested.[23] Four days later Asquith announced that in the next Parliament the government would introduce a bill to extend the franchise. He made only the vaguest gesture towards the women's vote, announcing that the bill would be 'so framed as to admit of free amendment'. The following morning, as Asquith was hustled into a taxi, Mrs Pankhurst led an attack on Downing Street which broke Asquith's car windows and injured Augustine Birrell, the Chief Secretary for Ireland.[24] Churchill arrived to see a suffragette leaning against a wall. 'Drive that woman away,' he told a policeman, even though he knew she was Mrs Cobden Sanderson, an intimate friend of his wife's family.[25]

Christabel was delighted that the truce was over. She announced at a breakfast for released prisoners: 'Ladies! The truce was all very well, but there is nothing like militancy. We glory in this fight because we feel how much it strengthens us.'[26] Meanwhile Lloyd George complained that revolt was spreading through the country 'like foot-and-mouth disease'. Rebellion was growing in Ulster over Home Rule, there was violence in the docks and rioting in the streets.[27] On 15 December 1910 Emily

Wilding Davison was arrested for stuffing paraffin-saturated linen into a pillar box.

The truce resumed, however, with a second attempt at a conciliation bill. On 5 May 1911 this bill achieved an even larger majority on its Second Reading than the first: 255 to 88.[28] However, the drama was to undergo yet another twist. Lloyd George, the Cabinet's most vocal suffragist, now declared himself against the bill on the grounds that it would add Tory voters to the electorate – the old argument against 'equal' suffrage. In September 1911 he wrote to the Liberal Chief Whip: 'We have never really faced the situation manfully. I think the Liberal party ought to make up its mind as a whole that it will either have an extended franchise which would put working men's wives on to the register as well as spinsters and widows, or that it will have no female franchise at all.' The bill as it stood, he claimed, was 'playing into the hands of the enemy', since it would 'add hundreds of thousands of votes to the strength of the Tory party'.[29]

On 7 November 1911 Asquith torpedoed the bill and with it the best chance yet for women's suffrage. Instead he announced that a reform bill would be introduced in 1912 basing the franchise on 'all persons of full age and competent understanding', but doing nothing for women – although the House could amend it if it so desired. When he was asked about this apparent volte-face, he replied curtly that his views were well known and hadn't changed. On 18 November 1911 Asquith received a suffragist deputation in conciliatory mood, indicating that he would look favourably on any women's amendments to the reform bill. On 12 December 1911 he received an anti-suffrage deputation including Lord Curzon, Mrs Humphry Ward and Miss Violet Markham. Asquith indicated his sympathies were with them and advised them to put more vigour into their opposition. Granting the vote to women, said this Janus of the Liberal government, 'would be a political mistake of a very disastrous kind'.[30]

'If Mr Asquith desired to revive a violent outbreak of militancy,' Mrs Fawcett was to remark later, 'he could not have acted differently or done more to promote his end.'[31]

In fact, Asquith saw militancy as a means of defeating the whole movement for women's suffrage. Just as Mrs Pankhurst and Christabel thought violent martyrdom was the way to engage popular sympathy with them and impatience with the government, so conversely Asquith viewed the popular recoil from unacceptable extremism as the best weapon against the cause itself. He never distinguished between militancy and non-militancy. For him, Mrs Fawcett's constitutionalism was no less an irrelevant irritant than the militant suffragettes. He compared himself to Orpheus and the whole suffrage movement to the wild women of Thrace.[32]

But why was he so opposed to the very idea of giving women the vote? For, as his biographer Roy Jenkins has noted, his opposition was as bizarre as it was pivotal. His hostility placed him in opposition to the majority of his own Cabinet, the parliamentary Liberal Party and even the Conservative leader, Arthur Balfour (whose own support for the women's cause put *him* in conflict with most Tories).[33]

Asquith had opposed women's suffrage as early as 1882 before any militancy had started. In part this was because he shared certain Gladstonian views. William Gladstone had supported the principle of universal manhood suffrage but had spoken against 'sudden, violent, excessive or intoxicating change'. Asquith's views were similar, and like Gladstone he believed that popular agitation should not be confused with public opinion.[34]

More to the point, perhaps, Asquith's attitude derived from his character as a dry, pedantic, unemotional lawyer. He was not an ideological anti-suffragist. For him, it was not a matter of abstract right or wrong; the only question was whether what was being proposed would improve the system of government. His lawyer's logic answered in the negative, because the suffragists' claim was innately undemocratic. He acknowledged as much in his memoirs. Although he claimed to have been an advocate of the admission of women on the same terms as men to the professions and to business, as well as to the administration of municipal and local affairs, he admitted that until nearly the end of the war he was a strenuous opponent of extending the parliamentary franchise to women. He had always said, he wrote, that if such a change were to be made it must be carried to its logical conclusion, 'which the more timid of the suffragists were loath to face' – the 'assimilation in all material conditions of the male and female franchise and the eligibility of women to the House of Commons'.[35]

But this was not a complete answer. The most plausible explanation is that Asquith found the very idea of women voters so utterly foreign to his view of the world that he could not believe that any woman other than the most atypical, unwomanly extremist, could possibly want it. For confirmation he had only to turn to his wife, Margot, and their elder daughter, Violet, who were vehement anti-suffragists.

The first suffragist deputation he had met, who had seen him while he was still Chancellor of the Exchequer, had included Mrs Fawcett, Emily Davies, Lady Strachey, Miss Frances Sterling, Miss I. O. Ford and others. Asquith took Mrs Fawcett aside and asked for her word that no delegation member would employ physical violence. But she saw in the room a woman she didn't recognise and said so. 'Oh that,' he said in some agitation, 'that lady is Miss Asquith.' He had 'yet to learn', he told the women, 'that there was any widespread desire among the women themselves for their enfranchisement'. Miss Ford said she would show him thousands of working women in Yorkshire who wanted the vote. 'He replied in his most forbidding air: "The prospect does not greatly attract me".'[36]

Believing there was no great female appetite for the vote, and with so many other intractable problems on his plate – Ireland, industrial unrest and above all the crisis over the House of Lords – Asquith refused to treat the cause of women's suffrage as a priority. Instead, his instinct was to play the issue down. He told the House of Commons in May 1913: 'There are very few issues in politics upon which more exaggerated language is used both upon the one side and upon the other. I am sometimes tempted to think, as one listens to the arguments of supporters of woman suffrage, that there is nothing to be said for it, and I am sometimes tempted to think, when I listen to the arguments of the opponents of woman suffrage, that there is nothing to be said against it.'[37]

He hoped the issue would simply go away. But what he could not ignore was the mounting and violent threat to public order to which it gave such dramatic rise. It was not merely a matter of window-breaking. The suffragettes made many attempted assaults on him, and others were hurt on his behalf. On the golf links at Lossiemouth, in Scotland, militants tried to tear off his clothes and were prevented from doing so only by the intervention of his daughter Violet, who protected him with her fists. In November 1913, while driving to Stirling, Asquith's car slowed down to avoid a woman lying in the road; whereupon other women promptly jumped on the car and belaboured him over the head with dog whips, his head protected only by his top hat. A peer, Lord Weardale, was mistaken for him and was whipped at Euston; the Ireland Secretary, Augustine Birrell, had his kneecap damaged when accompanying him in Whitehall; John Redmond, the leader of the Irish Nationalists in Parliament, who was sitting in the same carriage as the Prime Minister in Dublin, was wounded in the ear by a hatchet. There was no relief at social events, where Asquith found himself hectored by fashionable women – which, as Roy Jenkins observes, he particularly resented, and which contrasted sharply with the form which he believed conversation between the sexes should take on such occasions.[38]

Asquith found all this as distasteful as it was mystifying. As Roger Fulford wrote in Votes for Women: 'The idea of converting a human being's reason by parades, marching and fighting the police was incomprehensible to him. The more the women marched, the less his reason marched with them. Therefore the work of the militants strengthened his opposition to the vote.'[39] And the more violence there was, the more he felt he had to uphold the principle of parliamentary sovereignty against the suffragettes, along with the anarchical trade unionists and rebellious Ulstermen.[40]

It was particularly unfortunate that a man with Asquith's characteristics should have been Prime Minister at this point in history. For his unimaginative obtuseness only served to inflame still further the pathological self-importance and urge to martyrdom of Christabel Pankhurst and her mother. Yet now their fury was directed not so much at

Asquith, whose hostility had long been a byword within the suffrage cause, as at Lloyd George, their erstwhile ally, whose backing for adult suffrage was seized upon as the act of treachery that proved beyond peradventure the utter perfidy of male politicians and indeed the whole male sex.

'War is declared on women!' declared Christabel (again). 'The government's latest attempt to cheat women of the vote is of course inspired by Mr Lloyd George. The whole crooked and discreditable scheme is characteristic of the man.'[41]

By now the cause of militant suffrage had constellated around the person of Christabel. At a rally at the Albert Hall on 16 November 1911 Christabel told her audience they were soldiers and, like Joan of Arc, 'Our voices are of God.'[42]

These latter-day saints now included arson in their repertoire of violence. On 21 November a mass outbreak of window-breaking caused Elizabeth Garrett Anderson to resign from the WSPU. Even Annie Kenney had her doubts about the violence but 'would go through fire for Christabel'.[43]

The editor of the *Manchester Guardian*, C. P. Scott, recorded the Chancellor of the Exchequer Lloyd George as saying: 'They are mad; Christabel Pankhurst has lost all sense of proportion and reality. It's just like going to a lunatic asylum and talking to a man who thinks he is God.' Scott, himself an admirer, wrote of Christabel that she 'envisaged the whole suffrage movement in its present phase as a gigantic duel between herself and Lloyd George whom she desired to destroy. She had lost all sense of proportion and honestly believed she could force the government to yield.'[44] Adela Pankhurst said she realised that militancy was out of control and tried to tell Christabel – but her sister merely thought she was trying to set up a rival organisation.[45]

On 16 February 1912 Charles Hobhouse, then Chancellor of the Duchy of Lancaster, said in a speech in Bristol that until there were scenes comparable to the Hyde Park riots of 1867 there could be no evidence of popular support for the women's cause. As the former (but now anti-) WSPU paper *Votes for Women* expostulated, this was surely 'the most calculated and wicked incitement to violence that any responsible man, and more especially any minister of the Crown, has ever uttered'. Hobhouse himself claimed in debate that 'the absorption of women in politics would prejudice the number, character and vigour of our future race, would lead to the limitation of their capacity and inclination for maternity, and to their unwillingness and incapacity to manage their home and home was the primary and eternal unit of social life in all countries'. A hay-fever sufferer, he received from the suffragettes in his morning post a letter filled with grass seed and pepper.[46] On the evening he made his speech, Mrs Pankhurst told a dinner of released prisoners: 'The argument of the broken window pane is the most valuable argument in modern politics.'[47]

The violence now translated itself into a change of political mood. The revised Conciliation Bill, which was still limping through Parliament despite Asquith's promotion of an alternative franchise reform measure, reached its Second Reading in March 1912. Although this was essentially the same measure that had obtained a majority of 167 the previous year, it was now defeated by fourteen votes. Asquith had been up to his old tricks. His supporters had adroitly detached the Irish Nationalists from supporting women's suffrage. One MP, T. P. O'Connor, described the tactic in the *Chicago Tribune*. A Liberal master of intrigue, sauntering through the tea-room, would chat with a group of Irish Nats and observe what a pity it would be if Home Rule were to be thrown away, since if the Conciliation Bill was passed and Asquith forced to keep his promises, the government would break up and be followed by the reactionary Tories. As a result all but three Irish Nats voted against the bill.[48] However, the bill was not lost merely because the Irish had changed sides. Some forty-two previous parliamentary friends had voted against and ninety-one had abstained because of the militants' violence.

Later that year, at the Second Reading of the 1912 Reform Bill, Asquith nailed the lid down even further. 'The bill does not propose to confer the franchise on women,' he said flatly. 'The House at an earlier stage of the session rejected with sufficient emphasis the proposal . . . and, so far as I am concerned, I dismiss at this moment as altogether improbable the hypothesis that the House of Commons is likely to stultify itself by reversing in the same session the considered judgement at which it has arrived.'[49]

The defeat of the Conciliation Bill had two direct effects. The first was that the constitutional suffragists abandoned their non-party strategy and threw in their lot with Labour. In an agreement negotiated between the NUWSS and Arthur Henderson MP, the suffragists agreed to support certain Labour candidates and campaign against anti-suffrage Liberals, while Labour agreed to vote against any franchise bill which failed to include women. This was significant, because in the country the Liberals depended upon electoral co-operation with the Labour Party.[50]

The second effect was a dramatic upsurge of suffragette violence. On 4 March 1912 windows were smashed throughout central London on a huge scale. There was general uproar. *The Times* called for penal servitude for the WSPU leaders. Fred and Emmeline Pethick-Lawrence were arrested with Mrs Pankhurst, Mabel Tuke and others and charged with conspiracy to incite malicious damage.

In May they were found guilty and sentenced to nine months in the Second Division, a punishment which shocked even those who did not support militancy. Mindful of his celebrity prisoners, the Home Secretary ordered that Mrs Pankhurst and the Pethick-Lawrences be moved to the First Division. However, when they discovered that the others had been left behind, all three went on hunger strike and were forcibly fed. Mrs Pankhurst was released in June after she threatened the force-feeders with an earthen toilet ewer; Mrs Pethick-Lawrence was forcibly fed only once; Mr Pethick-Lawrence was forcibly fed for five days. He was singled out for harsher retribution because he was a man who had had the temerity to fight for the suffragettes, and for good measure he was thrown out of the Reform Club.[51]

In the House of Commons the Labour MP George Lansbury strode up to Asquith and announced that he would 'go down in history as the man who tortured innocent women'.[52] The Labour leader, Ramsay MacDonald, on the other hand, took a very dim view indeed of the women's performance. In a letter to the *Daily Chronicle* he wrote that hunger striking and rioting were marked not by heroism but 'pettifogging qualities which, insultingly to women, used to be known under the generic title of "feminine" . . . The whole of this tomfoolery is the creation of women who are in a position to throw into collecting plates £10,000 at a moment's notice. It in no way represents either the mind or the manners of the great mass of working women whose well-being is cruelly sacrificed. Is the work of women who have stood by the National Union of Women's Suffrage Societies to be swept away in the deluge of reaction which must follow this hysterical campaign?'[53]

But in the middle of these histrionics, the queen of melodrama herself was nowhere to be seen. Christabel Pankhurst had determined that her own days of martyrdom were over. Now she would merely direct other women to martyr themselves. Prison was no longer an option she wanted to take. In the wake of the arrest of her mother and the Pethick-Lawrences, she fled to a nursing home in Pembridge Gardens, Notting Hill Gate, where she dressed in a nurse's uniform. The next day she slipped away to Paris, where she took refuge with her friend the Princesse de Polignac, who softened her exile by furnishing her with an entrée into fashionable French society. From here Christabel wrote to her most devoted acolyte, Annie Kenney, asking her to take control of the movement and to visit her in France in disguise. To the public, she had simply disappeared. Her mythological power would now be enhanced; but she was never to recover the position of pre-eminence she had lost.[54]

Christabel was later to claim that she had fled on the spur of the moment, having previously considered sharing the fate of her mother and the Pethick-Lawrences, but all the signs were that her flight was premeditated. She had decided to go to France to control the movement from there because she was worried about losing control if she were to be jailed. Every Friday, Annie Kenney visited her, returning on Sunday with Christabel's latest instructions on tactics, articles, raising money and lobbying and an editorial for *Votes for Women*. The choice of Annie Kenney was shrewd. Christabel was anxious lest the WSPU be either manoeuvred into surrender or infiltrated by those who put peace and party politics before votes for women. She knew that Annie would resist either development, and that she would be a pliable and utterly loyal instrument through which Christabel could continue to control the WSPU from behind the scenes.[55]

For the rest of the time, Christabel spent her days shopping, visiting friends or strolling in the Bois de Boulogne. Her sister Sylvia, who visited her fresh from the traumatic horrors of hunger strikes and forced feeding, was rather less impressed than Annie Kenney. Indeed, Sylvia was appalled. She found Christabel serene and gay, enjoying her new life in Paris and ready for sightseeing and visiting fashionable shops. Sylvia, traumatised by the suffering and the loss of health of the suffragette militants, thought her approach was ludicrous and recoiled from the fact that Christabel simply thrust aside anyone who dared disagree with her tactics at all.[56]

In London, a great suffragette meeting was held in Hyde Park on 14 July 1912, the anniversary of the fall of the Bastille and Mrs Pankhurst's birthday. There were twenty platforms with twelve banners for each suffrage organisation, topped with the scarlet caps of liberty and supported by women in white. Some 150 brass bandsmen marched at the foot of a huge, laurel-wreathed flagpole swathed in the WSPU colours. The park was a blaze of colour; scarlet caps flaming red on long poles, wide banners floating like sails above a sea of people: purple, white and green for the suffragettes, orange and green for the Irish, black and white for writers, green and gold for Wales, black and brown for tax-resisters, red and white for Labour. The only jarring note, wrote Sylvia, was that the demand was only for a limited vote on the existing terms and not for womanhood suffrage. Then she received a message from Christabel in Paris. Would Sylvia burn down Nottingham Castle? Sylvia was shocked. Such a request, she thought, was morally wrong. The most she would do, she replied, was lead a torchlight procession to the castle and fling symbolic torches at it.[57]

But that summer Christabel was to direct a campaign of arson from her Parisian exile. On 12 July two militants equipped themselves with inflammable oil, pick-locks and glass cutters to set fire to the home of the anti-suffragist minister Lewis Harcourt. They were caught at 1 a.m., crouching among the ivy.[58] The suffragette Mary Richardson said that, like the window-smashing, the arson campaign was intended to put pressure on the government through the insurance companies.[59] Young women carried petrol and paraffin across the country at night. Pillar boxes were set on fire; works of art and historic relics were attacked; golfers found 'Votes for Women' burned on to their greens.

Sylvia regarded it all with 'grief and regret' as she thought it mistaken and unnecessary. Annie Kenney justified it, but still reflected the unease caused by the tactic. 'Both Christabel and her mother were against the taking of human life,' she later wrote, 'but Christabel felt the times demanded sterner measures, and burning she knew would frighten both the public and parliament. "But no life must be taken on our side", she said, "we alone are the ones who are prepared to give our lives, if necessary".' Nevertheless, Annie conceded, the public had been endangered. 'We did risk human life when we burnt houses, in spite of the care we took to see that all buildings were untenanted, but Providence protected us. No life was lost except on the militants' side . . . I was thankful when the burning days were over. I felt they were necessary, but I was never quite happy about them, and I do not think Mrs Pankhurst ever felt so comfortable about this phase of militancy as she did about the milder forms.'[60]

The government felt more than uncomfortable. On 5 September Lloyd George encouraged his supporters to beat up suffragette disrupters; on 21 September, when he addressed his constituents in Llanystymdwy, militants were assaulted and stripped almost naked.[61]

In October 1912, at a meeting at the Albert Hall, Mrs Pankhurst produced her justification of terrorist violence. Militancy, she defiantly declared, was necessary to save women's souls and thereby the souls of men too:

Until by law we can establish an equal moral code for men and women, women will be fair game for the vicious section of the population, inside Parliament as well as out of it . . . When I began this militant campaign I was a Poor Law guardian, and it was my duty to go through a workhouse infirmary, and never shall I forget seeing a little girl of thirteen lying in bed playing with a doll . . . I was told she was on the eve of becoming a mother, and she was infected with a loathsome disease, and on the point of bringing, no doubt, a diseased child into the world. Was that not enough to make me into a militant suffragette? We women suffragists have a great mission – the greatest mission the world has ever known. It is to free half the human race, and through that freedom to save the rest.[62]

Having provided the moral justification, Mrs Pankhurst cried: 'I incite this meeting to rebellion! Be militant each in your own way, I accept the responsibility for everything you do!'[63] The intoxication from such a performance led to even more hero worship; money poured in and some even threw jewels and watches at her feet.[64]

But the fact was that militancy had run out of steam and had become counterproductive. In 1912 George Lansbury fought a by-election in Bow and Bromley, in east London, after he resigned his seat to obtain a specific mandate for the women's franchise. This turned into a quite unanticipated disaster. The constituency regarded the suffragettes as an imposition; the well-to-do suffragettes refused to acknowledge the socialism in their candidate's programme.[65] The result was that although Lansbury had won his seat comfortably in 1910, he was now trounced by an anti-suffragist Unionist.

The message was not understood. The following day the WSPU poured acid, ink, lamp-black and tar into pillar boxes in London and the provinces. Two thousand letters were damaged. The tactics had now changed dramatically, from attempting to win public support to coercion. As *The Suffragette* made plain: 'The suffragists who have been burning and otherwise destroying letters have been doing this for a very plain and simple reason. They want to make the electors and the government so uncomfortable that, in order to put an end to the nuisance, they will give women the vote.'[66] The new policy of indiscriminate harm was the public's own fault. 'The public acquiesced far too widely and easily in the sufferings of women; its dishonour is on its own head.'[67]

With women portraying themselves as victims of oppression, all violence was justified – even murder. A Metropolitan Police report of a WSPU meeting recorded a Miss Gilliatt responding to the remark that they had never taken human life and that it was impossible for them to do so. 'As regards the impossibility of killing a Cabinet minister, she [Miss Gilliatt] and her followers knew different. "Attend their [Cabinet ministers'] political meetings", Miss Gilliatt said, "and you will find out for yourselves what an easy matter is their destruction".'[68]

Although most people were not engaged by the issue either way but were curious or just indifferent, hostility was growing. Opinion had turned; speakers' platforms were rushed with cries of 'You ought to be hung!', and Sylvia's appeals on behalf of the hunger strikers were received with howls of derision. Suffragette-baiting became a popular sport. Helena Swanwick wrote: 'They have appealed to the mob and the mob, another Frankenstein monster, has turned upon them and on suffragists generally.'[69] The Pankhursts' tactics had backfired badly.[70]

The reaction against the militants' behaviour fed existing prejudices against women's suffrage. At a time of gathering international tensions and fears about Britain and its Empire, the relationship between the right to vote and the responsibility to fight for one's country was a strong factor behind the hostility to the women's cause. This may strike us today as strange, even preposterous; but it is important to realise that voting then meant something completely different from what it does today. Modern democracies regard the vote as a universal human right. To the Victorians and Edwardians, by contrast, voting was a serious business requiring political judgement and expertise. Indeed, some were troubled by the fact that the women's cause seemed to be precisely about moving from responsibility to rights. Violet Markham wrote to Lord Cromer: 'I feel . . . that alongside liberty it is essential that discipline and reverence should grow up as well.'[71]

Since the vote carried serious responsibilities, the character of women and their fitness to discharge such responsibilities was in question. And for opponents, it was those characteristics associated with femininity that not only made women unfit for the responsibility of the vote but potentially might endanger the nation. Women, it was feared, not only had opinions which were unstable, uneducated and irrational, but they would introduce pacifism and enhance the danger of invasion. Lord Cromer, who was particularly fearful of German armament, warned: 'The German man is manly and the German woman is womanly; can we hope to compete with such a nation as this if we war against nature and endeavour to invert the natural roles of the sexes? We cannot do so.'[72]

The opposition to women's suffrage was complex and crossed political boundaries. Many opponents were instinctive conservatives, such as the historian and Conservative politician Sir Charles Oman, the eminent jurist Professor A. V. Dicey and the one-time Foreign Secretary Lord Curzon. They feared disorder and anarchy in a world of ever-extending democracy. Dicey recalled the Chartists and the sight of the ammunition carts passing his parents' house in the cause of defending public order against the mob. Yet hostility to women's suffrage was by no means confined to Conservatives. Although Liberals and Radicals had formed the bulk of supporters of women's suffrage, there were powerful Liberal voices in opposition too, such as Gladstone, Harcourt, Asquith and Rosebery.[73] Opponents included, too, many cross-bench thinkers: Herbert Ryle, Henley Henson, Lord Cromer, Mrs Humphry Ward. Many of these were deeply affected by the Irish crises of the 1880s, as were Liberal Unionists like Dicey. To the militant suffragettes, however, Ireland was merely a goad. As Sylvia Pankhurst noted, 'the Irish conflict remained a permanent incitement to intensified militancy'.[74] The suffragettes were fond of comparing the severity of the government's response to their campaign with the apparent immunity of the Ulster rebels. Repeated concessions by the Liberal government to the Ulster militants brought new recruits and supporters to the WSPU and spurred on feminine militancy.[75]

This militancy was about far more than the suffrage. To the women who were taking part, their deeds wrapped them in a romantic, heroic image which liberated them – by the most dramatic means possible – from the conventional image of womanhood, which to them was the creation of men. As the suffragette Mary Richardson wrote later:

> Our suffragette campaign was for much more than 'Votes for Women'. We were women in revolt, led and financed by women. We were inaugurating a new era for women and demonstrating for the first time in history that women were capable of fighting their own battle for freedom's sake. We were breaking down old senseless barriers which were the curse of our sex, exploding men's theories and ideas about us. We proved in our movement that many of men's accusations were untrue. We were not jealous; we did work together; we did know our own minds and our courage was beyond the wildest imagining of the Early Victorian – man or woman![76]

However, militancy also had the effect of alienating many women who had previously been stalwart supporters of the suffragette campaign. It was generally agreed that when the WSPU had first started, it had revitalised the campaign but after 1910 the violence had impeded it. The most devastating criticism of the WSPU's tactics came from Teresa Billington-Greig, the WSPU's erstwhile star speaker, who had split in 1907 over the autocracy of the Pankhursts. In a coruscating and merciless book, she exposed the dishonesty of deliberately courting martyrdom. 'What I condemn in militant tactics,' she wrote:

> is the . . . crooked course, the double shuffle between revolution and injured innocence, the playing for effects and not for results – in short, the exploitation of revolutionary forces and enthusiastic women for the purposes of advertisement. These are the things by which militancy has been degraded from revolution into political chicanery . . . The chorus of approval . . . confirmed in us the pose of martyrdom of which we had been rather ashamed until then, and it strengthened that curious mental and moral duplicity which allowed us to engineer an outbreak and then lay the burden of its results upon the authorities . . . We were

accepted into respectable circles not as rebels but as innocent victims,
and as innocent victims we were led to pose.[77]

In other words, the WSPU had used violence deliberately to provoke a
counter-reaction so extreme that it would produce the impression that
innocent women were being 'martyred' by an oppressive state. Such
manipulative cynicism is the hallmark of terrorism the world over.
Moreover, in Mrs Billington-Greig's view it had been counterproductive. The resumption of militancy after the breakdown of the
Conciliation Bill was a suicidal policy, she wrote. It turned MPs against
the cause just when their opinions were most important. Worse still, the
WSPU leaders would not accept responsibility for the violence perpetrated by their followers, a repudiation characterised by monstrous
cowardice and deceitfulness and which made victims of the very women
they were purporting to lead to liberation. 'Women who have been
worked up to fanaticism by years of influence are now to be given rein,
but the sins of their befoolment are to be upon their own heads and those
who made them fanatics are to escape ... Violence under these conditions is not only vindictive and unnecessary, it is victimisation ... do not
let any supporters of these leaders talk to me again of the iniquities of the
government. Here is iniquity enough for me.'[78]

She reflected that the Women's Freedom League, the organisation
she had founded when she split from the WSPU, had also failed because
it had fallen between two stools. 'It was not strong enough to cast off
the obsession of the earlier movement and at the same time it exhausted
itself in excessive recoil from the earlier excesses.' But the split resulted
in the growth of evil within the WSPU, whose horizons became increasingly limited the more extreme its actions. 'The pose of convention
became universal; the movement became honeycombed with snobbery.
The door was shut upon the real revolutionary spirit and purpose and at
the same time the functions of politics were glorified and exaggerated in
order to make sacrifice and subscription worthwhile. Extravagant
expectations were deliberately awakened on the one side to stir the
rebel women to take part in protests while on the other side no definite

or concrete ground for fear was allowed to disturb the most intolerant conventionalists.'[79]

No less serious was her charge that the WSPU had not faced up to the real implications of giving women the vote. It had glossed over the like-lihood of women MPs, for example, and had restricted its call for the vote to women taxpayers. 'All the way along the line similar sacrifices have been made, and gradually the movement has lost status as a serious rebellion and become a mere emotional obsession, a conventional cam-paign for a limited measure of legislation, with militancy as its instrument of publicity and the expression of its hurry,' she wrote. The leaders of the WSPU had imposed emotional control to produce mental and emotional slavery:

> The yoke is imposed by a mingling of elements of deliberately worked up emotion, by the exercise of affectional and personal charm, by an all-pervading system of mutual glorification in which each of the three leaders by turn sounds the praises of the others, by the deliber-ate exclusion of other women from all positions of prominence, by shameless boasting and booming, by an ingenious system of clever special pleading through which everything the political union does is chronicled and magnified, and everything that other suffragists do is belittled or ignored, and by that undoubted financial and political stage management which caters for all the elements of snobbery and narrowness and intolerance while employing the language of out-laws in revolt.[80]

The WSPU leaders used absurd hyperbole, she said, to exaggerate the effects of both militant and anti-government activity, serving up the same oratorical fare week after week. But it was all a gigantic game of bluff. All militant demonstrations were publicly announced through the press or through handbills and posters. So the authorities were always given notice. Blame for disorder was always placed on the government and police. These had abused their power; but the policy of planning out-breaks of violence and then using the resulting imprisonments as a stick to beat the government was an unworthy game. 'One cannot at the same time be the aggressor and the innocent victim . . . From the beginning the tactics have been deliberately intentioned to produce retaliation in order to work up the martyr cry and the martyr spirit . . . The policy, in brief, was to irritate the government until it should strike back and then to exploit the forces of feeling aroused; and the government lent itself to the game.'[81]

And in doing so women had squandered the moral superiority they had so brazenly appropriated from the separate spheres theory they purported to despise.

The claim that women would purify politics, said Mrs Billington-Greig, was a platform trick to awaken a sentimental response based on the discredited old 'angel-idiot' theory. Suffragists who claimed that women had a higher moral nature than men were ridiculous because they were playing men at their own game. 'The woman's boasted standard of morals in public life has come down to the standard that she has so loudly condemned . . . The militant movement has definitely encouraged its supporters to act as though they believed that women were the superiors of men. It has encouraged a system of stupid sex-glorification. The future is referred to with capital letters as The Woman's Age, and language is employed of which the only inference is that in the glorious coming days man will be as much repressed and discriminated against as woman is now.' Such a degradation of woman's outlook and expectations was much more disastrous than mere legislative disabilities.[82]

At the beginning, wrote Mrs Billington-Greig, she had been 'a feminist, a rebel and a suffragist – a believer, therefore, in sex-equality and militant action', and in the 'sacred duty of insurrection' to free women from their shackles. But now, she wrote, 'I do not believe in votes for women as a panacea of all evils.' She still believed in women's suffrage, but not at any price. 'I do not believe that woman is the superior of man any more than I believe she is his inferior . . . I do not believe that the best avenue for the emancipation of women is through emotionalism, personal tyranny and fanaticism.'[83]

This comprehensive shredding of the tactics and philosophy of the militant suffragettes was all the more deadly because of its authoritative insider's provenance. Mrs Billington-Greig's assault hit its target because she had so clearly recognised the contradictions, self-deceptions and rank deceit in the militant movement – not to mention the way a movement purporting to be about equality was actually simply trying to reverse the power of one sex over the other. But she was far from alone. Many other progressive women were appalled by the Pankhursts and what they had done to the women's movement.

The editor of *The Freewoman*, Dora Marsden, wrote contemptuously that Christabel had run away when it seemed she would have to pay the penalty for her bombast. 'The precious "leaders" continue to pile blunders on the end of blunders,' she wrote. 'After driving independence out of their ranks, after crystallising the forces of their enemies and splitting the forces of their friends, by their big words and small deeds they virtually lay militancy as a task upon the few – militancy which to make itself felt has to be such as to "stagger humanity".'[84]

Dora Marsden and Mary Gawthorpe had left the WSPU to become joint editors of *The Freewoman* in November 1911. Their view of feminism was much broader than the vote. In their first issue Dora Marsden wrote that the suffragist societies, 'with their half-hearted and sentimental allusions to prostitution, sweating, child assault and what not', had barely brushed the surface of the question. Women should realise that 'feminism is the whole issue, political enfranchisement a branch issue and that methods, militant or otherwise, are merely accidentals . . . We do not regard the vote as a symbol of freedom, nor do we understand those who do.'[85]

In the same issue, H. G. Wells put his finger on the fundamental and glaring contradiction at the heart of the suffrage campaign. 'I rarely walk upon Hampstead Heath,' he wrote, 'without hearing some devoted woman doing her best to persuade a group of ribald hearers that women are entirely different from men and should therefore be given the vote upon identical terms.' And he urged the WSPU to cure itself of its 'morbid infatuation' with Asquith. 'He has become the Antagonist of

Women ... the State Husband, the Official Wretch of the Woman Movement, the Depository of Feminine Repartee, the Public Henpeckee. He plays the role of Devil just as the two Misses Pankhurst are the radiant angels in the struggle for emancipation.'[86] Both Wells and George Bernard Shaw were amazed that women didn't realise that by following Christabel they were insulting their intelligence and stunting their emancipation. Christabel responded by calling Wells a 'spiteful little worm', and complained that intellectuals disliked suffragettes.[87]

However, the Pankhursts were to claim two more victims, this time at the very heart of the WSPU. Emmeline and Fred Pethick-Lawrence, the organisational geniuses who had effectively created the mass militant suffragette movement, were now to find out how the Pankhursts rewarded loyalty to the cause if anyone dared question the wisdom of their policy. The Pethick-Lawrences were extremely concerned about the rise in suffragette violence. Close to Christabel, they blamed Mrs Pankhurst for influencing her daughter. Since Christabel had gone to live in Paris, they said, she had become more extreme and had gone over to her mother's point of view. The issue came to a head over a heated quarrel in Paris when Mrs Pankhurst outlined her idea for 'civil war' and, wrote Mrs Pethick-Lawrence, 'appeared to resent the fact that I had even ventured to question the wisdom of her daughter's policies'. 'If you do not accept Christabel's policy', cried Mrs Pankhurst, 'we shall smash you!'[88]

And so they did. On Mrs Pankhurst's urging, the Pethick-Lawrences went on a trip to Canada. On their return in October 1912 they discovered that Mrs Pankhurst had simply thrown them out of the WSPU. The shocked Pethick-Lawrences could not bring themselves to believe that Christabel, to whom they had been so attached, was party to such an action. Their naïvety was finally shot to pieces when Christabel herself, summoned by her mother, arrived in London in disguise to express her complete agreement. 'She made it quite clear that she had no further use for us,' wrote Mrs Pethick-Lawrence.

They left the movement with only Votes for Women, the WSPU's erstwhile paper, which the Pankhursts allowed them to take, to show for their years of sacrifice for the organisation. 'There was something quite ruthless about Mrs Pankhurst and Christabel where human relationship was concerned,' wrote Mrs Pethick-Lawrence. This was surely something of an understatement. Yet despite the way she and her husband had been treated, she still struck a restrained, even respectful note. 'Men and women of destiny are like that. They are like some irresistible force in nature – a tidal wave, or a river in full flood . . . From that time forward I never saw or heard from Mrs Pankhurst again, and Christabel, who had shared our family life, became a complete stranger. The Pankhursts did nothing by halves!'[89]

But the Pethick-Lawrences faced further tribulations. Fred was pursued for the costs of the conspiracy trial and went bankrupt, and although this was later annulled he was not restored to membership of the Reform Club. His wife recorded, again with a remarkable absence of bitterness: 'Thus he underwent every variation of the sacrifice demanded for the freedom of women – imprisonment, hunger strike, forcible feeding, bankruptcy, loss of financial substance, expulsion from his club. All this he went through unflinchingly on account of the faith that was in him . . . many men did not hesitate openly to ally themselves with us and to fight what to them was a peculiarly difficult battle: there were men who suffered financial loss, men who went to prison, men who drew down upon themselves the vengeance of the police, or who risked life and limb when they challenged the brutality of the Liberal stewards.'[90]

The treatment of the Pethick-Lawrences shook even the Pankhursts' most devoted acolytes. Annie Kenney, known derisively as 'Christabel's blotting paper', wrote: 'To question policy with Christabel meant everything. Once people questioned policy her whole feeling changed towards them.' Christabel may have won, she observed, but when the Pethick-Lawrences – the creative geniuses of the 'constructive side of a world-famed fight' – departed, the movement lost.[91]

The split had a further resonance. Fred Pethick-Lawrence had been the only man at the heart of the WSPU. His departure powerfully symbolised a further change that had come over the organisation for which he had done so much. For the WSPU had become explicitly anti-male. Yet as Annie Kenney pointed out, men had supported militancy; they had helped in the processions, sacrificed their own businesses or professions and some had even been force-fed.[92]

Meanwhile there was a suffragette split even closer to home. Sylvia Pankhurst, the child who had always tried and failed to gain her mother's affection, passionately disapproved of the policy and ethos of the WSPU. It was too conservative, narrowly based and above all was not fighting for universal suffrage. Sylvia, a socialist who had an affair with Keir Hardie, started up her own suffrage campaign in the East End. To the white, purple and green of the suffragette colours, Sylvia added the socialist red. Sylvia was now in competition against her mother and sister.

The composition of her East London Federation (ELF) was very different from the upper-class, radical-chic socialites of the WSPU, who tended to be young and unmarried. ELF members tended to be married with families, and had a very different attitude to life. The suffragettes were more likely to shrug off sexual convention as repressive. The working-class suffragists' frame of reference was family life and community politics. Speakers who denounced marriage would have got short shrift. Free love was unrealistic for women for whom birth control was unobtainable. They worked with sympathetic men like Philip Snowden or Keir Hardie; there was none of the man-hating rhetoric of the WSPU.

There were, however, dilemmas for these women over the Labour Party policy of universal suffrage and over pay. Many women thought the vote would equalise women's pay, but Labour believed in the family wage idea that a man should earn enough to keep his wife and children. When the Liberal government decided that working wives should be squeezed out to solve unemployment, and married women's work in factories and sweatshops should be limited, many women socialists agreed. Under socialism, wrote Ethel Snowden, 'married women with children will not work in the factory; at least not until the children are out of their hands. They will not wish to do so, for they will be free and their children will claim them.'[93] Some thought that co-operative solutions to child-care was the ideal solution to the need for married women to work, but the idea was never taken further.[94]

Mrs Pankhurst and Christabel could not stomach what Sylvia was doing. So, in February 1914, they cast her off in a breach which, on a personal level too, was never healed. The split with Sylvia was not the only Pankhurst rupture at this time. As Martin Pugh has documented, the youngest daughter, Adela, was regarded as even more of a threat to her mother and Christabel than Sylvia. Adela, constantly rebuffed by her mother and feeling unloved, had been in fragile emotional health. Lonely and depressed, she wanted to take a speaking role in the suffragette campaign. But her mother regarded her independent streak with alarm, particularly since Sylvia had invited Adela to join her. Two sisters united by their left-wing views, and their common grief and resentment at their mother, was a threat that Mrs Pankhurst could not tolerate. So, at the age of twenty-eight, the crushed and vulnerable Adela was simply banished by her mother to Australia. 'Of course, now all is settled,' wrote Mrs Pankhurst, 'I have pangs of maternal weakness, but I harden my heart.'[95]

Pugh counsels against taking too severe a view of Mrs Pankhurst's behaviour, on the grounds that Victorian parents routinely separated themselves from their children in what may appear to us to be a heartless manner. But this *was* heartless. And it was all of a piece with Mrs Pankhurst's ruthless behaviour towards Sylvia and towards Harry. The only child whom Mrs Pankhurst did not abuse was Christabel, her favourite from childhood and with whom her relationship was unhealthily close and introverted.

In January 1913 the Franchise Bill was due to be debated. Various amendments giving the vote to women in differing circumstances stood in the names of Labour, Liberal and Conservative MPs. There was a cross-party consensus that – in however limited a form – women should be given the vote. At last, the suffrage was within women's grasp. Before these amendments could be considered, it was necessary to strike out the word 'male' from the bill, a proposal moved by Sir

Edward Grey. But then an extraordinary development occurred. The Speaker of the House of Commons suddenly declared that the adoption of any amendment would so alter the bill that it would no longer be the same measure, and so it would have to be killed and reintroduced in new form.

Was this an extraordinarily ill-timed accident, a blunder – or was it a malicious plot? Certainly the Speaker, the Conservative Sir James Lowther, was personally opposed to women's suffrage.[96] Suspicion naturally fell on Asquith, who was accused of plotting with the Speaker against the cause. It would seem, however, that although Asquith was certainly not sorry about what had happened, writing in a private letter: 'The Speaker's coup d'état has bowled over the women for this session – a great relief', he was as surprised as anyone and wrote to King George V that the Speaker had been 'entirely wrong'.[97]

In vain did Asquith deny that this was not a government plot. At the eleventh hour the suffragettes had once again been defrauded of their opportunity, one they thought would never come again. Asquith refused to draft a replacement government bill. The outcome was militant fury and violence on an unprecedented scale. Mrs Pankhurst announced that the suffragettes were 'guerrillists' justified in employing all the methods of war; human life was sacred but as much damage should be done to property as possible.[98]

A package containing sulphuric acid addressed to Lloyd George burst into flames when opened. An attempt was made to burn down his country house at Walton-on-the-Hill, Surrey, with the only trace of the culprits being a car passing through the village at four a.m. and two broken hat pins, a hairpin and a ladies' galosh found on site. Old ladies applied for gun licences. Street lamps were broken, keyholes stopped with lead pellets, chairs flung in the Serpentine, the cushions of train carriages slashed, flower beds damaged, golf greens burnt with acid, phone wires severed, windows smashed, envelopes containing red pepper and snuff sent to every Cabinet minister, boathouses and sports pavilions burnt down, thirteen paintings hacked to bits in a Manchester art gallery and bombs placed near the Bank of England. The *Weekly Dispatch* said the government had created a new type of woman, 'the Outragette'. Sylvia was jailed after stone-throwing in the East End and undertook a hunger and thirst strike. Emily Wilding Davison threw herself under the King's horse at the Derby and was killed. Mrs Pankhurst boasted about blowing up Lloyd George's house. She was charged with incitement to commit a felony and sentenced to three years' penal servitude.[99]

In response to the violence the Liberal government became increasingly repressive. It raided the WSPU's offices, tried to suppress *The Suffragette* and threatened the sources of WSPU financial support. To widespread revulsion, it also introduced the 'Cat and Mouse' Act, under which jailed women on hunger strike were released only to be reimprisoned once they had regained their health. Mrs Pankhurst went on hunger strike until she nearly died and was released, re-imprisoned and released again. Mary Richardson then took an axe to the Velázquez painting of Venus in the National Gallery, as a protest against the persecution of Mrs Pankhurst, 'the most beautiful personality of this age'.[100]

Militancy had hit the buffers. The WSPU had begun to decline. The constitutional suffragists, however, had their tails well up. They could see that, notwithstanding the débâcle over Speaker Lowther, the intellectual battle for the suffrage had been won. The Labour Party, thanks to Mrs Fawcett's shrewdness, was on side. At the same time, Conservative support was significantly increasing. In 1911 the conference of the National Union of Conservative and Unionist Associations had endorsed the Conciliation Bill, which was supported by both Balfour and Bonar Law. The Liberals were becoming alarmed by the squeeze, causing Asquith to meet with Sylvia Pankhurst's ELF and offer to intercede with the Home Secretary about an unconditional release from prison for Sylvia, who was putting her mother in the shade by the spectacle of her clashes with the police.[101]

Christabel, however, observing the eclipse of militancy and potentially of herself from centre stage, now tried one last throw of the dice. Mrs Fawcett had always wanted feminists to work closely with men for suffrage and social reform. In 1910 she had written to Lady Frances Balfour: 'I never believe in the possibility of a sex war. Nature has seen after that; as long as mothers have sons and fathers daughters, there can never be a sex war.'[102] But a sex war was precisely what Christabel now tried to start as a way of regaining the jaded attention of the public. She tried to revive support for militancy by proclaiming a moral crusade against male lust.

15

THE GYNAE-CENTRIC UNIVERSE

In the first decade of the new century, repression of prostitutes had reached a zenith. This phase of the campaign was shot through with unpleasant prejudices and phobias. Its proponents claimed that prostitutes and brothel keepers were foreigners and, in particular, Jews. In 1905 the Aliens Act was passed under social purity and eugenist pressure to keep out Jewish prostitutes. The National Vigilance Association advocated repatriation, even though Jews were fleeing the Czarist pogroms in Russia. In December 1912 a new Criminal Law Act known as the 'White Slave Act', supported by an alliance of feminists, social purists and the Liberal government, tightened up the law against prostitution even further. Nevertheless, the Metropolitan Police's White Slave Traffic branch reported little evidence of actual trafficking and complained that Britain had 'been aroused by a number of alarming statements made by religious, social and other workers, who spread the belief that there was a highly organised gang of "White Slave Traffickers" with agents in every part of the civilised world, kidnapping and otherwise carrying off women and girls from their homes to lead them to their ruin in foreign lands'.[1]

White slavery, however, resonated with a public mood that was convulsed by tumultuous uncertainties and insecurities, as late-Victorian society tried to grapple with the most fundamental questions about human existence and man's place in the world, against a background of deep-seated fears about underpopulation, the threat to Empire and the distant rumble of social insurrection and war. A host of theories crowded into the space between science and religion: psychic research, spiritualism, telepathy, mesmerism, clairvoyance. Above all, the evolutionist controversies brought to a head by Charles Darwin dominated popular thinking and had a profound influence on the reinterpretation of female sexuality and on the women's movement.

Darwin had published *The Origin of Species* in 1859 and *The Descent of Man* in 1871. Evolutionary theories had overshadowed thinking for decades previously, and the naturalist Alfred Russel Wallace had come up with a similar theory of natural selection at the same time as *The Origin of Species* appeared. There were, however, significant differences between Darwin and what Wallace and other evolutionary theorists were saying. Wallace, who was drawn to spiritualism and mesmerism, was attracted to evolutionary theory because it elevated man above the world of nature. T. H. Huxley believed that natural selection reduced man to the level of an ape. Social Darwinists seized upon the notion of sexual selection, and the idea that evolution depended on innate differences between the sexes – a notion that made use of the earlier theory by Jean-Baptiste Lamarck in the late eighteenth century, that organisms evolved by acquiring characteristics and then passing them on to their offspring in altered genetic information.

What was notable about feminism in the late nineteenth century was that it synthesised all these evolutionary theories and incorporated them into the women's cause. *The Descent of Man* showed how moral faculties like self-control, love and altruism were key elements in progressing towards a higher moral culture. Purity workers interpreted this by arguing that, as Elizabeth Blackwell said in *The Human Element*, morality involved the evolution of self-consciousness, which developed only in humans. Chastity, continence and self-control were the highest forms of sexual development as regulated by reason and knowledge of the laws of human nature. Blackwell wrote: 'Sex is capable of great devotion towards good or towards evil ... It may grow into a noble sympathy, self-sacrifice ... and joy ... It also allows that perversion and extreme degradation of sex observable in the human race.'[2]

Women would thus not merely transform relations between the sexes and improve male behaviour, but as a result they would also cause the human stock to improve and save the Empire and the race. For evolutionary thinking had fomented a new and widespread alarm.

The birth rate was now in decline, due to a combination of pessimism caused by the depression in agriculture and trade and an increase in birth-control practices.[3] But under the particular influence of social Darwinism and its offshoot, the new eugenics movement, concern about the quantity of the population was exceeded by a preoccupation with its quality. Eugenics, defined as the science of selective breeding to encourage the 'fit' to propagate and the 'unfit' to desist, had been dreamed up in 1883 by Darwin's cousin, the scientist and geographer Francis Galton. It was a widespread doctrine among the progressive intelligentsia, with noted eugenists including the sexual purity feminist Lady Isobel Somerset, Lady Ottoline Morrell, Winston Churchill, Maynard Keynes, George Bernard Shaw, H. G. Wells, Sidney and Beatrice Webb and the sex theoretician Havelock Ellis. Undoubtedly it was fuelled by the fact that the highest reductions in fertility had occurred within the upper and middle classes. The poor, by contrast, were actively feared as degenerates whose animalistic behaviour was regarded as a kind of throwback to an earlier stage of evolution. At the same time the preeminence of the Empire was under attack from a number of different directions: economic rivalry from Germany, the USA and Japan; the struggle with the Boers for control of South Africa's minerals; and, at home, threats from labour unrest, socialism, Irish Home Rule and the suffragettes.

Such cosmic insecurities were hugely amplified by perceived threats to the sacred refuge of the home. The Victorian family was invested with such exaggerated virtues that threats to domestic life easily morphed into scenarios of disintegration and ruin. The 'woman question', which challenged the stability of the family, the nature of authority and the basis of gender itself, became a magnet for the most deep-seated dread as well as hope.[4]

For some eugenists, feminism was directly responsible for the decline in the birth rate of the upper classes. In 1911 the eugenist doctor Arabella Kinealy wondered whether 'the refined and highly organised but neurotic mothers of our cultured classes' had sufficient 'mother power' to produce enough quality children. She thought the evidence already showed that the educated woman, 'all nerves and restless activity', was begetting 'offspring of the crude, rough hewn and unintelligent peasant type'.[5]

But other eugenists were more ambivalent about feminism. They recognised in it the potential to recruit women to the cause of remoralising the human race. The claim that women were morally superior so easily translated into the belief that they were evolutionarily superior. It was only natural that women should spearhead the drive for responsible motherhood that would rescue the race. 'The breeding of man lies largely in the hands of women,' said Havelock Ellis. 'That is why the question of eugenics is to a great extent one with the woman question. The realisation of eugenics in our social life can only be attained with the realisation of the woman movement in its latest and completest phase as an enlightened culture of motherhood, in all that motherhood involves alike on the physical and psychic sides.'[6]

And the feminists agreed. Male carnality was the cause of racial impurity and had to be curbed in the interests of all. The social purity feminist Ellice Hopkins wrote that 'all history teaches us that the welfare and very life of a nation is determined by moral causes; and that it is the pure races – the races that respect their women and guard them jealously from defilement – that are the tough, prolific, ascendant races'.[7] And she quoted Olive Schreiner's claim that the low standard of purity among men was held responsible for the 'Eurasian' population in India and half-castes in general, both of whom were seen as anti-social, possessing 'the vices of both parent races and the virtues of neither . . . with a tendency to be a liar, cowardly, licentious and without self-respect'.[8]

According to Alice Ravenhill, writing in the *Eugenics Review*, women should maintain a high standard of morality, produce and correctly rear children, provide health efficiency and happiness and cultivate the aesthetic qualities which make for physical intellectual and moral progress. As far as she was concerned, 'upon womanhood largely depends the standard attained by the world's ethical code ... women hold in their hands the health of the community and exercise far-reaching influence on human life'.[9] Civilisations, according to Ellice Hopkins, were defined by the way they treated their women: 'You will never find a permanently progressive race where the position of women is low, the men libertine, and the state of society corrupt.' England was the mother of all nations; decadence there would pollute the rest of the world, while moral improvement would correspondingly elevate the rest of the human race. 'The great British empire,' she wrote, 'the greatest civilising, order-spreading, Christianising world-power ever known, can only be saved by a solemn league and covenant of her women to bring back simplicity of life, plain living, high thinking, reverence for marriage laws, chivalrous respect for all womanhood and a high standard of purity for men and women alike.' Even Mrs Fawcett subscribed to this sexual jingoism. She had told a meeting at the Free Trade Hall in Manchester 'that the great question whether the relations of men and women shall be pure and virtuous or impure and vile lies at the root of all national well-being and progress ... self control and respect for the rights of others are the only cure for the terrible national danger that threatens us'.[10]

Mrs Wolstenholme Elmy spelled out just how the behaviour of women could affect the race. In 1893, in her book *Woman Free*, written under the pseudonym Ellis Ethelmer, she quoted Alfred Russel Wallace from the previous year:

When such social changes have been effected that no woman will be compelled, either by hunger, isolation or human compulsion to sell herself, whether in or out of wedlock, and when all women alike shall feel the refining influence of a true humanising education, or beautiful and elevating surroundings, and of a public opinion which shall be founded on the highest aspirations of their age and country, the result will be a form of human selection which will bring about a continuous advance in the average status of the race. Under such conditions, all who are deformed either in body or mind, though they may be able to lead happy and contented lives, will, as a rule, leave no children to inherit their deformity. Even now we find many women who never marry because they have never found the man of their ideal. When no woman will be compelled to marry for a bare living or for a comfortable home, those who remain unmarried from their own free choice will certainly increase, while many others, having no inducement to an early marriage, will wait till they meet with a partner who is really congenial to them. In such a reformed society the vicious man, the man of degraded taste or feeble intellect, will have little chance of finding a wife, and his bad qualities will die out with himself. The most perfect and beautiful in body and mind will, on the other hand, be most sought and therefore be most likely to marry early, the less highly endowed later and the least gifted in any way the latest of all, and this will be the case with both sexes.[11]

Thus women's emancipation, by enabling women to discard inadequate mates, would breed out the unfit and improve the race.

Women doctors were in the forefront of the doctrine of fit mothering. Dr Mary Scharlieb, a suffragist and gynaecologist, saw mothers as 'race regenerators'. The welfare of the race, she thought, depended on women who therefore needed motherhood training and the inculcation of their racial duty to breed eugenically to counter the moral and physical deterioration of the Empire.[12] Dr Elizabeth Sloan Chesser, a lecturer in hygiene with the Women's Imperial Health Association, called the sexual instinct the 'racial instinct', and informed adolescent girls that by their conduct they helped 'keep the life stream pure, help uplift the race'.[13] Constance Hartley, a writer and suffragist, also stressed women's racial duty to breed. 'Just as at the dawn of civilisation society was moulded . . . by women . . . so, in the future our society will be carried on and humanised by women, deliberately working for the race, their creative energy having become self-conscious and organised.'[14] She believed evolution was moving from natural selection towards conscious moral selection, with women's selective power the main factor in spiritual evolution of race.[15]

For the man-hating Mona Caird, eugenics merely amplified the lethal threat posed by men, who imperilled the well-being not only of women, but of the whole human race. The average man, she averred, was doomed to corruption. 'Man, the creature of his conditions, out of which he is fashioned and compounded, body and soul, has small hope indeed of resisting the influences at work upon his character, from the cradle to the grave. Liberty being denied to a whole sex, what can be expected from the other but licence?' And if this savage male element was not held in check, the evil and difficulty of a cure could only increase. 'After a certain time, the strength and life of the people must become exhausted, and then we shall be threatened with the fate that has overtaken so many nations after a certain stage has been reached – decadence through corruption, or through failure to produce varieties of type. It is in fact inconceivable that a people can go on progressing while they continue to cripple half their numbers.' Evil instincts, she maintained, gathered strength through heredity. Nature maintained a kind of 'mystic storehouse' in which she gathered together the many influences of daily life. 'Such facts, while adding to the sense of moral responsibility, must make clear the utter folly of accepting the leading characteristics of the average man of today as the final type of humanity.'[16] This biological and racial determinism sealed in pseudo-scientific certainty the damnation of half of the human race.

Yet although feminism so deeply absorbed eugenic thinking, there were many eugenists who were deeply worried by the apparent threat to sexual differentiation. Karl Pearson, professor of applied maths and mechanics at University College London, was a prominent eugenist who was hostile to female emancipation because of its implications for the future of the Empire and the race. He believed that the Darwinian struggle for survival had shifted from individuals to nations and peoples, and he reminded his readers that 'those nations which have been the most reproductive have, on the whole, been the ruling nations in the world's history; it is they who have survived the battle for life'.[17]

In his lecture notes on 'The Woman's Question', privately circulated in 1885, he suggested that although the effects of female emancipation could not yet be determined, women's duty to society was paramount. It was to breed. Feminists had to show that emancipation would improve the stability of society, the general happiness of mankind and the physique and health of both sexes. Pearson's major concern was for the future of marriage, for which his predictions were uncannily prescient. Emancipated women, he suggested, might demand an end to discrimination against children born outside wedlock. If granted, this might involve revolutionary changes to property and inheritance laws, and a return to the ancient matriarchal principle of tracing descent through the female. Faith in the religious nature of marriage would collapse, questions would arise of its duration and form, and 'a characteristic prop of existing society may rightly or wrongly be shaken by the complete emancipation of women'. If women were breadwinners of equal education and social weight with men, what woman would want to continue in a union which had become distasteful to both?

'With the past to guide us,' Pearson wrote, 'it seems not improbable that, when woman is truly educated and equally developed with man, she will hold that the highest relation of man and woman is akin to that of Lewis and George Eliot, of Mary Wollstonecraft and Godwin; that the highest ideal of marriage is a perfectly free, and yet generally life-long, union. May it not be that such a union is the only one in which a woman can preserve her independence, can be a wife and yet retain her individual liberty?' And yet, since a woman was always dependent during the bearing and rearing of children, she could not be independent without 'a complete reorganisation of society'. So his conclusion was that women would have to be martyrs for the race. 'If child-bearing women must be intellectually handicapped, then the penalty to be paid for race predominance is the subjection of women.' Equality, he said, meant either that men must desist from prostitution or women must be given the same freedom – which would mean that the state would decay. 'We shall have the choice between equal promiscuity and equal restraint. The misfortune for society is that the former is a much easier course to take than the latter, and one which history shows us has generally been adopted.'[18]

So worried was Pearson about the eugenic threat from female emancipation that he helped found the Men and Women's Club specifically to draw insights from women members into female nature and sexuality. The club, he laid down, was to 'discuss woman, her needs, her mental and physical nature, and man only in as far as he throws light upon her question'. Some fourteen middle-class men and women – lawyers, doctors, university lecturers – met there for the first time in July 1885. Most of the men were married and all but two of the women single, and all of the members were active in philanthropy, reform movements and women's suffrage.[19]

But although eugenic thinking was common among these women, the club polarised between men and women members over morality and sexuality. The women repeatedly criticised the men for treating male sexuality as a given and only female sexuality as problematic.[20] The men saw women as eugenic breeders; the women wanted emancipation and independence and for men to transform their own sexual practices and eradicate the double standard.

Henrietta Muller, an active feminist and Girton classicist, laid out the case against men in an argument with Pearson in 1885.[21] Mrs Elizabeth Cobb, a founder of the club, described her as a 'man-hater', 'one-sided' and 'warped in her moral nature'. Muller saw the division between the sexes as 'man's licence and woman's self-control'. 'Self-control is the basis of all moral life and . . . the characteristic which distinguishes humanity from the rest of the animal world,' she wrote. Men were inferior 'by reason of a natural slavery to sexual instinct'. Women were the moral saviours of humanity. 'The sons of earth have done their task and nature now calls upon her daughters to fulfil theirs – as the one has conquered the physical world, the other shall conquer the moral . . .'[22]

Miss Muller was supported by another member, Mrs Walters, who agreed that the sexes could be characterised as 'woman the slave to man, man to his own passion'.[23] Two solutions were possible: either women's independence from men, meaning their refusal of marriage, sex and child-bearing; or a change in men to become 'altruistic, in which case sexual instinct would be no longer ugly, but directed towards getting beautiful children, its only natural raison d'être'.[24]

The women repeatedly urged chastity for both sexes. The Fabian novelist Miss Emma Brooke warned Pearson that once women had economic independence, men would be forced to learn self-restraint and 'to stop being a beast of prey'.[25] Spiritual love was urged as a replacement for physical sexuality. Henrietta Muller wrote to Pearson: 'If our past race experience [in relation to sex] has failed then nothing is left to us but to try another way and to see whether the spiritual basis doesn't answer better; a spiritual love between a man and a woman would certainly . . . develop a passionate feeling, but one which differs so widely from the average feeling as to be almost of another kind. It is only then that passion can be "as intense as fire, as clear as the stars, as wide as the universe".'[26]

When Annie Besant spoke in favour of birth control, most men were in favour but the women were split; even those who were in favour saw it as a necessary evil, with abstinence the preferred option. Contraception was said to be brutalising as it 'vulgarised the emotions', encouraged promiscuity and made women subject to men's whims. Significantly, it was viewed as removing a bar to sexual pleasure among men – but not among women. Only the bohemian Olive Schreiner believed that many women experienced sexual pleasure. After she left the club, Pearson horrified the remaining women members by suggesting that sex involved pleasure, prompting Maria Sharpe to equate this scornfully with 'a taste of a strawberry and a kiss of a friend'.[27]

This severe but abstract difference of perspective was to become very personal. For Pearson wanted to marry Maria Sharpe. But the idea of physical union repelled her. Unlike men, she told him, women entered marriage with 'repulsion toward the exercise of the sex function'.[28] The reason for this wild and inaccurate generalisation was inextricably bound up with her feminism. She believed that a woman gave a man not just her virginity but her very being. Sexual intercourse was therefore not so much a union as a surrender; and self-surrender was of course the enemy of women's emancipation.[29]

Maria Sharpe eventually changed her mind and married Pearson. But when she was dying thirty-seven years later, she wrote that although she had been a splendid wife and mother, she did it out of duty and he had never won her.[30]

The issue of sexual pleasure became a most significant totem for the women's movement, and one that was to divide them bitterly. A huge fissure developed between those feminists who believed that freedom meant emancipation *from* sex, and those who believed that emancipation meant the freedom to practise it without conventional social constraints.

The first group – with many shades of opinion within it – constituted the majority. For them, the women's movement amounted to a transmutation of the physical evolution of humanity into moral evolution. This was a process that depended entirely upon the agency of women to transform and elevate the moral behaviour of men. What this involved was leaving behind physical sexuality – identified with men – and moving on to a 'higher' spiritual and psychic plane of existence altogether.

In books, pamphlets and speeches, feminists stressed celibacy, evolutionary superiority and spirituality, where physical passion would be transmuted by a higher form of love. A heightened, quasi-religious language drawing on mysticism and theosophy was used to formulate a new spiritualised conception of sex relations freed from male control.[31] In 1897 Mrs Wolstenholme Elmy envisaged an initiation into a higher psychic existence of love beyond the physical. Even the widely accepted emphasis on the dignity and sanctity of womanhood, she declared, had denied the all-important psychic capacity of women. Man's 'lower passion – untempered by psychic considerations – had attained a disordinate proportion, not without evil results on both sides . . .' This was harmful to the 'growing intellect of the race'. Many writers had wrongly identified lust as love, not realising 'that only by the accession of reason and justice could physical impulse be elevated to a psychic position worthy of the name of love'. And it was men alone whom she blamed for the mistake. Nature offered equally the spiritual as well as the physical; it was man's own doing to choose the latter, resulting in women's suffering. Women, diffident to their own potential, had acquiesced in their own subjection. But now the higher phase of evolution was becoming evident. 'The history of human love,' she concluded, 'has been and is the story of the upward effort of the race; the progression from the brute to the human, and from the human still onward to the psychic; the development and maturing of the very psyche or soul itself.'[32]

Annie Besant's study of Darwin, Spencer and others convinced her that theosophy and evolution together could redeem the feminist cause. All the evil, anti-social side of man's nature was an inheritance from his brute ancestry, and could be gradually eradicated.[33] Human evolution, she decided, was a journey of the soul to perfection in which man had to fight against the constant temptations of his lower nature. Renouncing such brutish gratification of the male sexual instinct would result in the elevation of the race, the progress of evolution and the realisation of the harmony of the universe.[34]

This argument was pushed to the outer limits of bizarre, man-hating fantasy. From the swirling intellectual fads and charlatanries of these fevered times, feminists conjured up a mystic Utopia which ventured far beyond the reformation of male manners into the prospective eradication of masculinity altogether. Since evolution taught that organisms constantly adapted for the better by eradicating degenerate features, and since male sexuality and the very masculinity that engendered it were so degenerate, surely evolution would come to the aid of women by eradicating masculinity altogether? At the Men and Women's Club, Kate Mills wrote to Maria Sharpe: 'I am not an ascetic or a prude but . . . I say it is the cursed thing that pulls men and women down and holds them down . . . this mad craving to find a heaven in the absorption in to another life which takes the form of sexual intercourse . . . It is fatal because it does it while it throws over us a beautiful, incomprehensible, mysterious feeling of devotion and self-surrender . . . But since we are Darwinians . . . may we not reasonably suppose that the animal kingdom in its highest genus may evolve a more perfect specimen of the perfect man (which would surely be hermaphroditic – only man and woman together forming the perfect creature . . .)'[35]

Her suggestion of hermaphroditism found its most enthusiastic echo in the extraordinary writings of the prominent suffrage speaker Frances Swiney. President of the Cheltenham branch of Mrs Fawcett's sedate National Union of Women's Suffrage Societies, and the mother of six children, Mrs Swiney showed by her virulent hatred of men that sexual extremism was embedded in the mainstream of the suffrage movement. Brought up in colonial India and married to a military man, she developed in her fifties an elaborate theory of the natural supremacy of women and the need to return to a matriarchal society, ideas which circulated in her theosophical society, the League of Isis.

Drawing on some of the more colourful misapprehensions entertained by contemporary medicine about sexuality, Mrs Swiney effectively rewrote evolution to construct a preposterous gynae-centric universe and write men out of the script of human progress altogether. Men, she declared, were far down the ladder of evolution; nature had bestowed the most care, provision and attention instead upon the female organism. The superstructure of sex showed that:

the motherhood of the universe is the natural vehicle of determinate progression; that the female is the handmaid and co-worker with the infinite; and that the distinctive feminine organs are the chosen tools for the highest form of workmanship on the material plane, transmuting the grosser physics into ever finer grades of psychic force . . . and it is through this all-abiding, all-controlling, all-constructive feminine element that creation works towards the perfection of the universe. It absorbs that evil, the waste, the katabolic energies and forces that, if left to themselves, would produce universal anarchy, but purified, utilised afresh by the creative feminine principle, conduce to further construction, further development and a higher stage of evolution.

Men were a lower form of animal life; indeed, Mrs Swiney wondered if they might not be properly alive at all. She quoted the opinion of various contemporary writers that 'males are rudimentary females', 'biologically the male is secondary' and 'the female not only typifies the race but, metaphor aside, she is the race'. Man, on a lower plane, was actually an undeveloped woman, resulting from a female failure in creative power in not reabsorbing what had been left over in the creative process. 'In fact, we may call the male Nature's greatest experiment in the utilisation of waste products.'[36]

Not surprisingly, as the garbage of human history, men were without any redeeming feature. 'The male is inherently errant, restless and variable, having no continuous specific sphere of action assigned by nature other than that of fertilisation, while on the female organism is thrown the whole responsibility of construction and production of kind . . .' Given the utter superiority of women to this excrescence of evolution, sexual reproduction was clearly insupportable. Parthenogenesis was a far more natural and ideal type of reproduction – and of course, only females were worthy of being born at all. 'The female being the standard in nature, relative harmony with the environment precludes the birth of males.'[37] Maleness, in short, had to be obliterated altogether. And women's emancipation was the means to bring this about.

Men's moral evolution had been abnormally slow, she continued, because they had treated women as chattels, ignoring the fact that women were the key to evolution. Yet, despite this oppression, somehow women had still managed to be entirely responsible for male achievements: 'It is in a large measure to their mothers that men owe their powers of organisation and their ability in shaping national polity; women, having through the wise, tactful, methodical and thrifty ordering and management of their households inculcated in their sons the qualities requisite for the wider field of civic and political administration.'[38]

Inverting altogether the Victorian medical representation of femininity as the fount of diseased pathology, Mrs Swiney portrayed men as the source of putrefaction. It was men's sexual impositions upon their wives during pregnancy, she confidently claimed, that produced the vernix in which newborns were enrobed, a 'cheesy mess' formed from 'inanimate decomposed zoosperms' – since sperm in excess was a 'virulent poison'. Sexual intercourse too soon after childbirth, she added for good measure, led to the human species becoming 'diseased by sexual vice, overpopulated with degenerates, imbeciles and mal-formed individuals'.[39]

Men were indeed the source of all disease. In a footnote Mrs Swiney added:

> The first drunken woman was the daughter of the male drunkard . . .
> The human race is suffering from over-fertilisation and enforced repro-
> duction. Man the destroyer has been at work, not woman the
> constructor. When man is continent the mysterious origin of cancer
> will be solved and cancer, with other kindred horror, will disappear.
> Sexual germs are not confined to the reproductive organs; they perme-
> ate the whole body. Assimilation and absorption by the female
> organism cannot divest them of their potential properties of stimula-
> tion and disintegration, of decay and corruption. Hence the terrible
> increase of cancer among the western races, who for so long have
> ignored the law.[40]

Motherhood, by contrast, determined the health of the human race:

> The mother's mental influence upon the brain structure of her off-
> spring can alone produce a better standard of brain power. She alone
> can retard or reduce the pathological condition of suffering mortality.
> With her rests the responsibility of eliminating suicidal tendencies, of
> preventing the increase of insanity, epilepsy, imbecility and idiocy. She
> has to build up the nobler, purer, brighter, and happier manhood and
> womanhood of the future, evolving the race to a higher plane of
> being – the outcome of maternal impressions, rightly dirigated, con-
> trolled and synthesised. Her creative powers range from the strictly
> material to the sublimest spirituality; and through and by that spiritu-
> ality she will, as the highest evolved organism, and as the chosen
> medium to achieve the greatest results in the process of evolution,
> gradually uplift humanity.[41]

Male vice was the root cause of national decline. Vices, however, like curses, came back to wreak vengeance on man for his treatment of woman. 'In his own enfeebled frame, in his diseased tissue, in his weak will, his gibbering idiocy, his raving insanity and hideous criminality, he reaps the fruits of a dishonoured motherhood, and outraged woman-hood, an unnatural, abnormal stimulated childbirth and starved poison-fed infancy.'[42]

And of course it went without saying that women would preserve the racial superiority of the British Empire. Modern civilisation would count for little, Mrs Swiney thought, if the great Anglo-Saxon nation couldn't keep its blood-royal 'pure and undefiled'. Women as mothers must there-fore bring their knowledge to bear on transmitting untainted 'the purity and nobility of racial characteristics', and fight the anarchy and animal-ism which threatened modern civilisation. Although men had sexual relations with the 'lowest and most disgusting females of the most degraded races', most women were always careful to keep their offspring 'free from tainted blood'. 'The Aryan woman, happily, has never stooped to the sexual degradation of the Aryan man; and it is to the influence of the white woman in the future, that we must look for the enforcement of that high and pure morality which will restrain the conquering white man from becoming the progenitor of racial crossing with a lower and more degraded type, dangerous to social and ethical advancement, in the lands that come under his sway.'[43] In these utterances of this most advanced and progressive Edwardian feminist could be heard a precur-sor of the genocidal horrors of thirty years later.

Women's suffrage, said Mrs Swiney, was needed because these old savage virtues were at a discount, and

> the factor to bring about the gradual extinction of the more virile qual-
> ities of mankind so as to inculcate in their place the mild and gracious
> virtues of the higher dispensation is the influence of woman in every
> sphere of public life. Women will plead for arbitration between
> nations; they will be the universal peace-makers; they will bring into
> public administration that element of stability, of sterling moral worth,

of justice and equality, upon which alone depends a nation's true progress ... the lower animal instincts and passions of man will be held under control and ultimately eliminated when the great chastity of paternity, to match the great chastity of maternity, will have brought the ideal union of the sexes to its consummation.[44]

The suffragists, however, were as divided over sexuality and family issues as they were over almost everything else. Some who were profoundly hostile to marriage arrived at that position from a diametrically opposite direction from the purity lobby. For they believed not in chastity but in free love. At the end of the century, under the influence of new continental theories of sexology and psychology, including the work of Sigmund Freud, a new science of 'sexology' arose, with writers such as Grant Allen, Edward Carpenter and Havelock Ellis projecting sexual liberation as part of a wider utopian socialist vision, or a radical liberal ideal of self-liberation. Such ideas were promoted by the Legitimation League, founded in 1893 with the American feminist Lilian Harman as president. This advocated not libertine sexual intercourse but free love, which was said to combine the aesthetic and spiritual sides of the personality with a frank and open attitude towards sex. It stressed the importance of female sexuality and women's right to sexual pleasure with men.

However, free-love movements were dominated by men, and there were tensions among feminists in committing themselves to such libertarian politics. Lilian Harman herself warned that the libertarianism of men meant in practice that women merely became the property of the herd rather than of one man – hardly an advance for freedom. Men and women, she warned, had a different understanding of free love. Men thought it meant that women would enjoy those sexual pleasures that previously only men had enjoyed. But what Harman meant was that women could define an autonomous sexuality free of the constraints of marriage and family which had been used by men to oppress them.[45]

To most such feminists, indeed, free love meant not unbridled promiscuity but an end to monogamous marriage and its replacement by spiritually meaningful love affairs based on ties between individuals freely entered into. This was the way they thought women could free themselves from male oppression. Love was something on a higher plane altogether than mere carnal lust, which was a male deficiency, had been legitimised through marriage and legitimated in turn prostitution. Thus Arabella Dennehy wrote: 'Is woman to remain the physical and moral slave of man, or is she to determine her own future? Is marriage a mere piece of mechanism for subjugating women and allowing men to gratify their basest desires while outwardly conforming to conventional regulations? If so, then true morality would lead to this inevitable result – abolish marriage, establish free union in which each sex would have an equal voice, and make love the only law regulating the relationship of the sexes.'[46]

Effie Johnson wanted free love because 'that most effectively leads to the goal towards which both evolution and progress press – viz, spiritually'. And spiritual love was 'the apex of all material evolution, the flower which aeons of slowly developing animal organisms at length bear'. Marriage, by contrast, had evolved 'into that terrible growth, prostitution, linked with a miscalled monogamy, which admits a one-sided licentiousness under monogamic laws, truly appalling to contemplate'. Free love was not 'excess', and women who chose it did so in revolt against the injustice of marriage laws.

Annie Besant was also at one stage a strong propagandist for sexual intercourse. She argued that celibacy was a mark of imperfection causing diseases such as spermatorrhoea, chlorosis and hysteria in women, a list that rivalled Frances Swiney's equivalent set of horrors attendant on sexuality.[47] Annie Besant had an affair with George Bernard Shaw, after which it was said, her hair turned grey and Shaw later told an interviewer that she had 'absolutely no sex appeal'.[48] When she later turned to theosophy, however, she came to a rather different conclusion and became an advocate of sexual self-control. 'Now the sexual instinct that he [man] has in common with the brute is one of the most fruitful sources of human misery . . . to hold this instinct in complete control . . . is the task to which humanity should set itself . . . It follows that Theosophists should sound the note of self-restraint within marriage and the restriction of the marital relation to the perpetuation of the race.'[49]

In common with other suffragists, Annie Besant's personal life failed to live up to the grand theories feminism was promoting of a higher plane of love between the sexes. In the Men and Women's Club, the writer Olive Schreiner had been a lone voice promoting the idea of female sexual pleasure. In her book *Woman and Labour*, she mapped out a sexual utopia in which both sexes would reach their full evolutionary potential. She hoped that the women's movement could be 'called a part of the great movement of the sexes towards each other, a movement towards common occupations, common interests, common ideals, and an emotional tenderness and sympathy between the sexes more deeply founded and more indestructible than any the world has ever seen'.

Like another club member, Eleanor Marx, Olive Schreiner suffered for much of her life from crippling psychosomatic diseases and nervous symptoms. Eleanor Marx lived with the critic Edward Aveling, and they presented their union as a model for the future of free men and women. In their book *The Woman Question* they wrote that there would no longer be 'the hideous disguise, the constant lying, that makes the domestic life of almost all our English homes an organised hypocrisy'. Yet Aveling was one of the most notorious liars and philanderers in London, a hypocrite who secretly married a much younger woman in 1897. In 1898, having discovered his infidelity, Eleanor Marx killed herself at the age of forty-three by taking prussic acid. Olive Schreiner, meanwhile, had a series of self-destructive relationships with men in England, returned to South Africa and married a younger man who took her name. For her, marriage never met the expectations of equal intellectual partnership that she had recommended to everyone else.[50]

The feminist debates about sexuality raged particularly in the pages of *The Freewoman*, which promoted free-love unions. Although this was a tiny publication, running from November 1911 to October 1912 – resurfacing briefly as *The New Freewoman* in 1913 – it was disproportionately influential among suffragists, who read it widely. Mrs Fawcett, however, tore it up in disgust and Maude Royden, a fellow member of the NUWSS executive, thought it 'nauseous'. *The Freewoman* was started by Dora Marsden and Mary Gawthorpe, both former members of the WSPU but who had left in protest at the narrowness of the suffrage campaign and the autocracy of the Pankhursts. Dora, a feminist anarchist individualist whose mill-owner father had deserted his wife and five children when Dora was eight years old, was described by Emmeline Pethick-Lawrence as 'the sweetest, greatest and bravest of suffragettes' and by Sylvia as having 'a face like a Florentine angel'.[51] Like so many feminists, Dora was later to became engrossed in religion; she wrote three incomprehensible books about spirituality and claimed that 'spiritual consciousness' would eventually 'constitute a higher development in the evolution of the human race and of human achievement'.[52] But first she ignited feminist debates which the suffrage movement was ignoring.

The paper was radical and freethinking, drawing on the work of such progressive thinkers as Rebecca West, H. G. Wells, Edward Carpenter, Havelock Ellis, the socialist Ada Neild Chew, the anarchists Guy Aldred and Rose Witcop and the free-love feminist Stella Browne. It promoted revolutionary ideas about women's sphere, marriage, sexuality and reproduction which interpreted feminism far more widely and radically than either Mrs Fawcett's NUWSS or the Pankhursts' WSPU. Indeed, the paper specifically attacked both the militant movement and the preoccupation with the vote. The message that shone through its debates was that many positions taken up by both the suffragists and the militant suffragettes were based on stereotyped roles that would only contribute to the continued oppression of women. Explicitly contemptuous of Parliament, the paper argued also for revolutionary politics – or force – and even, in 1911, for civil war if Asquith broke his promise and didn't allow a women's amendment to the forthcoming Reform Bill. 'Could anyone ask a young movement to ally itself with so hopeless and hapless a baby as the Labour parliamentarians?' it asked. 'We think not. The women's ranks have shown themselves far too liable to the same kind of disease as the parliamentary Labour party; the childish belief in parliamentary action; the vain imagining that the masses do not count; that they are to be led up the parliamentary stairs, in fact.'[53]

Suffragism, it said, was a side issue to feminism which had misdirected women's reforming efforts.[54] It criticised militancy as a narrow policy preventing genuine radical thinking, and described Christabel Pankhurst as a leader of 'bondswomen'.[55] It claimed that there 'is no idea behind English suffragism . . . no feminism' and that its leaders stood to 'defend the capitalist monopoly [and] the marriage monopoly'.[56]

It was the marriage monopoly that was squarely in Dora Marsden's sights. Sex roles, she thought, had to be abandoned if women were to be free. Marriage was just another form of prostitution, as Edward Carpenter had argued. Monogamous morality, she wrote, was 'based on the intellectual apathy and insensitiveness of married women, who fulfilled their own moral ideal at the expense of the spinster and prostitute. 'Indissoluble monogamy is an unjustified tyranny,' she stormed. 'It is blunderingly stupid and reacts immorally, producing deceit, sensuality, vice, promiscuity, prostitution, spinsterdom and a grossly unfair monopoly.'[57] Marriage was a 'deliberate abrogation of freedom' and limited sexual expression while debasing women 'to the level of common merchandise'.[58] Instead, writers for *The Freewoman* suggested new forms of sexual union. Some proposed an exclusive relationship without a contract; others said brief sexual encounters were to be recommended. Free-love unions were frequently proposed. One vicar's wife claimed most women 'give themselves for love', although there were 'women who disassociate the spiritual from the bodily appetite and satisfy the latter without the former, just as a man can. There are some in fact to whom it is a necessity of health to do so.'[59]

In 1912 the paper hosted a heated debate between new moralists and purity feminists. Celibacy for women was said to be unhealthy. Stella Browne wrote: 'The sexual experience is the right of every human being not hopelessly afflicted in mind or body and should be entirely a matter of free choice and personal preference, untainted by bargain or compulsion.'[60] In response to critics who emphasised the values of marriage and domesticity, Rose Witcop, who lived with Guy Aldred, wrote back that she wanted them to become 'disgusted with the barrack-like existence you are leading today, to fill your minds with thoughts higher than sex . . .'[61]

The debate broadened into advocating sex without conception. Motherhood – that sacred state for female triumphalists – was denounced instead as a major factor in women's enslavement. According to Stella Browne, women must freely choose or reject maternity on their own terms and their 'right to refuse maternity is an invulnerable right'.[62] The maternal role, said Dora Marsden, was the cause of women's oppression: 'To the door of the "legitimate mother" and to the "protection" accorded to her by popular sentiment is to be traced the responsibility for most of the social ills from which we suffer.'[63]

Ada Neild Chew argued that motherhood was an obstacle to women's economic independence. 'The greatest obstacle to economic freedom is the deeply rooted notion, in the minds of many of themselves, and in the minds of almost all men, that they are merely playing at work for a time until they undertake the "duties of wife and mother".'[64] Women, she contended, could not 'live individual lives and develop on individual lines' if they were forced to become mothers or be dependent on either the state or upon men.[65] Dora Marsden thought the solution lay in state-run nurseries for babies of two weeks and above because 'if women's work has to assume the permanent character of that of men, it must be of a permanent nature'.[66] H. G. Wells advocated the state endowment of motherhood, but Dora said this would encourage the 'captivity of woman', and if the state was to pay women to become mothers, then why not pay for their sexual services too?[67] Housework, she said, had no economic value and made the housewife into a drudge because 'she creates nothing'.[68]

But who, then, should perform the domestic and maternal roles? There were no clear answers – hardly surprising, since these dilemmas remain unresolved even today. Some, like Fanny Johnson, wanted men and women to share housework and childcare equally. She asked: 'Might not the advice to go home and mind the baby sometimes be applied to fathers?'[69] Others proposed 'group houses' where individuals would share the housework or employ professionals.

There was, of course, another way of preventing motherhood – contraception. Yet this was an incendiary issue which was to divide the women's movement. The majority of feminists were either ambivalent or deeply hostile to contraception. Some believed that sex was solely about reproduction; others, that birth control would awaken the 'slumbering beast' of sex, which would become unmanageable. Most opposed contraception on the grounds that it would both encourage sex outside marriage and dehumanise sexual relations. The root of the feminist objection to birth control was that it would only promote more male sexual activity. Margery Smith wrote in 1925: 'We regard artificial birth control as wrong. We know well that it would open the way to demands from men that would amount to a new tyranny. We do not want more tyrannies but more practical love.'[70]

But there were other feminists – a vociferous minority – who argued that birth control involved prudence, foresight, responsibility and rational control. They drew such sentiments from Thomas Malthus, the eighteenth-century prophet of population increase – even though Malthus had been virulently opposed to contraception. Yet these neo-Malthusians believed that birth control would permit normal sexual relations while bringing procreation under rational control. After the sensational trial of Annie Besant and Charles Bradlaugh, the Malthusian League was formed, with Annie Besant as Honorary Secretary and Dr Charles Drysdale, who had stood bail for them, as President.

This corruption of Malthus to promote birth control drew a furious response from the feminist pioneer Dr Elizabeth Blackwell. The message of the neo-Malthusians was getting in the way of the campaign to curb male sexuality, the real cause of the problem. As if it was not bad enough to have surgeons and physicians claiming that chastity was bad for unmarried men, she fumed, now these false Malthusians were polluting marriage. Childless union, she asserted, was a risk to woman's health. Contraception indulged a husband's sensuality while counteracting nature with uncertain or bad effects upon a woman. 'Her internal structure fights against the success of unnatural arts; her tissues imbibe any poisonous drug, and resent the absence of what is natural ... no considerable improvement which may be called national can be hoped for until women insist on exacting from men the chastity which we claim of them. Under this wholesome pressure we shall learn new lessons; the true doctrine of sexual purity will seem an obvious necessity for virtue, manliness, honour and self-respect.'[71]

In the book's notes, Dr Blackwell worried further that only the upper classes would practise contraception. 'If the morally and physically superior portion of the population can become infatuated enough to obey the teaching of those who advocate artificial checks to population, criminals and rogues, the dwarfed and degenerate will out-breed all the nobler forms and nobler minds,' she wrote.[72]

Despite the opposition to birth control of the majority of feminists, by the early twentieth century the Malthusian League was actively courting the women's movement. Against the opposition of Mrs Fawcett, they not only promised feminists that birth control would give women greater control than ever in determining the size of their families, but coupled this with demands for votes for women as they said both would give mothers the right to refuse to bring children into an overcrowded world. Female inferiority, they said, had been perpetuated by cycles of high fertility that kept women in maternal bondage. Most feminists refused to associate themselves with such arguments. But the fact was that family planning had been quietly adopted by millions. By 1906, according to Beatrice and Sidney Webb, between half and two-thirds of families were practising some kind of family limitation.[73] Moreover, some feminists, including Mrs Mona Caird, Mrs Wolstenholme Elmy and Lady Florence Dixie, assumed that smaller families would result from greater sexual equality and that this was a good reason to battle for the vote.

This reinforced the popular resentment that feminism was depleting the national breeding stock. Under the influence of eugenic thinking, it was widely feared, the modern educated women of superior breeding would be unwilling or unfit for motherhood. So even suffragist sympathisers agreed with their opponents that too many 'feminine literati' and 'married school mistresses' were avoiding their primary biological and social duties. Had not Herbert Spencer warned in his *Principles of Biology* in 1864 that mental exertion in upper-class women would cause a reduction in reproductive power, and even absolute sterility? He wrote of 'flat-chested girls who survive their high-pressure education [but who] are incompetent to bear a well-developed infant and to supply it with the natural food for the natural period'.

All of this left the Eugenics Education Society, founded in 1907 to promote the acceptance of eugenics, in something of a quandary. Some forty per cent of its members were unmarried and many were active in the moderate suffrage movement, although they rarely spoke out on women's rights. But the eugenists were divided over their attitude to women's emancipation. Some thought that women should be given the vote to clear them to make enlightened marriages which would produce genetically valuable children. By contrast, Francis Galton and others thought that female emancipation would interfere with natural selection by reducing the availability of eugenically preferred women. Galton opposed admitting women to universities, lent his name to an anti-suffrage statement in 1908 and was unpersuaded that educated women would contract racially advantageous marriages based on mutual respect, compatibility and attraction.[74]

Eugenists' doubts about birth control were reinforced by medical evidence of the effects of 'unnatural' feminine activity and deferred fertility. Mrs E. M. Somervell, president of the Anti-Suffrage Society and a eugenist, reported health authorities' findings of high childhood mortality, maternal deaths, disease and moral decay in those manufacturing districts with substantial female employment. Physicians reported more female hysteria and obstetric problems, which they ascribed to the confusion of sex roles stirred up by the suffrage campaign. Dr Hope Grant claimed in the *British Medical Journal* in 1904 that the new woman was becoming masculine; she cycled, played golf and hockey and other sports which increased her muscles while diminishing her pelvis. The sexually rebellious nature of the women's movement troubled doctors, who thought it showed a deep disturbance in the 'emotional nature' of the modern female, leading to an 'atrophied maternal instinct, loss of femininity and a lessened development of women's ways'. Dr R. Murray Leslie believed 'sex starvation' and sterility stimulated by the women's movement might be a major cause of increased female insanity. Dr Francis Freemantle, Medical Officer of Health for Hertfordshire, believed that the demand for the vote directly stemmed from sexual indulgence stimulated by the Besant–Bradlaugh trial, luring women in the upper classes to limit their families, thus corrupting moral and social ideals.[75]

Mainstream suffragists were highly sensitive to charges of perverted femininity and refused to be seduced by the neo-Malthusian push for birth control. Mrs Fawcett denied there was any logical connection between the suffrage campaign and the rise of family limitation. In 1910 Emmeline Pethick-Lawrence denied that the movement had ever disputed the supreme importance of motherhood; its concerns were rather with the debased position of women and of mothers.[76] Nevertheless, there was clearly evidence of antipathy to motherhood itself by some in the women's movement. Teresa Billington-Greig agreed that modern women were in revolt 'against unwilling and too frequent motherhood', although she thought that in the main this was a rebellion for liberty.[77]

Most feminists were opposed to free unions. They feared women's vulnerability to desertion and betrayal too much. In any event, for the majority of feminists male sexuality was the evil to be confronted and tamed. Female sexuality and motherhood were not the problem, only the male laws and social conventions which exploited or abused them. Men, not women, were the issue. And as the suffrage struggle intensified, male sexuality came to the fore as the dominant problem to be resolved. Female rights of citizenship were increasingly seen as the means to curb male sexuality. The suffragette Lucy Re Bartlett claimed that the struggle was nothing less than a sex war. 'The public roughly seems divided between people who deny the struggle any sexual significance at all, and those who, seeing the significance, attribute it to sexual morbidity and hysteria. The situation with which we are face to face represents indeed a sex war ... it is a war which signifies vitality, not decadence.'[78]

And it was as a sex war that Christabel Pankhurst now attempted to kick back into life the stalemated suffrage campaign.

The ferment about prostitution and sexuality that characterised the Victorian period had never gone away. In the fevered climate of the times many suffragettes thought the White Slave Act of 1912 had been watered down. This gave added impetus to the pathological sense of grievance and persecution that characterised the militant movement. The issues of male sexuality, prostitution and white slavery became increasingly conflated in suffragette thinking.

This was not confined to the militants. When it came to prostitution, the sedate Mrs Fawcett was as much a sex warrior as any suffragette. In 1910, at the request of the NUWSS, Dr Louisa Martindale published *Under the Surface*, a book about prostitution which was sent to every MP. She wrote: 'My one object has been to prove to those who do not yet believe it that the existence of prostitution in our land is due to the fact that women are not treated as, or believed to be, the equals of men.' The prostitute, she said, had been from her earliest days 'imbued with the belief in the superior knowledge of the other sex. She has been taught to be affectionate and charming, and above all to be unselfish. She has been taught to regard her future husband as master, and one she must obey ... She has been trained from her earliest years in the very qualities which make her an easy prey to the professional seducer or procurer.' Men, she said, had deliberately trained a whole class of women to minister to their alleged sexual needs. 'Even further, it is these men who have instilled into their womenfolk the idea that sexual indulgence is a necessity to their health – one of the greatest fallacies that ever existed.'[79]

In November 1912 Mrs Drummond wrote in *The Suffragette*:

There are three questions which, above all others, are firing our indignation and making us determined that we will now get the vote once and for all. These questions are: 1. The sweating of women workers. The starvation of women is undermining the health of the mothers of the race and is driving thousands to a life of shame. 2. The White Slave Traffic. Even under the new Bill which is now being carried a man can get less punishment for trapping an innocent girl and forcing her to a life of shame than for stealing a loaf of bread. 3. The outrages committed upon little girls, some of them only babies. This is a growing evil, which working-class mothers are determined to stamp out, and to do this they must have the vote.[80]

That year the Recorder of Sandwich, Kent, became a suffragist *cause célèbre* when he gave only a nominal sentence to a man convicted of child violation on the grounds that he had succumbed to a normal, momentary temptation.[81] In July 1913 the scandal of the Piccadilly flat case inflamed the issue still further. Young girls barely over the age of consent were being procured to work in a brothel run by a woman called Queenie Gerald, allegedly servicing upper-class men, including MPs and judges. Feminists demanded their names be revealed; Keir Hardie was persuaded to raise the issue in the Commons. Mrs Pankhurst claimed that the WSPU offices were raided to seize evidence which the suffragettes could have used to expose the role of government in the affair. Christabel, milking the scandal for all it was worth, wrote: 'In the Piccadilly flat case, with its foul revelations and still fouler concealments, is summed up the whole case against Votes for Women.'[82] A few days later she added for good measure: 'The men patrons . . . after their share in degrading young girls, after wading through physical and moral filth, went home and doubtless forbade any meddling with the suffrage question . . .' Women who wanted to see 'humanity no longer degraded by impure thought and physical disease' would realise how vital it was to enter the ranks of the WSPU to win the vote.[83]

The issue of the parliamentary vote was being increasingly swept along by a rising tide of sexual hysteria. Militant violence was being justified as a response to male sexual excess. Lucy Re Bartlett wrote that women could not remain indifferent when faced with the horror of the white slave traffic, the ruin of little children and the total inadequacy of law and the indifference of the legislators. Suffragettes were being called unwomanly, she said indignantly, but women were called by their status as women and mothers to redress these wrongs. Militancy, she claimed, was the direct result. 'It is moved by some, as an objection to giving the

vote to women, that it will cause dissension in the home, through differing opinions. There is no fair difference of opinion which can have the
power to rouse anything like the feeling which is rising in some women
now as they feel the awfulness of certain wrongs, the indifference of
men, and their own helplessness to bring any remedy. It is the sense of
helplessness, more than any other thing, which brings the touch of "madness" to many women.' And even among those who were not engaged in
violent acts, militancy was to be justified in the home in the form of a sex
strike. 'In the hearts of many women today is rising a cry somewhat like
this: "If I cannot help, at least I will not acquiesce . . . I will know no
man, and bear no child, until this apathy be broken through – these
wrongs be righted!"'[84]

As militancy ran into the political quicksand, the Pankhursts cranked
up the supremely emotive issue of the sexual abuse of women and children in order to regain the momentum. As repression against militancy
deepened, the WSPU increasingly presented their opponents as the
embodiment of sexual evil. The hostile press, said Mrs Pankhurst, were
deliberately rousing 'that element from which the White Slaver is drawn;
from which the brute who lives on the immoral earnings of his own
child is drawn'.[85] Militancy was the means of drawing the sexual poison
from society. 'The chief fruits of woman slavery is the Social Evil [pros-
titution]. As a result of the Social Evil, the nation is poisoned morally,
mentally and physically. Women are only just finding this out. As their
knowledge grows, they will look upon militancy as a surgical operation – a violence fraught with mercy and healing.'[86] The stone-throwing,
arson and physical attacks were all a means of cleansing society. 'The
militancy of women is doing a work of purification. Nowhere was purification more needed than in the relationship between men and women . . .
When militancy has done its work then will come sweetness and clean-
ness, respect and trust, perfect equality and justice into the partnership
between men and women.'[87]

Purification was a word not used lightly. For male sexual profligacy
was blamed for spreading venereal disease, the preoccupation with
which had scarcely diminished since the days of the Contagious Diseases

Acts. The subject was still the most inflammatory and sensational, and could be relied on to boost the circulation of a flagging periodical.[88] In 1913 Christabel published a series of articles in *The Suffragette* which were later collected in a book entitled *The Great Scourge and How to End It*.

Claiming that man was 'the exterminator of the species', she presented a dire picture of men as the fount of sexual disease which threatened the health and lives of women, not just in the brothels but within the sacred marriage bed itself. A diseased man was more dangerous than a diseased prostitute because he could pass VD on to his wife and children. Men were infecting their wives with syphilis and gonorrhoea, she said, without their knowing it. It was a huge cause of physical, mental and moral degeneracy. She quoted various doctors as estimating that seventy-five to eighty per cent of men were infected with gonorrhoea, and twenty per cent with syphilis, before the age of thirty. Sexual vice, she said, was rampant in all classes. Marriage didn't satisfy men, and carried an appalling risk to women. Many wives contracted 'conditions which alter life and even character ... headache, backache, irregular and painful menstruation, urinary disorders, localised peritonitis, loss of healthful beauty, lassitude, hysteria, sterility, miscarriages'. Men were consistently infecting the race with vile disease and threatening the downfall of the nation. Marriage was to be avoided as an 'appalling danger to women'. 'Never again must young women enter into marriage blindfolded. From now onwards they must be warned of the fact that marriage is intensely dangerous, until such time as men's moral standards are completely changed and they become as chaste and clean-living as women.'[89]

Female infirmities, used by some as an argument against giving women the vote, were in fact caused by VD. The re-education of men on sexual matters was one of the most urgent issues. 'Until men in general accept the views on the sex question held by all normal women, and until they live as cleanly as normal women do, the race will be poisoned, as it is today, by foul disease.' But men instinctively wanted to keep women in economic dependence and have them at their mercy, at the root of their opposition to women's employment. This would continue as long as men had a monopoly of political power. They wanted the lewdness and obscenity they couldn't get with their wives, preferably with young virgins.

Intelligent women knew that the physical and spiritual consequences of sexual union were profound. 'When women have the vote they will be more and not less opposed than now to make a plaything of sex and of entering casually into the sex relationship,' Christabel confidently predicted.[90] Again, one wonders what she would have made of the sexually licentious women of today. She even managed to blame the Prime Minister for destroying women's health. The cause of sexual disease was the subjection of women; therefore Asquith's opposition to the suffrage meant that he was an overwhelming public danger.

She rejoiced in doctors' failure to find a cure for VD, for their quest was a wicked attempt to enable men (no mention of women) to 'go and sin in safety'. Like the doctors and purity campaigners in the previous century, she argued that continence was 'the surest guarantee against atrophy of the sexual organs' and that 'the proper subjugation of the sexual impulses and the conservation of the complex seminal fluid, with its wonderfully invigorating influence, develops all that is best and noblest in man'.[91]

The cure, in short, was votes for women and chastity for men. Regulation of vice was futile. 'Chastity for men – or, in other words, their observance of the same moral standard as is observed by women – is therefore indispensable.' When they became citizens equipped with the vote, women would feel more respect for themselves and be more respected by men. The vote would give them power to secure the enactment of laws for their protection and would strengthen their economic position.[92]

The facts she was presenting, wrote Christabel, made an overwhelming case for votes for women. The knowledge of this hidden scourge would put new and greater passion into the movement for political enfranchisement and make it more than ever like a war against slavery. Criticism of the militant policy of destroying property in the fight for the vote would be silenced by the retort that men were destroying the health and life of women in pursuit of vice. The true reason behind the opposition to the vote, she claimed, was nothing other than sexual vice. 'Those who want to have women as slaves obviously do not want women to become voters.'[93] Men knew that when women became politically free and economically strong they would not be purchasable for vice. One wonders what she would have made of London's King's Cross a century later.

It was certainly true that the extent of VD was still a significant problem – but nowhere near as bad as Christabel had made out. Her figures were a wild exaggeration. In 1916 the Royal Commission on Venereal Disease said that, in 1912, up to twelve per cent of adult males and at least seven per cent of adult females in the working population had acquired syphilis, and that school leavers should be given moral instruction and warned against sexual temptation.

Some feminists were horrified by Christabel's sensational claims. Rebecca West wrote in the *Clarion* that 'her remarks on the subject are utterly valueless and are likely to discredit the cause in which we believe . . .'[94] Dora Marsden said in *The New Freewoman* that there was more danger to health from the misery of renunciation and virginity than from VD.[95] But sales of *The Suffragette*, which had sunk to ten thousand a week by January 1913, now shot up to nearly thirty thousand. The Daily Herald League suggested forming a Guild of Honour for mothers who vowed to remain chaste until the vote was won. *The Eye-Opener*, the organ of the Men's Society for Women's Rights, condemned male voters as 'sexually depraved degenerates who are spewed out nightly from taprooms or even more evil resorts'.[96] *The Great Scourge* rescued Christabel from oblivion.

As her sister Sylvia mordantly observed: 'She who had deprecated and shunned every mention of her sex now hinged the greater part of her propaganda upon the supposed great prevalence of venereal diseases and the sex excesses of men.' The great advantage to the WSPU of the *Great Scourge* propaganda was that it didn't offend the class consciousness of the Tories, and by its inflammatory nature spurred women on to more serious acts of destruction. Sylvia wrote despairingly:

Christabel was now, in effect, preaching the sex war deprecated and denied by the older suffragists. Mr [Pethick-]Lawrence had often said he had thrown in his lot with the militant women in order that the suffragette struggle might not become a 'sex war'. Not from the speeches of Mrs Pankhurst, who never lost her gift of sympathy with her audiences, but from the columns of the *Suffragette* the deduction was clear: women were purer, nobler and more courageous; men were an inferior body, greatly in need of purification, the WSPU being the chosen instrument capable of administering the purge. Masses of women, especially of the middle class, were affected by this attitude even though they remained outside the ranks of the union.[97]

Events, however, were to intervene: The sex war was superseded by a real war. In August 1914 Britain found itself at arms against Germany. The Great War had begun, and the world would never be the same again.

16

WAR AND VICTORY

The immediate reaction of the suffragists to the outbreak of war in 1914 was confused and uncertain. Had not feminism, after all, stood for peace and harmony against the bellicose nature of men? Was not war an anathema to all that the suffragists believed in and had fought for? On 4 August Mrs Fawcett called on governments to avert war, but by the following day she had changed her tune. Women, she said, should realise that their country needed them and they should now show themselves worthy of its citizenship.[1]

This brief vacillation was as nothing compared to the spectacular volte-face performed by the Pankhursts. Christabel immediately decided that the war was a judgement on the iniquity of men. She wrote in *The Suffragette* on 7 August 1914: 'A man-made civilisation, hideous and cruel enough in time of peace, is to be destroyed ... This great war ... is nature's vengeance – is God's vengeance upon the people who held women in subjection ... that which has made men for generations past sacrifice women and the race to their lusts, is now making them fly at each other's throats and bring ruin upon the world ... Women may well stand aghast at the ruin by which the civilisation of the white races in the Eastern Hemisphere is confronted.

This, then, is the climax that the male system of diplomacy and government has reached.'[2]

Mrs Pankhurst too had previously said: 'War is not women's way! To the women of this union human life is sacred!' But the government had offered a truce; and she knew that to oppose war would almost certainly destroy the WSPU. The week after *The Suffragette*'s loud damnation of male diplomatic stupidity, the paper failed to appear; the jailed suffragettes were freed from prison and on 13 August Mrs Pankhurst suspended militancy, which, she said, would be pointless in the face of the infinitely greater violence of war.[3] In 1914 she wrote: 'So ends, for the present, the war of women against men. As of old the women become the nurturing mothers of men, their sisters and uncomplaining helpmates.'[4]

Christabel told the *Daily Telegraph* on 4 September that a German victory would be a disaster for women. 'We suffragists . . . do not feel that Great Britain is in any sense decadent. On the contrary, we are tremendously conscious of strength and freshness.'[5] This from a woman who only the previous year had been representing Britain as putrefying from corruption and disease. She told an audience the same month that militant women must rouse men to match the sacrifice of France and Belgium. Pacifist talk was a luxury which could no longer be afforded. 'In the English-speaking nations under the British flag and the Stars and Stripes,' she said, 'woman's influence is higher, her political rights more extended than in any other part of the world . . .'[6] One has to rub one's eyes in disbelief. The militant who had gone to war against the government, who had been jailed and gone on hunger strike, who had commanded violent deeds and mounted a decades-long propaganda offensive, all in the cause she had endlessly proclaimed of freeing oppressed women from slavery and worse, was now effectively airbrushing all of that from history. The story now was to be completely different.

It was the end of the campaign by Mrs Pankhurst and Christabel for women's suffrage. Now they were to adapt and reinvent themselves once again in a world that had changed. From the enemy within, they were to be transformed into the most strident of patriots. This was not, however, as strange as it may seem. They had been reliant for years on the support of upper-class women for whom patriotism was axiomatic.[7] On a more profound level, the spiritual crusade they represented was intimately bound up with imperialist beliefs about the superiority of the British Empire and the assertion of its values over lesser breeds.

For these Manicheans of feminism, the Liberal government was now joined in its familiar role of devil by the male-chauvinist Germans.[8] Mrs Pankhurst portrayed Germany as militaristic, tyrannical and male; Belgium and France were innocent, threatened, invaded and – of course – female.[9] Indeed, male chauvinism was now replaced by real chauvinism as Mrs Pankhurst and Christabel rapidly turned into the most strident belligerents. They thought the war was a process of national purification and condemned Asquith, Haldane and Grey as military fainthearts. The war provided a fresh and more savage stick with which to beat male politicians. Christabel came out against Irish Home Rule as she thought it would result in German infiltration. They portrayed Keir Hardie and Ramsay MacDonald as being tools of the Kaiser. Soon after war was declared Christabel appeared at the Opera House in London with a speech on the 'German peril', but then went abroad, and spent much of the war as an armchair general issuing weekly broadsides against the conduct of the war from her pleasant retreat at Deauville – 'a nice quiet little place with such a good climate'.[10]

Mrs Pankhurst, meanwhile, continued to make platform speeches up and down Britain but this time casting herself as a recruiting sergeant-in-chief and browbeater of men for failing to be belligerent enough; her supporters handed out white feathers to every young man in civilian dress, and held placards saying, 'Intern them all.'[11] In a speech at Plymouth she declared: 'The war has made me feel how much there is of nobility in man, in addition to the other things which we all deplore.' The Pankhursts organised yet another women's procession, this time demanding that women be given work in munitions factories: this to oblige Lloyd George, until recently the object of their contempt and hatred, who said he was facing opposition in Cabinet. In November 1917 the WSPU became the Women's Party, standing for opposition to

Home Rule, the abolition of the trade unions and the elimination of all persons of non-British descent from government departments and essential industries.[12]

This startling transformation of Christabel and her mother caused no small degree of shock. To the anguished Sylvia, it was simply a betrayal of the women's movement. In 1916 two breakaway organisations were formed as a result: the Suffragettes of the WSPU and the Independent WSPU. Sylvia's own suffrage organisation, the East London Federation, became an important focus of anti-war activity. Sylvia, who saw the struggle more as a class than a gender conflict, changed its name in 1916 to the Workers' Suffrage Federation.[13] The WSPU paper *The Suffragette* vanished, to be reborn as *Britannia*, advocating military conscription, the internment of aliens and a war of attrition against Germany, under the slogan: 'It is a thousand times more the duty of the militant suffragettes to fight the Kaiser for the sake of liberty than it was to fight anti-suffrage governments.' Sylvia wept. 'To me,' she wrote, 'this seemed a tragic betrayal of the great movement to bring the mother-half of the race into the councils of the nations. "Women would stand for peace!" How often, how often had they and all of us averred it!'[14]

The peace movement was, in fact, to split not just the Pankhursts but the whole suffrage movement. Many thought that pacifism was inseparable from the women's cause. Emmeline Pethick-Lawrence wrote that since women had shown solidarity as the guardians of the human race, how could they stand aside now while the flower of manhood was slaughtered?[15]

Mrs Fawcett, by contrast, viewed the war as being fought for the sanctity of treaties, the rights of small nations and the overthrowing of military tyranny. The Empire was at war, she said, to preserve democracy against Prussian authoritarianism; a Prussian victory would make women's suffrage even more difficult.[16] She also knew the danger of the suffrage movement being branded pro-German. Men would say women were politically hopeless and unfit to have the vote. The anti-suffragists were only too keen to claim that women would hinder governments from waging a just war. As it was, the *Anti-Suffrage Review* could only lament instead that suffragists were knitting and sewing for soldiers, 'but with such a perpetual running accompaniment of suffragist self-laudation that they might as well embroider the sacred name of Mrs Pankhurst or Mrs Fawcett on every sock and every muffler, so as to give notice to the soldiers as well as to the country at large that suffragism alone has the trademark of thoughtful and benevolent patriotism'.[17]

So Mrs Fawcett turned the NUWSS over to war-relief work. But the pacifists, who were numerous, were very angry, and said that she was acting unconstitutionally and imposing her own personal view on the union. In April 1915 Dutch suffragists and English pacifists urged the formation of an international congress of women to promote pacifism. Mrs Fawcett rejected it, but Maud Royden and others said the women's movement was an attempt to assert the supremacy of the spiritual over physical force and eleven anti-war NUWSS members resigned. That year the Women's International League for Peace and Freedom was formed, with Mrs Swanwick as chairman, Miss Irene Cooper as secretary and Mrs Pethick-Lawrence as treasurer.[18] It gained the support of both Sylvia's East London Federation and Adela Pankhurst, who in Australia had become an outspoken opponent of the war – whereupon their mother publicly repudiated them. 'I am ashamed to know where you and Adela stand!' she told Sylvia curtly.[19] Adela described her mother's reaction as ridiculous. 'But it was the family attitude – Cause first and human relations – nowhere ... [if] Emmeline had been tolerant and broad-minded, she would not have been the leader of the suffragettes.'[20]

Mrs Fawcett was deeply disturbed by the split in the movement since her opponents carried a great deal of weight. Nevertheless, the union as a whole was strongly behind her; women as much as men were generally standing by their country at war.[21] The NUWSS now suspended its political work and threw itself instead into the relief of war distress.

The emergence of women in the war effort was to have a tremendous and decisive impact, although it was still not without its difficulties. For example, when women doctors approached the War Office with the offer of fully staffed medical units, they were told 'to go home and keep quiet', and that commanding officers 'did not want to be troubled with hysterical women'. But thousands of women were absorbed by the expansion of nursing; they worked in Voluntary Aid Detachments, which expanded rapidly and helped house and resettle refugees; women took on men's jobs and released them for fighting duties. The women were eager and enthusiastic and although they were mainly untrained, they displayed astonishing quickness and aptitude, turning into charge hands, tool setters and factory supervisors with remarkable success. Employers who had been apprehensive found such women willing, skilful and patient. But male workers were often jealous and hostile. Men were already facing the subdivision of skilled work and a threat to their shift system. Fearing for their own position after the war, in many factories they refused to work with women or to teach them anything. In March 1915 agreement was reached with the unions by which the government undertook to protect wage rates, ensured equal piece-work rates to both sexes and promised to restore pre-war industrial practices.[22]

In Whitehall 162,000 women were employed in new ministries, even though the civil service was reluctant to entrust this new army of clerks with any responsibility. Women were taken on in banks and businesses; they became window cleaners and plumbers, signalmen and porters, bus conductors, van drivers, shepherds and electricians. Women worked in men's jobs such as the munitions industry, stoking furnaces, unloading coal wagons and building ships. The Land Army put uniformed girls on to farms to plough, milk and weed.

The Prefect of Constanza said of women orderlies in hospitals in Serbia: 'It is extraordinary how these women endure hardships; they refuse help and carry the wounded themselves. They work like navvies. No wonder England is a great country if the women are like that.'[23] A ship coming from Australia bringing troops and nurses was torpedoed in the Mediterranean. The captain ordered the lifeboats out and ordered that the women should be saved first; but the nurses drew back and said: 'Fighting men first; they are the country's greatest need.' This was the stuff of legend. As Mrs Fawcett observed: 'Men could hardly speak of these things without tears in their eyes.'[24]

By mid-1916 women were the objects of a chorus of praise. Newspapers began to say 'the nation is grateful to the women', not realising, of course, that the women were of the nation.[25] After the British Red Cross had rejected women in 1914, they set up hospitals in France under Dr Elizabeth Garrett and Dr Flora Murray which were so successful that in 1915 the War Office put these two in charge of a military hospital in London.

As Ray Strachey of the NUWSS remarked: 'It was wildly illogical to be converted to women's suffrage because a girl who had been a good milliner could also be a good lift attendant; but so it was.' Even more crucially, the war changed the outlook of women themselves. They were now doing things that they knew to be important; they were encouraged to show enterprise and ambition, they had been paid, they were better fed.[26] Lloyd George said he was anxious 'to bear testimony to the tremendous part played by the women of England in this vital epoch of human history'. Winston Churchill said: 'Without the work of women it would have been impossible to win the war.'[27] Even Herbert Asquith said, on the heroic death in October 1915 of Nurse Edith Cavell: 'She has taught the bravest man among us a supreme lesson of courage; yes, and in this United Kingdom and in the Dominions there are thousands of such women, but a year ago we did not know it.' 'Pathetic blindness!' remarked Mrs Fawcett.[28] But it made the difference. The first hint came that the main impediment to the women's vote was finally crumbling. On 7 May 1916 Asquith wrote to Mrs Fawcett that he recognised the magnificent contribution that women were making to the war, and that in due course he would impartially consider the women's franchise.

Mrs Pankhurst, meanwhile, was continuing to make a spectacle of herself. In the summer of 1915 she announced that the WSPU would adopt up to fifty 'war babies', born to thousands of unmarried mothers who had been left stranded when Kitchener's recruits departed for the front. Her members were underwhelmed by the call. The response was small; instead, there was a revolt against the neglect of votes for women in favour of tasks that were regarded as the responsibility of the state. At least two splinter groups were formed as a result. Undaunted, Mrs

Pankhurst herself adopted four three-year-old girls. In view of her record as a biological mother, such a stunt was, to say the least, ill advised, and predictably enough the care of the children was entrusted to a nurse.

She continued with her wild recruiting harangues, and was asked to apologise publicly for calling those suffragettes who didn't agree with Christabel's views 'pro-German'. Mrs Swanwick remembered Mrs Pankhurst talking 'unbelievable nonsense about the Germans' at a meeting that year. A man who was present claimed that stewards at Liberal meetings between 1906 and 1914 had been Huns. '"You will remember," he roared, "with what brutality these stewards treated the women?" Then, after a dramatic pause, he leant forward and snarled, "It was not for nothing that they spoke with a foreign accent and in a guttural tongue." Mrs Pankhurst nodded approval. I was so startled by this absurdity that I let out a shout of laughter. But the audience turned on me with a shocked "Hush!" as though I had brawled in church.'[29]

Far from being eclipsed, however, the cause was to resurface again in dramatic and unexpected form as a direct result of the war. The outbreak of hostilities had made the electoral register completely unworkable. To get on to the register, a man had to show uninterrupted occupation of his premises for twelve months to the preceding July. So the men most eager to join up had forfeited their votes. Not one in five men was now located where he was registered to vote, or was likely to be in the same place for long enough to be re-registered. There would have to be a new register; and this of course raised the question of who should be entitled to be on it.

In May 1916 Sir Edward Carson and others pressed for a new register based on war service. That summer the NUWSS resumed lobbying for the suffrage. The coalition government had seen the departure of some veteran anti-suffragists and the substitution of supporters such as Lord Robert Cecil, Lord Selborne and Arthur Henderson. On 4 May 1916 Mrs Fawcett wrote to Asquith asking for women to be included in any change to the franchise. Asquith replied: 'No such legislation as you refer to is at present in contemplation; but if and when it should become necessary to undertake it you may be certain that the consideration set out in your letter will be fully and impartially weighed without any pre-judgement from the controversies of the past.'³⁰ The women were now pushing at a door whose bolts were finally being removed.

On 14 August 1916, in the House of Commons, Asquith finally threw in the towel. Acknowledging the women's war effort, he said: 'These abnormal and, of course, to a large extent transient conditions have to be revised and when the process of industrial reconstruction has to be set on foot, the House will agree that the women have a special claim to be heard on the many questions which will arise directly affecting their interests, and possibly meaning for them large displacements of labour. I cannot think that the House will deny, and I say quite frankly that I cannot deny, that claim.'³¹

Undoubtedly the women's war effort had knocked away the last vestiges of Asquith's personal opposition. By demonstrating not only their patriotism and usefulness but also that they could do work that had hitherto been a male preserve, they both repaired the damage done by the militant violence and made the separate spheres approach look out of date. In a subsequent debate in the Commons on 28 March 1917, Asquith claimed that his opposition had always been based on public expediency and he had thought that women should work out their own salvation. Now, they had done so through their war work, and there had been no recurrence of 'that detestable campaign which disfigured the annals of political agitation in this country'. This was a shade disingenuous. His opposition to votes for women had predated the militant suffragette campaign; and his prejudices were still to surface years later. In 1920 he said of the women of Paisley, where he was fighting a by-election: 'There are about 15,000 women on the register – a dim, impenetrable, for the most part ungettable element – of whom all that one knows is that they are for the most part hopelessly ignorant of politics, credulous to the last degree, and flickering with gusts of sentiment like a candle in the wind.'³² Yet he also said of the electors of Paisley generally: 'They are among the most intelligent audiences I have ever had ...' and of his daughter: 'Violet is a marvellous success as a speaker.'³³

Even so, the suffragists were greatly alarmed by the proposal to enfranchise the troops, since military service would have been an insuperable hurdle for women. But few could have predicted the extraordinary attitude adopted by Mrs Pankhurst. After all her years of fighting for the vote, at the moment that her old enemy Asquith had finally conceded she flipped over and declared that women would not be used to deny the vote to the fighting men of Britain. Determined now to paint the Liberals as the enemies of patriotism, she used the offer of votes for women as further proof of Asquith's perfidy. She had simply departed from reality.

In August 1916 she authorised a Tory MP, Commander Bellairs, a veteran opponent of the women's franchise, to state on her behalf in the Commons that the WSPU would not use the enfranchisement of soldiers and sailors as a reason for agitating for women's votes.³⁴ Bellairs told the House: 'They will not allow themselves to be used to prevent soldiers and sailors from being given the vote.' Sylvia reported her mother's position: 'The men had proved their claim to the vote by making it possible to keep a country in which to vote. Could any woman face the possibility of the affairs of the country being settled by conscientious objectors, passive resisters and shirkers? . . . In the name of the women she declared that they were ready to make every sacrifice, in order that the sacrifices already made should not be made in vain.'³⁵ Mrs Pankhurst herself wrote in *Britannia* on 18 August 1916: 'Before the war, Mr Asquith used the question of more votes for men to "dish" the women who want votes. Now he reverses the process and uses the women to "dish" the men who are heroically sacrificing themselves in defence of the nation . . . we indignantly resent the Prime Minister's attempt to exploit, for his own political purposes, the women's cause, of which he has been, and still is, the determined enemy.'³⁶

One might further surmise that such extraordinary perversity and twisted thinking was rooted in a determination that Asquith should never get the glory for delivering votes for women, an honour which could only be claimed by the Pankhursts themselves.

Many have assumed that the change in mood caused by the women's war work meant that the battle for the vote was now won. Not quite. A significant change had certainly occurred, but there was still considerable resistance. The Cabinet was in fact deadlocked, with many pushing for soldiers alone to be registered, but with Arthur Henderson and Lord Robert Cecil threatening to resign if women's suffrage was not included.[37]

A Speaker's Conference was appointed from both Houses of Parliament, presided over by Speaker Lowther – the very Speaker who had caused such uproar when he had ruled the amended reform bill unconstitutional in 1913 – to consider the whole issue of electoral reform. Asquith's coalition was replaced by one under Lloyd George as Prime Minister. Although he personally was sympathetic to women's suffrage, his Cabinet now included two powerful opponents, Lord Curzon and Lord Milner. In January 1917 the Speaker's Conference recommended that the vote should be given to all adult men and to women on the local government register, as well as those women whose husbands were on the register. The qualifying age was fixed at thirty for women and twenty-one for men.[38]

This left a lot of women still disenfranchised and so was, of course, contrary to the suffragists' demand for equality with men. Mrs Fawcett, convinced that if this was rejected the government would drop women's suffrage from its proposals, persuaded her fellow suffragists to accept this compromise. Although Eleanor Rathbone objected that it excluded most women factory workers, the NUWSS executive endorsed the proposal, with only one dissension.[39]

There was still no guarantee that the Speaker's Report would be accepted by the government. Mrs Fawcett lobbied hard, and undertook that if the proposals were accepted the women would not agitate for equal parliamentary franchise. Other suffragists, such as Sylvia Pankhurst and Margaret Llewellyn Davies, were continuing to press for full adult suffrage. But within the Cabinet there was a struggle to get even the Speaker's Conference proposal accepted. The Conservatives, led by Lord Curzon, opposed it, and although Bonar Law and Balfour accepted it the government was reluctant if it was to be so controversial.[40]

In the end it was Asquith, of all people, who helped break the impasse with a proposal that franchise reform should be a House of Commons rather than a government bill. This enabled the Cabinet to proceed without forcing opponents such as Lord Curzon to resign. The deadlock in Cabinet, though, continued and it was Arthur Henderson's insistence that eventually proved decisive. In the Commons, Asquith moved that a Commons bill be introduced embodying the Speaker's Conference proposals. He argued not that the women's war effort had earned the vote but rather that, after the war, important issues about women in the labour force would have to be resolved and that women should have the right to express their views. The House endorsed his motion by 343 to 64; all the opponents were Conservatives, of whom only seventy-nine supported the measure.[41]

On 19 June 1917 the House of Commons voted by 385 to 55 to accept the Representation of the People's Bill's women's suffrage clause. In the Commons debates on the measure, Lloyd George said the women's vote would 'bring into public life a point of view and spirit which will be of incalculable value to the progress of democracy in these islands'; Asquith said it was 'a privilege which carries with it a great responsibility'; Balfour said he'd always supported women's suffrage, now granted 'mainly due to universal recognition of the magnificent work performed by the women of Britain in the country's cause'.[42] Among the Conservatives, resistance had declined dramatically. Some anti-suffragists had changed sides, partly because they thought reform was now inevitable, or because most constituency parties favoured reform. But as Harold Smith has observed, the overwhelming support was undoubtedly due to the fact that this was an extremely conservative measure. Despite all the huzzahs over women's war work, most female munitions workers remained disenfranchised because they were under thirty. Older women were believed to be less likely to support feminist or radical reforms. Many other women remained without the vote. The NUWSS campaigned hard to remove an anomaly which would have prevented many enfranchised women from voting in local government elections. It was a sign of the persistent sensitivity around the issue that the government at first refused, although it later relented.[43]

The women's suffrage clause was debated in committee. Women packed the Ladies' Gallery behind the grille. In the division, the clause enfranchising women was carried by 385 to 55, with a majority within each political party. Asquith likened himself to Stesichorus, who had been blinded for insulting Helen of Troy. 'Some of my friends may think that, like him, my eyes which for years in this matter have been clouded by fallacies and sealed by illusions, at last have been opened to the truth.'[44]

The biggest fight was always likely to take place in the House of Lords, led by the implacable foe of the suffragettes, Lord Curzon. True to form, he protested that the bill would ruin the country, that women were politically worthless and that the women's movement was disastrous and wrong. But the majority in the Commons had simply been too big. One hundred and forty-three peers voted for the measure, seventy-one against and thirteen abstained.[45]

The Representation of the People Act 1918 enfranchised 8.4 million women and thirteen million men. At the Queen's Hall the suffrage societies threw a victory party for which William Blake's poem 'Jerusalem' was set to music as the suffrage hymn. Mrs Fawcett regarded the passing of the suffrage legislation as the greatest moment of her life.[46] It was indeed a remarkable triumph after all the years of struggle, for which she could justifiably claim the lion's share of the credit.

To Mrs Fawcett, the war had been a truly liberating force. 'The war revolutionised the industrial position of women. It found them serfs and left them free,' she wrote. It had opened up both opportunities and men's minds. It had made both men and women aware of the waste involved in condemning women to work which needed only mediocre intelligence. 'It was almost ridiculous to watch the amazement of the ordinary man when he saw how rapidly women learned men's jobs and how, by their patriotic zeal and entire innocence of the trade union practice of ca'canny, their output frequently exceeded, and exceeded largely, the output of men working the same machinery for the same number of hours.'[47]

How decisive was the war in finally securing the women's franchise? It is simplistic to single out any one factor in the complex process that takes place whenever a culture shifts its attitudes. The movement in public opinion towards the women's vote was undoubtedly rooted in the changes in women's position in society, much of which was due to the wider activities of the women's movement – the entry of women into higher education and the professions, for example. As women became so much more visible in the public sphere, it became progressively less threatening to envisage their being able to vote.

Mrs Fawcett's patient, painstaking lobbying achieved untold results in helping persuade MPs and others in the establishment of the justice and sense of the women's cause. For her part, Mrs Pankhurst thought that the vote was finally granted because of the fear of resumed suffragette militancy. All the evidence, to the contrary, encourages the view that militancy became a serious impediment to reform as it polarised opinion and hardened political opposition. But although the militants had boxed politicians into a corner, their activities – as Mrs Fawcett was quick to acknowledge – so heightened feminist consciousness that the non-militant, constitutional cause received a very important shot in the arm.

Clearly the war played a significant part in the final breakthrough, but it has to be viewed against that wider context. Judging from the majorities in the House of Commons, the battle of public opinion had been won as far back as 1884. Progress was then thwarted by two related factors: the personal hostility of politicians such as Gladstone and Asquith, and the fact that neither main political party thought women's suffrage would be in its own electoral interests. The war, and the social changes it ushered in, helped transform Asquith's hitherto implacable opposition into support, and the development of coalition government helped resolve the party political deadlock.

For Sylvia Pankhurst, the women's movement was a wiser and better enterprise as a result of the war. 'The suffrage movement, which lived through the vast holocaust of peaceful life, was a more intelligent and informed movement than that which, gallant as it was, had fought the desperate pre-war fight. Gone was the mirage of a society regenerated by enfranchised womanhood as by a magic wand. Men and women had been drawn closer together by the suffering and sacrifice of the war. Awed and humbled by the great catastrophe, and by the huge economic problems it had thrown into naked prominence, the women of the suffrage movement had learnt that social regeneration is a long and mighty work.'[48]

Adela Pankhurst developed a more bitter and cynical view about democracy itself. She was later to write to Helen Fraser Moyes:

One thing I am sure of . . . that women did not get the vote for supporting the war because Christabel and my mother did so. The real reason for the capitulation of the government was that the war really crushed the old faith in voting and Parliaments among the men who had votes, and the political parties were therefore only too anxious to give votes to women who really wanted them . . . at least until the second war came. After which neither men nor women cared tuppence about them. They'd had Liberals, Tories and Labour and since wars and the aftermath of wars kept on coming whichever party was the government – they lost all faith in the whole business.[49]

Ordinary feminists simply hailed the new dawn for which they had so striven and longed. Now they could put their grand ideals into practice. Alice Abadam, who had left the WSPU in the 1907 split, waxed particularly lyrical. In *The Feminist Vote, Enfranchised or Emancipated?* she wrote: 'Do you feel the spirit of a Great Crusade, a Great Adventure, stirring within you? Do you realise you are a New Force in the New World which is destined to rise clean, sweet and white on the ruins of the Old Order now expiring amidst blood, savagery, lust, disease and famine? . . . The Constructive Feminist has to be no man's shadow. She must be herself – free to the very soul of sex servility. So and only so can she save a stricken world . . . Let her bathe her spirit in Freedom and wash away in the waters of a new baptism the dark secretions of her long sex slave existence . . . O femina gloriosa! Procede, prospere et regna.'[50]

Sylvia Pankhurst, now a revolutionary communist, thought the women's vote was a 'fancy franchise' designed to avoid making women electors the majority; both the vote and the subsequent right to become an MP were a trick to revive public interest in an institution which was manipulated by capitalists and their Labour lackeys and should be abolished. In November 1917 the WSPU had become the Women's Party, which demanded equality of employment, pay, marriage laws, parental rights, a raised age of consent and political rights. It also campaigned against Bolshevism.[51] This meant effectively campaigning against Sylvia and Adela, who had herself become a revolutionary socialist in Australia. Once again, sex and politics were intertwined. One of the most disgusting aspects of capitalism, wrote Adela, was its deliberate exploitation of sexual lust. 'Communism will abolish prostitution and enable young people to attend schools and universities where every influence will be used to encourage purity and sexual restraint.' After a visit to Russia in 1920, H. G. Wells remarked that the naïve utopianism of the Bolsheviks reminded him of the suffragettes, 'who used to promise us an earthly paradise as soon as we escaped from the tyranny of man-made laws'.

In November 1918 a bill was passed enabling women to stand as parliamentary candidates. Mrs Pankhurst now had a new platform from which to attempt to rewrite the history of the world with herself and her daughter at centre stage. The Women's Party, she said, with its sole parliamentary candidate, Christabel, would bring a new and noble spirit into the Commons. For them, the sex war was not dead. Their manifesto said that 'while the Women's Party is in no way based on sex antagonism, it is felt that women can best serve the nation by keeping clear of men's party political machinery and traditions which, by universal consent, leave so much to be desired'. Indeed, it was clearly the world's misfortune that Christabel and her mother had not been running it. For Mrs Pankhurst said of her daughter: 'Had her war policy prevailed in the early years, many thousands of lives would have been saved. A prominent American assured me that if Miss Pankhurst had been in the government, most of the mistakes made by the allies would have been avoided.'[52]

Nevertheless, despite their disdain for male politics, when they realised that Lloyd George was issuing sponsorship letters for his coalition ticket to candidates he saw as reliable supporters, Mrs Pankhurst and Christabel abandoned their separatist position and pressed for sponsorship.

Under pressure from her mother to stand for Parliament, Christabel forced herself into the selection for Smethwick in 1918, but she had no clear platform and no appeal. She was viewed as little more than a condescending, jumped-up grande dame in furs. The press baron Lord Northcliffe referred to her as a 'political flibbertigibbet' who had whipped on young women to futile violence from her comfortable flat in Paris; he labelled her supporters as 'Christabelligerents'. Despite feverish attempts by Mrs Pankhurst, Christabel lost the election by 775 votes. In the event, the first woman be elected to Westminster turned out to be a damp squib. The Sinn Feiner Countess Markievicz was returned for the Dublin constituency, but was unable to take up her seat since she happened to be incarcerated in Holloway jail at the time. In 1919 the first woman actually to take her seat in the House of Commons was an American, Nancy Astor. She became MP for Plymouth Sutton, stepping into her husband's constituency shoes when he inherited the viscountcy. Her place in history was galling to Mrs Pankhurst, since although she was a temperance fanatic and a champion of old-fashioned values, Nancy Astor had played no part in the cause.

Christabel wanted to fade away, but Mrs Pankhurst declared that her daughter would contest Westminster at the next election. So Christabel wrote articles in the *Daily Sketch* with headlines such as: 'If a woman were premier! Famous suffragist leader shows how she would solve the strike crisis in Britain.' On 10 April 1919 she warned the Prime Minister to choose between the great patriotic majority and the 'gang of Asquithian pacifists, pro-German money grabbers' and 'bolshevists and cranks of all sorts who compose the unpatriotic minority'. Women, she said, wanted a national government with a programme based on reality rather than on Marxist jargon. As David Mitchell has observed, her 'Britain for the British policy', with its references to the conspiracy of the

Unseen Hand, strongly resembled the line soon to be taken by the groups fused in Oswald Mosley's British Union of Fascists, with which two ex-suffragettes, Mary Richardson and Mrs Dacre Fox, were to be associated. By the end of the summer of 1919 the Women's Party ceased to exist. Mrs Pankhurst and Christabel, it turned out, would have no part to play in the long agitation ahead for equality of franchise, pay, opportunity, divorce and inheritance.[53]

It would be several more years before women were elected on their own worth. In 1921, after the death of Tom Wintringham, the Liberal MP for Louth in Lincolnshire, his widow Margaret was elected to the seat. In the 1922 general election thirty-three women stood, but since they were all in unwinnable seats only Lady Astor and Mrs Wintringham were re-elected. In 1923 they were joined by Mrs Mabel Hilton Philipson, who was keeping the Berwick-on-Tweed seat warm for her husband, who had been unseated because of his agent's fraud. In the general election of that year five more women were elected, four of them – at last – on their own account.[54]

After the war, however, feminism went off the boil. Women were more interested in other things. Freedom was the motif, a reaction against the war. Skirts stayed short, as did hair, and clothes became more convenient; women scandalised their elders with their cigarettes, motor cars, latchkeys and athletics. The most popular women's organisations catered for a conventional domestic role with broader interests: the Women's Institutes and Townswomen's Guilds.[55] Dr Marie Stopes pushed Annie Besant's birth-control crusade with a flair similar to the old Pankhurst style, and wrote a book telling ignorant husbands how to give their wives the sexual satisfaction which was their right. Feminist communists and anarchists such as Elinor Burns, Mary Patricia Willcocks, Alexandra Kollontai, Rose Witcop and Sylvia Pankhurst were criticising once again the 'legal prostitution' of marriage, but this time advocating early sex education and universal co-education and scorning the 'spinsterly ideals' of earlier feminists.[56]

Some in the NUWSS felt that they must now work only for the removal of women's remaining disabilities; others believed there was broader work to be done, such as promoting the welfare of children, improving health education and sanitation and developing international understanding. The NUWSS became the National Union of Societies for Equal Citizenship; its objectives were still feminist, but with an added phrase authorising it to work 'to educate women in the duties of citizenship'. Mrs Fawcett resigned and was succeeded by Miss Eleanor Rathbone. Much still needed to be done. Women still suffered many flagrant injustices: unequal divorce, inheritance and nationality laws, a limited franchise, and still no equality over the guardianship of children, conditions of employment and pay.

With the end of the war, indeed, women's new prosperity shuddered to a halt. Many were sacked and became unemployed. Jobs were kept open instead for the returning soldiers. Because of the carnage at the front, there was now an enormous number of surplus women; as a result, almost one in three had to be self-supporting. But public opinion assumed that women could still be supported by men and that women were wicked to continue working. So the press turned once again, and women were transformed from heroines and saviours to parasites, blacklegs and limpets. Yet the women were docile, as they did not want to stand in the way of the returning soldiers. There was still a shortage of domestic servants, however; but women no longer had the necessary experience, as they could no longer cook or sew and knew little about health or cleanliness.

Women's opportunities nevertheless continued to broaden in the decade after the war. The Sex Disqualification Removal Act opened up the legal profession, magistracy and jury service to women. In 1920, a year before Emily Davies died, women were admitted as full students to Oxford. Cambridge held out for longer. In 1921 the civil service was opened to women, and in 1925 three women passed the entrance exam and became 'administrative cadets'. Teachers fought for equal pay but were awarded five-sixths of men's pay. In 1922 the Law of Property Act made men and women equals in cases of intestacy. By 1923 there were eight women MPs, and that year the Matrimonial Causes Act made the grounds for divorce the same for men and women. In 1925 the

Guardianship of Infants Act gave mothers and fathers equal rights over their children. And so on.

But reform was far from complete. Women were still different and inferior under franchise law. During the 1920s the final struggle took place for equality in the franchise. Although the Coalition government's manifesto in 1918 undertook to remove inequalities between men and women, Conservative backbenchers were opposed. In 1919 Labour introduced a Women's Emancipation Bill to allow women to vote at twenty-one, but it was blocked. Such bills were introduced almost every year during the 1920s and blocked by the government. Although the Labour Party had consistently advocated equality in the franchise, the 1924 Labour government was reluctant to sponsor reform. It was worried that feminism would undermine Labour's class base. The issue had become stalemated. It was an all too familiar story. Political leaders expressed support for the principle but were reluctant to put it into practice.[57] But the age limit had become an absurdity. For Miss Jennie Lee, the daughter of a Fifeshire miner, was elected as an MP at the age of twenty-four, six years before she was entitled to vote. (In 1964 Lee was to become Britain's first minister for the arts.)

In the end, reform came from the Conservative Party. It became aware that women were vital to its interests since they were its main recruiters, canvassers and fundraisers. In addition, more women than men were likely to vote Conservative. The party's shattering defeat in the 1923 election was blamed on the loss of the women's vote because of the threat of dearer food. Shortly before the 1924 election Stanley Baldwin declared that the party supported equal rights for women and proposed an all-party conference on franchise reform. His intentions were ambiguous and the party was divided. There were fears that an equal franchise would make women a majority of the electorate, which they would use to introduce feminist legislation. Some objected that men would be ruled by women. Others thought women would vote en bloc to transform male political culture.[58]

During 1927, however, the Conservatives finally became reconciled to equality at age twenty-one. They decided that the alternative under consideration, setting the age at which women could vote at twenty-five, was impractical; and since Labour would lower the age to twenty-one, this would mean that newly enfranchised women would vote Labour.[59]

In March 1928 the Representation of the People (Equal Franchise) Bill passed its Second Reading by 387 to 10. The Prime Minister, Stanley Baldwin, said in the debate: 'The subjection of women, if there be such a thing, will not now depend on any creation of the law, nor can it be remedied by any action of the law. It will never again be possible to blame the sovereign state for any position of inequality. Women will have, with us, the fullest rights. The ground and justification for the old agitation is gone, and gone for ever.'[60]

Sylvia Pankhurst delivered a misleadingly complacent view of this final act of the great struggle. 'The profound divergences of opinion on war and peace had been shown to know no sex,' she wrote. 'The Act of 1928, which swept away the absurd restrictions of 1917, came virtually without effort. It was quietly received. Women had already taken a wide and important part in parliamentary politics, and both men and women had completely assimilated the view that all women were potential voters. Thus the extension was regarded as a matter of course.'[61]

Far from it. Equality had been intensely opposed, and women had once again had to fight hard for it. As Harold Smith observes, the huge majority in the Commons reflected prudence by MPs, who realised that the bill would pass and that their political futures depended on female voters who would be watching carefully how they had voted.[62] Right to the end, therefore, the women's vote was a battle against men who were terrified they would be swamped by this new, alien political force and lose their power over the public sphere.

As for the Pankhursts, their political drama was to become ever more bizarre. Mrs Pankhurst progressed from opposing the Bolshevik terror to become the star speaker at the Canadian National Council for Combating Venereal Diseases. Social hygiene, she told them, was the crying need of the time. VD was closely linked to the disease of Bolshevism by the widespread tendency to sneer at traditional Christian morality. Her experiences as a Poor Law guardian and registrar in Manchester had revealed a cesspool of perversion so vile that to cleanse it had been one of the main purposes of her fight for women's suffrage. What was needed, she said, were chastity and sexual self-control. With this familiar refrain, she designed the NCCVD's badge in the purple, white and green colours of the WSPU, and it was bought and worn by thousands.[63]

Christabel, meanwhile, had turned to God. She returned from her tour of the United States to find Dora Russell, in *Hypatia* in 1925, urging feminists to take forward the sexual revolution. Sex starvation of young women, she declared, was a sin since 'sex, even without children and without marriage, is a thing of dignity, beauty and delight'. Continuing agitation for political and legal equality was all very well, she went on, but feminism was needed in the home. Women needed contraception and an adequate wage for housework. Only by risking reckless love could men and women transform the world.[64]

Christabel's answer was to become the implacable foe of the hedonism of the twenties. She became the darling of fundamentalist Christians in both Britain and America, preaching imminent Armageddon and lambasting modern degeneracy and indecent literature. 'This is not the kind of liberty mother and I set out to get,' she raged. 'I do not consider that art justifies the writing of books which *even men* are horrified to read.' She was now a sadder and wiser woman, with her illusions about women apparently shattered. 'The shallow optimism of yesterday has vanished. Some of us used to imagine that the world must get better and better under the treatment of its many reformers. That illusion surely perished during the war.' It had been necessary to believe that votes for women would bring the millennium because only powerful illusions could overcome human inertia. But women were no more perfect than men. 'Those days of the suffrage fight were the days of political childishness. Now is the time to put away childish things. The one thing that counts . . . is whether an individual or a nation is for or against the Lord Jesus Christ and His Supremacy.' She now looked forward to the war to end all wars. When she made her debut as a preacher in the Knox Presbyterian church in Toronto, it was packed to capacity and the doors were locked against the crowds outside.[65]

In the summer of 1925 Mrs Pankhurst, Mabel Tuke and Christabel opened a tea shop in Juan-les-Pins, on the Côte d'Azur. It failed, and in December Mrs Pankhurst returned penniless to London. She refused to work for the Six Point Group, one of several fighting for full equality, as she said there were already sufficient women voters to secure the desired legislative reforms. In a letter to the newspapers Sylvia expressed 'profound grief' that Mrs Pankhurst had 'deserted the cause of progress'.[66]

In 1926, in admiration at the way the Tory Prime Minister Stanley Baldwin had handled the General Strike, Mrs Pankhurst joined the Conservative Party as the key force that would uphold the British constitution and Empire, support democracy, advance the cause of women and resist communism. In 1927 she was adopted as the Conservative candidate for Whitechapel and St George's in London's East End. When Sylvia heard the news, she wept.[67]

In February 1927 Sylvia announced she was pregnant. When her son Richard Keir Pethick Pankhurst was born, she left the name of his father ostentatiously blank on the birth certificate. In an interview she asked why a woman shouldn't have children without being married. 'Free' marriage, responsibly entered into, was the ideal towards which society must move. She had waited until the pace of her own life had slackened and her health was good. To this extent the baby was 'eugenic'. But she disapproved of play-girl emancipation; smoking, wearing short skirts and messing about with cosmetics betokened 'the slave woman's sex appeal rather than the free woman's intelligent companionship'.[68]

News of Sylvia's baby had been kept from Mrs Pankhurst, but she was asked about it at a political meeting.[69] On Easter Sunday 1928 she read about the baby's scandalous birth in the *News of the World*. She wept uncontrollably, and said she would abandon politics and never speak in public again. She would never see nor forgive Sylvia. Already in poor health, she deteriorated.

On 14 June 1928, a month before her seventieth birthday and three months after women finally achieved franchise equality with men, Emmeline Pankhurst died in Dr Chetham Strode's nursing home, following the shock of learning that her forty-one-year-old daughter had become an unmarried mother.[70]

EPILOGUE

The battle for the vote was over. But the issues that galvanised the Victorian and Edwardian women's movement did not go away. Indeed, one might say that the questions at the very heart of the cause, concerning the relationship between men and women and the dilemmas posed by the entry of women into the public sphere, remain unresolved to this day. Is it possible for women to straddle both the public and the domestic domains, the world of work and the world of home, without demanding immense sacrifices, both of themselves and of others? Is marriage a trap for women, or does it offer them the best advantages in life? Are women's interests best served by freedom in sexual encounters or by monogamy? Is masculinity a problem and a threat from which women should protect themselves by independence, or are men the life partners who provide women with the passport to self-fulfilment?

These are the same battle-lines over sex, family and men behind which the feminists of the nineteenth and early twentieth centuries were marshalled. The same arguments that consumed them are still raging today. Among modern women, it is possible to spy the direct descendants of the marriage-hating Mona Caird and the marriage-loving Millicent Fawcett, of the sexually liberated Dora Marsden and the purity campaigner Ellice Hopkins, of the birth controller Annie Besant and the chastity-promoting Elizabeth Blackwell, all struggling from opposing sides to lay claim to the mantle of feminism. Indeed, it is even possible to detect, in today's encouragement of the feminised 'New Man' and the attempt to remove men altogether from the reproductive process, the ghost of the would-be exterminator of the male sex, Frances Swiney.

Nor have modern women solved the paradox that was such a notable feature of the suffrage cause. Women claimed to want equality with men; but, from Mary Wollstonecraft to Christabel Pankhurst, the core belief was that women's virtues were needed in the public sphere in order to purify it and to elevate base men on to a higher plane of being. In other words, women saw themselves not as the equals of men, but as their superiors. Fighting against the sexual double standard by which men were allowed a sexual licence for which women were punished, they introduced a double standard of their own: equality *and* superiority.

The same double standard persists to this day, with women claiming 'equality' and yet insisting, for example, that mothers have prior claim over fathers to their children after divorce; or that women must be economically independent of their husbands, unless they separate, in which case men must turn back into breadwinners; or that if a man is violent to a woman or a child, he is an irredeemable savage, but if a woman is violent towards a man or a child, she must be suffering from an emotional problem.

One wonders what the suffragettes would have made of today's women. Those who fought for women's emancipation were convinced that their freedom would be a weapon of social reform. Have enfranchised women made a better world? Has their freedom elevated humanity on to a more spiritual plane? Have they transformed male sexual appetites – or simply added their own? If Mrs Fawcett were now to enrol on a university gender-studies course, or if Christabel Pankhurst were to spend time on a shattered housing estate where fathers were virtually unknown, would they both say, 'Yes, this is what we were fighting for'?

Women take for granted nowadays their place in the public sphere, in education, work and politics: roles for which the Victorian and Edwardian feminists battled for more than a century. Some modern feminists believe that the cards are still stacked against women and so they continue to press for more flexible work hours, more childcare, rates of pay and promotion that are identical with men, and more representation on public bodies. Other women, however, are wondering whether emancipation may have gone too far, as mothers give up highly paid careers to care for their children at home, or single women race desperately in middle age against the biological clock to have a child.

At the heart of it all, women have still not settled the great questions and dilemmas about their place in the world, which have remained unresolved for at least three centuries. Can women really have it all? they constantly ask. The world still waits for an answer.

NOTES

PREFACE

1　Pankhurst, Sylvia, *The Suffragette Movement*, Longman, 1931.
2　Mitchell, David, *Women on the Warpath*, Jonathan Cape, 1966.

1 HOW IT BEGAN

1　Rousseau, Jean-Jacques, *Emile*, Everyman, 1993 edn.
2　Stone, Lawrence, *The Family, Sex and Marriage in England 1500–1800*, Weidenfeld & Nicolson, 1977.
3　Porter, Roy, *English Society in the Eighteenth Century*, Penguin, 1991 (rev. edn.).
4　Ibid.
5　Brody, Miriam, Introduction to Wollstonecraft, Mary, *A Vindication of the Rights of Woman*, Penguin, 1992.
6　Ellis, Gran A., *Life and Works of Mrs Barbauld*, Boston, 1874.
7　More, Hannah, *Strictures on the Modern System of Female Education*; quoted in Brody, Introduction to Wollstonecraft, Mary, *A Vindication of the Rights of Woman*.
8　Strachey, Ray, *The Cause*, G. Bell, 1928.
9　Stone, *The Family, Sex and Marriage in England 1500–1800*.
10　Barker-Benfield, G. J., *The Culture of Sensibility: Sex and Society in Eighteenth Century Britain*, University of Chicago Press, 1992.
11　Bennett, John, *Letters to a Young Lady*, 1789.
12　Porter, Roy and Hall, Lesley, *The Facts of Life: The Creation of Sexual Knowledge in Britain, 1650–1950*, Yale University Press, 1995.
13　Porter, *English Society in the Eighteenth Century*.
14　Barker-Benfield, *The Culture of Sensibility: Sex and Society in Eighteenth Century Britain*.
15　Porter, *English Society in the Eighteenth Century*.

2 MARY WOLLSTONECRAFT AND THE FRENCH REVOLUTION

1   Plumb, J. H., *England in the Eighteenth Century*, Penguin, 1990 edn.
2   Tomalin, Claire, *The Life and Death of Mary Wollstonecraft*, Weidenfeld & Nicolson, 1974.
3   Ibid.
4   Brody, Miriam, Introduction to Wollstonecraft, Mary, *A Vindication of the Rights of Woman*.
5   Godwin, William, *Memoirs of Mary Wollstonecraft*, Haskel House, 1927.
6   Tomalin, *The Life and Death of Mary Wollstonecraft*.
7   Brody, Introduction to Wollstonecraft, Mary, *A Vindication of the Rights of Woman*.
8   Wollstonecraft, Mary, *A Vindication of the Rights of Woman*.
9   Tomalin, *The Life and Death of Mary Wollstonecraft*.
10 Wollstonecraft, Mary, *An Historical and Moral View of the Origins and Progress of the French Revolution*, London, 1794; quoted in Blakemore, Steven, *Crisis in Representation: Thomas Paine, Mary Wollstonecraft, Helen Maria Williams, and the Rewriting of the French Revolution*, Associated University Presses, 1997.
11 Wollstonecraft, *A Vindication of the Rights of Woman*.
12 Ibid.
13 Ibid.
14 Ibid.
15 Ibid.
16 Ibid.
17 Godwin, *Memoirs of Mary Wollstonecraft*
18 Tomalin, *The Life and Death of Mary Wollstonecraft*.
19 Holmes, Richard, Introduction to *Mary Wollstonecraft and William Godwin*, Penguin, 1987.
20 Ibid.
21 *Anti-Jacobin Review*; quoted in Barker-Benfield, *The Culture of Sensibility: Sex and Society in Eighteenth Century Britain*, University of Chicago Press, 1992.
22 *The Lady's Monthly Museum* 1, 1798; quoted in Stone, Lawrence, *The Family, Sex and Marriage in England 1500–1800*, Weidenfeld & Nicolson, 1977.
23 Porter, Roy, *English Society in the Eighteenth Century*, Penguin, 1991 (rev. edn.).
24 Taylor, Barbara, *Eve and the New Jerusalem*, Virago, 1983.

3 THE ANGEL IN THE HOUSE

1   Fulford, Roger, *Votes for Women*, Faber and Faber, 1957.
2   Thompson, William, *An Appeal of One Half the Human Race, Women,*

Against the Pretensions of the Other Half, Men, to Retain Them in Political and Thence in Domestic Slavery, in Reply to a Paragraph of Mr Mill's Celebrated 'Article on Government', 1825.

3 Ibid.

4 Ibid.

5 Ibid.

6 Ibid.

7 Wright, Frances, Course of Popular Lectures, New York, 1829; quoted in Taylor, Barbara, *Eve and the New Jerusalem*, Virago, 1983.

8 Taylor, *Eve and the New Jerusalem*.

9 Petrie, Glen, *A Singular Iniquity: The Campaigns of Josephine Butler*, Macmillan, 1971.

10 Rosen, Andrew, *Rise Up Women!*, Routledge and Kegan Paul, 1974.

11 Banks, J. A. and Olive, *Feminism and Family Planning in Victorian England*, University of Liverpool, 1964.

12 Wollstonecraft, Mary, *A Vindication of the Rights of Woman*, 1792, Penguin, 1992.

13 *Westminster Review*, April 1862.

14 Pinchbeck, Ivy, *Women Workers and the Industrial Revolution, 1750–1850*, Frank Cass, 1969.

15 Shoemaker, Robert B., *Gender in English Society 1650–1850*, Longman, 1998.

16 *Quarterly Review*, vol. 123, 1867.

17 Pinchbeck, *Women Workers and the Industrial Revolution, 1750–1850*.

18 Ibid.

19 Ruskin, John, 'Of Queens' Gardens', in *Sesame and Lilies*, Smith, Elder, 1865.

20 Ibid.

21 Himmelfarb, Gertrude, *Marriage and Morals Among the Victorians*, I. B. Tauris, 1989.

22 *Edinburgh Review*, vol. 73, 1841.

23 Hardy, Edward, *Manners Makyth Man*, T. Fisher, Unwin, 1887.

24 Walker, Alexander, *Woman Physiologically Considered as to Mind, Morals, Marriage, Matrimonial Slavery, Infidelity and Divorce*, A. H. Baily, 1839.

25 Stickney Ellis, Sarah, *The Women of England, Their Social Duties and Domestic Habits*, Fisher, 1839.

26 Ibid.

27 Ibid.

28 Ibid.

29 Stickney Ellis, Sarah, *The Wives of England, Their Relative Duties, Domestic Influence and Social Obligations*, Fisher, 1843.

30 Brown, James Baldwin, *The Home Life: In the Light of its Divine Idea*, 1866; quoted in Houghton, Walter E., *The Victorian Frame of Mind 1830–1870*, Yale University Press, 1957.

31   *The English Matron*, 1846, in Shoemaker, *Gender in English Society 1650–1850*.

32   Gisborne, Thomas, *An Enquiry into the Duties of the Female Sex*, 1797, in Shoemaker, *Gender in English Society 1650–1850*.

33   Ovington, John, *The Duties, Advantages, Pleasures and Sorrows of the Married State*, 1813, in Shoemaker, *Gender in English Society 1650–1850*.

34   *The English Matron*, 1846, in Shoemaker, *Gender in English Society 1650–1850*.

35   Farnham, Eliza W., *Woman and Her Era*, A. J. Davis, 1864.

36   Chambers, Robert, *Vestiges of the Natural History of Creation*, 1844.

37   Quoted by Bury, J. B., *The Idea of Progress*, 1913.

38   Darwin, Charles, *The Origin of Species*, 1859.

39   Woodham-Smith, Cecil, *Florence Nightingale*, Fontana, 1951.

40   Blackstone, William, *Commentaries on the Laws of England*, 1847.

41   Walker, *Woman Physiologically Considered as to Mind, Morals, Marriage, Matrimonial Slavery, Infidelity and Divorce*.

42   Hollis, Patricia, *Women in Public: The Women's Movement 1850–1900*, George Allen and Unwin, 1979.

43   Blackstone, *Commentaries on the Laws of England*.

44   Norton, Caroline, *English Law for Women in the Nineteenth Century*, privately circulated, 1854.

45   Stone, Lawrence, *Roads to Divorce, England 1530–1987*, Oxford University Press, 1982.

46   Strachey, Ray, *The Cause*, G. Bell, 1928.

47   Kamm, Josephine, *Rapiers and Battleaxes*, George Allen and Unwin, 1966.

48   Hon Caroline Norton, *A Letter to the Queen on Lord Chancellor Cranworth's Marriage and Divorce Bill*, 1855.

49   Stone, *Roads to Divorce, England 1530–1987*.

50   Ibid.

51   Divorce and Matrimonial Causes Bill, House of Commons, Hansard, 7 August 1857.

52   Cobbe, Frances Power, *Celibacy v Marriage*, *Fraser's Magazine*, February 1862.

53   Cobbe, *Celibacy v Marriage*.

54   Stone, *Roads to Divorce, England 1530–1987*.

4 THE EMBERS SMOULDER

1   Houghton, Walter E., *The Victorian Frame of Mind 1830–1870*, Yale University Press, 1957.

2   Strachey, Ray, *The Cause*, G. Bell, 1928.

3   Houghton, *The Victorian Frame of Mind 1830–1870*.

4   Briggs, Asa, *Chartism*, Sutton Publishing, 1998.
5   Ibid.
6   Liddington, Jill and Norris, Jill, *One Hand Tied Behind Us*, Virago, 1978.
7   Fulford, Roger, *Votes for Women*, Faber and Faber, 1957
8   Smith, Harold L., *The British Women's Suffrage Campaign 1866–1928*, Longman, 1998.
9   Briggs, *Chartism*.
10 Ibid.
11 Strachey, *The Cause*.
12 Ibid.
13 Bentley, Michael, *Politics Without Democracy 1815–1914*, Blackwell, 1996 (2nd edn.).
14 Gay, Peter, *The Bourgeois Experience: Victoria to Freud*, vol. 1: *Education of the Senses*, Norton, 1984.
15 Zola to Jean-Baptistin Baille, 2 June 1860; quoted in Gay, *The Bourgeois Experience: Victoria to Freud*, vol. 1: *Education of the Senses*.
16 Houghton, *The Victorian Frame of Mind 1830–1870*.
17 Froude, James Anthony, *Thomas Carlyle: A History of His Life in London, 1834–1881*, 1884.
18 Morley, John, *Recollections*, in Houghton, *The Victorian Frame of Mind 1830–1870*.
19 Houghton, *The Victorian Frame of Mind 1830–1870*.
20 Best, Geoffrey, *Evangelicalism and the Victorians*, in Symondson, Anthony, ed., *The Victorian Crisis of Faith*, SPCK, 1970.
21 Briggs, Asa, *The Age of Improvement 1783–1867*, Longman, 2000 (2nd edn.).
22 *The Christian Observer*, January 1861.
23 Cobbe, Frances Power, *Essays on the Pursuits of Women*, 1863.
24 Prochaska, Frank, *Women and Philanthropy in Nineteenth Century England*, Oxford University Press, 1980.
25 Lewis, Sarah, *Women's Mission*, 1839; quoted in Rendall, Jane, *The Origins of Modern Feminism*, Palgrave Macmillan, 1985.
26 Shoemaker, Robert B., *Gender in English Society 1650–1850*, Longman, 1998.
27 Stickney Ellis, Sarah, *The Wives of England, Their Relative Duties, Domestic Influence and Social Obligations*, Fisher, 1843.
28 Nightingale papers, British Library.
29 Linton, E. Lynn, *Ourselves, A Series of Essays on Women*, 1870, in Prochaska, *Women and Philanthropy in Nineteenth Century England*.
30 Platt, Elspeth, *The Story of the Ranyard Mission*, 1937.
31 Strachey, *The Cause*.
32 Mort, Frank, *Dangerous Sexualities: Medico-Moral Politics in England Since 1830*, Routledge and Kegan Paul, 1987.
33 Edward Sieveking, in Maurice, F., ed., *Lectures to Ladies*, 1855.

34   Mort, Frank, *Dangerous Sexualities: Medico-Moral Politics in England Since 1830*.
35   Ibid.

5 THE LADIES OF LANGHAM PLACE

1   Strachey, Ray, *The Cause*, G. Bell, 1928.
2   Ibid.
3   Ibid.
4   Strachey, Ray, *Women's Suffrage and Women's Service*, London and National Society for Women's Suffrage, 1927.
5   Grey, Maria M., *The Women's Educational Movement*, in Stanton, Theodore, *The Woman Question in Europe*, Sampson Low & Co., 1884.
6   Strachey, *The Cause*.
7   Strachey, Ray, *Millicent Garrett Fawcett*, John Murray, 1931.
8   Ibid.
9   Strachey, *The Cause*.
10   Strachey, *Millicent Garrett Fawcett*.
11   Strachey, *Women's Suffrage and Women's Service*.
12   Hollis, Patricia, *Women in Public: The Women's Movement 1850–1900*, George Allen and Unwin, 1979.
13   Ibid.
14   Mill, John Stuart (Harriet Taylor), *Enfranchisement of Women*, *Westminster and Foreign Quarterly Review*, July 1851.
15   Kraditor, Aileen S., *The Ideas of the Woman Suffrage Movement 1890–1920*, Columbia University Press, 1965.
16   Mill, John Stuart (Harriet Taylor), *Enfranchisement of Women*.
17   Ibid.
18   Ibid.
19   Gaskell, Elizabeth, *The Life of Charlotte Brontë*, 1857, quoting a letter by Brontë, 20 September 1851; quoted in Himmelfarb, Gertrude, *On Liberty and Liberalism: The Case of John Stuart Mill*, Alfred Knopf, 1974.
20   Himmelfarb, Gertrude, *On Liberty and Liberalism: The Case of John Stuart Mill*.
21   Mill, J. S., *Autobiography*, 1873; Penguin edn., ed. John Robson, 1990.
22   Himmelfarb, Gertrude, *On Liberty and Liberalism: The Case of John Stuart Mill*.
23   Ibid.
24   *National Review*, 1862
25   Woodham-Smith, Cecil, *Florence Nightingale*, Fontana, 1951.
26   Ibid.
27   Ibid.
28   Ibid.

6 THE SEXUAL DOUBLE STANDARD OF VICTORIAN ENGLAND

1 Himmelfarb, Gertrude, *On Liberty and Liberalism: The Case of John Stuart Mill*, Alfred Knopf, 1974.

2 Mason, Michael, *The Making of Victorian Sexuality*, Oxford University Press, 1994.

3 Pethick-Lawrence, Emmeline, *My Part in a Changing World*, Gollancz, 1938.

4 Mahood, James and Wenburg, Christine, eds, *The Mosher Survey: Sexual Attitudes of 45 Victorian Women*, 1980, quoted in Gay, Peter, *The Bourgeois Experience: Victoria to Freud*, vol. 1: *Education of the Senses*, Norton, 1984.

5 Hill, Bridget, *Women, Work and Sexual Politics in Eighteenth Century England*, Blackwell, 1989.

6 Cobbett, William, *Advice to Young Men (And Incidentally to Young Women)*, 1837.

7 Macfarlane, Alan, *Marriage and Love in England: Modes of Reproduction 1300–1840*, Blackwell, 1986.

8 Taine, Hippolyte, *Notes on England*, 1972; trans. Edward Hyams, 1957.

9 Gay, *The Bourgeois Experience: Victoria to Freud*, vol. 1: *Education of the Senses*.

10 Plumb, J. H., *England in the Eighteenth Century*, Penguin, 1990 (rev. edn.).

11 Porter, Roy and Hall, Lesley, *The Facts of Life: The Creation of Sexual Knowledge in Britain, 1650–1950*, Yale University Press, 1995.

12 Mason, *The Making of Victorian Sexuality*.

13 Chadwick, Edwin, *Report on the Sanitary Condition of the Labouring Population of Great Britain, 1842*, ed. M. W. Flinn, Edinburgh University Press, 1965.

14 *Appendix C to Report of Poor Law Commissioners*, Parliamentary Papers 1834.

15 Davenport-Hines, Richard, *Sex, Death and Punishment*, Collins, 1990.

16 Kay, James Phillips, *The Moral and Physical Condition of the Working Classes Employed in the Cotton Manufacture in Manchester*, 1832, in Mort, Frank, *Dangerous Sexualities: Medico-Moral Politics in England Since 1830*, Routledge and Kegan Paul, 1987.

17 Percival, Thomas, *Medical Ethics*, 1803.

18 Mort, *Dangerous Sexualities: Medico-Moral Politics in England Since 1830*.

19 Ibid.

20 Acton, William, *The Functions and Disorders of the Reproductive Organs, in Childhood, Youth and Advanced Life*, John Churchill, 1857.

21 Ryan, Michael, *The Philosophy of Marriage in its Social, Moral and Physical Relations*, John Churchill, 1839.

22 Cooke, William, *Mind and the Emotions Considered in Relation to Health*

and Disease, 1830, in Mort, *Dangerous Sexualities: Medico-Moral Politics in England Since 1830*.

23 Children's Employment Commission, *First Report, Mines*, 1842, in Mort, *Dangerous Sexualities: Medico-Moral Politics in England Since 1830*.

24 Acton, William, *The Functions and Disorders of the Reproductive Organs, in Childhood, Youth and Advanced Life*, 6th edn., 1875.

25 Mason, *The Making of Victorian Sexuality*.

26 Porter, Roy and Hall, Lesley, *The Facts of Life: The Creation of Sexual Knowledge in Britain, 1650–1950*.

27 Acton, *The Functions and Disorders of the Reproductive Organs, in Childhood, Youth and Advanced Life*.

28 Alcott, W. A., *The Physiology of Marriage*, 1855; quoted in Gay, *The Bourgeois Experience: Victoria to Freud*, vol. 1: *Education of the Senses*.

29 *The Westminster and Foreign Quarterly Review*, April–July 1850, 457; quoted in Thomas, Keith, *The Double Standard, Journal of the History of Ideas*, vol. 20, 1959.

30 Platt, Smith H., *Queenly Womanhood. A Private Treatise, for Females Only, on the Sexual Instinct, as Related to Moral and Christian Life*, 1875.

31 *Woman in her Psychological Relations, Journal of Psychological Medicine and Mental Pathology*, 4, 1851, in Moscucci, Ornella, *The Science of Woman: Gynaecology and Gender in England, 1800–1929*, Cambridge University Press, 1990.

32 Darwin, Charles, *The Descent of Man*, 1871.

33 Clarke, Edward, *Sex in Mind and in Education, or a Fair Chance for the Girls, Fortnightly Review* 21, 1874.

34 Moscucci, *The Science of Woman: Gynaecology and Gender in England, 1800–1929*.

35 Walker, Alexander, *Beauty Illustrated by an Analysis and Classification of Beauty in a Woman*, 1852, in Moscucci, *The Science of Woman: Gynaecology and Gender in England, 1800–1929*.

36 Moscucci, *The Science of Woman: Gynaecology and Gender in England, 1800–1929*.

37 Ibid.

38 Manton, Jo, *Elizabeth Garrett Anderson*, Methuen, 1965.

39 Bland, Lucy, *Banishing the Beast: English Feminism and Sexual Morality 1885–1914*, Penguin, 1995.

40 Jackson, Margaret, *The Real Facts of Life: Feminism and the Politics of Sexuality c1850–1940*, Taylor and Francis, 1994.

41 Blackwell, Elizabeth, *The Human Element in Sex: Being a Medical Enquiry into the Relation of Sexual Physiology to Christian Morals*, J. & A. Churchill, 1884.

42 Ibid.

43 Ibid.

44 Ibid.

45 Ibid.

46 Shoemaker, Robert B., *Gender in English Society 1650–1850*, Longman, 1998.

47 Blackwell, Elizabeth, *Essays in Medical Sociology*, 1902, in Jackson, *The Real Facts of Life: Feminism and the Politics of Sexuality, c1850–1940*.

48 Stone, Lawrence, *The Family, Sex and Marriage in England 1500–1800*, Weidenfeld & Nicolson, 1977.

49 Parliamentary papers 1881, House of Commons paper no. 448, vol. 9; quoted in Fisher, Trevor, *Scandal: The Sexual Politics of Late Victorian Britain*, Alan Sutton, 1995.

50 Taine, *Notes on England*.

51 Stone, *The Family, Sex and Marriage in England 1500–1800*.

52 Blackwell, Elizabeth, *Purchase of Women: The Great Economic Blunder*, John Kensit, 1887.

53 Petrie, Glen, *A Singular Iniquity: The Campaigns of Josephine Butler*, Macmillan, 1971.

54 Ibid.

55 Tait, William, *Magdalenism. An Inquiry into the Extent, Causes and Consequences of Prostitution in Edinburgh*, P. Rickard, 1840.

56 Ryan, Michael, *The Philosophy of Marriage in its Social, Moral and Physical Relations*.

57 Bartley, Paula, *Prostitution: Prevention and Reform in England, 1860–1914*, Routledge, 2000.

58 Walkowitz, Judith R., *Prostitution and Victorian Society*, Cambridge University Press, 1980.

59 Prochaska, Frank, *Women and Philanthropy in Nineteenth Century England*, Oxford University Press, 1980.

60 Heasman, Kathleen, *Evangelicals in Action: An Appraisal of their Social Work in the Victorian Era*, Geoffrey Bles, 1962.

61 Marcus, Steven, *The Other Victorians*, Weidenfeld & Nicolson, 1966.

62 Acton, William, *Prostitution*, 1857, 1869 (10th edn.), ed. Peter Fryer, MacGibbon and Kee, 1968.

63 Ibid.

64 Davenport-Hines, Richard, *Sex, Death and Punishment*.

65 Walkowitz, *Prostitution and Victorian Society*.

66 Mort, Frank, *Dangerous Sexualities: Medico-Moral Politics in England Since 1830*, Routledge and Kegan Paul, 1987.

67 Briggs, Asa, *The Age of Improvement, 1783–1867*, Longman, 2000 (2nd edn.).

68 *Lancet*, 3 March 1860.

69 Mort, Frank, *Dangerous Sexualities: Medico-Moral Politics in England Since 1830*.

70 Fisher, *Scandal: The Sexual Politics of Late Victorian Britain*.

71 Butler, Josephine, *Personal Reminiscences of a Great Crusade*, Horace Marshall, 1896.

72 Walkowitz, *Prostitution and Victorian Society.*
73 Davenport-Hines, *Sex, Death and Punishment.*
74 Ibid.
75 Petrie, *A Singular Iniquity: The Campaigns of Josephine Butler.*
76 Moscucci, *The Science of Woman: Gynaecology and Gender in England, 1800–1929.*
77 Blackwell, *The Human Element in Sex: Being a Medical Enquiry into the Relation of Sexual Physiology to Christian Morals.*
78 Hall, Marshall, *On a New and Lamentable Form of Hysteria,* Lancet 1, 1850.
79 Carter, R. B., *On the Pathology and Treatment of Hysteria,* 1853.
80 Moscucci, *The Science of Woman: Gynaecology and Gender in England, 1800–1929.*
81 Blackwell, *Purchase of Women: The Great Economic Blunder.*
82 Acton, *Prostitution.*
83 Garrett, Elizabeth, *An Enquiry into the Nature of the Contagious Diseases Acts, Pall Mall Gazette,* 25 January 1870, in Manton, *Elizabeth Garrett Anderson.*
84 Butler, *Personal Reminiscences of a Great Crusade.*

7 JOSEPHINE BUTLER AND THE REVOLT OF THE WOMEN

1 Walkowitz, Judith R., *Prostitution and Victorian Society,* Cambridge University Press, 1980.
2 Ibid.
3 Petrie, Glen, *A Singular Iniquity: The Campaigns of Josephine Butler,* Macmillan, 1971.
4 Ibid.
5 Butler, Josephine, *Personal Reminiscences of a Great Crusade,* Horace Marshall, 1896.
6 Butler, Josephine, *The Duty of Women,* in Petrie, *A Singular Iniquity: The Campaigns of Josephine Butler.*
7 Butler, *Personal Reminiscences of a Great Crusade.*
8 Stead, W. T., *Josephine Butler,* Morgan and Scott, 1887.
9 Petrie, *A Singular Iniquity: The Campaigns of Josephine Butler.*
10 *Saturday Review,* 19 March 1870; quoted in Walkowitz, *Prostitution and Victorian Society.*
11 Morley, John, *Short Letter to Some Ladies, Fortnightly Review* 7, 1870; quoted in Walkowitz, *Prostitution and Victorian Society.*
12 Fisher, Trevor, *Scandal: The Sexual Politics of Late Victorian Britain,* Alan Sutton, 1995.
13 Butler, *Personal Reminiscences of a Great Crusade.*
14 Ibid.
15 Strachey, Ray, *The Cause,* G. Bell, 1928.

16 Petrie, *A Singular Iniquity: The Campaigns of Josephine Butler*.

17 Hume-Rothery, Mary, *A Letter Addressed to the Rt Hon W. E. Gladstone MP*; quoted in Walkowitz, *Prostitution and Victorian Society*.

18 Walkowitz, *Prostitution and Victorian Society*.

19 Josephine Butler to Albert Ruston, 22 February 1868.

20 Walkowitz, *Prostitution and Victorian Society*.

21 Ibid.

22 Mort, Frank, *Dangerous Sexualities: Medico-Moral Politics in England Since 1830*, Routledge and Kegan Paul, 1987.

23 Scott, Benjamin, *A State Iniquity: Its Rise, Extension and Overthrow, 1890–1894*, reprinted Augustus M. Kelley, 1968; quoted in Fisher, *Scandal: The Sexual Politics of Late Victorian Britain*.

24 Fisher, *Scandal: The Sexual Politics of Late Victorian Britain*.

25 Ibid.

26 Letter to LNA branches, 1872, quoted in Fisher, *Scandal: The Sexual Politics of Late Victorian Britain*.

27 Fisher, *Scandal: The Sexual Politics of Late Victorian Britain*.

28 Butler, *Personal Reminiscences of a Great Crusade*.

29 Ibid.

30 Walkowitz, *Prostitution and Victorian Society*.

31 Ibid.

32 Stead, *Josephine Butler*.

33 Butler, *Personal Reminiscences of a Great Crusade*.

34 Josephine Butler to Vernon Lushingham, PRO Admiralty papers, 12 January 1870, quoted in Walkowitz, *Prostitution and Victorian Society*.

35 *The Shield*, 8 July 1871.

36 Butler, *Personal Reminiscences of a Great Crusade*.

37 Social Purity Alliance annual report 1880.

38 Mrs Butler's third letter from Kent, *The Shield*, 9 March 1870.

39 Stead, *Josephine Butler*.

40 *Opinions of Women on Women's Suffrage*, 1879, in Prochaska, Frank, *Women and Philanthropy in Nineteenth Century England*, Oxford University Press, 1980.

41 *Opinions of Women on Women's Suffrage*.

42 Prochaska, *Women and Philanthropy in Nineteenth Century England*.

43 Davenport-Hines, Richard, *Sex, Death and Punishment*, Collins, 1990.

44 Petrie, *A Singular Iniquity: The Campaigns of Josephine Butler*.

45 *Pall Mall Gazette*, 3 March 1870.

46 Hume-Rothery, *A Letter Addressed to the Rt Hon W. E. Gladstone MP*; quoted in Walkowitz, *Prostitution and Victorian Society*.

47 Acton, William, *A Practical Treatise on Diseases of the Urinary and Generative Organs*, 1875, quoted in Walkowitz, *Prostitution and Victorian Society*.

8 THE CHALLENGE TO POLITICS

1 Rosen, Andrew, *Rise Up Women!*, Routledge and Kegan Paul, 1974.

2 Caine, B., *Victorian Feminists*, Oxford University Press, 1992.

3 Strachey, Ray, *Women's Suffrage and Women's Service*, London and National Society for Women's Suffrage, 1927.

4 Rosen, *Rise Up Women!*.

5 Fulford, Roger, *Votes for Women*, Faber and Faber, 1957.

6 Smith, Harold L., *The British Women's Suffrage Campaign 1866–1928*, Longman, 1998.

7 Liddington, Jill and Norris, Jill, *One Hand Tied Behind Us*, Virago, 1978.

8 Harris, Josie, *Private Lives, Public Spirit: Britain 1870–1914*, Penguin, 1994.

9 Hansard, 20 May 1867.

10 Himmelfarb, Gertrude, *On Liberty and Liberalism: The Case of John Stuart Mill*, Alfred Knopf, 1974.

11 Mill, John Stuart, *The Subjection of Women*, 1869, Oxford University Press, 1912.

12 Ibid.

13 Ibid.

14 Himmelfarb, *On Liberty and Liberalism: The Case of John Stuart Mill*.

15 Mill, John Stuart, *The Subjection of Women*.

16 Hansard, 20 May 1867.

17 Himmelfarb, *On Liberty and Liberalism: The Case of John Stuart Mill*.

18 Briggs, Asa, *The Age of Improvement 1783–1867*, Longman, 2000 (2nd edn.).

19 Rosen, *Rise Up Women!*.

20 Strachey, Ray, *The Cause*, G. Bell, 1928.

21 Smith, *The British Women's Suffrage Campaign 1866–1928*.

22 Pankhurst, Sylvia, *The Suffragette Movement*, Longman, 1931.

23 Lewis, Jane, ed., *Before the Vote Was Won: Arguments For and Against Women's Suffrage 1864–1896*, Routledge and Kegan Paul, 1987.

24 Strachey, *The Cause*.

25 Harris, *Private Lives, Public Spirit: Britain 1870–1914*.

26 Ibid.

27 Fawcett, Millicent Garrett, *What I Remember*, Fisher Unwin, 1924.

28 Hollis, Patricia, *Women in Public: The Women's Movement 1850–1900*, George Allen and Unwin, 1979.

29 Grey, Maria M., *The Women's Educational Movement*, in Stanton, Theodore, *The Woman Question in Europe*, Sampson Low & Co., 1884.

30 Strachey, *The Cause*.

31 Ibid.

32 Ibid.

33 Fawcett, *What I Remember*.

34 Strachey, Ray, *Millicent Garrett Fawcett*, John Murray, 1931.

35 Fawcett, *What I Remember*.
36 Strachey, *Millicent Garrett Fawcett*.
37 Ibid.
38 Ibid.
39 Fawcett, *What I Remember*.
40 Ibid.
41 Strachey, *Millicent Garrett Fawcett*.
42 Harrison, Brian, *Separate Spheres: The Opposition to Women's Suffrage in Britain*, Croom Helm, 1978.
43 Heyck, T. W., *The Transformation of Intellectual Life in Victorian England*, Croom Helm, 1982.

9 THE AGE OF CRUSADES

1 Bagehot, Walter, *Physics and Politics*, 1872.
2 Heyck, T. W., *The Transformation of Intellectual Life in Victorian England*, Croom Helm, 1982.
3 Smith, Warren Sylvester, *The London Heretics*, 1870–1914, Constable, 1967.
4 Ibid.
5 Himmelfarb, Gertrude, *Darwin and the Darwinian Revolution*, Chatto and Windus, 1959.
6 Heyck, *The Transformation of Intellectual Life in Victorian England*.
7 Smith, Warren Sylvester, *The London Heretics*, 1870–1914.
8 Henderson, Archibald, *George Bernard Shaw, Man of the Century*, 1956, in Smith, *The London Heretics*, 1870–1914.
9 Davies, Charles Maurice, *Heterodox London*, in Smith, *The London Heretics*, 1870–1914.
10 Heasman, Kathleen, *Evangelicals in Action: An Appraisal of their Social Work in the Victorian Era*, Geoffrey Bles, 1962.
11 Stephen, George, *Anti-Slavery Recollections in a Series of Letters Addressed to Mrs Beecher Stowe*, 1854.
12 Howard Temperley, in Hollis, Patricia, ed., *Pressure from Without in Early Victorian England*, Edward Arnold, 1974.
13 Brian Harrison, in Hollis, *Pressure from Without in Early Victorian England*.
14 Harris, Josie, *Private Lives, Public Spirit: Britain 1870–1914*, Penguin, 1994.
15 Johnson, George W. and Johnson, Lucy, eds., *Josephine Butler, An Autobiographical Memoir*, Arrowsmith, 1911.
16 Blackwell, E., 'Scientific Method in Biology', *Essays in Medical Sociology*, Ernest Bell, 1902.
17 Moscucci, Ornella, *The Science of Woman: Gynaecology and Gender in England, 1800–1929*, Cambridge University Press, 1990.

18 Cobbe, Frances Power, *Life of Frances Power Cobbe*, R. Bentley and Son, 1894.

19 Ibid.

20 French, Richard D., *Antivivisection and Medical Science in Victorian Society*, Princeton University Press, 1975.

21 Lilly, W. S., 'The New Naturalism', *Fortnightly Review* xxxviii, 1885.

22 Butler, Josephine, ed., *Woman's Work and Woman's Culture*, Macmillan, 1869.

23 Cobbe, *Life of Frances Power Cobbe*.

24 Ibid.

25 Cobbe, Frances Power, *The Duties of Women*, Williams and Norgate, 1881.

26 Ibid.

27 Ibid.

28 Taylor, Helen, address to the third annual meeting of the Edinburgh branch of the NSWS, 1872.

29 Hollis, Patricia, *Women in Public: The Women's Movement 1850–1900*, George Allen and Unwin, 1979.

30 Fawcett, Mrs Henry, *Home and Politics*, Women's Printing Society, 1894, in Lewis, Jane, ed., *Before the Vote Was Won: Arguments For and Against Women's Suffrage 1864–1896*, Routledge and Kegan Paul, 1987.

31 Fawcett, *Home and Politics*.

32 Fawcett, Millicent Garrett, *What I Remember*, Fisher Unwin, 1924.

33 Garrett, Rhoda, *Electoral Disabilities of Women*, lecture, 3 April 1872.

34 Bodichon, Barbara, *Reasons For and Against the Enfranchisement of Women*, 1869.

35 Butler, ed., *Woman's Work and Woman's Culture*.

36 Ibid.

37 Cobbe, Frances Power, *Wife Torture in England*, 1878, in Jeffreys, Sheila, *The Sexuality Debates*, Routledge and Kegan Paul, 1987.

38 Cobbe, Frances Power, *The Duties of Women*.

39 L.S., *The Citizenship of Women Socially Considered*, *Westminster Review*, July 1874.

40 Butler, ed., *Woman's Work and Woman's Culture*.

41 Ibid.

42 Ibid.

43 Grey, Maria and Shirreff, Emily, *Thoughts on Self-Culture*, 1872.

44 Butler, ed., *Woman's Work and Woman's Culture*.

45 Paper read by Mrs McIlquham to the Bedminster (Bristol) Champion Habitation of the Primrose League, Women's Emancipation Union, 11 December 1891.

46 Ibid.

47 *The Nineteenth Century*, July 1889.

48 Smith, Harold L., *The British Women's Suffrage Campaign, 1866–1928*, Longman, 1988.

49 *Women's Suffrage Journal*, 1 April 1874.

50 Debate on Women's Disabilities Removal Bill, May 1872.

51 Strachey, Ray, *The Cause*, G. Bell, 1928.

52 Harris, *Private Lives, Public Spirit: Britain 1870–1914*.

53 Harrison, Brian, *Prudent Revolutionaries*, Clarendon Press, 1987.

54 Besant, Annie, *An Autobiography*, 1893, with an additional survey of her life by George S. Arundale, Theosophical Publishing House, 1939.

55 Ibid.

56 Ibid.

57 Besant, Annie, *The Political Status of Women*, 1874.

58 Ibid.

59 Mitchell, David, *Queen Christabel*, Macdonald and Jane's, 1977.

60 Hollis, *Women in Public: The Women's Movement 1850–1900*.

61 Fawcett, *What I Remember*.

62 Letter to Samuel Smith, 11 April 1892.

63 Lewis, *Before the Vote Was Won: Arguments For and Against Women's Suffrage 1864–1896*.

64 Smith, Harold L., *The British Women's Suffrage Campaign, 1866–1928*.

65 Hansard, 3 May 1871.

66 Speech to Electoral Reform Conference, 1874.

67 *Quarterly Review*, vol. 126, 1869

68 Commons debates, 7 March 1879, quoted in Harrison, Brian, *Separate Spheres: The Opposition to Women's Suffrage in Britain*, Croom Helm, 1978.

69 Harrison, *Separate Spheres: The Opposition to Women's Suffrage in Britain*.

70 Wilson, D. A. and MacArthur, D. W., *Carlyle in Old Age*, 1934, quoted in Harrison, *Separate Spheres: The Opposition to Women's Suffrage in Britain*.

71 Harrison, *Separate Spheres: The Opposition to Women's Suffrage in Britain*.

72 Maudsley, H., *Fortnightly Review*, April 1874, in Hollis, *Women in Public: The Women's Movement 1850–1900*.

73 *The Girl of the Period*, *Saturday Review*, March 1868, quoted in Gay, *The Bourgeois Experience: Victoria to Freud*, vol. 1: *Education of the Senses*, Norton, 1984.

74 Martineau, Harriet, *Harriet Martineau's Autobiography*, James R. Osgood & Co., 1877.

75 Smith, Harold L., *The British Women's Suffrage Campaign, 1866–1928*.

76 Fawcett, *What I Remember*.

10 SLOUCHING TOWARDS MILITANCY

1 Smith, Harold L., *The British Women's Suffrage Campaign 1866–1928*, Longman, 1998.

2   Ibid.
3   Strachey, Ray, *The Cause*, G. Bell, 1928.
4   Montefiore, Dora, *From a Victorian to a Modern*, Archer, 1927.
5   Mitchell, David, *Queen Christabel*, Macdonald and Jane's, 1977.
6   Smith, Warren Sylvester, *The London Heretics, 1870–1914*, Constable, 1967.
7   Showalter, Elaine, *Sexual Anarchy: Gender and Culture at the Fin de Siècle*, Bloomsbury, 1991.
8   Smith, Warren Sylvester, *The London Heretics, 1870–1914*.
9   Ibid.
10 Harris, Josie, *Private Lives, Public Spirit: Britain 1870–1914*, Penguin, 1994.
11 Hollis, Patricia, *Women in Public: The Women's Movement 1850–1900*, George Allen and Unwin, 1979.
12 Morgan, David, *Suffragists and Liberals: The Politics of Woman Suffrage in Britain*, Blackwell, 1975.
13 Ibid.
14 Pankhurst, Emmeline, *My Own Story*, told to Rheta Childe Dorr, Eveleigh Nash, 1914.
15 Pankhurst, Sylvia, *The Suffragette Movement*, Longman, 1931.
16 Pankhurst, E. Sylvia, *The Life of Emmeline Pankhurst*, Werner Laurie, 1935.
17 Pankhurst, Emmeline, *My Own Story*.
18 Pugh, Martin, *The Pankhursts*, Penguin, 2001.
19 Mitchell, *Queen Christabel*.
20 Pankhurst, Sylvia, *The Suffragette Movement*.
21 Pugh, *The Pankhursts*.
22 Pankhurst, Sylvia, *The Suffragette Movement*.
23 Pugh, *The Pankhursts*.
24 Pankhurst, Christabel, *Unshackled*, Hutchinson, 1959.
25 Mitchell, David, *The Pankhursts*, Heron, 1970.
26 Mitchell, *Queen Christabel*.
27 Ibid.
28 Pugh, *The Pankhursts*.
29 Mitchell, *Queen Christabel*.
30 Pankhurst, Sylvia, *The Suffragette Movement*.
31 Mitchell, *Queen Christabel*.
32 Pugh, *The Pankhursts*.
33 Ibid.
34 Pankhurst, Sylvia, *The Suffragette Movement*.
35 Mitchell, *Queen Christabel*.
36 Mitchell, *The Pankhursts*.
37 Pankhurst, Sylvia, *The Suffragette Movement*.
38 Mitchell, *Queen Christabel*.
39 Pugh, *The Pankhursts*.

40   Ibid.
41   Pankhurst, Sylvia, *The Suffragette Movement*.
42   Ibid.
43   Strachey, Ray, *Millicent Garrett Fawcett*, John Murray, 1931.
44   Pankhurst, E. Sylvia, *The Life of Emmeline Pankhurst*.
45   Pankhurst, Sylvia, *The Suffragette Movement*.
46   Mitchell, *Queen Christabel*.
47   Fenwick Miller, Mrs F., *On the Programme of the Women's Franchise League*, an address delivered at the National Liberal Club, 25 February 1890, Tracts 1890–95.
48   Pankhurst, Sylvia, *The Suffragette Movement*.
49   Gay, Peter, *The Bourgeois Experience: Victoria to Freud*, vol. 1: *Education of the Senses*, Norton, 1984.
50   Fenwick Miller, *On the Programme of the Women's Franchise League*.
51   Strachey, *The Cause*.
52   *The Nineteenth Century*, June 1889.
53   Ibid.
54   Ibid.
55   Fawcett, Millicent Garrett, *What I Remember*, Fisher Unwin, 1924.
56   Houghton, Walter E., *The Victorian Frame of Mind 1830–1870*, Yale University Press, 1957.
57   Harris, *Private Lives, Public Spirit: Britain 1870–1914*.
58   Paper read by Mrs McIlquham to the Bedminster (Bristol) Champion Habitation of the Primrose League, Women's Emancipation Union, 11 December 1891.
59   Strachey, *The Cause*.
60   Harrison, Brian, *Separate Spheres: The Opposition to Women's Suffrage in Britain*, Croom Helm, 1978.
61   Helen Taylor to Barbara Bodichon, 9 May 1866, McCrimmon Bodichon collection, Fawcett Library.
62   Fawcett, Mrs, *A Reply to the Letter of Mr Samuel Smith MP*, NUWSS, 1892.
63   Commons debates 27 April 1892; quoted in Harrison, *Separate Spheres: The Opposition to Women's Suffrage in Britain*.
64   Fawcett, Mrs Henry, *Home and Politics*, Women's Printing Society, 1894.
65   Morgan, *Suffragists and Liberals: The Politics of Woman Suffrage in Britain*.
66   Pankhurst, E. Sylvia, *The Life of Emmeline Pankhurst*.
67   Fawcett, *Home and Politics*.
68   Pugh, *The Pankhursts*.
69   Mitchell, *Queen Christabel*.
70   Ibid.
71   Ibid.
72   Pugh, *The Pankhursts*.
73   Ibid.

74 Ibid.
75 Pankhurst, E. Sylvia, *The Life of Emmeline Pankhurst.*
76 Swanwick, Helena Maria, *I Have Been Young*, Gollancz, 1935.
77 *Labour Leader*, 30 May 1903.
78 Mitchell, *Queen Christabel.*
79 Pankhurst, Sylvia, *The Suffragette Movement.*
80 Ibid.
81 Pugh, *The Pankhursts.*
82 Macaulay, Thomas Babington, *The Complete Writings*, ed. Lady Trevelyan, 1898.
83 Houghton, *The Victorian Frame of Mind 1830–1870.*

11 THE WOMEN'S NAPOLEON

1   Smith, Harold L., *The British Women's Suffrage Campaign 1866–1928*, Longman, 1998.
2   Strachey, Ray, *The Cause*, G. Bell, 1928.
3   Pugh, *The Pankhursts*, Penguin, 2001.
4   Thompson, Paul, *The Edwardians: The Remaking of British Society*, Weidenfeld & Nicolson, 1975.
5   Thompson, Laurence, *The Enthusiasts: A Biography of John and Katharine Bruce Glasier*, Gollancz, 1971.
6   Snowden, Philip, *An Autobiography*, vol. 1, Nicholson and Watson, 1934.
7   Pugh, *The Pankhursts.*
8   Mitchell, David, *Queen Christabel*, Macdonald and Jane's, 1977.
9   Pugh, *The Pankhursts.*
10 Mitchell, David, *Queen Christabel.*
11 Pankhurst, Sylvia, *The Suffragette Movement*, Longman, 1931.
12 *Labour Leader*, 19 May 1905, in Rosen, Andrew, *Rise Up Women!*, Routledge and Kegan Paul, 1974.
13 Pugh, *The Pankhursts.*
14 Pankhurst, Emmeline, *My Own Story*, told to Rheta Childe Dorr, Eveleigh Nash, 1914.
15 Ibid.
16 McPhee, Carol and Fitzgerald, Ann, eds., *The Non-Violent Militant: Selected Writings of Teresa Billington-Greig*, Routledge and Kegan Paul, 1987.
17 Ibid.
18 Mitchell, Hannah, *The Hard Way Up*, ed. Geoffrey Mitchell, Faber and Faber, 1968.
19 Ibid.
20 Kenney, Annie, *Memories of a Militant*, Edward Arnold, 1924.
21 Pankhurst, Sylvia, *The Suffragette Movement.*
22 Kenney, Annie, *Memories of a Militant.*

23 Pugh, *The Pankhursts*.
24 Pethick-Lawrence, Emmeline, *My Part in a Changing World*, Gollancz, 1938.
25 Ibid.
26 McPhee, Carol and Fitzgerald, Ann, eds., *The Non-Violent Militant: Selected Writings of Teresa Billington-Greig*.
27 WSPU pamphlet, Museum of London.
28 Lytton, Constance, *Prisons and Prisoners*, Heinemann, 1914.
29 Pethick-Lawrence, *My Part in a Changing World*.
30 Pankhurst, Christabel, *Unshackled*, Hutchinson, 1959.
31 Ibid.
32 Fawcett, Millicent Garrett, *What I Remember*, Fisher Unwin, 1924.
33 Ibid.
34 Pankhurst, Emmeline, *My Own Story*.
35 Strachey, *The Cause*.
36 Pankhurst, Sylvia, *The Suffragette Movement*.
37 Mitchell, Hannah, *The Hard Way Up*.
38 Nevinson, Margaret Wynne, *Life's Fitful Fever*, A. & C. Black, 1926.
39 Swanwick, Helena Maria, *I Have Been Young*, Gollancz, 1935.
40 Margaret Ashton to Mrs Fawcett, 16 January 1906, Manchester Central Library.
41 Billington-Greig papers, Fawcett Library.
42 Nevinson, *Life's Fitful Fever*.
43 Morgan, David, *Suffragists and Liberals: The Politics of Woman Suffrage in Britain*, Blackwell, 1975.

12 THE THEATRE OF VIOLENCE

1   Pankhurst, E. Sylvia, *The Life of Emmeline Pankhurst*, Werner Laurie, 1935.
2   *Diary of Alice Milne*, 22 October 1906, copied by Teresa Billington in Billington-Greig papers, box AK/WSPU/P, in Rosen, *Rise Up Women!*, Routledge and Kegan Paul, 1974.
3   Strachey, Ray, *The Cause*, G. Bell, 1928.
4   Fawcett, Millicent Garrett, *What I Remember*, Fisher Unwin, 1924.
5   Pethick-Lawrence, Emmeline, *My Part in a Changing World*, Gollancz, 1938.
6   Rosen, *Rise Up Women!*.
7   Pethick-Lawrence, *My Part in a Changing World*.
8   Rosen, *Rise Up Women!*.
9   Kenney, Annie, *Memories of a Militant*, Edward Arnold, 1924.
10 McPhee, Carol and Fitzgerald, Ann, eds., *The Non-Violent Militant: Selected Writings of Teresa Billington-Greig*, Routledge and Kegan Paul, 1987.
11 Rosen, *Rise Up Women!*.

12   Billington-Greig, Teresa, *The Militant Suffrage Movement*, Frank Palmer, 1911.

13   McPhee, Carol and Fitzgerald, Ann, eds., *The Non-Violent Militant: Selected Writings of Teresa Billington-Greig*.

14   Ibid.

15   Ibid.

16   Quoted in Fulford, Roger, *Votes for Women*, Faber and Faber, 1957.

17   Strachey, *The Cause*.

18   Mitchell, David, *Queen Christabel*, Macdonald and Jane's, 1977.

19   Ibid.

20   Ibid.

21   Billington-Greig, *The Militant Suffrage Movement*.

22   Fawcett, *What I Remember*.

23   Mitchell, *Queen Christabel*.

24   Ibid.

25   Ibid.

26   25 October 1906; quoted in Liddington, Jill and Norris, Jill, *One Hand Tied Behind Us*, Virago, 1978.

27   Pankhurst, Christabel, *Unshackled*, Hutchinson, 1959.

28   Christabel Pankhurst to Henry Harben, 1 August 1913, Harben papers, in Pugh, Martin, *The Pankhursts*, Penguin, 2001.

29   Strachey, *The Cause*.

30   Smith, Harold L., *The British Women's Suffrage Campaign 1866–1928*, Longman, 1998.

31   *Daily Chronicle*, 14 February 1907, in Pugh, *The Pankhursts*.

32   Pugh, *The Pankhursts*.

33   Pankhurst, Sylvia, *The Suffragette Movement*, Longman, 1931.

34   Strachey, *The Cause*.

35   Ibid.

36   Women's Suffrage collection, London Museum, folder, Constitution-Organisation, H. Fraser to I. Seymour, Glasgow, 6 July 1908, in Rosen, *Rise Up Women!*.

37   Mitchell, *Queen Christabel*.

38   *Daily News*, 2 July 1908.

39   *Votes for Women*, 10 December 1908.

40   Fawcett, *What I Remember*.

41   Rosen, *Rise Up Women!*.

42   Smith, *The British Women's Suffrage Campaign 1866–1928*.

43   Mitchell, *Queen Christabel*.

44   Smith, *The British Women's Suffrage Campaign 1866–1928*.

45   Mitchell, David, *The Pankhursts*, Heron, 1970.

46   Linklater, Andro, *An Unhusbanded Life: Charlotte Despard, Suffragette, Socialist and Sinn Feiner*, Hutchinson, 1980.

47   Bartley, Paula, *Votes for Women 1860–1928*, Hodder and Stoughton, 1998.

48   Pankhurst, Sylvia, *The Suffragette Movement*.

49   Ibid.

50 Ibid.
51 Mitchell, *Queen Christabel*.
52 Pankhurst, Emmeline, *My Own Story*, told to Rheta Childe Dorr, Eveleigh Nash, 1914.
53 Bartley, *Votes for Women 1860–1928*.
54 Billington-Greig, *The Militant Suffrage Movement*.
55 Linklater, *An Unhusbanded Life: Charlotte Despard, Suffragette, Socialist and Sinn Feiner*.
56 Verbatim Report of Debate on 3 December 1907, *Votes for Women*, 1908.
57 Ibid.
58 Pankhurst, Sylvia, *The Suffragette Movement*.
59 Mitchell, *Queen Christabel*.
60 Smith, *The British Women's Suffrage Campaign 1866–1928*.
61 Pankhurst, Sylvia, *The Suffragette Movement*.
62 Pugh, *The Pankhursts*.
63 Quoted in St John, Christopher, *Ethel Smyth*, Longman, 1959, in Pugh, *The Pankhursts*.
64 *Votes for Women*, 31 December 1908.
65 Mitchell, *Queen Christabel*.
66 Pankhurst, Sylvia, *The Suffragette Movement*.
67 Mitchell, *Queen Christabel*.
68 Nevinson, Henry, *More Changes, More Chances*, Nisbet, 1925
69 Swanwick, Helena Maria, *I Have Been Young*, Gollancz, 1935.
70 Billington-Greig, *The Militant Suffrage Movement*.
71 Fawcett, *What I Remember*.
72 Lady Frances Balfour letter in Fawcett Library Autograph Collection.
73 Mitchell, *Queen Christabel*.
74 Ibid.
75 Ibid.
76 Mitchell, *The Pankhursts*.
77 Strachey, Ray, *Millicent Garrett Fawcett*, John Murray, 1931.

13 THE DAMNATION OF MEN

 1 Fawcett, Mrs Henry, *Home and Politics*, Women's Printing Society, 1894.
 2 Ibid.
 3 Mort, Frank, *Dangerous Sexualities: Medico-Moral Politics in England Since 1830*, Routledge and Kegan Paul, 1987.
 4 Fisher, Trevor, *Scandal: The Sexual Politics of Late Victorian Britain*, Alan Sutton, 1995.
 5 Ibid.
 6 Petrie, Glen, *A Singular Iniquity: The Campaigns of Josephine Butler*, Macmillan, 1971.
 7 Fisher, *Scandal: The Sexual Politics of Late Victorian Britain*.

8   *Pall Mall Gazette*, 29 October 1885.
9   Petrie, *A Singular Iniquity: The Campaigns of Josephine Butler.*
10 *Pall Mall Gazette*, 6 June 1885.
11 Fisher, *Scandal: The Sexual Politics of Late Victorian Britain.*
12 Ibid.
13 Strachey, Ray, *Millicent Garrett Fawcett*, John Murray, 1931.
14 *Common Cause*, 19 May 1910.
15 *The Contemporary Review*, 1885, in Jackson, Margaret, *The Real Facts of Life: Feminism and the Politics of Sexuality c1850–1940*, Taylor and Francis, 1994.
16 Fisher, *Scandal: The Sexual Politics of Late Victorian Britain.*
17 Josephine Butler to Mrs Priestman, 1883.
18 Mort, Frank, *Dangerous Sexualities: Medico-Moral Politics in England Since 1830.*
19 Bland, Lucy, *Banishing the Beast: English Feminism and Sexual Morality 1885–1914*, Penguin, 1995.
20 Barrett, Rosa, *Ellice Hopkins: A Memoir*, Wells Gardner Darton, 1907.
21 Ibid.
22 Ibid.
23 Hopkins, Ellice, *Drawn unto Death: A Plea for the Children Coming Under the Industrial Schools Amendment Act 1880*, Hatchards, 1884.
24 *Journal of the Vigilance Association for the Defence of Personal Rights*, 15 November 1882.
25 *The New Woman*, 29 November 1894.
26 Address by R. A. Bullen, Social Purity Alliance, c.1900, in Bartley, Paula, *Prostitution: Prevention and Reform in England, 1860–1914*, Routledge, 2000.
27 Ibid.
28 Barrett, *Ellice Hopkins: A Memoir*; quoted in Bartley, *Prostitution: Prevention and Reform in England, 1860–1914.*
29 Schreiner to E. Carpenter, 11 November 1888, Edward Carpenter Collection, in Bland, *Banishing the Beast: English Feminism and Sexual Morality 1885–1914.*
30 Caird, Mona, 'Marriage', *Westminster Review*, no. 130, 1888, in Bland, *Banishing the Beast: English Feminism and Sexual Morality 1885–1914.*
31 Bland, *Banishing the Beast: English Feminism and Sexual Morality 1885–1914.*
32 Schreiner, Olive, *Woman and Labour*, 1911.
33 Braby, Maud, *Modern Marriage and How to Bear It*, 1909.
34 Thompson, Paul, *The Edwardians: The Remaking of British Society*, Weidenfeld & Nicolson, 1975.
35 Caird, Mona, *The Morality of Marriage and Other Essays on the Status and Destiny of Woman*, George Redway, 1897.
36 Swanwick, Helena M., *The Future of the Women's Movement*, Bell, 1913.
37 Ibid.

38 Hamilton, Cicely, *Marriage as a Trade*, Chapman and Hall, 1909.
39 Ibid.
40 Engels, Frederick, *Origin of the Family, Private Property and the State*, 1884.
41 Lerner, Gerda, *The Creation of Patriarchy*, Oxford University Press, 1986.
42 Ibid.
43 Caird, *The Morality of Marriage and Other Essays on the Status and Destiny of Woman*.
44 Ibid.
45 Hamilton, *Marriage as a Trade*.
46 Chare, Hope, *Stagnant Virginity, Free Review*, January 1897, in Bland, *Banishing the Beast: English Feminism and Sexual Morality 1885–1914*.
47 Gallichan, Walter, *Modern Woman and How to Manage Her*, 1909, in Jackson, Margaret, *The Real Facts of Life: Feminism and the Politics of Sexuality c1850–1940*, Taylor and Francis, 1994.
48 Jackson, Margaret, *The Real Facts of Life: Feminism and the Politics of Sexuality c1850–1940*.
49 Eckenstein to Pearson, 24 April 1890, in Bland, *Banishing the Beast: English Feminism and Sexual Morality 1885–1914*.
50 Hamilton, *Marriage as a Trade*.
51 Mason, Michael, *The Making of Victorian Sexuality*, Oxford University Press, 1994.
52 Blackwell, Elizabeth, *Rescue Work in Relation to Prostitution and Disease*, *1881*, in Jackson, *The Real Facts of Life: Feminism and the Politics of Sexuality c1850–1940*.
53 Blackwell, Elizabeth, in Jackson, *The Real Facts of Life: Feminism and the Politics of Sexuality c1850–1940*.
54 J. S. Mill to Lord Amberley, 2 February 1870, *Later Letters IV*, 1893, in Himmelfarb, Gertrude, *On Liberty and Liberalism, The Case of John Stuart Mill*, Alfred Knopf, 1974.
55 Geddes, Patrick and Thompson, J. Arthur, *The Evolution of Sex*, W. Scott, 1889.
56 Ethelmer, Ellis, *The Phases of Love*, Congleton, 1897.
57 *Shafts*, March 1897.
58 Ethelmer, Ellis, *Woman Free*, 1893.
59 Ethelmer, *The Phases of Love*.
60 Ibid.
61 Barrett, *Ellice Hopkins: A Memoir*.
62 Ibid.
63 Ibid.

14 MARTYRS AND HYPOCRITES

1 Smith, Harold L., *The British Women's Suffrage Campaign 1866–1928*, Longman, 1998.

2   Mitchell, David, *Queen Christabel*, Macdonald and Jane's, 1977.
3   Kenney, Annie, *Memories of a Militant*, Edward Arnold, 1924.
4   *Votes for Women*, 17 September 1909.
5   Gladstone papers, in Mitchell, *Queen Christabel*.
6   Mitchell, David, *The Pankhursts*, Heron, 1970.
7   Pankhurst, E. Sylvia, *The Life of Emmeline Pankhurst*, Werner Laurie, 1935.
8   Pankhurst, Sylvia, *The Suffragette Movement*, Longman, 1931.
9   Pugh, Martin, *The Pankhursts*, Penguin, 2001.
10 Pankhurst, Sylvia, *The Suffragette Movement*.
11 Rosen, Andrew, *Rise Up Women!*, Routledge and Kegan Paul, 1974.
12 Pugh, Martin, *The Pankhursts*.
13 Pankhurst, Sylvia, *The Suffragette Movement*.
14 Fawcett, Millicent Garrett, *What I Remember*, Fisher Unwin, 1924.
15 Smith, *The British Women's Suffrage Campaign 1866–1928*.
16 Pankhurst, Sylvia, *The Suffragette Movement*.
17 Ibid.
18 Ibid.
19 *The Nation*, 20 March 1909, in Mitchell, *Queen Christabel*.
20 Pankhurst, Sylvia, *The Suffragette Movement*.
21 Fawcett, Millicent, *The Women's Victory and After: Personal Reminiscences, 1911–1918*, Sidgwick and Jackson, 1920.
22 Mitchell, *Queen Christabel*.
23 Pankhurst, Sylvia, *The Suffragette Movement*.
24 Ibid.
25 *Votes for Women*, 9 December 1910.
26 Ibid.
27 Pankhurst, Sylvia, *The Suffragette Movement*.
28 Smith, *The British Women's Suffrage Campaign 1866–1928*.
29 Rosen, *Rise Up Women!*.
30 Fawcett, Millicent, *The Women's Victory and After: Personal Reminiscences, 1911–1918*.
31 Fawcett, *What I Remember*.
32 Ibid.
33 Jenkins, Roy, *Asquith*, Collins, 1978.
34 Koss, Stephen, *Asquith*, Allen Lane, 1976
35 Asquith, Herbert, *Memories and Reflections 1852–1927*, Cassell, 1929.
36 Strachey, Ray, *Millicent Garrett Fawcett*, John Murray, 1931.
37 Jenkins, *Asquith*.
38 Ibid.
39 Fulford, Roger, *Votes for Women*, Faber and Faber, 1957.
40 Koss, *Asquith*.
41 *Votes for Women*, 10 November 1911.
42 *Votes for Women*, 24 November 1911, in Mitchell, *Queen Christabel*.
43 Nevinson journals, Bodleian Library, Dep.e 73/1, 6 December 1911.

44   Scott, C. P., *Political Diaries*, ed. Trevor Wilson, Collins, 1970.
45   Helen Fraser Moyes papers, Museum of London, in Mitchell, *Queen Christabel*.
46   David, Edward, ed., 'Inside Asquith's Cabinet', in *The Diaries of Charles Hobhouse*, John Murray, 1977.
47   Dangerfield, George, *The Strange Death of Liberal England*, Constable, 1936.
48   Fawcett, *What I Remember*.
49   Strachey, Ray, *The Cause*, G. Bell, 1928.
50   Pugh, *The Pankhursts*.
51   Pankhurst, Sylvia, *The Suffragette Movement*.
52   Ibid.
53   Mitchell, *Queen Christabel*.
54   Pugh, *The Pankhursts*.
55   Kenney, Annie, *Memories of a Militant*.
56   Pankhurst, Sylvia, *The Suffragette Movement*.
57   Ibid.
58   Ibid.
59   Richardson, Mary, *Laugh a Defiance*, Weidenfeld & Nicolson, 1953.
60   Kenney, Annie, *Memories of a Militant*.
61   Mitchell, *Queen Christabel*.
62   *Votes for Women*, 18 October 1912, in Rosen, *Rise Up Women!*.
63   Strachey, *The Cause*.
64   Ibid.
65   Pugh, *The Pankhursts*.
66   *The Suffragette*, 13 December 1912.
67   *The Suffragette*, 6 December 1912, in Rosen, *Rise Up Women!*.
68   PRO, HO 45.231366/3, Metropolitan Police report on WSPU meeting, Wimbledon Common, 8 December 1912, in Rosen, *Rise Up Women!*.
69   Swanwick, Helena Maria, *I Have Been Young*, Gollancz, 1935, in Mitchell, *Queen Christabel*.
70   Pugh, Martin, *Electoral Reform in War and Peace, 1906–18*, Routledge and Kegan Paul, 1978.
71   Cromer papers, PRO, FO 633/19, in Harrison, Brian, *Separate Spheres: The Opposition to Women's Suffrage in Britain*, Croom Helm, 1978.
72   *Anti-Suffrage Review*, November 1910.
73   Harrison, Brian, *Separate Spheres: The Opposition to Women's Suffrage in Britain*.
74   Pankhurst, Sylvia, *The Suffragette Movement*.
75   Rosen, *Rise Up Women!*.
76   Richardson, Mary, *Laugh a Defiance*.
77   Billington-Greig, Teresa, *The Militant Suffrage Movement*, Frank Palmer, 1911.
78   Ibid.
79   Ibid.

80 Ibid.
81 Ibid.
82 Ibid.
83 Ibid.
84 *The Freewoman*, 22 August 1912.
85 *The Freewoman*, 23 November 1911.
86 Ibid.
87 24 February 1917, Baronne de Brimont papers, in Mitchell, *Queen Christabel*.
88 Mitchell, *Queen Christabel*.
89 Pethick-Lawrence, Emmeline, *My Part in a Changing World*, Gollancz, 1938.
90 Ibid.
91 Kenney, Annie, *Memories of a Militant*.
92 Ibid.
93 Snowden, E., 'The Woman Socialist', in *The Labour Ideal*, 1907.
94 Liddington, Jill and Norris, Jill, *One Hand Tied Behind Us*, Virago, 1978.
95 Pankhurst, Adela, *My Mother*, Pankhurst-Walsh papers, in Pugh, *The Pankhursts*.
96 Smith, *The British Women's Suffrage Campaign 1866–1928*.
97 Jenkins, *Asquith*.
98 *The Globe*, 28 January 1913, in Rosen, *Rise Up Women!*.
99 Strachey, *The Cause*.
100 Mitchell, *The Pankhursts*.
101 Pugh, *The Pankhursts*.
102 Harrison, Brian, *Prudent Revolutionaries*, Clarendon Press, 1987.

15 THE GYNAE-CENTRIC UNIVERSE

1 Special report, CID, 7 November 1913; quoted in Bartley, Paula, *Prostitution: Prevention and Reform in England, 1860–1914*, Routledge, 2000.
2 Mort, Frank, *Dangerous Sexualities: Medico-Moral Politics in England Since 1830*, Routledge and Kegan Paul, 1987.
3 Soloway, Richard Allen, *Birth Control and the Population Question in England, 1877–1930*, University of North Carolina Press, 1982.
4 Soloway, Richard Allen, *Demography and Degeneration*, University of North Carolina Press, 1990.
5 *Eugenics Review*, vol. 3, no. 1, April 1911, in Soloway, *Demography and Degeneration*.
6 Ellis, Havelock, *The Task of Social Hygiene*, Constable, 1912, in Bland, Lucy, *Banishing the Beast: English Feminism and Sexual Morality 1885–1914*, Penguin, 1995.

7   Hopkins, Ellice, *The Power of Womanhood, or Mothers and Sons*, Wells Gardner, 1899, quoted in Bartley, Paula, *Prostitution: Prevention and Reform in England, 1860–1914*, Routledge, 2000.

8   Schreiner, Olive, quoted in Hopkins, *The Power of Womanhood, or Mothers and Sons*.

9   Ravenhill, Alice, *Eugenic Ideals for Womanhood, Eugenics Review*, vol. 1, April 1909–January 1910.

10 Hopkins, Ellice, *The Power of Womanhood, or Mothers and Sons*.

11 Ethelmer, Ellis, *Woman Free*, 1893.

12 Scharlieb, Mary, *Womanhood and Race Regeneration*, Cassell, 1912, in Bland, *Banishing the Beast: English Feminism and Sexual Morality 1885–1914*.

13 Chesser, Elizabeth Sloan, *Perfect Health for Women and Children*, Methuen, 1912; *From Girlhood to Womanhood*, Cassell, 1914; both in Bland, *Banishing the Beast: English Feminism and Sexual Morality 1885–1914*.

14 Hartley, Constance, *The Truth About Women*, Everleigh Nash, 1913, in Bland, *Banishing the Beast: English Feminism and Sexual Morality 1885–1914*.

15 Bland, *Banishing the Beast: English Feminism and Sexual Morality 1885–1914*.

16 Caird, Mona, *The Morality of Marriage and Other Essays on the Status and Destiny of Woman*, George Redway, 1897.

17 Pearson, Karl, *The Ethic of Free Thought*, 1901.

18 Ibid.

19 Bland, *Banishing the Beast: English Feminism and Sexual Morality 1885–1914*.

20 Jackson, Margaret, *The Real Facts of Life: Feminism and the Politics of Sexuality c1850–1940*, Taylor and Francis, 1994.

21 Pearson collection, University College London, in Bland, *Banishing the Beast: English Feminism and Sexual Morality 1885–1914*.

22 Pearson collection, University College London, in Bland, *Banishing the Beast: English Feminism and Sexual Morality 1885–1914*.

23 Minutes, November 1885, in Bland, *Banishing the Beast: English Feminism and Sexual Morality 1885–1914*.

24 Bland, *Banishing the Beast: English Feminism and Sexual Morality 1885–1914*.

25 E. Brooke to K. Pearson, 14 March 1886, Pearson collection, University College London, in Bland, *Banishing the Beast: English Feminism and Sexual Morality 1885–1914*.

26 29 April 1887, in Bland, *Banishing the Beast: English Feminism and Sexual Morality 1885–1914*.

27 Sharpe, M., on Karl Pearson's Paper, 2 June 1887, in Bland, *Banishing the Beast: English Feminism and Sexual Morality 1885–1914*.

28 Sharpe to Pearson, 15 November 1885, in Bland, *Banishing the Beast: English Feminism and Sexual Morality 1885–1914*.

29 Sharpe to Pearson, 30 May 1889, in Bland, *Banishing the Beast: English Feminism and Sexual Morality 1885–1914*.

30 Bland, *Banishing the Beast: English Feminism and Sexual Morality 1885–1914*.

31 Mort, *Dangerous Sexualities: Medico-Moral Politics in England Since 1830*.

32 Ethelmer, Ellis, *The Phases of Love*, Congleton, 1897.

33 Besant, Annie, *An Autobiography*, 1893, with an additional survey of her life by George S. Arundale, Theosophical Publishing House, 1939.

34 Besant, Annie, *In the Outer Court*, Theosophical Publishing Society, 1895.

35 K. Mills to M. Sharpe, 24 April 1889, in Bland, *Banishing the Beast: English Feminism and Sexual Morality 1885–1914*.

36 Swiney, Frances, *The Cosmic Procession, or the Feminine Principle in Evolution*, 1906.

37 Ibid.

38 Swiney, Frances, *The Awakening of Women; or Women's Part in Evolution*, William Reeves, 1908.

39 Swiney Frances, *The Bar of Isis*, Open Road, 1907.

40 Ibid., in Jeffreys, Sheila, *The Sexuality Debates*, Routledge and Kegan Paul, 1987.

41 Swiney, *The Cosmic Procession; or the Feminine Principle in Evolution*.

42 Swiney, *The Bar of Isis*.

43 Swiney, *The Awakening of Women; or Women's Part in Evolution*.

44 Ibid.

45 Harman, Lilian, *The Adult*, 1898, in Mort, *Dangerous Sexualities: Medico-Moral Politics in England Since 1830*.

46 *Westminster Review*, July 1899.

47 Besant, Annie, *The Law of Population, Its Consequences and Its Bearing Upon Human Conduct and Morals*, Freethought Publishing Co., 1878.

48 Fryer, Peter, *The Birth Controllers*, Secker and Warburg, 1965.

49 Besant, Annie, *Theosophy and the Law of Population*, 1901, in Jeffreys, Sheila, *The Spinster and Her Enemies: Feminism and Sexuality 1880–1930*, Pandora, 1985.

50 Showalter, Elaine, *Sexual Anarchy: Gender and Culture at the Fin de Siècle*, Bloomsbury, 1991.

51 *The Freewoman*, 11 July 1912.

52 *The Freewoman*, 30 November 1911

53 *The Freewoman*, 11 May 1912.

54 *The Freewoman*, 14 December 1911.

55 *The Freewoman*, 7 December 1911.

56 *The Freewoman*, 4 July 1912.

57 *The Freewoman*, 4 January 1912.

58 *The Freewoman*, 20 June 1912.

59 *The Freewoman*, 21 March 1912.

60 Ibid.

61   *The Freewoman*, 22 February 1912.
62   *The Freewoman*, 1 August 1912.
63   *The Freewoman*, 11 January 1912.
64   *The Freewoman*, 11 July 1912.
65   *The Freewoman*, 22 August 1912.
66   *The Freewoman*, 8 February 1912.
67   *The Freewoman*, 29 February 1912.
68   *The Freewoman*, 8 February 1912.
69   *The Freewoman*, 7 December 1911.
70   Letter to *The Woman's Leader*, 1925, in Jeffreys, *The Spinster and Her Enemies: Feminism and Sexuality 1880–1930*.
71   Newman, Francis William, *The Corruption Now Called Neo-Malthusianism*, with notes by Dr Elizabeth Blackwell, Moral Reform Union, 1889.
72   Ibid.
73   Hollis, Patricia, *Women in Public: The Women's Movement 1850–1900*, George Allen and Unwin, 1979.
74   Soloway, *Birth Control and the Population Question in England, 1877–1930*.
75   Ibid.
76   *Votes for Women*, 23 September 1910.
77   *Contemporary Review*, no. 24, 1908.
78   Re Bartlett, Lucy, *The Coming Order*, Longman, 1911, in Mort, *Dangerous Sexualities: Medico-Moral Politics in England Since 1830*.
79   Martindale, Louisa, *Under the Surface*, 1910.
80   *The Suffragette*, 29 November 1912.
81   Mitchell, David, *Queen Christabel*, Macdonald and Jane's, 1977.
82   *The Suffragette*, 18 July 1913.
83   *The Suffragette*, 25 July 1913, in Mitchell, *Queen Christabel*.
84   Re Bartlett, Lucy, *Sex and Sanctity*, Longman, 1912.
85   PRO, HO, 45.231366. Transcript of speech, E. Pankhurst, London Pavilion, 3 March 1913.
86   *The Suffragette*, 11 April 1913.
87   *The Suffragette*, 2 May 1913.
88   Pugh, Martin, *The Pankhursts*, Penguin, 2001.
89   Pankhurst, Christabel, *The Great Scourge and How to End It*, Lincoln's Inn House, 1913.
90   Ibid.
91   Ibid.
92   Ibid.
93   Ibid.
94   *Clarion*, 17 October 1913.
95   *The New Freewoman*, 15 June 1913.
96   Mitchell, *Queen Christabel*.
97   Pankhurst, Sylvia, *The Suffragette Movement*, Longman, 1931.

16 WAR AND VICTORY

1   Mitchell, David, *Women on the Warpath*, Jonathan Cape, 1966.
2   *The Suffragette*, 7 August 1914.
3   Mitchell, David, *Queen Christabel*, Macdonald and Jane's, 1977.
4   Pankhurst, Emmeline, *My Own Story*, told to Rheta Childe Dorr, Eveleigh Nash, 1914.
5   *Daily Telegraph*, 4 September 1914.
6   Mitchell, *Women on the Warpath*.
7   Pugh, *The Pankhursts*, Penguin, 2001.
8   Mitchell, *Queen Christabel*.
9   *Daily Sketch*, 25 March 1913, in Rosen, Andrew, *Rise Up Women!*, Routledge and Kegan Paul, 1974.
10 Pugh, *The Pankhursts*.
11 Pankhurst, Sylvia, *The Suffragette Movement*, Longman, 1931.
12 Pugh, Martin, *Electoral Reform in War and Peace, 1906–18*, Routledge and Kegan Paul, 1978.
13 Smith, Harold L., *The British Women's Suffrage Campaign 1866–1928*, Longman, 1998.
14 Pankhurst, Sylvia, *The Suffragette Movement*.
15 Pethick-Lawrence, Emmeline, *My Part in a Changing World*, Gollancz, 1938.
16 Smith, *The British Women's Suffrage Campaign 1866–1928*.
17 *Anti-Suffrage Review*, 77, March 1915.
18 Pethick-Lawrence, *My Part in a Changing World*.
19 Pankhurst, E. Sylvia, *The Life of Emmeline Pankhurst*, Werner Laurie, 1935.
20 Pankhurst, Adela, *My Mother*, Pankhurst-Walsh papers, in Pugh, *The Pankhursts*.
21 Strachey, Ray, *Millicent Garrett Fawcett*, John Murray, 1931.
22 Strachey, Ray, *The Cause*, G. Bell, 1928.
23 Fawcett, Millicent Garrett, *What I Remember*, Fisher Unwin, 1924.
24 Ibid.
25 Strachey, *The Cause*.
26 Ibid.
27 Fawcett, *What I Remember*.
28 Swanwick, Helena Maria, *I Have Been Young*, Gollancz, 1935.
29 Ibid.
30 Fawcett, *What I Remember*.
31 Ibid.
32 Bles, Geoffrey, *Letters from Lord Oxford to a Friend*, 1933.
33 Pugh, Martin, *Electoral Reform in War and Peace, 1906–18*.
34 Ibid.
35 Pankhurst, Sylvia, *The Suffragette Movement*.
36 Pankhurst, E. Sylvia, *The Life of Emmeline Pankhurst*.

37 Smith, *The British Women's Suffrage Campaign 1866–1928*.
38 Ibid.
39 Fawcett, *What I Remember*.
40 Smith, *The British Women's Suffrage Campaign 1866–1928*.
41 Ibid.
42 Mitchell, *Queen Christabel*.
43 Smith, *The British Women's Suffrage Campaign 1866–1928*.
44 Fawcett, *What I Remember*.
45 Smith, *The British Women's Suffrage Campaign 1866–1928*.
46 Ibid.
47 Fawcett, Millicent, *The Women's Victory and After: Personal Reminiscences, 1911–1918*, Sidgwick and Jackson, 1920.
48 Pankhurst, Sylvia, *The Suffragette Movement*.
49 Mitchell, *Queen Christabel*.
50 Ibid.
51 Ibid.
52 Ibid.
53 Ibid.
54 Phillips, Melanie, *The Divided House*, Sidgwick and Jackson, 1980.
55 Harrison, Brian, *Prudent Revolutionaries*, Clarendon Press, 1987.
56 Mitchell, *Queen Christabel*.
57 Smith, *The British Women's Suffrage Campaign 1866–1928*.
58 Ibid.
59 Ibid.
60 Hansard, 29 March 1928.
61 Pankhurst, Sylvia, *The Suffragette Movement*.
62 Smith, *The British Women's Suffrage Campaign 1866–1928*.
63 Mitchell, David, *The Pankhursts*, Heron, 1970.
64 Ibid.
65 Ibid.
66 Ibid.
67 Purvis, June, *Emmeline Pankhurst*, Routledge, 2002.
68 Mitchell, *The Pankhursts*.
69 Purvis, *Emmeline Pankhurst*.
70 Mitchell, *Queen Christabel*.

BIBLIOGRAPHY

Acton, William, *Prostitution*, 1857, 1869 (10th edn.), ed. Peter Fryer, MacGibbon and Kee, 1968.
—— *The Functions and Disorders of the Reproductive Organs, in Childhood, Youth and Advanced Life*, John Churchill, 1857, 1875 (6th edn.).
—— *A Practical Treatise on Diseases of the Urinary and Generative Organs*, 1875.
Asquith, Herbert Henry, *Memories and Reflections 1852–1927*, Cassell, 1929.
Balfour, Betty, ed., *Letters of Lady Constance Lytton*, Heinemann, 1925.
Balfour, Lady Frances, *Ne Obliviscaris*, Hodder and Stoughton, 1930.
Banks, J. A. and Olive, *Feminism and Family Planning in Victorian England*, University of Liverpool, 1964.
Barker-Benfield, G. J., *The Culture of Sensibility: Sex and Society in Eighteenth Century Britain*, University of Chicago Press, 1992.
Barrett, Rosa, *Ellice Hopkins: A Memoir*, Wells Gardner Darton, 1907.
Bartley, Paula, *Votes for Women 1860–1928*, Hodder and Stoughton, 1998.
—— *Prostitution: Prevention and Reform in England, 1860–1914*, Routledge, 2000.
Bax, E. Belfort, *The Fraud of Feminism*, Grant Richards, 1913.
Bentley, Michael, *Politics Without Democracy 1815–1914*, Blackwell, 1996 (2nd edn.).
Besant, Annie, *The Law of Population, Its Consequences and Its Bearing Upon Human Conduct and Morals*, Freethought Publishing Co., 1878.
—— *An Autobiography*, T. Fisher Unwin, 1893.
—— *Women and Politics*, Theosophical Publishing Society, 1914.
Billington-Greig, Teresa, *The Militant Suffragette Movement*, Frank Palmer, 1911.
Blackstone, William, *Commentaries on the Laws of England*, 1847.
Blackwell, Elizabeth, *The Human Element in Sex: Being a Medical Enquiry into the Relation of Sexual Physiology to Christian Morals*, J. & A. Churchill, 1884.

—— *Purchase of Women: The Great Economic Blunder*, John Kensit, 1887.

—— *A Medical Address to the Benevolence of Malthus, Contrasted with the Corruption of Neo-Malthusianism*, Darks and Co., 1888.

—— *Essays in Medical Sociology*, vol. 2, Ernest Bell, 1902.

Blakemore, Steven, *Crisis in Representation: Thomas Paine, Mary Wollstonecraft, Helen Maria Williams, and the Rewriting of the French Revolution*, Associated University Presses, 1997.

Bland, Lucy, *Banishing the Beast: English Feminism and Sexual Morality 1885–1914*, Penguin, 1995.

Briggs, Asa, *Chartism*, Sutton Publishing, 1998.

—— *The Age of Improvement 1783–1867*, Longman, 2000 (2nd edn.).

Brown, James Baldwin, *The Home Life: In the Light of its Divine Idea*, Smith, Elder and Co., 1866.

Browne, Alice, *The 18th Century Feminist Mind*, Harvester Press, 1987.

Burton, Antoinette, *The Feminist Quest for Identity: British Imperial Suffragism and Global Sisterhood, 1900–1915*, Journal of Women's History, vol. 3, no. 4, 1990.

Butler, Josephine, ed., *Woman's Work and Woman's Culture*, Macmillan, 1869.

—— *Personal Reminiscences of a Great Crusade*, Horace Marshall, 1896.

Cady Stanton, Elizabeth, *80 Years and More: Reminiscences 1815–1897*, T. Fisher Unwin, 1898.

Caird, Mona, *The Morality of Marriage and Other Essays on the Status and Destiny of Woman*, George Redway, 1897.

Carpenter, Edward, *Love's Coming-of-Age*, Manchester Labour Press, 1896.

Chadwick, Edwin, *Report on the Sanitary Condition of the Labouring Population of Great Britain, 1842*, ed. M. W. Flinn, Edinburgh University Press, 1965.

Chance, Lady, *Women's Suffrage and Morality; An Address to Married Women*, NUWSS, January 1913.

Climenson, E. J., *Elizabeth Montagu, Queen of the Bluestockings*, 1906.

Close, David, *The Collapse of Resistance to Democracy: Conservatives, Adult Suffrage and Second Chamber Reform 1911–1928*, Historical Journal 20, 1977.

Cobbe, Frances Power, *Essays on the Pursuits of Women*, 1863.

—— *Why Women Desire the Franchise*, National Society for Women's Suffrage, 1877.

—— *The Duties of Women*, Williams and Norgate, 1881.

—— *Life of Frances Power Cobbe*, R. Bentley and Son, 1894.

Dangerfield, George, *The Strange Death of Liberal England*, Constable, 1936.

Davenport-Hines, Richard, *Sex, Death and Punishment*, Collins, 1990.

David, Edward, ed., *Inside Asquith's Cabinet: From the Diaries of Charles Hobhouse*, John Murray, 1977.

Delamont, Sara and Duffin, Lorna, eds., *The Nineteenth Century Woman: Her Cultural and Physical World*, Croom Helm, 1978.

Donzelot, Jacques, *The Policing of Families*, Hutchinson, 1979.

Ethelmer, Ellis, *Woman Free*, 1893.
—— *The Phases of Love*, Congleton, 1897.
Fawcett, Millicent Garrett, *Home and Politics*, Women's Printing Society, 1894.
—— *Women's Suffrage: A Short History of a Great Movement*, T. C. and E. C. Jack, 1911.
—— *The Women's Victory and After: Personal Reminiscences, 1911–1918*, Sidgwick and Jackson, 1920.
—— *What I Remember*, Fisher Unwin, 1924.
Fenwick Miller, Mrs F., *On the Programme of the Women's Franchise League*, an address delivered at the National Liberal Club, 25 February 1890, Tracts 1890–95.
Fisher, Trevor, *Scandal: The Sexual Politics of Late Victorian Britain*, Alan Sutton, 1995.
Foyster, Elizabeth A., *Manhood in Early Modern England: Honour, Sex and Marriage*, Longman, 1999.
French, Richard D., *Antivivisection and Medical Science in Victorian Society*, Princeton University Press, 1975.
Fulford, Roger, *Votes for Women*, Faber and Faber, 1957.
Garner, Les, *Stepping Stones to Women's Liberty: Feminist Ideas in the Women's Suffrage Movement 1900–1918*, Hutchinson, 1984.
Gawthorpe, Mary, *Uphill to Holloway*, Traversity Press, 1962.
Gay, Peter, *The Bourgeois Experience: Victoria to Freud*, vol. 1: *Education of the Senses*, Norton, 1984.
Geddes, P. and Thompson, J. A., *The Evolution of Sex*, W. Scott, 1889.
Godwin, William, *Memoirs of the Author of the Rights of Woman*, 1798, Penguin, 1987.
Halevy, Elie, *History of England in the 19th Century, Book 2, 1905–1914*, Benn, 1952.
Hamilton, Cicely, *Marriage as a Trade*, Chapman and Hall, 1909.
Harris, Josie, *Private Lives, Public Spirit: Britain 1870–1914*, Penguin, 1994.
Harrison, Brian, *Separate Spheres: The Opposition to Women's Suffrage in Britain*, Croom Helm, 1978.
—— *Prudent Revolutionaries*, Clarendon Press, 1987.
Hay, Douglas and Rogers, Nicholas, *Eighteenth Century English Society*, Oxford University Press, 1997.
Heasman, Kathleen, *Evangelicals in Action: An Appraisal of their Social Work in the Victorian Era*, Geoffrey Bles, 1962.
Heyck, T. W., *The Transformation of Intellectual Life in Victorian England*, Croom Helm, 1982.
Hill, Bridget, *Women, Work and Sexual Politics in Eighteenth Century England*, Blackwell, 1989.
Himmelfarb, Gertrude, *Darwin and the Darwinian Revolution*, Chatto and Windus, 1959.
—— *Marriage and Morals Among the Victorians*, I. B. Tauris, 1989.

Hollis, Patricia, *Women in Public: The Women's Movement 1850–1900*, George Allen and Unwin, 1979.

Hollis, P., ed., *Pressure from Without in Early Victorian England*, Edward Arnold, 1974.

Holton, Sandra Stanley, *Feminism and Democracy: Women's Suffrage and Reform Politics in Britain 1900–1918*, Cambridge University Press, 1986.

Hopkins, Ellice, *The Power of Womanhood, or Mothers and Sons*, Wells Gardner, 1899.

—— *Drawn unto Death: A Plea for the Children Coming Under the Industrial Schools Amendment Act 1880*, Hatchards, 1884.

Houghton, Walter E., *The Victorian Frame of Mind 1830–1870*, Yale University Press, 1957.

Hynes, Samuel, *The Edwardian Turn of Mind*, Princeton University Press, 1968.

Jackson, Margaret, *The Real Facts of Life: Feminism and the Politics of Sexuality c1850–1940*, 1994, Taylor and Francis, 1994.

Jeffreys, S., *The Spinster and Her Enemies: Feminism and Sexuality 1880–1930*, Pandora, 1985.

—— *The Sexuality Debates*, Routledge and Kegan Paul, 1987.

Jenkins, Roy, *Asquith*, Collins, 1978.

Johnson, George W. and Johnson, Lucy, eds., *Josephine Butler, An Autobiographical Memoir*, Arrowsmith, 1911.

Kamm, Josephine, *Rapiers and Battleaxes*, George Allen and Unwin, 1966.

Kenney, Annie, *Memories of a Militant*, Edward Arnold, 1924.

Kent, Susan Kingsley, *Sex and Suffrage in Britain, 1860–1914*, Routledge, 1987.

Kitchen, Paddy, *A Most Unsettling Person: An Introduction to the Ideas and Life of Patrick Geddes*, Gollancz, 1975.

Koss, Stephen, *Asquith*, Allen Lane, 1976.

Kraditor, Aileen S., *The Ideas of the Woman Suffrage Movement 1890–1920*, Columbia University Press, 1965.

Lerner, Gerda, *The Creation of Patriarchy*, Oxford University Press, 1986.

Lewis, Jane, ed., *Before the Vote Was Won: Arguments For and Against Women's Suffrage 1864–1896*, Routledge and Kegan Paul, 1987.

Liddington, Jill and Norris, Jill, *One Hand Tied Behind Us*, Virago, 1978.

Linklater, Andro, *An Unhusbanded Life: Charlotte Despard, Suffragette, Socialist, Sinn Feiner*, Hutchinson, 1980.

Lytton, Lady Constance, *Prisons and Prisoners*, Heinemann, 1914.

Macfarlane, Alan, *Marriage and Love in England: Modes of Reproduction 1300–1840*, Blackwell, 1986.

Mahood, Linda, *The Magdalenes: Prostitution in the Nineteenth Century*, Routledge, 1990.

Manton, Jo, *Elizabeth Garrett Anderson*, Methuen, 1965.

Marcus, Steven, *The Other Victorians: A Study of Sexuality and Pornography*, Weidenfeld & Nicolson, 1966.

Martineau, Harriet, *Harriet Martineau's Autobiography*, James R. Osgood & Co., 1877.

Marwick, Arthur, *Women at War 1914–1918*, Fontana, 1977.

Mason, Michael, *The Making of Victorian Sexuality*, Oxford University Press, 1994.

Maurice, Frederick, *Lectures to Ladies*, 1855.

McLaren, Angus, *Birth Control in Nineteenth Century England*, Croom Helm, 1978.

McPhee, Carol and Fitzgerald, Ann, eds., *The Non-Violent Militant: Selected Writings of Teresa Billington-Greig*, Routledge and Kegan Paul, 1987.

Meikle, Wilma, *Towards a Sane Feminism*, Grant Richards, 1916.

Mill, John Stuart, *The Subjection of Women*, reprinted in Alice Rossi, ed., *Essays on Sex Equality*, Chicago University Press, 1970.

—— *Autobiography*, 1873; Penguin edn., ed. John Robson, 1990.

Mitchell, David, *Women on the Warpath*, Jonathan Cape, 1966.

—— *The Fighting Pankhursts*, Jonathan Cape, 1967.

—— *The Pankhursts*, Heron, 1970.

—— *Queen Christabel*, Macdonald and Jane's, 1977.

Mitchell, Hannah, *The Hard Way Up*, ed. Geoffrey Mitchell, Faber and Faber, 1968.

Montefiore, Dora, *From a Victorian to a Modern*, Archer, 1927.

Morgan, David, *Suffragists and Liberals: The Politics of Woman Suffrage in Britain*, Blackwell, 1975.

Mort, Frank, *Dangerous Sexualities: Medico-Moral Politics in England Since 1830*, Routledge and Kegan Paul, 1987.

Moscucci, Ornella, *The Science of Woman: Gynaecology and Gender in England, 1800–1929*, Cambridge University Press, 1990.

Murby, Millicent, *The Common Sense of the Woman Question*, Frank Palmer, 1908.

Nevinson, Henry, *More Changes, More Chances*, Nisbet, 1925.

Nevinson, Margaret Wynne, *Life's Fitful Fever*, A. & C. Black, 1926.

Newman, Francis William, *The Corruption Now Called Neo-Malthusianism*, with notes by Dr Elizabeth Blackwell, Moral Reform Union, 1889.

Pankhurst, Christabel, *The Great Scourge and How to End It*, Lincoln's Inn House, 1913.

—— *Unshackled*, Hutchinson, 1959.

Pankhurst, Emmeline, *My Own Story*, told to Rheta Childe Dorr, Eveleigh Nash, 1914.

Pankhurst, Sylvia, *The Suffragette Movement*, Longman, 1931.

—— *The Home Front*, 1932.

—— *The Life of Emmeline Pankhurst*, Werner Laurie, 1935.

Pearson, Karl, *The Ethic of Free Thought*, 1901.

Perrin, Noel, *Dr Bowdler's Legacy*, David Godine, 1969.

Pethick-Lawrence, Emmeline, *My Part in a Changing World*, Gollancz, 1938.

Petrie, Glen, *A Singular Iniquity: The Campaigns of Josephine Butler*, Macmillan, 1971.

Plumb, J. H., *England in the Eighteenth Century*, Penguin, 1990 (rev. edn.).

Porter, Roy, *English Society in the Eighteenth Century*, Penguin, 1991 (rev. edn.).

Porter, Roy and Hall, Lesley, *The Facts of Life: The Creation of Sexual Knowledge in Britain, 1650–1950*, Yale University Press, 1995.

Prochaska, Frank, *Women and Philanthropy in Nineteenth Century England*, Oxford University Press, 1980.

Pugh, Martin, *Electoral Reform in War and Peace, 1906–1918*, Routledge and Kegan Paul, 1978.

—— *The Pankhursts*, Penguin, 2001.

Purvis, June, *Emmeline Pankhurst*, Routledge, 2002.

Ravenhill, Alice, *Eugenic Ideals for Womanhood, Eugenics Review*, vol. 1, April 1909–January 1910.

Re Bartlett, Lucy, *The Coming Order*, Longmans, 1911.

—— *Sex and Sanctity*, 1912.

Richardson, Mary, *Laugh a Defiance*, Weidenfeld & Nicolson, 1953.

Roberton, J., *The Relative Proportion of Male and Female Population: Report of the Manchester Statistical Society*, 1840.

Rosen, Andrew, *Rise Up Women!*, Routledge and Kegan Paul, 1974.

Rover, Constance, *Women's Suffrage and Party Politics in Britain 1866–1914*, Routledge and Kegan Paul, 1967.

Royden, Maude, *A Threefold Cord*, Gollancz, 1947.

Rupke, N. A., ed., *Vivisection in Historical Perspective*, Croom Helm, 1987.

Ruskin, John, 'Of Queens' Gardens', in *Sesame and Lilies*, Smith, Elder, 1865.

Ryan, Michael, *The Philosophy of Marriage in its Social, Moral and Physical Relations*, John Churchill, 1839.

Scharlieb, Mary, *Womanhood and Race Regeneration*, Cassell, 1912.

Schreiner, Olive, *Woman and Labour*, 1911.

Shoemaker, Robert B., *Gender in English Society 1650–1850*, Longman, 1998.

Showalter, Elaine, *Sexual Anarchy: Gender and Culture at the Fin de Siècle*, Bloomsbury, 1991.

Smith, Harold L., *The British Women's Suffrage Campaign 1866–1928*, Longman, 1998.

Smith, Warren Sylvester, *The London Heretics, 1870–1914*, Constable, 1967.

Smyth, Dame Ethel, *Female Pipings in Eden*, 1933.

Soloway, Richard Allen, *Birth Control and the Population Question in England, 1877–1930*, University of North Carolina Press, 1982.

—— *Demography and Degeneration: Eugenics and the Declining Birthrate*, University of North Carolina Press, 1990.

Spencer, Herbert, *Social Statics, or the Conditions Essential to Human Happiness*, 1851.

Stanton, Theodore, *The Woman Question in Europe*, Sampson Low and Co., 1884.

Stead, W. T., *Josephine Butler*, Morgan and Scott, 1887.

Stickney Ellis, Sarah, *The Women of England, Their Social Duties and Domestic Habits*, Fisher, 1839.

——*The Wives of England, Their Relative Duties, Domestic Influence and Social Obligations*, Fisher, 1843.

Stone, Lawrence, *The Family, Sex and Marriage in England 1500–1800*, Weidenfeld & Nicolson, 1977.

Strachey, Ray, *Women's Suffrage and Women's Service*, London and National Society for Women's Suffrage, 1927.

—— *Millicent Garrett Fawcett*, John Murray, 1931.

—— *The Cause*, Virago, 1978

Swanwick, Helena Maria, *The Future of the Women's Movement*, G. Bell and Sons, 1913.

—— *I Have Been Young*, Gollancz, 1935.

Swiney, Frances, *The Cosmic Procession; or the Feminine Principle in Evolution*, 1906.

—— *The Bar of Isis*, Open Road, 1907.

—— *The Awakening of Women; or Women's Part in Evolution*, William Reeves, 1908.

Symondson, Anthony, ed., *The Victorian Crisis of Faith*, SPCK, 1970.

Tait, William, *Magdalenism: An Inquiry into the Extent, Causes and Consequences of Prostitution*, P. Rickard, 1840.

Taylor, Barbara, *Eve and the New Jerusalem*, Virago, 1983.

Thomas, Keith, 'The Double Standard', *Journal of the History of Ideas*, vol. 20, 1959.

Thompson, Laurence, *The Enthusiasts: A Biography of John and Katharine Bruce Glasier*, Gollancz, 1971.

Thompson, Paul, *The Edwardians: The Remaking of British Society*, Weidenfeld & Nicolson, 1975.

Thompson, William, *An Appeal of One Half the Human Race, Women, Against the Pretensions of the Other Half, Men, to Retain Them in Political and Thence in Domestic Slavery, in Reply to a Paragraph of Mr Mill's Celebrated 'Article on Government'*, 1825.

Thomson, David, *England in the Nineteenth Century*, Penguin, 1955.

Tomalin, Claire, *The Life and Death of Mary Wollstonecraft*, Weidenfeld & Nicolson, 1974.

Walker, Alexander, *Women Physiologically Considered as to Mind, Morals, Matrimonial Slavery, Infidelity and Divorce*, A. H. Baily, 1839.

Walkowitz, Judith R., *Prostitution and Victorian Society*, Cambridge University Press, 1980.

Watts, Duncan, *Tories, Conservatives and Unionists 1815–1914*, Hodder and Stoughton, 1994.

Wollstonecraft, Mary, *A Vindication of the Rights of Woman*, 1792, with an Introduction by Miriam Brody, Penguin, 1992.

Woodham-Smith, Cecil, *Florence Nightingale*, Fontana, 1951.

Wright, Sir Almroth, *The Unexpurgated Case Against Woman Suffrage*, 1913.

INDEX